The Last First Sergeant

To Asher Sweeney
from Mike Durfey
1/12/00

Layton Black

Griffith Publishing
Caldwell, Idaho

Printed in the United States of America

ISBN 0-9665140-0-4

Copyright © 1998 by Jeanne Black

All rights reserved

Edited, designed and produced by
GRIFFITH PUBLISHING Caldwell, Idaho 83606

*Dedicated to Nathan—
Layton and Jeanne Black's
grandson*

Contents

Foreword ix
Leadership in World War II x
Introduction xii
1. Camp Denford—Hungerford England 1
2. The Big Buildup 5
3. Normandy! 13
4. Capture the Flag 23
5. Firing Ammo at the Enemy 33
6. The Move on Carentan, France 41
7. Attack Underway 49
8. After a Great Battle 71
9. Twelve Days on the Battle Line 81
10. The Corridor Fight 95
11. Defending St. Oedenrode 103
12. The British Are Here 117
13. What's in a German Musette Bag? 123
14. The Big Battle on the Road to Schijndel 137
15. The Steel Helmet Is Part of Your Head 149
16. Stuck in a Two-Man Foxhole 165
17. A Box From Home 179
18. "Get in and Shut Up!" 187
19. My Last Fast Draw 205

20. Frolic in Paris 213
21. How I Heard about the German Breakthrough 225
22. Christmas in Bastogne 241
23. "Where the Hell Did that Shell Hit?" 251
24. Holly's Great Escape 263
25. Mad as Hell 275
26. One Down, Four to Go 291
27. Back to France 303
28. Filling in the Ranks 319
29. Slam the Door 325
30. Bales of Silk 331
31. Schnapps by the Barrel 339
32. When Your Home Isn't Your Castle 345
33. Unconditional Surrender 349
34. Alles Kaput! 355
35. Crashing an SS Party 361
36. In Hitler's Back Yard 369
37. The Last First Sergeant 379

Snapshots 384
Epilog 386
Appendix I: A Guide to WWII Rhetoric 387
Appendix II: Military Organizational Structure 388

Foreword

The paratroopers of World War II were the epitome of the term, "the process of elimination." They were all volunteers to a new form of warfare called "airborne." In the U.S. they formed four great airborne division units—the 82nd, the 101st, the 11th and the 17th.

Layton Black's story is about the 502nd Parachute Infantry Regiment from the 101st Airborne Division, especially Company "C" of this regiment. He shares his experiences day to day, foxhole to foxhole, with the Second platoon of his company. This book will take you back to those wonderful GIs of the 1940s.

This book does not dwell on either the gore or the heroism in war. It does not speak for the acclaim of high rank or military achievements. The author makes the point that the front line soldier won the war; everybody else helped. Fifty of Black's "C" Company troopers gave their lives; he knew them all. Not one hesitated in his duty. "Every trooper who jumped behind the enemy," Black writes, "and lived or died, served his country to the hilt."

Sadness and joy march step for step with front-line soldiers as the author brings them through the war. His writing makes these paratroopers so real that in the end you will swear you knew them. He does not leave out details that make him look foolish. All was part of a combat trooper's life in a far-off land.

Leadership in World War II

An explanation of the leadership is in order, beginning with the head man of Germany—the Fuhrer, Adolf Hitler. He was a "dictator" in the true sense of the word. During World War II he functioned as the army commander-in-chief, especially on the Russian front from June 22, 1941, to November 22, 1944. Hitler at times was a military genius; it was foolish of his enemies to consider him anything less. His faults were isolating his headquarters from the action and rejecting bad news. His success lay in his ability to inspire a devoted following, bordering on the fanatical.

Hitler's armies had many victories and pushed their supply lines simultaneously across three continents. His uncanny ability to rally his armies from what appeared to be certain defeat was a remarkable talent. His last great battle was a stroke of genius, carried off as a complete surprise to the Americans. It was his last Ardenes Offensive, Christmas 1944, which was to become America's greatest battle of World War II, the Battle of the Bulge.

The head man for England was Sir Winston Churchill, who took over as Prime Minister at the time Hitler began World War II. Churchill's ability to get the British people to endure the hardships of England's darkest hour and then sustain the war effort for over five years was his triumph. He was the opposite of Hitler in every way. He let his military people run the war on the battlefields. He told his people the truth about the war.

In my opinion Churchill was the major force in the course of victory for the Allies. Still, I will fault him for the course of peace in the end, although I realize that one cannot bargain from a bankrupt position. The war had broken England, and his great friend, the leader of the U.S., had just died. In this setting the cold war between capitalism and communism was to begin and continue for forty-five years.

The head man for the U.S. was President Franklin D.

Roosevelt. Our American form of government steers away from military control even in a time of war. Our war policies stem from the State Department. The most important single action Roosevelt took in World War II was naming General George C. Marshall his chief of staff. Later a young major, Paul Robinett, who worked on Roosevelt's staff, said, "Marshall was the consummate army politician." Beyond his statesmanship was General Marshall's ability as the leading planner of strategy in World War II. His major contribution was convulsing President Roosevelt in early 1940 to prepare for war before it would be too late. Marshall was notable for his steadfastness in supporting Eisenhower as the Supreme Commander of Europe. His "Marshall Plan" was a great help in winning the peace.

I should mention Joe Stalin, the Russian dictator who outfoxed us in the end. He beat us to Berlin! My belief is that was our biggest mistake in Europe. In spite of the fact that the USSR lost many more soldiers in the war than we did, I find it hard to praise a man who was such a butcher of his own people. But I do understand the great effort they put forth against a much stronger Germany on their eastern front than Germany was able to muster against us on the western front.

The USSR lost by far the most people and fought the greatest battles of World War II, but they had the best reason to do so: they were fighting on their own home land.

France played her part in a leadership role at the end, which returned her to a place of world power. This was accomplished by one man who fought for France's right to share in the victory of the Allied forces. He was Charles de Gaulle, who became the leader of France.

Introduction

I did not miss a single day once I joined the 101st Airborne (502nd Paratrooper Regiment, 1st Battalion, "C" Company, 2nd Platoon) in May of 1943 until November 1945. I spent all of this time in "C" Company moving from Private to First Sergeant. I did not get a scratch in all the division's time overseas. (By "scratch," I mean anything bad enough to put me out of action.) In fact, I never was on sick call!

I believe I have a story to tell, not because of me, but because of the times. It has been many decades since the end of World War II, the greatest war of all time. It was the first war we fought by jumping from airplanes high in the sky, landing by chance behind enemy lines in a mass army of thousands.

We were called Paratroopers because of the chutes that brought us to the ground. Our training was for mass use of Paratroopers in major invasions, several divisions at one time. Each of us knew the chances we took just to get to the ground alive, let alone to obtain a location for fighting from, always on the enemy's home ground. As we said, we had two chances: slim and none. We knew all of this and had asked for it.

The whole world looked up to the Paratroopers. We were the glory of our time. Now we are being phased out because of new forms of air travel. All the more reason to put down what I think made us tick.

I tell my story from a regular GI's point of view, without apologies. There wasn't any glamour down in 2nd Platoon "C" Company. Just pride.

Come along with my sharp memory of life in the military from the biggest airborne jumps ever made (D-day, the invasion of Normandy, France), to the daytime jump into Holland and the start of the great race to the north under British Field Marshall Montgomery. Then the call for help with the great German breakthrough and our ride into the "bulge." This time arriving by cattle trucks, we unloaded at a place in Belgium called Bastogne. Learn what it was really like at the "front" those last days of the war and into the first days of army occupation.

The following sentiment will not show up in the pages that follow, but it was always my true feeling at the sight of every dead enemy soldier.

> I came in haste with cursing breath
>   And heart of coldest steel.
> But when I saw thee cold in death
>   I felt as man should feel.
>
> For when I look upon that face
>   That cold, unheeding, frigid brow
> Where neither rage nor fear has place,
>   By Heaven! I cannot hate thee now.
>
> —"On a Dead Enemy," by Alfred Lord Tennyson

1

Camp Denford—
Hungerford England

The front door banged open and slammed back into the double-deck bunk bed of Sergeant Junior Nutter in II barracks of the 2nd Platoon, "C" Company, immediately followed by a fully packed duffle bag bounding all the way into the center of the small Nissenhut, just missing the small Victorian coal stove.

"Hey! Wake up in here, goddammit!" came the voice from a big bull of a paratrooper standing in the open doorway. All of us in that "hut" had been enjoying a quiet Sunday afternoon nap, but now we were wide awake, each of us up on one elbow, facing the open doorway. What we saw was a big kid, one we had never seen before. He was dirty from top to bottom, and even though he was wearing his O.D. (off duty) uniform, I noticed he wasn't wearing a tie.

It was plain to see this big kid was a "raw replacement" just landed from the States. We knew our platoon was short one trooper as time for the big invasion grew near. He spoke again and loud. "Has anybody in this chicken-shit outfit got a clean tie

I can use until tomorrow? Your chicken-shit First Sergeant won't let me go on pass unless I find one!"

Hell could freeze over before I was going to give him one of mine, and that was the feeling of everybody as we lay back down to continue our rest. "Hey, I'm talking to you guys," the big kid said. "Somebody give me a goddamn tie before I tear this place apart!"

With that remark Sergeant Nutter slipped out of his top bunk and got his own tie. He handed it to the big kid and said, "Is your name Private James Flanagan?"

"How did you know who I am?"

"Well, kid, I want you to know that General Eisenhower sent me a special delivery letter telling me you were coming. I'm Sergeant Nutter. Look me up when you get back from pass, early in the morning. You have a lot of training to catch up on."

Sergeant Junior Nutter closed the front door and climbed back on his bunk bed. Quiet prevailed.

Sometime toward evening when the men were stirring around—maybe it was when we were on our way to chow—someone said to Sergeant Nutter, "Who was that loud-mouthed kid you called Flanagan?"

Before he could answer I said, "Damned if I would have loaned him my tie if I was the sergeant of this hut. By God, he would have to stay here and learn some respect."

"I'll start teaching him respect tomorrow, Black, but I doubt if I'll have enough time to accomplish the task."

I asked Sergeant Nutter if there was a double meaning in what he'd just said. Yes, he told me, he did have another meaning about time growing short. "We are ready to go. Our company has been short one trooper, and today that last one came aboard. Look around you. Charlie's company is at full strength. See who is sleeping next to you—the cook, the medic, the radio man, the clerk, the platoon runner. We're all here. We are ready to make our next move. You and I know it's long overdue. It's time to go. That's what we were trained for."

Men on special duty slept with the rest of the platoon only when a big jump was at hand. Sergeant Nutter was right. The "great invasion," the start of the long talked-about "second front," was about to take place.

It is somewhere towards the end of May 1944. We are in our last week outside of "captivity" behind barbed wire where we would camp just before the invasion. Two weeks from tonight we will board the planes for the mass jump that will start the great Normandy invasion. The 101st Airborne is headed for our first combat jump.

One year back, on April 19, 1943, Jump Class #66 was graduating from the Parachute School in Fort Benning, Georgia. The word was going around that most of our "class of 66" would end up in the 82nd Airborne Division since it had just been ordered to move overseas—to Africa.

Few among us cared for that idea, and it wasn't because we disliked the 82nd; at that time we didn't know one airborne division from another. I wanted to go to the 508th parachute regiment because my best friend Junior Dries from Circleville, Ohio, was already in it. We had entered the Army one week apart, and he was the main reason I had gone to jump school in the first place. Junior joined the paratroopers immediately, and that put him into the 508th, a newly forming unit.

By the time I heard from Junior a few weeks after he signed up, I had already started basic training at Camp Wheeler. I checked into the Airborne and signed up for the paratroopers in December of 1942. I almost backed out at the end of basic when I was offered Corporal's rating to stay on as Cadre at Camp Wheeler.

While I was making up my mind, Junior invited me down to Columbus, Georgia, to take a look at jump school. I arrived there the day he got his "wings" (graduated). That did it for me. Those jumpboots, jump wings, the uniform! What a wonderful group of young men! What *esprit de corps!* Man, that was an army! The paratroopers reeked of confidence. Those men could lick twice their weight in wildcats. Junior made it in a breeze—five jumps in one week. "Nothing to it," he said. "What I can do, you can do better."

Six weeks later I made five jumps in a three-day period, all from a C-47 airplane at twelve hundred feet above the ground. All I wanted was to end up in the 508th with my friend from back home. Of course I didn't. The Army never works like that.

When my friends and arrived at Fort Bragg on Tuesday May 11, 1943, to join the 502nd Paratrooper Regiment, we were given a seven-day furlough starting the very next day. We knew we had come to the right place.

Many of the NCOs (noncommissioned officers) in 502 had been in the regular army before and were among the first to join the paratroopers. The "C" Company men were eager to find out what their first combat jump would be like. Since most of the N.C.O's were the original Cadre and had been at the helm for two years, their word was law. No one gave a thought about the possibility that an NCO might be killed.

Before the ball game they say, "Get your score card here! Know the names of each and every player!" In our situation I would add, "Look quickly, for some will hardly have time to run out into the field."

First to go out the door to land at Normandy Beach will be our "jump master," Sergeant Nutter; then the scout, Private First Class William A. Cooper (Kentucky); riflemen Private First Class Anthony F. Marcozzi (Delaware), Private First Class Jack L. Evans (Pennsylvania), Corporal Edwin E. Metz (West Virginia) and Private Ervine D. Goodwin (Rhode Island); bazookaman Private First Class Edwin E. Funk (Virginia); assistant bazookaman Private First Class L. D. Cissan (Georgia); First machine gunner Private First Class Vincent J. Folley (New York); Second machine gunner Private First Class Layton Black Jr. (Ohio); machine gun ammo bearer Private Robert E. Cahoon (Massachusetts); and last out of the plane, rifleman Private James W. Flanagan (Missouri).

These are the men who make up the cast of most of my stories of World War II. My world during the war was so small that what happened over the hill from me was someone else's story. I tell what I know best: the sights, sounds and feelings of the war as I experienced them.

2

The Big Buildup

We left for the marshalling areas of southwest England, where we were given our final instructions and our first look at the place we would be jumping into. Our "look" consisted of a layout on a sand table, plus maps and pictures showing every detail.

Since the 101st Airborne was spread out in small camps across a wide area in England, large marshalling areas sprang up in large open spaces with canvas tents and army cots for sleeping. Barbed wire enclosed these areas like a prison. To us it looked more like a place to keep wild animals than living space for soldiers. There was one point to this "captivity" business: to keep the time and place of the invasion secret. Although something of this magnitude was impossible to hide, the details were kept "classified secret." Once inside the barbed wire of our marshalling area, no one got out until the jump was on or the training exercise was over.

Our military leaders were putting the finishing touches on the 101st Airborne Division for the big invasion. Each exercise was coordinated with the assault forces that would invade Hitler's Fortress Europe. Three exercises would be dry runs, but we didn't know that until we were well into them. In every detail even the great amphibious operations using invasion-sized armadas were realistic, including the use of live ammunition.

All inhabitants were cleared from a large area of English coastline. The first exercise at Slapton Sands near Torquay, a seaport on the coast of southwest England, was called "Beaver." From March 27 through 31, 1944, we conducted a huge seaborne landing. While those of us in the airborne division didn't jump from anything higher than the back of a six-by-six truck, the exercise proceeded as closely as possible to a real airborne operation.

In two of the three exercises those of us in the "C" Company were housed in tourist hotels in the resort city of Torquay. These old hotels dotted the hillsides of the most beautiful places in all of old England. The streets climbed like terraces up the hillsides circling the bay on three sides. From the back porch of our hotel we could see the whole city stretched out below. It looked like a giant horseshoe-shaped stadium—the bay the playing field, the sailboats the players. The hotel sat on the rim of the highest hill at the top of the city. Although there was no barbed wire around our hotels, there was strict guard detail. The whole southwest coastal area had been taken over by the military. British and U.S. navy, army and air forces were poised to carry out the great invasion.

The airborne part of both exercises took very little of our time. They were overnight problems. By noon the next day we were free to lounge around in our hotels. Of course we had map reading and the sand table to study, but once we found out that each exercise was a dry run, it was hard for us paratroopers to do much more than go through the motions at playing soldier.

The biggest inspection jump was on March 23, 1944, when the British Prime minister himself, Sir Winston Churchill, and U.S. General Dwight Eisenhower came to look us over.

We "old timers" in the 502nd understood that every jump was serious business. We were always trying for a perfect "stick" jump, with all of us going out the door close together as fast as we could. The closer we were when we left the door, the closer together we would be on the ground.

The Big Buildup

We also wanted to land as close as possible to our equipment bundles containing machine guns and ammunition, food, medical supplies, radios, telewire and other supplies needed by a line infantry company. Different colored chutes helped us track different types of supplies. With perfect stick jumping as the main goal in the "Churchill" jump of March 23, our plane's jump master, Sergeant Nutter, had only one thing in mind: to kick out the plane's one equipment bundle and then jump out the door after it. Sergeant Nutter would jump on top of the bundle's chute if possible, and the rest of us would try to do the same to the trooper in front of us. This would give us the best company drop pattern.

"Check your equipment!" Sergeant Nutter called out. "Count off...Stand in the door!" His voice rang out. A lifetime went by waiting for the light to change from red to green. We heard the sergeant shout, "Let's go-o-o-o-o!" But the light did not turn green.

"No jump! Jump is off!" yelled one of the flight officers from up front. Our plane shot straight up in the air. The nose went up and the tail down as the pilot put the gas to our C-47 in a desperate climb. We paratroopers were standing up holding on to our static lines hooked to the plane's center cable. Most of us were able to keep from being slammed to the rear of the plane, but it was a struggle to hang on.

Our plane leveled off, and we were told to unhook, sit down and relax. The jump was off. Our plane flew out of formation and landed at the end of the series of planes that had taken off from our airfield. Had it been combat we would have just made another pass.

What had gone wrong?

The challenge of a C-47 pilot flying a mass operation is to maintain correct airspeed and altitude. The perfect airspeed for us jumpers was 110 miles per hour with the nose down somewhat and the tail up. We dreaded the dual possibilities of being blown off by the prop blast and of having our chutes catch on the plane's tail. The pilot's job was to fly in a three-plane "V" echelon formation in tight sequence so that a mass jump would have a good drop pattern.

In this maneuver the three planes in front of us were a little too high in relation to us. When our pilot put the nose of our plane down without cutting air speed enough, he saw that he was about to fly directly into the paratroopers floating through the air head of us. To avoid hitting them he aborted and climbed. It was a rough ride for us GIs from the 2nd Platoon that day, but not as scary as it must have been for those troopers falling through the air ahead of us.

I've often wondered what "Ike" and "Winnie" thought while watching the show.

A new man in our company—I think he was from California—joined the 2nd Platoon after the March jump. We called him "Kid." He was likable but just that, a kid—too damned young to be in the 502nd less than sixty days from combat.

Everything seemed to be going as smooth as silk for our second jump. "Stand up and hook up! Check your equipment! Sound off! Stand in the door!" Then the green light. Sergeant Nutter, our jump master, yelled, "Let's go-o-o-o-o!" and out the door he went.

Talk about silk! It was everywhere. The plane was full of parachute silk clear into the cockpit. Nobody could see anything. Everybody standing in line down the center of the plane was shoving, but nobody was going anywhere. The crew chief at the tail of the plane yelled, "Hold up! Hold up! Hold up!" Folley and I were the last two men in the jump stick's line of jump, just in front of Corporal Metz who yelled, "What the hell happened?"

I was sure our plane had run into a bunch of our paratroopers who had jumped out of the plane ahead of us. Why else all that silk? My squad was now two for two in extra thrills and no jumps. With any kind of mix-up, once the green light is on, you quickly pass over the "drop zone." The jump was off for our plane, except for Sergeant Nutter.

"Unhook your static lines and sit back down," the crew chief said, passing the word along as he helped each of us untangle ourselves from the white silk and riser lines. As the men in front of me sat down I saw what had happen.

The Kid had somehow pulled his reserve chute. The wind from the open door had caught it and sent it streaming back up through the plane. He was now trying to gather it all up in his arms, which wasn't easy to do. Corporal Metz gave the Kid hell in no uncertain terms, leaving little doubt that he felt sure it was no accident. As our plane was coming in for the landing, Corporal Metz said to the Kid in a voice loud enough for all of us to hear, "Enjoy this ride because you only get one chance to screw up in the Airborne, and you're out!"

I'm sure Corporal Metz meant every word of that, but Captain Hancock overruled him, and the Kid was given a second chance in the night-time jump on May 11, 1944. This was "Exercise Eagle," the dress rehearsal for the real thing. It had already become a joke in the 2nd Platoon about our non-jumping Second Squad mixed with a hint that maybe a jinx was underway. Whatever that may have meant to the rest of the men, I didn't take it seriously myself.

Once more we roared off into the sky and once more we reached our drop zone somewhere over the English countryside. I kept my eyes glued on the Kid and Corporal Metz. They were seated across from each other; Nutter and Metz had decided that the Kid would jump next to last in the stick. If he screwed up again he would have to do it right in front of Corporal Metz. I was next to him in the line.

The time was at hand. "Stand up and hook up!"

Dark as it was in the plane I could see white silk floating around. This time the Kid was sitting so close to the open door into the cabin that the silk was invading the cockpit, and the pilots were in trouble. The Kid hadn't even taken the chance of standing up. There was nothing to do but to abort the jump.

We left for the true marshalling area around the first of June. Historians say it was May 29, and it was if you were General Taylor's radio operator, T/3 George E. Koskimaki. But for others like Private David K. Webster of the 506th parachute regiment, it could have been May 30. Still another, Thomas B. Buff, of the Division H.Q. Company, said it was 1600 hours on the afternoon of June 5. Whenever it was, the preparation throughout the 101st Airborne Division was about the same for all of us.

To explain the significance of the marshalling area—"inside captivity" I call it—here are excerpts from the diaries and notes of other soldiers (used with their permission):

May 29, 1944. Packed all our equipment today ready for

shipment. Adjusted our chutes. Leave for marshalling area today sometime. Turning diary over to Hannemon until return.

May 30. I learned today our exact location and mission when I helped Lt. Bierce work on some maps. I hope we make a good show of it.

May 31. The entire division H.Q. Parachute echelon was briefed for the first time today. All boys were greatly surprised when they learned where we would jump.

June 2. Each man sketched the road network of the area in which we land, from memory. We get a good two hours briefing each day.

June 3. Each man was given his ammo and grenades. Today we had hot showers and some extra cigarettes and candy rations.

June 4. We were equipped and packed ready to leave today. Bad weather is said to have caused postponement of the invasion until tomorrow or the next day.

June 5. Tonight we ring the bell on the greatest invasion show in the world.

— History of the 101st Airborne Division

We were issued $10.00 worth of crisp new French money just minted in Washington for the invasion. Every man had three yard-square maps, which, when pieced together, represented the entire peninsula of Normandy, including a distorted photo map of the jump field (which nobody could figure out), and one or two diagrams and overlays of the village or strong point the soldier's platoon of company was assigned to take. Small pocket compasses were issued so that we could orient ourselves on the ground. We were given dime-store "crickets" for identification purposes: one squeeze (click-clack) to be answered by two (click-clack, click-clack).

We drew American flags about five inches by three and fas-

The Big Buildup 11

tened them to the right sleeves of our jump jackets. We shaved our heads. Boxes of machine gun and mortar ammo were rolled into the equipment bundles and attached to the bottom of the planes. Then we drew our "Mae West" life jackets from storage. We went down to the hangars, adjusted our chutes, put our rifles in their cases, checked our ammo, broke down our "K" rations and arranged our chutes in kit bags by companies. Then we waited.

The night of June 4 we were served an outstanding meal: steak, green peas, mashed potatoes, white bread, ice cream, coffee. All a soldier could ask for. A terrific wind was blowing, but we all felt our day had come. However, an officer told us to go to bed. We weren't leaving tonight.

By late afternoon June 5 the wind had died down. We were going! We ate a hurried meal of stew and left for the airport. Nobody sang. Nobody cheered. It was like a death march. After we found our kit bags, we boarded trucks and drove to our planes. We ended our equipment issue by receiving "seasick pills" and round cardboard ice cream containers in case the pills didn't work. We put on our gear and waited.

—Pfc. David Webster, 506th Regiment

We got to the air dome around three or four o'clock on the afternoon of June 5. Briefing was over. Everyone had been briefed and briefed again. All officers were there with the men of their section, casually going over plans and alternate plans, checking maps, checking technical equipment. Last-minute preparation for an early-morning "vertical invasion" of Hitler's Fortress Europe went forward in exactly the same manner as for our field exercises. There was no visible sign of nervousness, tension, brooding doubt, or fear.

While we were blackening our faces and hands, Butler, Bill Smith and Phil Romano completed their makeup and combined forces to put on an ad lib minstrel act for us. We laughed at their antics until our sides hurt.

General Taylor had already spoken to the officers and men.

He paid a tribute to his predecessor, Major General William C. Lee, and asked each of us to yell, "Bill Lee!" as we left the door of our planes over France.

—Sgt. Thomas B. Buff, Division H.Q. Company

What a thrill it was, having the head man, Ike himself, come to see us off! His presence built great personal courage in me and my fellow soldiers. When one is young it is easy to become inspired. When one is a young paratrooper from the 502nd he is the very best trained soldier in the world and knows it. He is unbeatable.

General Eisenhower left our 502nd area, and we started our move to the airfields. The whole First Battalion flew out of Membury, about ten miles northwest of Newbury, England. The Second and 3rd Battalions left from Greenham-Commons several miles to the southeast.

The ride in closed-in GI trucks from the marshalling area to the airfield was not a joyful one. The wind had calmed down somewhat, and it did not seem strong enough to stop a jump of this magnitude. I was sure we would go this time. Corporal Metz said, "It's a long time until 0130 hours, men." It was still light by the time we picked up our chutes and reached our own planes. We sat down and waited.

We had played the old hurry-up-and-wait game dozens of times, but it was easier this night. We had become accustomed to darkness, for England was in total blackout. However, when darkness fell on that historic night, the old man in the moon put on a show of his own. Thank God for that. It was never pitch black dark that night.

After 2200 hours (10 p.m.) the planes began to warm up their motors. One by one the word went out across Membury Airfield to put on our equipment. Once our equipment was in place and had been checked out by our squad sergeants, we climbed on board our planes to begin three hours of sheer agony. That was the total time we would sit on the plane with all of that heavy equipment tightly strapped to our bodies.

3

Normandy!

We race down the runway. At the last second we are airborne. We climb and climb and climb. Then we bank into huge turns. At last we circle into "V" formations. We meet up with other C-47 planes, and then other planes meet up with us. The sky is full of planes. I look out the open door. We are still over England, and all I can say is, "What a sight! What a sight!"

It has been said that we flew nine planes abreast and that we reached back for two hundred miles. We are told that four hundred ninety C-47 planes carried six thousand, six hundred paratroopers from the 101st Airborne Division alone. Besides our division, the U.S. 82nd Airborne Division and the British 6th Airborne Division were in the air that night. The total number of paratroopers to come down from the sky over Normandy some five hours before the start of D-day will be eighteen thousand, three hundred. The ships under us in the English channel were five thousand strong. Then there were fighter and bomber planes above us. It was a sight that man will never see again. To live to tell about it is a marvelous thing.

We were about to invade Europe, and the place we were going to land was Normandy, France. Our leaders told us that the first six "serials" to drop on Normandy would be "pathfinders." There would be three serials each from the 101st and the 82nd Airbornes, with three planes per serial. The first pathfinders from our 101st were to take off around midnight.

The main body of the invasion, the parachute regiments, were packed into ten 40-plane serials per division. The 101st was to take off first. Each of the serials was spaced at six-minute intervals. The first serial would leave the tip of England at 0021 hours (21 minutes past midnight), and in just 58 minutes they would reach the drop zone in Normandy, France. The 502nd Parachute Regiment made up serials seven, eight, and nine. My First Battalion was serial number nine. Thus it became true that the very first men to touch down on French soil in the big invasion, the start of the long awaited "second front" would be my fellow paratroopers of 502.

Nothing was said or done by any of the men in the plane on that flight to Normandy. Once I sat back in my seat after looking out the door, I did not get up again. I did not sleep as some men did—or appeared to do. I did not talk to anyone, nor did anyone else talk. No one got sick, either. It was an uneventful flight. I remember saying a prayer to my God and asking Him to bless all of my people. I asked God to forgive me for what I was about to do to the Germans. And I was gracious enough to ask Him to have mercy on them, for I felt the average German did not know what he had done.

My prayer was long and sincere, and when it was over I was ready for whatever was below me in Normandy, France. At that very moment in our flight I realized we were being fired on. It was flak from the German anti-aircraft guns. As if they were the signal, on came the red light. My plane was having no problems and was flying straight as a dart. We went through all the pre-jump procedures and stood in line waiting for the green light.

Suddenly it comes on. Without a hitch we all race down the corridor of the plane toward the open door. I am in the air, and my cry of "Bill Le-e-e-e-e!" has not ended when my chute cracks open. I look up to see if my chute is OK, and above me I see fireworks filling the sky.

Looking down I can see fire spewing out of patches of darkness everywhere. My eyes follow tracer bullets into the sky. They crisscross in patterns that seem aimless to me. Now and then I pick up a new stream of tracers headed straight at me. I think a tracer bullet went through my chute.

If I had to choose one word to describe my feelings as I flew to earth, it would be "fascinated." I was not scared. Nor was I unduly excited, nor overly anxious about what was happening around me.

As for my rapid descent, it ended with a bang. For the first time in eleven jumps I landed right on my ass. I fell on my back and lay there as my green camouflage parachute settled around me. It did not cover me, so I was able to see all around. "Man, I sure hit the ground hard," I thought to myself. "That was a fast trip to the ground!"

My first moves were reflex actions based on many hours of hard training. Self-preservation is the key word in the first minutes of a combat jump. I reached down to my right jump boot for my dagger-like trench knife, just in case I would have to fight from here, on my back, even before I could get out of my harness. Then I got ready to use my weapon. Mine was around my neck and stashed under my reserve chute, across my chest.

In order to get at my weapon, I had to release my reserve chute pack from my harness. Next in line was my Mae West life preserver, in case we went down in the ocean. It tied in the back, and there was no way I could reach it to untie it from my position there on my back—a position, I might add, that was more comfortable than the one I'd experienced for the past three hours.

My weapon was not going to be usable quickly enough to suit me. My next best tool was a hand grenade. I found one on me someplace and held onto it with one hand. I put my trench knife between my teeth, I guess to hold it so I could get to it if I needed it. I was still not out of my chute, nor was I ready to get up off my back.

I could hear small-arms fire coming from all directions. I thought I'd better see if anybody was nearby. Without standing up, I moved my head from side to side. Nothing came into view, but I could not see behind me because I didn't want to make undue movements that might give away my position until I was out of my harness and had my weapon to fight with. Seeing no one moving toward me, I laid my hand grenade on my chest and unsnapped my leg harness, then both chest snaps. All of these were difficult and seemed to take too much time. Free from my harness at last, I felt safe. Because of this feeling and because the opportunity presented itself, I took a foolish chance.

Call it young stupidity, youthful boldness or whatever. I decided I needed a personal souvenir from this jump. My paratrooper friend from back home, Junior Dreisbach, who was also making this same D-day jump but with the 507th Airborne Division, told me not to forget to bring back my rip cord from my reserve chute. It was a metal ring-like gadget with a cord tied to it. When pulled off the chute, it ripped the cord away, and the chute would spill open. Thus the name, "rip cord."

I took the rip cord and then used my trench knife to cut out one whole panel of my main chute. Even though my knife was sharp, it is not the easiest thing in the world to cut silk in a straight line. Not while lying on your back in the middle of the night in the middle of a French pasture with a hell of a war going on. Then I cut a big chunk out of my white reserve chute. All of this I put into my big pant-leg jump pocket.

These activities took up time, enough time for me to make three observations, all of which turned out to be true. First, that our C-47s were flying far too low. Those I saw go over were under six hundred feet, and many were as low as three hundred feet. Judging by the speed at which I hit the ground, I was sure my plane had been that low. Second, they were flying far too fast. The order of march for troop-carrier wings was seven hundred feet and one hundred and ten miles per hour when they reached the drop zones. The third point I observed while I lay there on my back was the absence of jumpers in my area. I swear, I did not see one of our C-47s unload its cargo anywhere near me. And it was moonlight.

Just as I was about to stand up, I heard someone behind me, walking in my direction. I was startled. I realized I'd made a bad mistake. Whoever it was, the footsteps were coming at me from my blind side in the rear, the area I had not bothered to check. There was no point in challenging them, I decided. They were too damned close by now. "I'll just fake injury," I thought. "They won't get me without a fight. Hell's fire! I haven't come all this way not to fire a shot!"

I'd put my trench knife away, but the hand grenade I'd held a few minutes back was now hanging by its handle from my jumpsuit's chest pocket. My weapon was still slung around my neck, loaded and ready. I could fire it from that slung position in a bat of an eye. Very slowly, I took the hand grenade in my right hand and pulled the pin. With my left hand I grabbed the stock of my weapon and waited. You're damned right I was scared now!

There was more than one. More than two. Now they were coming fast! One more second, and I would turn over onto my belly and let go with everything I had.

Then there was a loud "Mo-o-o-o-o-!" Any farmer knows only a cow makes that kind of noise. I didn't just roll over. I jumped straight up and waved both arms in a gesture that any cow in the world understands. Unless, of course, the cow isn't a cow, but turns out to be a bull!

As would happen so many times throughout the war, luck played her hand on my side. No bull. Just big, old French dairy cows. Seven of them. I counted them three times as I stood there. All seven cows had slid to a four-legged stop when I had jumped up suddenly. Now they stood frozen in their tracks, staring at me, the intruder from the sky who was messing up their midnight lunch.

Now that I was on my feet I looked all around. I saw that I was not alone in this small field. Two other paratroopers had landed here and had left their chutes. They had to be from my planeload, I figured, because I hadn't seen anyone come down after we jumped. Overhead plane after plane roared, all flying the same direction. The three parachutes in this pasture pointed like an arrow in that direction.

A row of trees surrounded the three acres or so of this French pasture. By daylight I would learn that they were hedgerows. I would also learn that I had landed dead center in the field. As I stood boldly in the open on the Normandy dairy farm I saw someone moving near the tree line. I had no doubt about it; this was someone I knew, a friendly trooper. I turned back to the French cows and said to them, "Thank God, you are cows and not German soldiers."

I walked straight over to the paratrooper. As I came closer he snapped his toy cricket once.

"That you, Sergeant Nutter?" I said.

"Goddamnit, Black. You are supposed to answer with a password or with your cricket."

As I approached the sergeant I saw that he was hurt. I asked him if he'd been hit, and he said he thought he may have broken his leg on the jump. It was his ankle, and with the jump boot still on, he wasn't sure. But it hurt like hell. Since we were at the wire fence on the border of the field, and he had checked it out (by eye only), Sergeant Nutter felt we should cross the fence. There were two lines of trees, and what appeared to be a road between. The area was elevated maybe three or four feet above the field, and there was a small drainage ditch between the fence and the road. The trees were very close together, and it was dark along the ditch.

Sergeant Nutter decided we should crawl over the fence, get into the ditch (which was dry), and then we could take a look at his ankle. We had just made it over the fence when we heard someone coming. Sergeant Nutter used his toy cricket. "Click-clack!"

Immediately came back, "Click-clack, click-clack" and then, "Flash! Thunder?"

It was Bob Cahoon, no mistaking that Boston brogue. He was our Second Squad's machine gun ammo bearer, with Folley and me. "That you Sergeant Nutter?" he said. "Great! Who else? Black! You made it? Great! Everybody OK?" Private Cahoon asked.

"Hell, no! Get over here in this ditch with us and shut up. Where do you think we are, at the local pub?" Sergeant Nutter made it clear to both of us squad men that he was in charge no matter how badly he was hurt.

None of us had any medical training to speak of, but we agreed his jump boot should be taken off or at least loosened. Cahoon tried to help the sergeant take off his jump boot while I kept a watchful eye out for anybody who might go by. The pain was too great for the sergeant to bear the unprofessional messing around of Private Cahoon. The jump boot would stay on. Sergeant Nutter had made up his mind. Broken leg or not, there was a war on. He had a job to do.

The first thing we had to do was figure out where we were. Down in the ditch, we could hear people talking. They were too far away for us to make out whether they were friends or foe. Sergeant Nutter felt we should go that way and investigate. We played safe by crawling on our hands and knees, staying in the ditch.

I led out as the scout, with the sergeant in the middle and Bob Cahoon guarding our rear. Until we started moving I hadn't seen anything on the roadway. My guess is that we crawled at least a hundred yards before I could make out a set of farm buildings in the moonlight. Then I could see people moving about on the road near the building. I could plainly hear their conversation. I stopped to listen to what they were saying. The Sergeant caught up to me. "What the hell is the holdup, Black?" he said.

I told him I was listening to a group of people talking just ahead of us. "Well, what the hell are they saying?"

"I can't understand one word," I said.

"Can you tell me if they're talking French or German?" Before I could answer, he said, "Godammit, Black, use your cricket. Hear that click-clack? Answer them!"

While I was looking for it Private Cahoon caught up with us. At last I found it, and on bent knee I gave the old one-two answer back: "Click-clack, click-clack!"

All hell broke loose. "Br-r-r-r-r-r-rt! Br-r-r-r-r-r-rt! Br-r-r-r-r-r-rt!" Right down our ditch about a foot over the top of our heads. Tree leaves, twigs and small branches fell on top of us.

"Don't those dumb bastards know the password?" said Nutter.

"Password be damned, Sergeant," I said. "That wasn't one of our guns. You know something else, Sergeant? Those guys were talking in German. I'm damned sure of that now, and I can't speak a word of it."

"You're right, Black! Turn around, and let's get the hell out of here."

We did. All three of us stood up and ran back down that ditch. We ran at least two hundred yards before we stopped, and then only because Sergeant Nutter couldn't keep up with Bob and me. He yelled at us to stop.

Sergeant Nutter caught up with us, and after we got ourselves together and talked over what we should or could do, he made a wise decision.

That little run had just about fixed Sarge's leg. He could not go on any longer. All around us were German soldiers. They were walking up and down the roadway in squad-sized patrols. Lying out of their sight in the ditch, we could almost reach up and touch them as they walked by.

It was obvious we had landed in a bees' nest. Sergeant Nutter's decision was for us to stay out of sight and wait until daylight. Then we could see where we were and try to get help. So the three of us sat down back to back in a vigil that for Private Cahoon and myself meant nothing less than the guarding of our wounded Sergeant. To both of us this became a deadly serious act. It could also have been our bravest act of D-day.

All night long our planes roared overhead. The sound of their engines was probably the eeriest sound of the whole war as far as I was concerned. We could hear our C-47s hedge-hopping their way back out to sea once they had cut their payloads. They flew so low over us that we could have tossed a stone and hit them. We always had the fear they were going to crash into us when they were hit, as we saw many that were hit and burst into flames. All night the Germans ran back and forth on the road in front of us stopping only to fire their small-arms weapons at the planes overhead.

It was an unforgettable night. It seemed it would never end. At dawn's early light, something new began. Offshore came the navy guns. Ours!

I remember Sergeant Nutter's words: "Take hope, men. The big invasion has begun."

Then it was daylight. Just like that, from dark to day. It was as if our big Navy guns pushed the sun up. For the first time on this long night the three of us could see each other. We were one hell of a sight. Our blackened faces, streaked from sweat, were smeared with splotches of dried blood from scratches on our run through the tree branches.

Sgt. Nutter looked at me and said, "What do you have in your hand?"

When he asked me that question, I had to look. I was gripping the hand grenade I'd been about to toss when those French dairy cows were charging at me. The sergeant took a closer look at me. "That godamned thing doesn't have a pin it. Throw the son-of-a-bitch!"

I did. "Bang!" My first shot in the war.

4

Capture the Flag

For half an hour since the offshore shelling had begun, no German soldiers had walked past us or could be seen. Nor could we hear any movement around the farm site. This was on the sergeant's mind when he said, "I think we should try to find out where we are and where the rest of our squad is. Let's try the farm site again. There must be a house there and Frenchmen around here somewhere."

Once more I became the scout, and Bob Cahoon let Sergeant Nutter lean on him. This time we walked on the roadway between the rows of trees and marched straight toward the main gate at the farm.

The gate was made of heavy boards, a true farm type. It was shut, closing in a rectangular area surrounded by a brick wall that linked the masonry farm buildings. One of the buildings was the dwelling. We could tell because in the row of farm buildings, a roof lined with several chimneys marked the farmhouse. Through the gate we walked into the brick and cobblestone farmyard, like being on a street in a small town. Trees lined the outside walls and draped their branches over the sides.

We saw evidence of plenty of Germany activity around the front gate. An assortment of military junk, both German and American, was spread around on both sides near the gate. Spent shell casings lay on the hard surface. Several parachutes hung from tree limbs inside the farmyard. Two of the chutes were equipment bundles; the others were the main chutes of troopers. We decided to inspect them later. Just then I caught movement at the doorway.

Private Cahoon and I dashed through the gate and divided in two directions in the courtyard. The Germans were no longer there. However, our little act did scare someone. The only trouble was it turned out to be our friends, the French. This hurt rather than helped us, because now the farmers were afraid to come outside for fear we would shoot at anything that moved.

Obviously, there were no Germans around here, but we needed to know where they had gone and when they left. Our communications had broken down before we started.

To those Normandy farmers we three paratroopers must have looked like men from outer space, and I can't blame them for looking at us from the relative safety of their windows. Bob and I tried what any Yank soldier in World War II would have done on his first try: talk them out.

"Hey, you guys in there. Come out here. We want to talk to you."

"Me A-mer-i-can!"

No show.

Bob and I walked back to the gate—without getting shot in the back—and told Sergeant Nutter what he had been watching all along. He told us to go back and try sign language. If that didn't work, he said, go on up and knock on their door.

We did. It must have been as funny as hell to watch us. First me, then Private Cahoon, went through motions. We waved. We stuck out our hand in friendship. We pointed to our American flag armbands. We took the bayonet off our one rifle. Then we tried the ultimate. We laid our firearms on the ground in a gesture of peace. Nothing worked.

Sergeant Nutter had seen enough. "Hey, you two troopers," he shouted. "Come here! Let's try something else." He had us go out the gate, out of sight of the farmers while he told us what he had in mind.

"Let an old soldier try a trick or two from the old book," he said. "Only this time we won't be tricking anybody, will we?" He handed me his Thomson submachine gun and gave his helmet to Private Cahoon. "Get me a stick of some kind, to use for a walking stick to lean on." I found something nearby. "Now watch this, men. No one can resist the plea for help by a wounded, helpless soldier." He started through the gate into the courtyard. "Or can they?" he added as he made his way toward the house.

Sergeant Junior Nutter was hurting, that was for damned sure. Bob and I knew that as we watched him struggle to walk. This was no act. He had no tricks up his sleeve. He was begging for help, it was plain to see in any language.

Before the sergeant got to the door the Normandy farmers came out to help him. Soon there were three men, and then three women. All were old. An old lady held out a cup and a pitcher of milk. The Sergeant drank the milk gratefully. They talked and pointed and waved and then looked at the sergeant's map. A little while later they helped Sergeant Nutter back to the gate where Bob and I were waiting. We shook hands all around. The Frenchmen repeated one phrase over and over: *"La boshe, kaput! La boshe, kaput!"*

We knew no French, but we knew what that meant. We felt good about our chances of getting away from this farm and finding help for the sergeant. Before heading back down the lane, we inspected the area around the empty parachutes hanging from the branches. Everything of any value was gone—taken by the Germans, we judged, according to the way the bundles were torn open. They could have been our own platoon's equipment bundles. Later we learned we had lost one. We were not positive who the trooper was who landed near one of those chutes, but it seemed clear that he was from our Company.

We left that Normandy farm by the front entrance, strolling down the country lane as the old French farmers were bringing their dairy cows in for the early morning milking.

From that first day of combat to the end of the war I observed that at or near the front lines, everything stops except for one thing—farming. The reason for this, I believe, is that food is needed for both sides. A sort of unwritten law seems to protect the farmers. We "sort of" fought around them. Add to that the fact that farmers are a hearty lot.

We reached the end of the lane and turned to the right, which led southeast. Sergeant Nutter told us we were near a place called Foucarville in the area of our First Battalion's (502) missions. Foucarville was a small village about two miles inland from Utah Beach, the key point of the northern boundary to the beach landing. Colonel Cassidy, our First Battalion Commanding Officer has as his "end mission" the task of establishing a northern defense line that would be a safeguard for keeping open Causeway #4 as well as Exit #3.

Our first job was to capture and hold the road net that ran through the first set of these small villages. This involved clearing out all the German strongholds, such as the known artillery garrison and barracks at St. Martin de Varreville where Exit #4 went straight through to the inland. This task was called "Objective X-X-Y-Z."

The objective of the 3rd Battalion under Lt. Colonel Cole was the capture of the two northern causeways, Exits #3 and #4. Colonel Chappuis' Second Battalion was assigned the mission of destroying a big coastal gun battery in the village of St. Martin de Varreville along Causeway #4, about two miles inland.

Speaking only for those of us with no rank, not the officer corps or the strategists, I would like to point out two serious problems at the Normandy invasion. First off, the drop itself was so badly bungled by the C-47 pilots that we found ourselves lost from the start. So bad was this night jump for most of us that the main advantage of the invasion, having the "element of surprise" on our side, was taken from us. The second serious problem was what to do with German soldiers who were surrendering in large numbers? Where do we put them? How do we move them? Who guards them while we fight?

As a result of these problems, many of us enlisted men didn't know who was giving out the orders after our landing. Should we try to find our own outfits to help carry out the job we were briefed to do? Should we join up with the first soldiers we saw and do

Capture the Flag

whatever the ranking man saw fit for us to do? The second option could leave a bad taste in your mouth if you lived through it. At best, you had a good chance of getting the short end of the stick.

Private Bob Cahoon and I moved slowly with our squad Sergeant. Marching straight down the center of the road in broad daylight, we came upon the dead body of one of our own 502 troopers. He was lying face down by the side of the road, so still that we were stunned at the sight. We stood and looked at him a long time. We could not see a mark on him. Sergeant Nutter told me to get one of his dog tags.

We put his rifle with the bayonet on it into the ground beside him and put his helmet on it. It seemed the right thing to do at the time, but I never did that again. I couldn't, after I found out how enemy soldiers treated the bodies of Americans lost in battle.

We moved on toward a group of buildings we thought was the village of Foucarville. We ran into a small patrol of our men led by Major Stopka from our 3rd Battalion. They were on their way to knock out a German machine gun nest back up the road a few hundred yards past the lane to the farmhouse we had visited.

"I could use your help," the Major said to Sergeant Nutter. "Besides, it might be fun."

Bob and I went with the men, leaving Nutter sitting by the road waiting for us to come back.

Boldly down the center of the road we marched. God, we were sure of ourselves. I sensed a feeling of excitement rising in me. There were eight of us in the patrol, and our heaviest weapon was a rifle. We attacked with a frontal assault, but the Jerry soldiers were too well dug in. The Major called it off, and we returned to the spot where Sergeant Nutter was waiting for us. Together we all moved on down the road southeast toward the village of Ravenoville. Along he way we ran into another group of paratroopers who were marching German prisoners to an old farm quadrangle they had just helped capture. These men had been part of Major Stopka's group and were out on a roundup of prisoners while the Major was taking us to the German machine gun nest.

The old farm quadrangle had been used as a German barracks, and the German soldiers tried their best to defend it. Many of them paid with their lives, but some had given up the fight and had run away. They were the ones being rounded up and herded back to their old barracks as our prisoners.

We three "C" Company men, along with the Major and his patrol, joined the paratroopers with the prisoners and followed them into the quadrangle. The area took on an atmosphere of celebration for the next few hours. Bob and I were glad not only because we found help in numbers, but also because we found a medic for our Sergeant. He was saved, though he would not reach the beach hospital for another twenty-four hours.

We met up with a few of our friends from our platoon and some from our very own squad. Corporal Metz and Lieutenant Cahill, our assistant platoon leader and our squad leader, were there. Also with them were Private Flanagan and Private Davis of our first squad. But no one knew where my first gunner, Pfc. Folley was or had any idea where "Big" Holly and W. O. Bird had come down. They did not know where Captain Hancock, Lieutenant Borcherd, or Sergeant. J. B. Shenk were. "But," said Corporal Metz, "We know where Pfc.'s Harry Dandorf and E. E. Funk are. Come, I'll show you."

Like a fool, I went. We walked through the back gate of the old farm to a wooded area with large trees. There, still hanging from their parachutes, were the bodies of Dandorf and Funk, both men from my Second Squad. Neither had a chance to fire a shot

Capture the Flag

because their chutes had been caught high in the trees. It was terrible to see. They were so high off the ground we couldn't reach them. Lieutenant Cahill sent a detail to cut them down.

As far as Private Flanagan was concerned, death was strictly for the enemy—or the unlucky, if it happened on our side. He gave no outward sign that he worried about it. James Flanagan started out like a wild man with absolutely no fear of the Germans. If there was a patrol to run anywhere near no-man's land, he was your man. Before the day ended, Major Stopka made him his right-hand man. He was the bravest damned trooper I'd ever seen.

Behind our circle of 2nd Platoon men I could hear a lot of excitement. Then Flanagan's loud mouth. "Hey, Black! You, too, Cahoon. Come over here! This guy's going to take your picture for the movies." He tapped me on the back and jerked me around to face him. "See this?" Private Flanagan said in another loud burst.

"Yeah? What the hell is it?" I said.

"Goddammit, can't you see? It's the first captured German flag of the war!" He was holding a small German flag he had taken down from the wall of the former German headquarters here, now our American stronghold. James Flanagan was generous as he tried again. "Come on, men! The 2nd Platoon is going to get credit for capturing the first German flag. This man wants to take a good action picture to show our people back home."

I suppose it was because of Flanagan's first entrance into our hut that Sunday afternoon back in England that all of us old-timers turned him off. Whatever the reason, to a man we all turned him down.

What none of us knew, not even Private Flanagan, was the fact that the very first newsreel seen in the movie theaters in the States included these pictures of Stopka's task force. The headline read, "101st Airborne Paratroopers Capture Flag!"

The day started to warm up towards noon. The good Lord, whom we thought was on our side, gave us warm sunshine, and the enemy put on the heat with counterattacks. Most of us were eating a dinner of K-rations when the Major asked if some of us wouldn't like to go on a little counterattack of our own. It seemed the Germans were about to zero an 88 in on our crossroad. "Hey, troopers! You all can finish your chow first!"

Two things about that interchange were never duplicated again in the war: first, our eagerness to volunteer and go along with him and, second, his polite and friendly manner as he offered to let us join him for some fun and excitement.

We had guards watching the German prisoners but had not yet set up roadblocks, not even outposts with guards to defend our stronghold. We had not dug our first foxhole. But, after all, no one was trying to capture us. Hell, so far into the war, *we* were doing the hunting. That had been the case at least since daylight.

Major Stopka was doing exactly what airborne troops were trained to do: raise hell with the enemy behind his lines. Whenever he heard they were nearby, he went after them. The major was always in the lead. Sometimes he would bite off more for us than we could chew. Then we would hit hard and fast and run back to our stronghold. We spent most of the afternoon doing this with good luck. We brought in prisoners from time to time, and no one on our side of these skirmishes was wounded. It was beginning to look easy. But, as we soon learned after our first day of combat, German soldiers will fight like hell against us and use every trick in their book.

Night time found us at this old farm quadrangle, now called "Stopka's Stronghold." Our outstanding officer called off the task-force patrols. He sent Second Lieutenant Cahill out to set up an outer defense of secondary outposts ringing the whole quadrangle. The defense consisted of roadblocks forming a tight ring around the stronghold. The Major set up several light air-cooled (30-C) machine guns with at least four riflemen to help protect each gun position.

Major Stopka used his daytime hours well. All the time he had us men out on hunting patrols, it wasn't just the enemy we were looking for. We were trying to reach other U.S. paratrooper strongholds in hopes of finding the other units of 502. There was no sign of the 4th Division from Utah Beach. We didn't know if they were even ashore yet. We were, in actuality, surrounded by enemy forces. Most of us didn't give that a thought, but the Major

Capture the Flag 31

and Lieutenant Cahill did. All day long we also hunted for any equipment bundles we could find.

By noon on D-day it was too late to worry about which division the bundles we found belonged to. We needed machine guns, mortars, ammo and food. Just as important, we didn't want the Germans to get their hands on them.

Because our hunt had been so successful, I was handed a 30-C machine gun and assigned as the first gunner on one of the outposts. My machine gun corporal, our platoon's highest ranking noncommissioned officer, was in charge of my gun position. My Second gunner was Pfc. William Cooper, who volunteered to help me. All four riflemen were "C" Company, 2nd Platoon men: Privates John L. Davis, George Blackburn, Robert Cahoon; and Corporal Metz.

Private James Flanagan would be our liaison between the Major and our post after dark. Also spending the night of D-day back in the quadrangle were Lieutenant Cahill and Private Rip Collins. Rip Collins was in the 3rd platoon, but he had overshot the drop zone and had landed in the ocean. He had worked his way inland and came across our stronghold later in the morning.

Since we were near the seashore in low-lying country, we knew that this part of Normandy was low-elevation country, and that the land around and leading to the largest city in the area, Carentan, was below sea level. The people needed drainage ditches and had built up a network of ditches like the one near the farm lane where I'd landed. There was no water in the ditches, and we used them as a means of movement back and forth from the Major's stronghold.

One ditch at the roadway where I had my machine gun set up ran north and south on one side of the road. Pfc. Cooper and I set the machine gun on the road bed without digging a hole. We stood in the deep ditch behind the gun just as if it were a man-made trench. Our four riflemen did the same.

Although by June 6 summer weather had not arrived, it would stay light until well past 2100 hours (9 p.m.). As Cooper and I stood at our positions waiting for whatever was in store, a single rifle shot rang out to our right. We heard the cry, "Medic!" Then the words, "Watch out! Lousy German sniper out in front of us!" The news traveled all the way around our outposts and back to the Major in the center of the stronghold.

Major Stopka came on the run to our area. "That dirty son-of-a-bitch got one of our boys right between the eyes," he said. So now there were four dead. I had yet to see anyone get hit, but I had heard my first one. Major Stopka had two troopers carry the dead boy back down the ditch past us all the way back to headquarters. Then the Major took Private Flanagan with several other troopers on one last "Stopka Task Force" patrol. It was an "eye for an eye" thing with our Major, and those lousy Krauts paid three times over. Not one but three German snipers fell dead from the tall trees in front of us.

Sometime before dark Major Stopka paid a visit to those of us on the outer perimeter with an extra box of 30-C machine gun ammo for each gun. He knew his two guns facing east toward the sea and Utah Beach would surely be tested before this night would end. To us two Pfcs the Major said, "Men, you have done a great job all day long. Let's hang on throughout this night. Come morning, we will have the 4th Division ashore to stay. Don't be afraid to burn up those barrels if you have to. We've got more where those came from. Give 'em hell, troopers. Give 'em hell!" He stood silently staring at the dense wooded area a few feet in front of our machine guns. For a long time he did not speak. He must have been thinking, "This is a hell of a spot for a machine gunner to be stuck. If the Germans had seen either one or both of these guns in the daylight...Man, just one hand-grenade at each gun site, and these guys are gone!"

The Major grabbed each of us by one arm and said, "Hey, godammit. If it gets too hot out here, beat it back down this ditch for the quadrangle. Do ya hear?" Then he left.

We watched him go back down the long ditch to the main gate of the old farm quadrangle where he had set up his headquarters for the long night ahead of us. Cooper and I did not speak to each other for a long time. Each of us was caught up in his own thoughts about this Major from our 502nd 3rd Battalion. When one of us did break the silence, it was Cooper who said, "There goes a real leader."

5

Firing Ammo at the Enemy

Our first long night in the war was underway. Our terrible gun positions, the Germans trying to free the prisoners we held, our uncertainty about the other Yankee soldiers who were strangers to us but sharing quarters with us, the loss of one of our men by a German sniper, three of us found dead in the trees nearby, and the pressure of feeling trapped with enemy troops out there—all of these contributed to our feelings of anxiety. But the hardest to overcome was loss of sleep. We were thoroughly fatigued by now, in no condition to fight. It was inevitable that the shooting was soon to start.

"Br-r-r-r-r-r-t!" The machine gun nest cut loose. This was not just a "tap off" as we were taught to do at night so we would not give our position away. A "tap off" was done by lightly tapping the machine gun trigger with your trigger finger in a quick jerky way so that only three bullets would fire at once. We would to this at spaced intervals. The "fire flash" with a "tap off" from the machine gun was hard for the enemy to pick up.

When a machine gunner cuts loose as this one did, either he has something in his sight or he is an inexperienced gunner. We saw and heard nothing so held our fire. On and on into the night Cooper and I lay behind our gun, straining our eyes and ears for the least sign of something to fire at. Private Flanagan was sent to find out the result of the shooting and why only one gun was involved. It was past midnight, Flanagan told us. We told him we had seen nothing to fire at and neither had any of our riflemen at this gun position. "The Major says if it gets too hot out here to pull back and bring your gun," Flanagan said. He dropped us off another box of ammo. We now had four boxes.

We kept our gun position quiet for at least another hour. Then our inexperience won over our better judgment. We both were sure we saw and heard the enemy in front of us. Now it was our turn to make war. I fired my machine gun in short bursts, tapping off three or four bullets at a time. It seemed the more we fired the gun, the more action took place in the pasture in front of us. We could see make out the forms running past us, as if they were trying to bypass our gun position and attack our quadrangle.

Time seemed to stand still. We were sure the Germans were infiltrating past our gun position by going through the field. We prayed for daylight. Riflemen back at the quadrangle began to fire a few shots as the skies grayed toward morning. By now we were on our fourth box of ammo. I told Pfc. Cooper to watch the gun while I went to find Corporal Metz. We had not seen or talked to anyone but Private Flanagan since Major Stopka had left us the third box of ammo back at the start of the darkness. It occurred to Cooper and me how strange it had been this whole night that our rifle support, which included Corporal Metz, had not fired a shot. Why?

I found the answer to that in a damned hurry. They had all been asleep—since sometime before we opened up with our machine guns around midnight! How in the world could anyone sleep through 750 rounds of machine gun firing? Not to mention all those hand grenades Cooper and I threw into the tree-covered area.

Damn, I was mad at those guys. All night long Cooper and I had felt sure that we had four riflemen guarding our flanks. I

Firing Ammo at the Enemy

raised so much hell up and down the ditches that everyone was awake for the rest of the time. I made sure of that. When I got to Corporal Metz, he gave me hell for making so much noise and awakening him. When I told him the Germans had been trying all night to break through our defense, he said, "What Germans?"

I said, "The ones Cooper and I have shot three boxes of ammo at!"

"Three boxes of ammo!" the Corporal yelled. "What in hell are you two men trying to do, win the war in one night?" He was wide awake. "Why didn't you wake me up sooner?" he said.

Much later I learned something that took away some of the sting of going it alone on this, the longest night of the war. To ward off air sicknesses, some of the airmen took two pills in the belief that if one is good, two is twice as good. Sooner or later, they became very drowsy and fell asleep no matter what was going on. Cooper and I had passed our pills on to someone else.

Dawn was beautiful. All was quiet. Not a shot was fired. The fog had settled in as it did almost every night here in the low country, rolling in from the sea and lifting as soon as the sun came up. We waited so we could count the dead.

We had the front seat on the stage of this war. On D plus one of this great invasion, that's how it looked to me. A big stage; the fog was the curtain. As it slowly went up, we knew it would reveal to Cooper and me the third act in our all-night drama.

Now on hand and wide awake was our supporting cast. Private John L. Davis from our 2nd Platoon's First squad kidded Cooper and me when he saw all of those empty 30-C shell casings. Davis was a handsome guy, always neatly dressed, and a sure-fire winner with the English gals. In a few days he would be killed in the line of action, and I would see it happen. But now he was enjoying being a tease. All day long he laughed about our valiant fight through the night. "Seven hundred and fifty of them," he told the boys, "I counted them!" It was funny. Seven hundred and fifty empty shell casings made a hell of a pile. What made it even funnier was that there was not one dead German soldier in front of our gun position.

The foggy curtain went up to reveal the damnedest war scene I ever saw. Out in that pasture lay the dead bodies of every horse and cow belonging to a French farmer who had the misfortune of choosing that field for them to spend the night of June 6, 1944.

In all, four horses and seven cows lay dead in the grass. So help me, there was not a single enemy soldier anywhere. I've never asked those machine gunners on our right about the few rounds of ammo they let fly. We had proof of our excuse. What was theirs?

We stayed in our position another two hours because of the pressure our American 4th Division was putting on the enemy as it moved in from the shores of Utah Beach.

Around 0700 hours I saw the first soldier from the 4th Division, the lead scout of one of the attacking regiments. He came straight at our gun down the roadway from our other gun position. I could always tell our infantry soldiers by their old-fashioned "leggins."

I do not remember any wild cheering or celebrating when the 4th Division arrived. Not even a handshake. An officer asked Corporal Metz a few questions. Metz ended the conversation by saying, "We are only a stronghold at this farmhouse, which has been a German headquarters. As far as we know, we are cut off from our main units of the 101st Airborne Division."

He directed the officer to Major Stopka back at the farm quadrangle for more information.

Thus, a meeting of the sea and airborne troops took place. As we sat and watched the men pass by, I felt that my part in the invasion was over and that we would be returning to England in a day or two. Little did I know.

One smart guy from the 4th made a remark he should have left unsaid. "You guys must have had a hell of a fight here!" he said.

"Yeah, we sure did," said Corporal Metz. "The Germans tried to lead a calvary charge through here."

We overheard a private from the 4th say to a buddy, "Hey, Joe. No one told us about the Germans having a calvary."

"There's a lot they didn't tell us, Willie," his buddy replied. "But by God they must. Take a look at all those dead horses over there in the field!"

Firing Ammo at the Enemy

Major Stopka's task force ended, we were told to chow down and stand by to move. The Major came by and shook hands with each of us. He said he was proud of our fine stand here through the night. He said the Germans had indeed tried to break through into the quadrangle and that our constant firing from the two machine gun positions kept them from mounting a sizable force to break through and release the prisoners. A search of the surrounding grounds, he said, had yielded several dead enemy soldiers. "I am going to recommend everyone for a medal," he said. "I want your names."

By afternoon we were formed up on the main road and soon met up with other First Battalion men. I saw Colonel Cassidy, our Battalion's Commanding Officer and with him some of our other "C" Company men, including Pfc. Marvin Milligan from our 2nd Platoon's First squad. He was assigned to help guard about forty German prisoners.

As the ranking officer, Colonel Cassidy took charge of those of us in the 502 group. His main interest was the rapid return of all men to their units so that a task force of strong units would be ready to strike out at the big city of Carentan. This was General Taylor's main concern for the Division. The high-ranking officers of the Division knew by now that the jump had been badly scattered, but at my level we had no idea how bad the jump had been. All I knew was that my "C" Company had been scattered. Now we would be meeting up with the rest of the "C" Company men.

We said good-bye to the men of the 501st and 506th Parachute Regiments. I never saw any of them again.

Colonel Cassidy told us as we got set to move out that we would be going through some enemy-held territory. A German officer taken prisoner had told Cassidy that he knew of no troops between the quadrangle and the place where we would meet our regiment. But in case he was lying, we were not going to take any chances.

After these many years I still feel that there are no rules in war, only in games. In war the winner makes the rules, but only in the end are they taken into account.

The Colonel ordered all of the prisoners in this "catch" to march at the head of the column with the German officer leading the way. For some reason our four troopers with Thompson submachine guns assigned to guard the prisoners on the march were all walking behind them. Because of the machine gun I was carrying, I was put in the rear.

At a bend in the road the Germans had a machine gun nest set up. Whether the German officer knew this all along or just picked it up as he walked by at the head of our column there is no way of knowing. The German machine gunners let all of the German prisoners pass. Then, "Br-r-r-r-r-r-t!" They let us have it.

Why they didn't get more of us I'll never know. We were stunned at first and waited too long to react. Some of our prisoners got away, including the sharp German officer.

Most of the prisoners hit the ground, as did all of us paratroopers. We recovered quickly enough to open fire and managed to knock out one of the machine gunners, while the other one ran away. How many prisoners got away I'm not sure. Those who didn't run off should have because the next thing I knew the guards were firing at all of the prisoners who were left. "Br-r-r-r-r-rt!"

People were going to die today. That much I was sure of. I knew that all of us men would have to help look out for one another.

It was a joy later that day when I met up with my fellow "C" Company men and officers. Our Commanding Officer Captain Hancock, First Lieutenant Jack Borcherd and the 1st Platoon's Second Lieutenant Morton Smit were there. Lieutenant Bernard Bucior had been wounded and was on his way back to England. Later we learned that he was KIA (killed in action) somewhere on the beach or at sea on his way to England.

Many of the men who were missing would trickle back to us in due time, delayed by small wounds or just from being lost on the jump. We learned that the "A" Company had lost a whole plane load, including their Commanding Officer R. L. Davidson, by overshooting the shoreline and crashing into the ocean where all drowned. Word was confirmed from rumors I heard on D-day that the Commanding officer of the "B" Company, Captain C. R. Fitzgerald, had taken enemy fire. Our 1st Battalion lost half of the

Firing Ammo at the Enemy

company's leaders. Captain Fitzgerald, however, lived and returned to lead the "B" Company in Holland.

Brigadier General Pratt, the Division's Assistant Commander, was killed when his glider crashed on the night glider landing on D-day. Our Regiment's Commanding Officer Colonel George Van Horn Moseley, Jr., broke his leg on the jump and stayed with us overnight, directing the Regiment from a French wheelbarrow. General McAuliffe had to order him to the rear, and General Taylor had him evacuated to England.

Our new Commanding Officer was Lieutenant Colonel John H. Michaelis. It was a quirk of fate that three of the 101st Airborne Division's oldest and most experienced leaders would miss out on the whole show. They had done their jobs well. That was for damn sure.

I stood as a posted guard in the early hours of the morning at our regimental bivouac. It was the last two-hour watch before daylight, a lonely watch. I found myself reflecting on what had happened the past two days.

6

The Move on Carentan, France

Those of us in the First and 3rd Battalions of the 502nd Regiment were to move out on the attack early in the morning heading toward the city of Carentan. The little village of Houesville was our immediate objective.

The day began as I came off guard at 0530 hours. The attacked developed slowly because of the difficulty in coordinating the artillery. It was the kind of attack with both Battalions going down the same road in single file. Our 1st Battalion would turn off to the right about a mile up ahead, while the 3rd would got off to the left. Since Company "C" was behind Company "A" and "B," we did a lot of standing around on the highway before we got into the fight.

As we came upon the main highway and made a turn to head down it, there in the crossroad, out in the open, in plain view of the enemy up ahead, was a French wheelbarrow in the middle of the highway. Sitting in it was our Regimental C.O.,

Colonel George Van Horn Mosely, Jr. His broken leg was in a cast, and he could not walk, but he was directing 502 just the same.

He looked each of us straight in the eye as we marched past. "Give 'em hell, men!" he said. I was sure he would lead us for the rest of the attack from that wheelbarrow, broken leg be damned. However, at this place General McAuliffe ordered him to the rear.

We pulled off the main Carentan highway to the right and started to flank the town of Houesville by going through the small fields near the seashore. French farmers used these fields, two or three acres in size, as cropland or pasture. Every field had a gateway, and surrounding each field was a mound of dirt, up to ten feet high, with trees and underbrush growing on it, making a perfect fence for livestock control. Some say that the fields were built to protect the Normans from invasion by sea. Others say they protected the crops from harsh winds and salt waters of the sea. I don't know, but one thing I am sure of. They were of damn little help to us Allied troops in 1944.

Field by field we cleared the space ahead of us. We used one platoon to a field to start. We went into the field by the main gate. Or tried to. The first man in was the scout. For our 2nd Platoon that was Pfc. John L. Davis. As the rest of us waited at the gate we watched Davis walk into the fields. About twenty yards in: "Br-r-r-r-r-rt!" John L. Davis fell dead.

We opened fire at the sound and blasted at the far hedgerow. We waited, then rushed into the field and searched it out. We found our empty shell casings where the Germans had been out of our sight. But they had gotten away.

Revenge was the cry. Out after them we went. We tried the front gate. To the next field we marched. Once more a single scout slowly moved out into the small field. "Br-r-r-r-r-rt!" This time it was Pfc. Norman Cournoyer from our 3rd squad who fell dead.

Hell! We could not keep this up. We were losing one man per field. The Germans were falling back a field at a time, fighting a delaying action, with the hedgerows furnishing perfect cover and protection. Lieutenant Thomas Cahill put his head together with Platoon Sergeant Jay B. Shenk, a man of quick wit and common sense. Since they huddled nearby, we could hear what was said.

The Move on Carentan, France

There weren't that many of us in the platoon, and we were losing them fast.

J. B. said, "By God, Sir, it's time we try going in some place besides the front gate—Sir. That is, if you ask me—Sir!"

"I am asking you, Sergeant," said the Lieutenant.

"If it were up to me, I would put Folley and Black on their machine gun up there on top of that hedgerow and let them spray hell out of those bastards the next hedgerow over. Give them a dose of their own medicine, by God! That's what I'd do—Sir!"

That is exactly what we did, and it worked. The rest of the men would rush into the field and spread out, firing as they ran in all directions. It was slow, hard and damned dangerous work. It took guts. But it worked. The only thing we did differently after that day in such a situation was to use our 60 mm mortars to soften them up whenever the Germans decided not to fall back when we rushed into a new field.

V. J. Folley and I were at last together on a machine gun and would stay that way throughout the whole Carentan battle. It took sixty hours for us to get together and work as the team we had trained so long to be.

The German line in this area had been broken down, and Houesville was ours. Our 3rd Battalion moved in and took over the town by 1300 hours (1 pm). About 1400 hours my 2nd Platoon walked through Houesville, France, a beautiful little place off the main highway.

Just like the residential section of any small town back home, I thought. No sign of war. Until I turned the last corner onto the main street of the town. There in the middle of the street lay one of the bloodiest sights of the war. A trooper had been shot through the head, cleanly, it appeared. He may have died instantly. We hoped so. For just below each knee his legs had been hacked off. Next to his body lay the "stumps" of his two legs, his feet bared. Nearby lay a pair of badly worn boots of a German soldier.

It was barbarian through and through. Somewhere there was a lousy Kraut, a low-down, bastard German, walking around in GI paratrooper jump boots. From that day on I never saw a German soldier without looking to see what he had on his feet.

From that terrible scene we moved on through the town of Houesville to a large field overlooking the countryside. Here we were told to dig in for our own protection from any German artillery shelling. It was the beginning of foxhole digging as a way of life whenever there was a break in the action. Foxhole digging was a good way to keep one's mind from running wild with fear or hate. Take it out on your GI shovel.

I was done with my foxhole and resting in it when someone came into the field where all of the "C" Company men had dug in. It was about 1600 hours (4 p.m.), and whoever it was announced that he had just heard over some radio that the Germans had surrendered and the war was over! I believed him. Every word. For the next half hour I felt great. "Hell," I said to V. J. Folley. "This war didn't turn out to be too bad after all!"

About then along came Sergeant Jay B. Shenk to straighten us out. "When are you men going to stop falling for every rumor that comes along?" he snapped at us. "Don't you forget it. We are on the attack, men! The 101st Division has the added job of taking the city of Carentan, and, mark my words, that ain't going to be easy." He ended his speech with, "All of you pack up. We're moving out in five minutes."

From our starting point for the attack we moved in single file because the company would be using a "skirmish line" style of attack, a favorite maneuver of Colonel Cassidy's 1st Battalion. First each platoon's scout would crawl up the ten-foot road bank to the top of the hedgerow and then move out thirty yards in front of the main body. Then the whole company would move out, except for the machine gunners who waited and stayed fifty yards behind.

The time was 1730 hours (5:30 p.m.), and we would be walking into the sun heading due west all the way to the river. Although we had never practiced it, we had read in the military newspaper, *Stars & Stripes*, and had been told that we could use a walking machine gun assault to spray more fire power into the attack. It would not be accurate, but if John Wayne could use it in those Marine movies, so could we.

The tricky part is draping all the ammo of that machine gun belt (250 rounds for a full belt) around your body. The belt had to be loose enough to feed freely into the gun when you fired, or it would jam on you and hang up. The best way to be sure that would not happen was to start the ammo belt from the gunner's neck and then drape several long loops around your left arm, like a cowboy's lasso rope.

Two important things you must keep in mind at all times: the weight you have to carry and the trigger, which was not protected by a guard ring as with other small arms. Anything that might bump the trigger could start it firing unexpectedly.

V. J. Folley helped me get all set up as everybody else climbed the bank and moved out into the field heading for the far-off river. To say our company was a little jumpy would be putting it mildly.

Folley had picked out a spot for me to go up the steep bank where there was enough space between the tree lines so that I could make my own effort. Since a 30-caliber air-cooled machine gun is a very heavy piece of military equipment, plus all of the other regular equipment a paratrooper must carry, there was only one way I was going to make it up and over: with a running start.

I backed up clear across the road and said to Folley, "Are you ready?" He stood at the top of the ten-foot hedgerow waiting to catch me and pull me over in case I did not make it all the way up the bank.

"Here I come!" I yelled and took off. I just made it, but teetered on the top edge. Folley thought I was going to slip back and grabbed for me. His jacket or something brushed the machine gun trigger. "Br-r-r-r-r-r-rt!" It took off. When the gun started to fire, I must have had it pointing in the direction of my company men. I didn't know about that. All of them were out in the center of that bare pasture. My thoughts were to keep the end of the barrel pointed up in the air because the gun was stuck in the firing position and would not stop. My teeth were chattering from the shaking that machine gun was giving me.

"Keep it pointed up! Keep it up! The barrel! The barrel up! Keep it up!" Folley shouted at me.

Then as if we were the enemy—V. J. Folley and Layton Black, Jr., just the two of us—we were now the subject of a vicious attack by our own men. Everybody was out there in front of us, standing spreadeagle, firing at just one point—us! Firing at our tracer bullets. At the fireflash and smoke. At the noise that came from just one place in their rear. At me! I headed down that hedgerow bank, down into the road ditch. Folley grabbed the gun barrel to help hold it straight up in the air, partly to save himself from being shot and partly to start both of us on a downhill slide on the seats of our pants to safety.

That did not stop the machine gun's firing. As we lay on our backs in the ditch looking up, I said to Folley, "Grab the belt and twist it!" At last it stopped. We lay in complete exhaustion, staring overhead at a steady hail of bullets from our own company.

The look on my face probably matched the fright on Folley's. "How do we stop that?" Folley said to me.

I said, "Try your helmet on the end of your carbine."

Before he could get it back down there were two holes in it, and the shooting kept on at the same pace. The next thing we tried was a white piece of my reserve parachute on a long stick. That worked. The firing stopped. But we did not stick our heads up right away. V. J. Folley was the first to speak out. "Hey! What the hell is the matter with you guys out there? It's Folley and Black from the 2nd Platoon back here. What the hell you trying to do, kill us?"

The next voice was Sergeant J. B. Shenk's. "Whose side do you two men want to be on?" he said. "Make up your mind before I get up off the ground."

I looked up and saw everybody from "C" Company stretched out flat on the ground facing back with their rifles pointed at us two machine gunners. A cold chill ran up and down my spine. "Pity the damned Germans when this outfit turns on them," I said out loud. "Damn, that was a close call."

No more shots were fired the rest of the day. We made it all the way to the river without seeing a single enemy soldier.

My 2nd Platoon was put into the "C" Company reserve. We had to move back up the hill away from the river, set back a quarter of a mile along a clean, new wire fence. We dug stand-up foxholes. We could see over the river past our own front lines to the far side where the enemy was well dug in, too. Between the two sides, at this point, was more than just the river. There was a good stretch of marshland on both sides. We were pretty certain that here in front of our "C" Company the area was almost impassable.

Our Assistant Platoon Leader, Lieutenant Thomas Cahill, came by each of our foxholes, probably to make us all feel better. He stopped to chat with V. J. Folley and me in our foxhole, where we had the only machine gun dug in. He asked if either of us had gotten hurt in any way when our machine gun jammed. It was the first time anyone had bothered to find out how Folley and I felt. We told him we had only hurt our pride, that tomorrow was another day, and that we would try to do better.

"I'm looking forward to tomorrow," Lieutenant Cahill said. "It seems yesterday was a year ago. I'm sorry we lost those two men today."

7

Attack Underway

The day was Friday, and our First Battalion was ordered to "stand in place," a military term for a unit that is on line but in "reserve" of another unit that is on the attack. Attacking for our Regiment was be the 3rd Battalion. The order came down the day before, D plus 2, "for the 101st to take the City of Carentan, France."

With a population of about 4,000 people, Carentan was the second largest city in the Cherbourg Peninsula, located about eight miles from the sea on the Douver River. A canal running into the city makes it possible for small boats to enter from the sea. A set of locks built into the canal controls the flow of the ocean's tide. North of the city is marshland, mostly below sea level. It would be easy to flood the entire area. The worst thing for us is the fact that there isn't any cover.

The Allies needed to capture the city of Carentan so that we could link up all the beaches. Only then could we think of breaking out. To the Germans, Carentan had great strategic importance. To Field Marshall Rommel and General Dollmann, the Commanding Officer of the 7th Army, losing Carentan would mean the loss of the main road, and only a short time until the whole peninsula would be cut in two at its base. The loss of the main seaport city of Cherbourg would then be inevitable. Helping the German officers decide on the importance of Carentan was their discovery the day before of an Allied operational order revealing our intentions.

At a road junction near the first of four bridges was "dead man's corner." The 506th and 501st Regiments had been in stiff fights here. The 327th Glider boys had helped out at "dead man's corner," too. Now, as we said in those days, "It's our turn!"

Most of our company had a good day's rest on Friday. I caught up on some sleep in the afternoon after cleaning my machine gun. I had no idea how important that small amount of sleep would turn out to be. However, I was learning fast to make sure to rest, sleep, eat, drink, and stay clean in order to keep some form of being regular.

As darkness took over, patrol-type guard duty became the orders for the night. Since our company lines were spread thin and my 2nd Platoon was a hundred yards to the rear in reserve, there was a great fear that the Germans might run an all-night patrol through our area. The tree-lined sunken roadway that ran right by my foxhole down to the Douve River made our area the most vulnerable.

Our platoon sergeant set up three-man patrols every two hours. I drew the first patrol out at 2200 hours (10 p.m.). As I got set to move out, the sergeant said, "Hey, you three troopers, be damned sure you remember the password tonight! We just got word that one of our own 'C' Company troopers from 1st platoon was shot and killed because he didn't know the password." We learned later it was one of his own 1st platoon men who fired the shot.

This news helped drive home the importance of carrying the password on our lips when walking around at night. This patrol was one of the toughest things I'd done so far in the war. The hardest part was not knowing where our "C" Company foxholes might be along the way. Making it worse was the pitch darkness of the

Attack Underway 51

narrow, sunken tree-lined roadway all the way down to the river. All three of us walked side by side on this patrol. Whenever we came upon one of our own men, now dug in deep in stand-up foxholes, we were challenged loud and clear. It was a long walk, and we made it safely, as did all the other patrols that night, but it was an ordeal I never forgot.

I was up bright and early next morning. The order for the day was passed down by Captain Hancock: "We are going back out onto the big highway. We will catch it at St. Come-du-Mont. Then head straight downhill, out across a causeway over four bridges; and, God willing, into the big city backing up the 3rd Battalion!"

The 3rd Battalion had moved out before midnight and, like so many times, a seemingly little thing popped up to halt big plans. Their problem lay at the feet of our Division's engineers, the 326th Airborne Engineer Battalion. They had failed to repair the Number 2 bridge in time for the 3rd Battalion to cross over on schedule.

Colonel Michaels saved the 3rd Battalion for the time being by having them march back to Les Quesnels and await a new Division order to re-attack Carentan, next time in the daylight. Sometime on Saturday afternoon (June 10, 1944) the attack was to resume.

All told, we would had a total of eighteen 105-millimeter self-propelled guns and thirteen 75-millimeter pack howitzers supporting our advance. With these weapons our 377th Field Artillery Battalion, and the 907th, along with the 65th Armored Field Artillery Battalion, provided substantial artillery fire. Not in our favor was the fact that we were making our attack in broad daylight.

It must have been at least 1200 hours when Lieutenant Gehauf went out to check on the engineers working on the bridge. Colonel Robert Cole went along with the lieutenant to see for himself. Nothing had been done. In fact, the engineers from the 326th had left the bridge.

In the Airborne, when something had to be done, even an officer with the rank of colonel could be counted on to pitch in. Colonel Cole set about the task with three other men, including the captain of the lead "G" Company for the 3rd Battalion. The four men worked hard for two hours and put together a foot bridge. It was wobbly, but it could support one trooper at a time.

At 1500 hours (3 p.m.) "G" Company's 1st Platoon started across the new foot bridge. Every time the troopers bunched up on the bridge the enemy let them have it from their 88s. It was more harassing fire than anything else, but it had run off the engineers.

After three hours all but one platoon from Company "H" of Colonel Cole's 3rd Battalion had crossed over Number 2 bridge and were strung out all the way up to Number 3 bridge. One platoon was over the third bridge and heading out to Number 4. Lieutenant Gehauf and his intelligence sections as well as a few troopers from "H" Company's 1st platoon had passed over Number 4 bridge to the Carentan side along the causeway road. About 1800 hours (6 p.m.) all hell let loose with small arms and automatic fire as well as mortar and continuous fire from the 88s.

Until then the 3rd Battalion had only the 88s to worry about. Only one trooper had been hit at the Number 2 bridge crossing. Our low casualty rate was due to the pleading and swearing of Colonel Cole as he moved up and down the causeway ordering his men not to bunch up. The officers of the 3rd Battalion were beginning to think they were going to pull off their advance over the causeway with little or no cost.

Where were the Germans? Had they pulled out of Carentan, as we had heard from one report? It seemed the enemy was not paying much attention to our advance.

We soon learned where they were: baiting the trap. Now it swung shut on the 34th Battalion of the 502nd Parachute Regiment, with two more battalions lined up on the road right behind them ready to go into the trap when the call went out. Talk about being bunched up! The regiment, the whole damned regiment, was on this road now.

We stopped dead still. The front line was the causeway. We in the 1st Battalion were in sight of the battlefield, in range of the 88s and at their mercy. There was no cover anywhere along this road.

The thought of taking a big city was terrifying to me, but I concealed my fear as did everyone else. We knew that this was it. We knew it would be just a matter of time until we in the 2nd Platoon would come under fire. "Hurry up and wait" was only a minor strain compared to the stress of what this day would bring.

Attack Underway 53

Walking through St. Come-Du-Mont, my first French town of any size, we saw no one. The town looked deserted. It was war torn to some degree, yet we felt it would survive because of its old stone and brick buildings and streets that had lasted so long. I was glad we were not going to fight here. By mid-morning the heat of this late spring day was getting to us. We knew it would be downright hot by mid-afternoon.

Once outside of St. Come-Du-Mont, we were on the main highway heading straight into Carentan. We had to go downhill quite a ways and were held up for several hours waiting for the change of orders from the Regiment to resume the advance by the 3rd Battalion. Most of us passed the time sleeping by the side of the road.

The war had raged on that highway in all of its terribleness, and no one had taken time to clean up the battlefield. Our "rear people" took care of our dead and wounded as they somehow always did. Even in the Airborne we had "rear echelons" who came in by sea to handle the dirty work, so to speak. Thank God that they did. But nothing else had been picked up. The German dead lay everywhere in every conceivable posture. Tools of war along with the plunder of both sides lay on the roadway, destroyed.

I was shocked at the manner in which the German dead had been disturbed. Always the soldier's personal items lay scattered about him as if he was carrying some great secret. The soldier was probably no more important than I was, and what the hell did I know or have on me that was of any importance? Among the personal effects were always black-and-white snapshots. The German soldiers carried more of these than we Americans did. Many of these photos lay on the ground, face up, for all of us to see. It seemed so unfair to have to bare one's soul. To give his life should be enough.

As high noon came and went, the head of a hot "near summer" day bore down. There was no shade of any kind. From time to time we moved slowly down toward the flat stretch of the causeway.

Sergeant Jay B. Shank told us we should eat one of our four "K" rations that we were carrying and moved us off the road bed into a dugout area that had once been some kind of a gravel pit. It was no bigger than a good-sized house and as hot as hell inside. No air was stirring, and it stunk to hell and back from all the dead bodies lying around.

We ate our "K" rations in front of several dead horses the Germans had used to haul their wagons. By now they were bloated and rolled up on their backs in the kind of death we called "ripe" back on the farm. We ate, however, and did not turn our heads away. It was Monday noon before my next meal, but due to total fatigue I wasn't hungry then.

I learned later that this place was called "dead man's corner" by the paratroopers of the 506th and 501st.

The day wore on. The movement had reached a standstill for us. Time lost all meaning for me. The ticking of a watch, the minutes and hours meant nothing. There was no hurry to die. Why should there be? Wasn't the 3rd Battalion doing that well enough for the rest of us? Our turn would come. We knew it would be only a matter of time until we would get the call to take over. Time simply meant daylight or darkness. We had great leadership, the greatest of the whole war, but there was nothing to lead. The 3rd Battalion was caught in a trap. The German 6th Paratroop Regiment opened up with everything they had at 1800 hours (6 p.m.) on that day. Our men dropped like flies.

The German guns zeroed in on the iron gate at Bridge Number 4 where they set up a roadblock. Their 88 millimeter guns raked the causeway from Bridge 2 all the way to Bridge 4. For four hours, the remaining daylight hours, the enemy poured bullets from machine guns and small arms into that roadblock. Movement stopped or, at the breach in the iron gate, slowed to a trickle. Soon it became a tangled mass of telephone and electric wires. Whenever the steel bullets struck the iron in the gate or bridge or a live downed electric wire, sparks flew like fireworks.

It was hell to watch a trooper run the gauntlet between bridges, let alone take one's own turn. The buildup of the 502nd Regiment ended with the coming of darkness. All of my Battalion was still back of Bridge 1, and as yet had not been called to take over. All of the "C" Company was yet to pass through Pont-De-Douve near Bridge 1. We had just reached the level part of the highway.

Attack Underway

With me at dusk on the machine gun was V. J. Folley, who was now the acting corporal for our Second Squad. We saw them at the same time. Several troopers yelled at the tops of their voices, "Enemy planes are upon us! Take cover! Take cover! Get down! Get down!"

But it was too late. I went flat out, face down, but only after I saw they were German (Stuka) dive bombers. Those planes were scary looking. They always had their wheels down. It looked like the planes were about to land on top of us when they dived down and made a fast machine-gun strafing run over the tops of our lines.

The noise was deafening: the bombs screaming down, the thud of the machine gun bullets striking the hard surface of the roadbed and bouncing off in every direction, the tremendous noise from the airplane's motor as it zoomed overhead in a great rush of air, and then the terrible, horrifying noise of the exploding bombs as they shook the earth where I lay.

"Damned, that was a close call!" I muttered. I was sure at least a hundred more enemy planes were coming right behind and stayed face down for what I felt was a very long time.

Everything grew deathly quiet from that point into the night, as if the Germans had said, "That's all for tonight. See you in the morning!" The only sounds we heard were the cries, "Med-ic! Med-ic!" up and down the causeway and the whimpering of pain and fear. But it was soft, and seemed suppressed. There was no sense of panic.

The "I" Company from the 3rd Battalion had taken the worst of it. They caught eight bombs at Bridge 3, and were practically eliminated from the main attack. Thirty troopers had been hit from the air raid alone; eight were dead.

This was one of the few times in my life that I felt total helplessness. When we got word at last to move up between Bridge 1 and 2, I thought, "Now we are getting someplace." For the first time in this long day I started digging a foxhole.

It was sometime after midnight, maybe 0100 hours. It seemed that all of "C" Company had crossed over to the east side of the road after crossing the first bridge. The "A" and "B" Companies were on the west side by then. Now the 502nd Regiment had two battalions packed in on this road where no cover existed. We were as close together as we could get. Too close to dig foxholes, but some of us dug, anyway. V. J. Folley and I were among those who did.

German shelling had let up but had not stopped completely. Any undue movement on our part or any kind of prolonged noise such as digging brought an 88 bullet to that spot. Since there was no protection and no warning, only a fool would take a chance and stand up. All our digging was done from one's belly while lying face down.

I lay on the hard roadbed digging through the tar-bound asphalt surface with my knife and my bare hands straight down through the roadbed. It was gravel and stone all the way down. It was slow work, and it took all night. By daylight it was deep enough that I could stand in it to my shoulders. Although I didn't have a chance to use it for very long—we started moving at daylight—I have always felt it was one of my best foxholes. It was a difficult but welcome challenge for me to dig through four feet of stone and gravel packed in tight without making any noise or movement the enemy could detect. Something about hard work cures the tricks one's mind can play on you.

"We're moving up!" These words we were more than ready to hear. Colonel Cassidy had been among us all night long. It was about 0700 hours, and he told us that we would have our turn at paying the lousy German bastards back. It would be "B" Company leading the attack followed by "A" Company with "C" Company following them. The HQ Company would be in the rear with reserve and support troops, heavy weapons and supplies for the attack.

Colonel Cassidy told us that Colonel Cole's 3rd Battalion had softened the Germans up for us. Now our battalion would teach them a lesson in airborne fighting. He knew that Cole's men had spent themselves by now.

It must have been two miles from "dead man's corner" to the city limits of Carentan. Maybe it was half a mile from Bridge 1 to 4 and another half mile to the city limits. The roadway was straight as a die, much of built up with no cover of any kind—not even a tree. The causeway was as high as ten feet above the two rivers.

Attack Underway   57

Off to each side was marshland stretching for miles—flooded land, below sea level and totally impassable. The land to the east, our left side as we faced the city, was perfectly flat and reached all the way into the city. The west side did not have as much flat land. The marshland was as wide as the two rivers flowing under the four bridges.

On all the high ground in northwest Carentan the German 6th Parachute Regiment made up its mind to stand. The ground to the west pitched upward a few hundred yards past Bridge 4 and circled back to the north in a half-moon shape of high ground. This region was farmland with well-concealed roads, farm building sites and, most important to the enemy, many hedgerows that ran at right angles to the main highway that we must cross.

The most frustrating part of the whole Carentan battle for us Americans was the fact that we could not see the enemy. He had every advantage. Every single one! He had set the trap, and we had taken the bait. But we refused to be caught. We simply kept on coming until our buildup became so great that they could not kill us all. Then it became a standoff.

The battle raged with one battalion at a time until it burned itself out. Then another moved up and took its place. Colonel Cole's 3rd Battalion failed to reach the high ground on the previous day. In fact, they barely made it past the roadblock at the fourth bridge. He would try again today at daybreak. At 0400 hours his "H" Company took over the lead. By 0530 hours Colonel Cole had what was left of his 3rd Battalion across Bridge 4, but they were stymied. Fire power from the Germans' parachute regiment was devastating.

Lieutenant Rogers took over leadership of the "B" Company after the news of the loss on D-day of their Commanding Officer, Captain Fitzgerald. Rogers was a big man, known by all the older enlisted men of the 1st Battalion as one of the best "snooping and pooping" officers in the Regiment. We gave him the nickname, "Buck Rogers." It was essential to the success of the company to be led in person at times like these. At Carentan we had three company commanders who demonstrated their leadership skills: Captain Hancock of "C," Lieutenant Swanson of "A," and Lieutenant

Rogers of "B." To me as an enlisted man at the lowest level in the Battle of Carentan, the courage of these men was infectious.

    Lieutenant Rogers led "B" Company down the road to the farmhouse where Colonel Cole had set up his command post and went on past the house to the roadway. German soldiers who had survived and run back under the bayonet charge of the 3rd Battalion were spilling back into the roadway. Lieutenant Rogers had Staff Sergeant Harrison Summers of "B" Company set up two of his platoon's machine guns just beyond the farmhouse where the road reached an orchard. The rest of the "B" Company set up a line of defense on the other side of the orchard near the roadway. These positions held as the battle increased and the day dragged on.

    Sometime after 0800 hours, "A" Company started their run over the open causeway and through the iron gate at Bridge 4. While "B" Company lost eight men crossing over the causeway, "A" Company lost only six. But disaster was waiting as they reached the open field at the end of the bridge.

    The Germans sent in one of the heaviest concentrations of artillery on the whole day. Two platoons of "A" Company troopers were caught out in the open and cut to pieces in nothing flat. German 88s and mortars fell on them. A total of 15 American paratroopers were hit, and the shock scattered the rest.

    After an effort to round up the two platoons of able-bodied "A" Company survivors, the 3rd platoon was sent across. Just as it reached the open field, it got the same treatment. All hell let loose again. Nine more troopers went down. Thirty men from "A" Company were gone, and they hadn't fired a shot.

    The shock to "A" Company was so great it took more than an hour to round them up into any kind of an effective fighting unit. Most of these men were placed on a line along a water-filled ditch about two hundred yards up the main highway toward Carentan and past the Number 4 bridge.

    Like the "B" Company, the "A" Company line held fast all day long, although the first few hours they spent recovering from their initial shock. Discounting the fact that the Germans had the high ground and the cover, I believe that the fact that our dead and wounded lay in our path of advance hurt us more than anything

Attack Underway   59

else. As the day wore on it grew worse, to the point that able-bodied men had to crawl over their fellow soldiers in the ditch, to keep ammo coming up. The ditches were our only cover from enemy fire, but it was little protection from the artillery that kept taking its toll.

Now it was time for my "C" Company to take our turn. By now our 502nd Parachute Regiment had only 39 men and officers. The jump and the five days since D-day had cut into our ranks even before we started the Carentan attack. The majority of platoons were down to fewer than thirty men, some as low as two dozen. Many had only one officer and half their noncommissioned officers; some had none. As we ran the open causeway and the gauntlet of the iron gate at the Number 4 bridge, our ranks were reduced even more. We were outnumbered by the Germans.

Our Company's movement along the causeway was painfully slow. V. J. Folley and I despaired that we would ever get our chance to stand up and run. Finally our turn came. Why we were in such a hurry to run through hell I'll never know.

I had the machine gun and my carbine, and a full machine gun belt of ammo wrapped around me. Folley had the machine gun's tripod and his carbine. Bob Cahoon, our ammo bearer, had two boxes of 30-caliber ammo and his rifle. We had some four hundred yards to run to reach any kind of safe cover. We were out in the open—sitting ducks for the enemy—from the time we started to run. Down the causeway, through the iron gate. Down off the bridge of the main road onto the road to the farmhouse. Off that road to the left and out across the bare field. Jump over the water-filled ditch. Run to the corner of the cabbage patch next to the hedgerow running parallel with the main road. Four hundred yards of sheer hell!

It was a "follow-the-leader" maneuver. Over and over, "old" Jay B. Schenk, our Platoon Sergeant, told us, "Men, remember your snooping-and-pooping training back in England, Bragg and Tennessee? Here it's no dry run, men. When Lieutenant Cahill starts out, one of you every five yards behind him. Goddammit! Zig! Then zag! All the way across that field. Stay bent over, low as you can get. Let a yell out as you go. Let the bastards know we're coming. Whatever you do, don't stop! Run, by God, run, till you make that hedgerow!"

It wasn't just a question of staying alive as far as "old" J.B. was concerned. It was the only way we could get enough troopers over to outflank the enemy and save the buildup at the farmhouse. Now, this moment, was what "old" J. B. had been training us for so long to do.

Lieutenant Tom Cahill, one of the nicest guys I was ever to know, led out first on a dead run. Five yards back it was Pfc. William Cooper, followed by Pfc. Anthony Marcozzy. Behind him five yards came Corporal Willie Craig, the head of our mortar squad. Next in line was Corporal John Whitlock, our radio man. For some reason, Private Herman Jones from the 1st Platoon was next up in our 2nd Platoon run. It was my turn after Jones, and V. J. Folley behind me. Private Bob Cahoon was next, and Pfc. Jack Evans was last.

Cahill, handsome and dashing man and as brave as any man, led the men across. Let me tell you, nobody went further on the flank at the Battle of Carentan on this day.

Fear stalks a front-line soldier every moment. Only the degree of fear fluctuates. It was not the time element but the degree of fear that determined how long we could endure. I had seen what happened to the men of the "A" Company. They were only one hundred yards in front of me when they got hit in broad daylight. But they took the blow, not me. That made a tremendous difference in the degree of fear I felt.

When Lieutenant Cahill yelled back at us, "Let's go!" and "old" J. B. repeated the cry, "Next trooper!" all that mattered was that I would stand up when it came my turn. I would run through hell as long as there was someone to follow. What would I do if everyone in front of me fell? I never once thought about it.

"Next trooper!"

It was my turn. Up onto the roadway I jumped. "Keep bent over! Don't straighten up! Zig and zag!" the old sergeant said to me.

I said out loud to myself, "J.B. knows what he's talking about. Keep bent over." I kept thinking, "It's harder to hit a mov-

Attack Underway 61

ing, bobbing and weaving target." I was sure a German soldier had me alone in his sights.

There it was! I was at Number 4 bridge, and there it stood—the iron gate! A roadblock. I had to stop dead still to squeeze the machine gun through. Bullets were zinging in every direction, and the cracking of the air over my head was terrifying. I had to get through the gate and off the bridge. Nothing could be as bad as it was up here, I thought.

I made it off the bridge, down onto the side road to the farmhouse, off that road and to the ditch beside it. Just as I started my spring to leap over the ditch, I looked down into the ditch to make sure I could jump it. For the first time I saw someone besides the man I was following, a "flash scene" that my eyes recorded forever. It was the worst sight I was to see in the war! As many as six American paratroopers had been hovered close together when a German 88-millimeter shell had hit dead center in the ditch on top of them. Now it was a dirty, bloody scene of arms, legs, heads and other body parts. I almost didn't jump, but my spring was already underway. I tried to increase my jump by trying to run on the air beneath my feet, the way a broad jumper does. I cleared the ditch and did not break stride.

Twice more I passed that spot. Once at the end of the battle as it grew dark and the next day just before it grew dark. Neither time could I look at the scene for fear that I would recognize a face.

Each of us made it all the way to the short hedgerow without stopping. Ten of the eleven men made it to the fourth bridge.

Only a few running steps later and my mind was back to the task at hand. The open field I entered was far worse, I was sure, than the "iron gate." Tracer bullets were as thick as fireflies on a hot summer's night. They were coming at us from three hedgerows straight ahead. All of us were running for the hedgerow at the corner of the cabbage patch.

Then it happened. Maybe I was halfway across the field. I saw a shell hit the dirt in front of me and instantly felt a terrific blow to the middle of my stomach. I was hit! I had seen it. It was a ricochet off the ground, but I was still running forward. Why hadn't I fallen down? I remember someone saying once that after you are hit you may take several steps before you fall over dead.

"Keep running," J. B. had said, "even if you are hit!" Somehow I was. Maybe all the other guys had been hit, too, and were still running. I felt a burning sensation in my midsection. Surely my guts must be about to fall out. Maybe I was bleeding to death. Still I ran on, and so did everybody else in front of me.

I thought about how I would fall down. How does one fall down with a full belt of 30-caliber machine gun ammo wrapped around him and a heavy machine gun on his shoulder without hurting himself? A day later I would laugh at that. If I was hit so hard that I was dying, what the hell did it matter how I hit the ground?

On I ran, zigging and zagging, still bent over. My training in the paratroops had been the best. Instinct took over. I was at the water-filled ditch. I made it in one leap. I was in the cabbage patch. The main hedgerow, the one that paralleled the Carentan highway, was just ahead. Lieutenant Cahill and Pfc. Cooper cut through the short hedge that jutted into the cabbage patch. Then Pfc. Marcozzi and Corporal Willie Craig disappeared out of my sight, followed by Private Jones and Corporal John Whitlock.

When I reached the hedgerow I hit the ground. I fell forward on my stomach as enemy bullets from machine guns ripped through the hedge trees just above me. I slowly reached my hand, finally free from the machine gun, back under me to my belt line. I rubbed it around my belly and then slowly brought it out before my eyes. I knew it would be covered with blood. Not a drop anywhere. I turned over and looked at myself. Nothing was wrong with me. Whatever had hit me had not hurt me.

All my fear was gone. It was like a heavy weight had been taken from me. I wasn't even tired from that long run. I felt strong, like now I would kick the shit out of these German bastards. I was brave as hell.

Folley, Cahoon and Evans were now beside me at the hedgerow. All of us were OK. Folley, now our Second Squad's assistant squad leader, asked me where everybody had gone. "Through there—that hedge!" I said. He took off yelling, "Follow me!" We did.

Attack Underway

I did not run. Once through the short hedgerow I felt the safety of the main hedgerow running alongside the Carentan highway with a four-foot mound of dirt before the thick hedge trees started. Fortified by the fact that all of the tracer bullets had come at me from the high ground to the right, I thought the enemy could not see me now.

All ten of us slowly moved along the main hedgerow. Lieutenant Cahill, still in the lead, must have been near the point where the fourth hedgerow meets the main hedgerow when he stopped to take a look through his field glasses. He went down on one knee, holding the glasses to his eyes with one hand. "Br-r-r-r-r-r-rt! Br-r-r-r-r-r-rt! Br-r-r-r-r-r-rt!" Three bursts of German machine gun fire filled the air.

I fell back into the dirt bank of the hedge, as did V. J. Folley who was near me. When Lieutenant Cahill stopped, we kept walking, and so were somewhat bunched up when it happened.

Since I still had the heavy machine gun on my shoulder, I leaned back into the dirt bank, thinking the well-being of that gun was important. I'd felt we were safe, and it was incredible to see what happened next. Every trooper in front of Folley and me was hit and hit hard.

The four of us in the rear had not been hit, but now the Germans were out to get us. "Br-r-r-r-r-r-rt! Br-r-r-r-r-r-rt! Br-r-r-r-r-r-rt!" They missed us, but they were damned close to Folley and me as we leaned back into the bank. Bob Cahoon and Jack Evans lay flat on the ground behind us, in better position to be hit than the two of us.

Folley spoke first. "We've got to get away from here!"

"Damned right! There's a shell hole. Let's jump in there," I said.

The hole was ten or twelve feet from us, away from the hedgerow and with no cover. I went first and landed in water up to my belt. V. J. arrived a few seconds behind me. When he landed he covered me with mud and water. Folley yelled to Lieutenant Cahill to find out what was happening up front. Cahill yelled back that everybody had been hit and that we should set up the machine gun and fire into the hedge spraying it all along on the way to Carentan.

We set the machine gun on its tripod at the edge of the shell hole. Then I saw that the belt of machine gun ammo was covered with mud and would not work in the gun. I had been so careful with the gun but had forgotten about the ammo belt! We lost time getting another box from Cahoon behind us. The Germans had zeroed in and were laying steady fire on us. At last we were ready.

"Keep your heads down. We're going to fire," Folley yelled. We did. I'm not sure how long. Maybe a whole box? I know I sprayed that hedgerow all the way into the City of Carentan and back. And we stayed in that water-filled shell hole a long time.

Our firing must have done the job because the enemy bullets stopped whizzing our way. Lieutenant Cahill had been hit by bullets from the enemies' machine gun, but what later cost him his left hand was not gunfire but the exploding of the glass in the field glasses he held. (Cahill survived but was done with the war. I saw him once more back in England after Normandy. He was on his way to the States and lived for many years after the war.)

Five men running with us paid the supreme price for their country. To the four of us who were left it was almost too much to bear. Five great guys, all close friends, had been cut down in their prime. William Cooper died without making a sound. Herman Jones was cut to pieces and died a slower, more horrible death. Corporal John Whitlock, our radio operator, must have been moving up to Lieutenant Cahill because he was hit next and died fast, face down. Behind him it was Corporal Willie Craig. Willie, when hit, spun around and sat down facing me. He was dead when he sat down. It was the damnedest sight. He sat down and slumped forward with his rifle across his knees and his legs crossed. I couldn't believe he was dead. Anthony Marcozzi was nearest to me. He was just in front of our shell hole and fell on his back when he was hit. Just once Marcozzi tried to rise up and say something, and then lay back down dead.

Five out of the six who were hit died. For Jack Evans it was too much. He broke under the strain and could not move after that. He had to be taken back to the rear. I saw him only once after that. With Evans gone, we had actually lost seven men. However, for the three of us who were left—Folley and I on the machine gun and Bob Cahoon our ammo bearer—we had just begun to fight.

Attack Underway 65

The small field where we were now was long and narrow. I assumed it was a truck patch, a place where garden vegetables were grown for the market. It was the spot where I saw Lieutenant Swanson for the first time. Lieutenant Swanson was a big man and as brave as they came. Later I would play football under his coaching with our regiment. Now he was walking down the middle of the field where disaster had just fallen on my 2nd Platoon. He was unaware of the fact that Lieutenant Cahill's platoon had taken a terrible loss or that Folley's machine gun had routed the German paratroopers who had covered this field so well or that the Germans were pulling back to outflank our machine gun position.

When Lieutenant Swanson saw we had no field of fire he asked us to move our gun into the truck patch and another hundred yards toward Carentan. We set up in a convenient shell hole. About then Sergeant Stanley Czarniak from our First Battalion's Headquarters Company approached us from the road to the truck patch. I had known Sergeant Czarniak well enough in England to pronounce his name right, and I knew he was a machine gun squad leader in our First Battalion Headquarters company. So when he asked us to move our machine gun over to an opening in the hedge along the main highway, I did not hesitate to pick up the gun and move on the run, again. I was sure he knew what he was doing.

Once at the opening in the hedgerow we saw it was a driveway into the truck patch. The road was much lower than the field, and it had a small culvert with a foot or so of dirt over it. By getting down in the ditch and setting the machine gun up on the driveway above the culvert, we had a fair spot to fire down the highway toward Carentan.

Enemy soldiers had been seen running across the highway near the city's first buildings. They were coming up the road in front of Colonel Cole's positions at the farmhouse and orchard that dead-ended into the main highway in Carentan.

"Fire when ready," Sergeant Czarniak said. "I will help you zero in on them as they cut across to the far side."

I was firing the gun, and Folley was feeding the belt. The sergeant was giving me firing directions. "Bring it down! Now to the left! Right! Right! More! Now you're on them. Let them have it! Attaboy! Kill the bastards!" he was standing straight up in the open, firing his rifle at the same Germans we were.

The German paratroopers were being cut down in bunches as they tried to cross the open highway. Suddenly the "cling" of his M-1 rifle's ammo clip drew my eyes toward the sergeant. His rifle was still at his shoulder in the aim position. In a flash I saw it happen. Blood flew. He got hit straight in the face. His M-1 rifle flew out of his hands, and in one motion he turned around and fell to the ground. He survived, and I saw him next back in England.

It was about 1200 hours. Lieutenant Swanson had disappeared, and so had Sergeant Czarniak. Lieutenant Cahill and two of our noncommissioned officers had fallen. We had not seen Sergeants Metz or Jay B. Shenk since the run for the iron gate. We did not know it then, but Sergeant Odom was just across the road out of sight from us. We wondered if all of our own "C" Company had made it across the last bridge. Where was our Company Commander, Captain Hancock? What about our Battalion Commanding Officer, Colonel Cassidy?

Folley and I had one thing in mind, to stop the German soldiers from turning our machine gun's position and outflanking us. We thought we were fighting the same soldiers we had routed at the hedgerow where we had lost so many of our 2nd Platoon people. We did not know that the German higher command at the 6th Parachute Regiment had started their first big counter attack of the battle.

For some reason the few soldiers walking in the road ditch behind us were reluctant to pass over or around the wounded soldiers and tended to bunch up. This made them good targets for artillery. They felt safe as long as our gun was firing, but when we ran out of ammo, they began to panic. We asked them to pass the word back, "We need machine gun ammo up here!" before we ran out. But no one got up and went after it.

Finally V. J. Folley sent Bob Cahoon on the run after ammo. As soon as our gun stopped firing the Germans increased their shelling of our road ditch. We said some harsh things, I'm sure, in the heat of the battle.

"Fall back! Fall back! The Germans are attacking! Fall back to the bridge!" came the words along the roadway all the way up

Attack Underway

to our machine gun position. Able-bodied men jumped up and started to run back down the open road. Many were hit as they ran. Others started to crawl over the wounded to get to the rear. It was near panic.

Our ammo bearer had not made it back yet, so there were only two of us left from the 2nd Platoon. By the looks of things we were damned fools if we tried to stay where we were and hold the Germans off with just our carbines. The two of us decided to get the hell out of there alive while we had a chance.

We could see German fire coming from the first buildings in town, straight down the roadway to our gun position and to the men in the road behind it. We knew there was no cover in the truck patch, just shell holes, so we chose an unknown way. We jumped up and cut across the highway to the far east side. We headed for a two-story stone house for cover. We made it. Once behind the house we saw US soldiers on the move back toward the Number 4 bridge. They were not running pell-mell but moving toward the river as if someone was leading them. Every now and then one of the retreating men would step out into the field and fire his rifle back at the Germans.

Folley and I came to a culvert where a small stream ran under the main highway back by the cabbage patch. We saw that "A" Company men had taken positions along it, too, so we decided to fall in with someone we knew. We moved into the water and crawled under the highway through the culvert and on up the ditch hoping to find some of our own "C" Company troopers. At the point where the ditch bends we fell in with a firing line for the rest of the day's battle. We did not see another 2nd Platoon trooper.

We heard word of a truce in the fighting, but it was ending by then; it had lasted only about an hour until about 1300 hours (1 p.m.). The truce was called by both sides to remove the badly wounded from the battlefields. We could see Major Davidson, the Regimental Surgeon, carrying a Red Cross flag and walking with two German officers down the center of the road from Carentan.

"That's nice," I said to Folley. "War really is just a game after all."

Years later I learned that during the truce our side sent the major from our Medic Corps into the City of Carentan to ask the German officer in command to surrender. He didn't.

The one-hour truce only served to make the German 6th Parachute Regiment even madder at us. The fight became worse, and the afternoon became sheer hell for anyone crossing the bridges. We American paratroopers were holding onto every inch of real estate we had gained after crossing the Number 4 bridge. The German paratroopers were after us, pressing one attack after another. There was no letup all afternoon. They came at us wave after wave, with rifles and burp guns (machine pistols) blazing from three directions.

Hour after hour they came out of the city, down both sides of ditches by the main highway. Down the four main hedgerows toward the cabbage patch the line at the culvert. Down from the railroad and the high ground at the orchard and our farmhouse defense position. Small arms bullets filled the air and found their mark as the afternoon wore on. Both sides paid a hell of a price on every attack and counter attack.

Folley and I picked up M-1 rifles to replace our carbines. By afternoon the battlefield was littered with firearms of all kinds from both sides. Because so many dead and wounded soldiers were out of the battle, you could take your pick of weapons.

Once Folley and I went to the water-filled ditch, we stayed there until the battle was over. For six and one-half hours from about 1300 hours (1 p.m.) we sat, stood, walked and even lay down in that muddy water. Even though it was summer, I felt chilled to the bone when the sun went down.

The farmhouse was soon retaken. Colonel Cole made plans with the Regiment to prepare for a withdrawal. Our Second Battalion was to build up a firing line on the causeway so that they would open fire on order so that all of us who were able-bodied from the First and 3rd Battalion could rush back across #4 bridge. The wounded would stay behind.

There was a grim feeling among us all. We could see it on everyone's face. I had not given up, and neither had anyone else. We were still holding on. There were so few of us left, but we kept

Attack Underway

firing our rifles in the direction of the enemy. We aimed at the sound of the bolt's action. We could not see him.

I stuck my rifle through the hedge and left it aimed at the enemy. When I heard them getting near I would fire it like a machine gun, a couple of shots at a time.

"For God's sake," we heard from the water-filled ditch around us, "why in hell are those boys sending out stuff so far over our heads. We need it right on top of us, and now!"

Suddenly (the "book" says it was 1800 hours, 6 pm.) it came, like rain from heaven. Our stuff fell just beyond our line at the ditch. Every gun in our possession opened up. It was the heaviest artillery from our guns I ever experienced. It lasted only five minutes, and we lost some American paratroopers who had stayed alive through the whole three-day fight. But it saved the day for 502. We won!

For the German 6th Parachute Regiment, it was the end at Carentan. Their fight was over. By midnight they had pulled back and by the next morning (D plus 6) they were leaving Carentan.

The Germans had taken tremendous losses, but they would rebuild their forces, and we would meet again.

I sat stunned like everyone else after the battle. I had no idea we had won, but for damned sure I knew the value of the artillery men. I don't even remember how we were told that the battle was over. Those of us in the water-filled ditch found ourselves out of the ditch standing on the far side of the main Carentan highway out in the open field. We were told to join up with survivors in each of our companies.

V. J. Folley and I were still together as we went looking for our "C" Company. When we found them, Captain Hancock told us to join our 2nd Platoon. We found Bob Cahoon, our ammo bearer still in one piece and asked him to lead us to the 2nd Platoon. Bob said, "This is it, right here." We turned around and saw only Sergeant Jay B. Shenk. I could not believe my eyes. Only four of us from the 2nd Platoon were left. To Folley I said, "Damn, that was close! They almost wiped out the whole platoon!" Even "old" Staff Sergeant Jay B. Shenk looked stunned. More significantly, he had nothing to say.

As darkness on that June night began to settle in, I saw the fires of the burning city off to the southeast. When we started moving back from Carentan to St. Come-Du-Mont we stood by the side of the big highway while the First Battalion of the 506th Regiment took over our places. One of the 506 boys called out, "Hey! You 5-0-Deuce boys sure look like you've been busy up here. Didn't anyone tell you you're not supposed to work on Sunday?"

It was midnight after our two-mile walk into Come-Du-Mont when I moved into a small field and found myself a spot along the fence under the hedge trees. I did not dig a foxhole because I couldn't stay awake to do so. Forty-four hours had passed since my last sleep.

8

After a Great Battle

It was 1200 hours (noon) before they woke us up the day after the battle. The pride of winning set in as we each retold our part in the battle. All afternoon we cleaned ourselves and our equipment and regrouped into companies and battalions. In the process we found plenty of time to visit back and forth.

What grew in my mind on that day after battle was the importance of not getting hurt. I knew I would be up front and not miss anything, and that became the whole point. I called it "the right to true pride," unparalleled glory. I believed I would survive.

I was awakened by W. O. Bird and William T. Hollingsworth, my two good friends. Bird crawled under the low-hanging branches of the hedgerow and shook me awake. He expected me to greet him with open arms, since neither of us knew the other one was alive. We hadn't seen each other since our two planes left the ground in England. But an odd thing had taken place in my soul. I showed no emotion whatsoever. "Where in the hell have you two guys been?" I said. Then I turned over on my side and went back to sleep.

This was a real blow to W. O. Bird, one he never understood. To him it was the cold shoulder. I was surprised at myself and did not understand why I had reacted that way.

The first thing I did after getting up was to take my trenching shovel off by myself and start digging a foxhole. While I was digging I decided to take off my pistol belt. It was too hot, or too heavy working with it, or something. I found that the simple movement of unsnapping a pistol belt, an action I could do in my sleep, did not work. The metal hook would not pass through the metal eye. It was bent out of shape.

"How could I have done that?" I asked myself. There was no way to get it unfastened, so the Supply Sergeant cut it off and gave me a new pistol belt. As an afterthought he said, "Looks like a bullet might have struck your belt. The webbing is torn, also." It came back to me. How could I not remember? It was that ricochet that kicked up the dirt in front of me after passing the iron gate at Number 4 bridge as I ran across the open field for the hedgerow at the cabbage patch. It had been a real blow to my midsection. Now I could see why it had not drawn blood.

"Good old GI belt buckle," Sergeant Anderson said to me. "Trooper, you sure are lucky. It's a damned good thing that buckles are made out of heavy brass, strong enough to turn a 30-caliber bullet, or you would have a new belly button here." As an afterthought he said, "Black, don't try to stop a 50-caliber next time or you'll lose more than a belt buckle!"

Several days went by before I was interested in what had happened to Bird or Holly or any other troopers back with us. It was like that for me after all great battles. I felt distant, detached, tough. It came from pride surging through me that I was still standing. Eventually the feeling dissolved, and I would lose my self-absorption and become a friendly human being again.

That feeling of pride developed into a sense that those of us who survived were worthy only of each other. We felt bad for the men who died in the line of duty around us. But the war was over for them, and that was acceptable while the battle was raging. It was almost the same feeling for the wounded, especially if they were headed back to the States. For those who came back to the front lines after missing great battles, I was glad for them and for

After a Great Battle

us, but I felt cheated. For anyone to let himself get captured, I felt that was a copout, a way to survive. Years later I realized I had been too far harsh in judging my fellow troopers, but those were my feelings on the front lines.

I was glad to have my two dear friends from the 2nd Platoon with me, unharmed. Friendship in the Airborne was a deep bond, and its greatest meaning was displayed in combat. "Big" Holly and I were never separated from the 2nd Platoon throughout the war.

Because of all the equipment nearby, a big radio jeep pulled into our First Battalion field to use it as a parking place. I asked the radio man in charge if he could pick up any good band music. To my surprise and everyone else's, he turned the knobs. Right there in the middle of the war was Glen Miller playing, "In the Mood," followed by Arttie Shaw's "Begin the Beguine," before the radio man went back to the war. For all of us who were not hillbillies or cowboys, it was an unforgettable treat. Many gathered around the jeep to hear better.

One big hillbilly sat on his steel helmet off by himself, cleaning his weapon. It was late afternoon by now, about 1700 hours (5 p.m.). As we stood there listening to the music, word came down for the 1st Battalion to prepare to move out. With that news the jeep pulled out of the field.

Someone who knew the hillbilly said, "Hey, Hank! You can quit cleaning your grease gun now! We're moving back up."

Someone else said, "What the hell you bucking for, Hank? You've broken down that gun a hundred times since you woke up this morning and cleaned each part ten times."

Hank came over to where we were standing and said in his slow drawl, "Goddammit, men, I don't want any more dreams like I had last night. I dreamed all night long that I was down in that water-filled ditch with German after German coming through the hedge after me. Every time I tried to fire this damned machine gun, it was plugged full of mud and water. So when I woke up this morning I took a look at this baby and, by God, she was plugged up, sure enough."

Once more the First Battalion was on the move. The battle for Carentan, we learned, was not quite over. The Germans were making a try at retaking it. Back down the main highway into the city we went. My "C" Company was in the lead this time in the battalion's line of march. A column of two spread out on each side of the big highway, at least five yards between each trooper.

On our way to the first bridge we hit the dirt whenever incoming 88s landed on our front column. I learned from this engagement that the Germans would never give up a town of any size without trying to retake it. Another thing I learned that no matter what country they are in, they will always have some friends on their side. The point was, don't trust anyone—man, woman or child—even if they hang out the American flag!

We had hardly recovered from the first shelling and were not moving yet when a line of big American semi trucks pulled up beside us. The lead truck slid to a stop at the front of the line of march. A big black First Sergeant jumped out as did all of the drivers that had come to a stop jammed behind. They were all black, too. The First Sergeant said, "Where in the hell..." and with that everybody hit Mother Earth in nothing flat as "Br-r-r-r-r-rt! Br-r-r-r-r-r-rt!" rang through the air. The big First Sergeant landed right beside me in the ditch, where he finished his question, "...are we?"

"Are you talking to me?" I asked.

"Not really. Anybody can answer."

"You are at a place called Carentan, France," I said.

"Carentan!" the black sergeant yelled. "There's a hell of a battle going on at the place. They told me at the beach. How far away is it?"

"This is it," I said. "You are there. Down this road is the front lines."

Right in my ear the sergeant blew his shrill whistle. By then we were all on our feet starting to move forward again.

"Turn 'em about, boys! Get the hell out of here! Every man for himself. We're at the front lines!" The sergeant yelled, "To the rear, march!"

Never have I seen a job of truck backing up that was pulled off with the speed those "Red Ball Express" soldiers undertook. They were gone in no time at all and did not upset one truck and even with all the shelling did not take any losses.

After a Great Battle

We moved across the first bridge, laughing and talking about the misfortune of the truck drivers. The tension from the German shelling had subsided. I cannot remember any close shelling for the rest of our march that day.

As we moved slowly along the causeway past the four bridges down the straight stretch leading into Carentan, grim reminders of Sunday's battle were still there. The bodies of the dead and wounded were gone, but the telltale signs of where they had fallen were not. We recognized the water-filled ditch, the culvert, the farmhouse off to the right, the crossroads, the orchard, the hedgerows, the cabbage patch, the truck patch, and, standing where we had left it, Folley and Black's machine gun. Only now it was pointed away from Carentan back at our lines.

Until that moment I had not given a second thought about our leaving the machine gun behind. Why had I not taken it with me when we fell back? Why had Folley let me leave it sitting there pointing to the Germans in Carentan? Yes, we had run out of ammo, but that was no reason.

We did not go into the center of the city. Our First Battalion turned to the right after a few blocks and left the city at the northwestern edge. The road went west out of Carentan onto the high ground where the 501st and 506th Parachute Regiments were already on line. I'm not sure what we were supposed to do there. I guess we were the reserve for the 501st Regiments, who were under a counter attack.

By this time it was pushing 2030 hours (8:30 p.m.), and darkness was not far off. Still, our Battalion Commanding Officer Colonel Cassidy marched us further on west of the city. Down the road we marched toward Periers. At a place called Auverville, Colonel Cassidy turned the battalion to the left off the Periers road. As we turned at the "Y" leading off the main highway into Auerville, our lead scouts were out of sight for a short period of time after making a turn at the bend in the road. Two rifle shots rang out in the early evening. We knew the shots were ours. We stopped in our tracks. You could damned near have heard a pin drop. One of the scouts ran back to us. He told us to come on, that it was only a lonely German soldier on his way to see his girlfriend.

As we followed the marching line around the bend in the "Y" going into the small sign we saw the grim sight of the price the two lovers at the front had paid. The German soldier boy on his bicycle had stopped in front of the French girl's home. Both now lay dead in the street, their blood mingling together. He had been caught by total surprise while astride his bike. She lay so close to him that they may have been in an embrace. The scene would shock the hardest of hearts. To my knowledge, no one ever spoke to the scouts about that shooting incident.

As we walked, I kept thinking about that German soldier. "Was he really there to see that girl? How far had he come from his own units? Damn it, there is something funny going on here."

I was not the only one thinking this way. Everyone around me suddenly felt uneasy. "Big" Holly, always with the outdoorsman's sense of the right feeling, said, "Hey, Black! What do you want to bet old Hop-along Cassidy's lost?" I did not answer Holly, but I was sure something was wrong, and if Holly was right the whole damned battalion was lost by now! It had been a long way back since we passed the last American foxholes. In fact by now, we of "C" Company, the lead unit of Colonel Cassidy's First Battalion were some four thousand yards past the front lines.

Put another way and it sounded even worse. "Sir, we are four thousand yards deep into enemy territory. Somewhere back there we made a bad turn. Now do an about face. Let us march back out of here, by God, with absolutely no noise whatsoever." That was Colonel Cassidy talking to our 2nd Platoon leader, Lieutenant Borcherdt as we stood on a sunken French road in no-man's land.

As we stood in a column of two on each side of the road, down the center between us roared an enlisted paratrooper from HQ company on a captured motorcycle with a sidecar attached to it. He stopped beside Holly and me. He did not turn off the motor. To make matters worse, that damned German motorcycle was only hitting on two (if it had four) cylinders. Every once in a while the thing would backfire, causing sparks to fly out of it in a stream three feet long. It was like someone beating a drum with a searchlight attached announcing to the Germans, "Hey! We're over here!" In the sidecar part of the motorcycle were all of the officer's bedrolls plus anything else he could get out of carrying.

After a Great Battle

Our Platoon Sergeant, "old" Jay B. Shenk, stood beside Lieutenant Jack Borcherdt while Colonel Cassidy was admitting that we were lost. Sergeant Shenk did not have to be hit over the head to get the point, especially since he knew his men were uneasy about something since the lover boy and his girlfriend were shot.

With a chew of tobacco jutting out his jaw and the Thompson submachine gun slung over his right shoulder pulling him somewhat off balance, he grabbed the butt of the gun, rested it on his pistol belt, and aimed the barrel straight up in the air. After punching the motorcycle driver with the barrel of his machine gun, he said out of the corner of his mouth, "Hey, you! Turn that godamned thing off!" The partaker did so at once. "Now hear this," Shenk went on, speaking to all who could hear him. "We are lost. What we are going to try to do is turn around and walk back outta here the way we came in. Ya hear? Fix, Bayonets! Any questions?"

The motorcycle driver had one. "What am I supposed to do?" he asked.

"Why, if you are smart, you will let that son-of-a-bitch sit right there and run like hell," said J.B.

Just then "Hop-along" Cassidy went by, and I heard him say, "Private! Turn it around! And push! Soldier, push! Whatever happens, don't start that motor!"

I don't know how we did it, but the whole battalion walked back those four thousand yards without a shot being fired on either side. I don't know how the enemy could help but hear us going in, but I know damned well he could not hear us going back out. I was a foot tall and no more than three inches wide by the time we crossed back over our MLD (Main Line of Departure).

Everyone else felt the same way. We were all laughing now, talking about how each soldier tried to make himself smaller and smaller as we walked back those four thousand yards. What happened to the trooper on the motorcycle? That question was on our minds, but nobody seemed to have the answer except for "Big" Holly, and he wasn't talking.

As if the forced march wasn't hard enough to go through, Colonel Cassidy had the "C" Company fall out along the side of the main road west out of Carentan and spend the night in the ditches. Along both sides of the road were Sherman tanks. All night long one after the other of those tankers was revving up its engine. When I finally fell asleep I dreamed that one of those tanks was about to back right over the top of me. When I was awake I was sure that German 88s were coming in on top of us because of all the tank noise. It was a hell of a night.

The tankers were a special breed of men. Most of the time they were great guys, as was the case the next morning. They were up with the sun cooking breakfast. The smell of coffee, real coffee, was in the air.

That day was a search-and-clearout day for "C" Company as we helped our sister regiments. By nightfall we came on line on their right flank. It was obvious that the 101st Airborne Division was preparing to defend Carentan from the south, east and west, as our armored infantry from the U.S. began to move west toward the sea.

I dug myself in along the tar-bound road between Carentan and Compagne near a small place called Douville. With me were V. J. Folley, James Flanagan and Corporal Metz. We were manning a listening post. Just before darkness we were given "C" rations for our supper. It consisted of one tin can, about half a pint of some mixture of food that was designed to be a meal in itself. I don't remember what it tasted like, but it was not good. I had to use a turn key to cut off the top, and this made the lid as sharp as a knife. I cut my finger, deep, on a "C" ration lid in the line of duty. It was embarrassing enough that a medic had to be called over to fix me up. Then, while Pfc. Marquart was working on my hand, a command car drove up from our armored infantry. They had been fighting near us all day. Out climbed a "full-bird" Colonel, and he walked over to where the three of us were standing with the medic giving him a hand salute. He was not West Point. I would have bet on that. It was not a crisp, snappy hand salute that he returned.

The visiting colonel joined us along with his sergeant and even drank some of our hot coffee. But he had not stopped by for coffee. He has something in mind. "How do you fight in hedgerow country?" he asked.

After a Great Battle

A seasoned soldier, he had fought in desert sand, on flat land, and in land with high hills. He had even fought among the rocks of Sicily. Now his men were stymied by these small fields surrounded by great mounds of dirt with thick hedges and large trees growing out of them.

"Tell me. How do you do it in the Airborne? You men just fought a great battle coming into Carentan. We know, because we have been following you in. I've learned one thing. When my main officers are stumped for an answer, I go ask the men who seem to know. How do you paratroopers pull it off?"

Corporal Metz spoke first. "Well, I'll tell you two things we won't do any more, Colonel Sir," he said. "We don't go through the gate, and we don't walk into just any field. This platoon lost a man who was killed each of the first two times we tried it. Now we pick our spot to go through the hedge. Then we all rush in at the same time and spray fire all around the next hedgerow." Corporal Metz ended by saying, "It would sure be a hell of a lot easier if tanks and infantry could work together."

I spoke up next as Private Markquart finished dressing my hand. "What we need to go ahead of us is a great big bulldozer. Let him plow a pathway through the hedgerow, and then we will coming running through right after him, sir."

"I believe you paratroopers may have the answer," the "full" Colonel said. "I've been thinking about some way I could weld a bulldoze blade on the front of a Sherman tank. How about that idea, men?"

V. J. Folley said, "That sounds like a better idea to me, sir. You might have trouble finding someone to get on a bulldozer and drive it since he would have to sit out in the open."

At that moment the third event of this evening opened up. "Look out! Here I come!" With that, crashing through the hedgerow where we all sat talking to the colonel came big Private James Flanagan, followed by three or four German mortar shells. All of us hit the dirt. When the dust cleared it was plain to see that Private Flanagan had landed right in the colonel's lap. Flanagan looked into the officer's face with a look of disbelief and said, "Sorry, sir. This is my foxhole!"

Soon after that the colonel left. But before he did, he said to me, "What happened to your hand, trooper?"

I told him about the C-ration can accident and he said to the medic, "Be sure to turn this soldier in for a purple heart. We did that back in Africa. I consider C-rations our worst enemy."

"We do, too," said Pfc. Marquart, "but our general thinks they are good for us, and he hates self-inflicted wounds."

The visit of the Armored Infantry's full colonel had been a pleasant one and pointed up the fact that some of the officers were genuine men, and not tin soldiers at all. His deep concern about the making of bulldozer tanks stayed with me. When I read about the breakthrough in hedgerow fighting later on in the *Stars and Stripes*, I wondered if this colonel had anything to do with it.

The hedgerows had been tough fighting. Some called it the worst fighting in the war. But it was made easier for American soldiers by a Sergeant Culin who developed a steel blade that mounted on the front of our tanks and made them into earth movers rather than incline climbers. This let the tank cut straight through the mound of earth and the hedges, leaving the tanker in a ready position to fire against the enemy.

Corporal Metz had said nothing to Private Flanagan while the colonel was visiting, but he was seething for the chance. In the end his lecture did little good. Private James Flanagan was a ball of fire, and nothing seemed to slow him down. If there was any action around "C" Company, you could bet that Private Flanagan was in on it. And when it was over you could find him looking for a German "Lugar" pistol. He was either brave as hell, or crazy.

9

Twelve Days on the Battle Line

By the dawn of the morning on Wednesday, June 14, the battle for the city of Carentan, France, had officially ended. The counterattack by the enemy's "elite" 17th SS Panzer Grenadier Division had failed to push us off the high ground, nor could the enemy retake the city. Had the Germans' 6th Parachute Regiment held off us Americans just one more day, or had the 17th SS Panzer Grenadiers not been late in their drive up from Brittany, the battle for all of Normandy might well have ended differently. The French Saboteurs made a major contribution to the Allied victory by imposing abnormal conditions on the 17th SS Panzer Grenadiers and delaying their counterattack.

The 501st and 502nd Regiments spent the day stretching our lines into a straight, long front. The 502nd dug in on the high ground west of Carentan extending from Auverville to an area northwest of La Compagne, on the road to Baupte. There we joined up with the 508th Parachute Regiment of the 82nd Airborne Division, which reached the Douve River. "C" Company dug in at La Compagne. My 2nd Platoon was stationed on the line just west of town on the main road to Baupte. The platoon's CP (command post) was set up in an apple orchard on the main road to Baupte. We set up one outpost—a listening post, actually—per platoon in each of the companies positioned up against the big swamp that ran across the whole 502nd front. The French called this swamp "Les Prairies Marecageuses de Georges."

By now my 2nd Platoon was so badly shot up that we were reorganized into two squads, one rifle and one mortar. That put "Big" Holly, Bird and myself back in the same squad again. The three of us plus another trooper (I think it was Goodwin) were sent out with a machine gun and a bazooka to man our outpost. We set up at a road junction near an old bombed-out farmhouse in front of us.

The dirt roads at this junction were sunken, with hedgerows on both sides. They were more like farm lanes than roads. I don't believe two tanks could have passed in them. With the hot summer sun above, it was nice and cool in the shade of the tree-lined hedgerows. We were also well concealed from enemy sight and thus free to move around in broad daylight.

Our fields of fire were at least two hundred yards down each roadway. The one on our left extended due west across the swamp. Our platoon leader, Lieutenant Borcherd, told us that tanks could not cross the swamp and that our main worry here would be German patrols at night. He also told us we were to let the French farmers pass through in the early morning so they could work on their farms. They would come back to their homes before dark. Most of the farms had dairy cattle, so they needed to see to their morning and night-time milking.

For most of the war in France the American GIs made good friends with the French farmers. Here along the swamp we did not, and with good reason. Since we had dug in on the high ground along the swamp, the farms were out in no-man's land, so to speak. For anyone passing in front of a front-line soldier it was touch-and-go at best.

Although we had a good daytime position, at night it was bad. On the narrow, dark, tree-covered roadway eerie shadows played in the moonlight. Guard duty involved two hours on and two hours off for the four of us twelve nights in a row. Fortunately, it was summertime, so the hours of darkness were short.

Life in combat for the 101st Airborne took on new meaning with a set of orders issued after the Carentan victory. "You will be clean in every way," the orders stated, "and shaven; your body, clothes, boots, haircuts, weapons, even your foxhole is to stay 'policed-up'—clean! You will have proper water on hand at all times." And one other order: "You will be properly camouflaged!" To back all this up there would be inspections by all COs (Commanding Officers) from bottom to top. That meant even General Taylor himself might stop by your foxhole.

In the Airborne few of us doubted for a minute that all of these orders would be carried out, and they were. Still, all that inspection stuff came as a shock to most of us after the killing and terrible life in the war itself.

Around 1600 hours (4 p.m.) I was told to report back to my 2nd Platoon's CP for a "spec duty" detail. "Be in proper dress." Two troopers from the platoon were going to be picked up by a regimental truck and hauled into the city of Carentan to stand in an "honor guard." Along with me would be V. J. Folley to represent "C" Company from the 502nd. It was truly an honor. Assignments like this were a privilege to carry out even if they were inconvenient or, in this case, hazardous.

I didn't look forward to the truck ride along the ridge road to each of the 502nd Regiment's companies on the way to Carentan. The road was exposed to enemy artillery fire and seemed to draw it every time I went for a ride. But we made it to the center of the city. It was my only war-time view of Carentan from inside the city.

We lined up in 24-man units to represent the four regiments and placed at "close order" in the town square. We were told that General Taylor would be there in a few minutes to present our Division's first medals of the war. These were "silver stars" that went to all four of the Regimental Commanders: Colonels Sink, Johnson, Harper and Michaelis. A few noncommissioned officers who had done something above and beyond the call of duty were also given medals.

The town square was large and displayed a big statue of Napoleon on a horse. All the buildings were two or three stories tall, and the streets as well as the buildings were made of stone. French people gathered around as the General drove up in his jeep. The impressive ceremony began. Each of the four Colonels was handed a bouquet of flowers by a young girl after receiving the Silver Star medal.

Then that sound we all knew so well began. A German 88 millimeter shell was on its way. We were all standing at attention in the center of the square near the big statue of Napoleon. The first shell landed in the side of a building facing into the square. The people screamed as steel fragments ricocheted wildly off the stone. As well-trained soldiers, we did not flinch and held our formation. Then another 88 millimeter shell ripped into the square. This time we did flinch. We ducked. On the third shell an officer yelled, "Take cover!" We broke ranks and ran for the cover of the buildings. The fourth shell landed near the statue, but by then the space had been emptied of people.

As far as I know not one trooper was hit, and that was a miracle. However, among the French townspeople several were wounded, including the little flower girl. "The party is over!" an officer yelled. Everyone ran for the trucks in order to get out of town before the next round of fire. In nothing flat every truck had cleared the center of the city.

But as far as the General was concerned, the awards ceremony was only half over, and that phrase could have been applied to the German part of it as well. General Taylor had his jeep driver speed up and stop two of the last trucks out of town. Would you believe it? Folley and Black were on one of those two trucks.

As we sat there General Taylor told both truckers to follow him while a few blocks behind us another four rounds of 88s landed in Carentan. The General led us to his Division's CP and there, in an open field, backed up against a wooded area, once more we formed in close order and stood at attention while General Taylor gave a little speech. He gave the Germans hell for upsetting the ceremony and assured all of us that he would pay them back double. He used the word, "Krauts," a term we Americans often used for the Germans when we were more than upset with them. This was the first of only three times I ever saw our General personally distraught. However, he was able to finish the job of awarding Silver Stars to four of the Division's Noncommissioned Officers, and we made it back to our own companies before dark. After that I was glad to be back on the front lines.

I told Bird and Holly what we went through back in Carentan. I commented that the Germans had to know exactly when and where to send in those 88s.

"By God!" Holly said. "These Frenchmen aren't on our side. They're tipping the damned Germans off to our every move. Hell! Blackie, they hit our platoon's CP while you were gone this afternoon, and we lost another trooper!"

That was enough proof for me. "What are we going to do about it?" I said.

"Big" Holly put his brain to work on a plan to teach a few French farmers a lesson or two about the ways of a North Carolina hillbilly. He planned on scaring them half to death. We had strict orders not to hurt any of the farmers, so his plan of attack took on a common-sense flavor. He would scare them so bad they would be afraid to come close to our gun positions.

Holly picked up some telephone line wire from the radio people at our company and set about stringing a line across each roadway from hedgerow to hedgerow. He stretched the wire tight about four feet off the ground and strung several C-ration cans with small stones in each can on the wire. Then he attached a trip wire from the long main wire to a hand grenade that he placed in a dugout on top of the hedgerow. The grenade was set so that it would explode upward into the trees, throwing dirt and tree limbs over the roadway. Its sole purpose this night was to scare. Later on there were nights when we would use it in a more serious fashion against German patrols.

At exactly 2200 hours (10 p.m.) "Big" Holly looked at his watch and said, "They're not coming back tonight!" Just then I heard something coming down the road from the west, straight at us. It was too dark to be sure who it was. It was a tense moment, and our guns were ready. By now combat experience had taught us to identify sound in terms of a number indicating quantity. This sound was a "one" of something but not the normal sound of marching feet. Holly's outdoor training did not desert him. He was the first to say, "That's him! Hear the clap of his wooden shoes? Be ready now. He's getting close!"

Then all hell let loose. It even scared me, and I knew it was coming. It was one hell of a sound, let me tell you.

The French farmer touched the wire to the hand grenade in the hedgerow, which exploded and sent dirt, gravel, tree limbs, twigs and leaves raining down on that poor farmer, now sitting on his rear some fifteen feet behind his wooden shoes. When my eyes picked him up in the light of the fire, he was looking straight into the air at a brilliant, burning light descending upon him from high above in what looked like a parachute. I hadn't been warned about that!

That French farmer jumped up, left his wooden shoes and walking stick in the roadway and took off for town. For the second time he hit that wire, only this time he was really moving. He "clothes-lined" that wire and stripped it off both hedgerow trees. He never broke stride. When he ran past Holly, Bird and me, he was wearing the machine gun ammo box for a necktie plus both ends of the wire, with all the cans streaming along behind him. As he ran he let out some kind of a yell that must have been French for something like, "Don't shoot! Don't shoot!" or "Help me! Help me!" But to us troopers it sounded like "O-o-o-o-e-e-e! O-o-o-o-e-e-e!"

That was the last time any of the French farmers went past our outpost for the next six days we spent there. We had everybody clear up to Regiment wanting to know what happened that night. I don't remember what we told him, but I'm sure it wasn't the truth.

The word about our little outpost must have gotten all the way back to General Taylor. In a few days we got word he was in our "C" Company area and on his way out to see us. Since the three of us lived a pretty clean life, especially around "Big" Holly, a general was as welcome in the field as our own captain.

We all got into our own foxholes with Holly on his machine gun dug back into the south hedgerow bank at the base of the road. We had dug clear through to the other side like a cave. This made it possible to cover the open field on our left that was our only blind spot. Plus it put all four of us troopers together at night. We had two more stand-up foxholes to use as rifleman positions in case of a fire fight. We were so well concealed that our camouflage blended us right into the hedgerow.

Captain Fred Hancock was a company commander who didn't do a lot of unnecessary walking around the front lines, stirring up the enemy until he drew shelling and then leaving. He believed in letting his platoon leaders lead their men. He gave orders to his leaders and they in turn to their NCOs (noncommissioned officers) in each platoon, who lived with the men and carried the orders out. Sometimes things went so well that the captain did not see some of us men for days. That had been the case here. In fact, Captain Hancock was so unfamiliar with us that he led the general and our regimental colonel down the road right past our gun position. We heard the colonel say, "Where did you say your outpost was, Captain?"

Captain Hancock said, "Right here at this road junction. Or it was. Lieutenant! Where are they?"

The four officers stopped and looked around. Our Captain looked like he was breaking out in a sweat. I bumped Holly with my elbow and whispered, "Say something!"

In his slow deep voice, Holly said, "We're still here, Captain! But you officers have all been dead for the past ten steps."

He was referring to the fact that if they had been the enemy they would have been dead by now. With that, Holly pushed away the camouflage revealing himself and W. O. Bird behind the machine gun. I climbed out of the foxhole from the other side.

The general wore a big smile on his face as he walked back to where Holly sat behind his gun. By then Bird had climbed out of our cave-like position and was standing with me in the roadway. He got into our dugout and sat behind the gun to examine its field of fire. He was pleased, and said so.

Overall our twelve-day stay at this outpost had not been that bad. We ate as well there as at any time in combat. We had the new "10-in-1" ration for all twelve days. I also made my first church call in combat at this spot in France. Church was held in a one-room schoolhouse on Sunday, June 25. "Chapie" Hall, the Protestant Chaplain, held forth, and there was a very good crowd, especially when you consider that each trooper had to leave the safety of his foxhole and take a chance to get there.

On our next-to-last day at this outpost, two burning desires reached Holly and me at the same time. One was the call of nature to relieve one's self, or in GI everyday language, we had to take a shit. The other burning desire was a growing curiosity that Holly and I had for that bombed-out farmhouse just two hundred yards in front of our outpost.

Each day we heard noise coming from that house as if someone was walking around down there. I say "down there" because it was slightly downhill from our position and not in clear view for us to pick up movement off the roadway. The time had come for someone to check out the area and see what was so important around a bombed-out farmhouse. "Big" Holly and I volunteered out of a necessity, one might say. Off we went with loaded weapons. We told W. O. Bird to keep a sharp eye out for any sign that we needed help.

We had to cross over a lot of rubble to go inside and look around. The tin in the trash made a hell of a noise as we stepped on it. The fire had left nothing of value that we could see except for a beautiful, green vegetable garden that had not been touched. The garden was protected by a six-foot brick wall with only a small wooden gate into it.

Whoever had lived here certainly had a green thumb, that was plain to see. Some of the vegetables were ripe. The garden had been tended right along with the war. It took a while before it dawned on us that it had been three weeks since D-day and that someone was obviously coming here every day. By then it was too late.

"Hey," Holly said, "here's the right place to dump our waste. We'll do the French a big favor and fertilize their victory garden. Come on, Black." In we went.

Even Holly and I knew enough to stay prepared. I remember making a point about us taking positions around the garden, putting each of us in a different location to cover the single gateway. The garden was maybe forty yards on each side. The gate was in the center on one side, and the rows of vegetables were planted in the same direction as the wall with the gate in it. So Holly chose to squat down directly across from the gate near the far wall. I chose the far wall to his left, the wall at a right angle to the gate wall. That gave me a lineup straight down the rows. This position gave Holly the advantage of the first shot.

We both carried rifles as well as our folding stock carbines. Holly had come up with a German P-38 pistol and the black German belt and holster that went with it. We put our rifles on the ground in front of us, at the ready. In my hand, ready to fire, was my carbine. "Big" Holly held the German P-38, fully loaded. Suddenly there was the noise of feet on tin beyond the garden wall. Both Holly and I were into our "act" to the point of no return. Get the job done. Hurry up, Nature!

Everyone knows there are times that nature cannot be rushed, and this was one of those times for both of us.

Those noisy feet are heading our way. Now they are at the gate. Since the gate is solid we can't see who is there until it opens. Our eyes glued on it, the door slowly swings open, back into the garden. I don't know why, but we don't fire. Probably we are stopped by the fear of shooting one of our own men. W. O. Bird might have been following us for some reason. So we wait.

Through the opening steps a pretty young French girl. She turns, takes down a hoe from the wall and slowly starts to hoe the first row, going down that row with her back to us.

I turned toward Holly. Moving only my lips, I said, "She didn't see us."

"What do we do now?" he mouthed to me.

I had no answer to his question. It never entered our minds to just stand up and pull our pants up.

I had a better location than he did at first, but once she reached the end of that first row, the point of which one of us she would see first depended on which row of vegetables she would choose to hoe next.

I've never been lucky at anything, and today was not going to be my day to start. She picked my row to hoe. The worst thing about that was the fact that my row did not have a weed in it!

Holly and I stayed frozen in our shameful positions as she came down the row toward us. I could not help but notice how painfully slowly she hoed. When she reached the halfway point in my row, in a straight line with the gate and "Big" Holly, she stopped to wipe her brow. That was the first time she saw us. First she saw me; then she turned her head and saw Holly. She said nothing but went on wiping her forehead. She took another long look at me and then at Holly. Still she said nothing. At last she turned around and started to hoe back on the next row. I was somewhat relieved, but "Big" Holly took it as an insult that she did not leave at once. He was upset and spoke out loud. "What the hell's the matter with these damned people, Black? Can't she see we came in here to be in private?"

"Yes, but it's her garden, Holly, don't forget," I said.

"The hell with her! She didn't even speak to us. Just stood there and looked a hole right through both of us."

I said, "Maybe she can't parlez-vous the Anglais," I said.

"Well, she could surely parlez-vous the Francais," he answered back.

"Yes," I said, "but which of us could understand what she was saying?"

Suddenly Holly stood straight up. At the top of his lungs he yelled, "Hey, you! Get the hell out of here. Goddammit!" Then he fired two quick shots from his pistol into the dirt just behind her. "Bang! Bang!"

He got her attention before he fired those shots. She turned around on his first two words, "Hey, you!" What she saw was a sight I never saw duplicated in the whole war. There stood Holly, bare naked from his belly button to his jump boots, with his arms outstretched toward the gate and a pistol in his hand.

When those shots went off and the dirt kicked up around her heels, that French girl left her wooden shoes sitting in the garden and made three leaps toward the gate. The fourth leap carried her out of the garden without opening the gate. The tin on the other side of the wall rattled like an army was crossing it as she left the area.

I've never been proud of the way Holly handled that situation, but don't forget it was the first time our "vanity" was at stake in the war.

When he heard the shots W. O. Bird came running. All he saw was the tail end of the whole thing, and I'll admit it looked

Twelve Days on the Battle Line 91

bad. A girl running down the road, and two half-naked men standing in her garden. He did not believe one word of our story.

"Today we are moving!" It was June 26. "Pack up everything and stand by."

We learned that the 101st Airborne Division was being relieved by the 83rd Infantry Division here, south of Carentan. We were to march out of this swamp area toward Baupte and spend the first night on the high ground north of the railroad.

Captain Hancock said, "Take the high ground, sergeants, and be sure your men pitch pup-tents tonight. Dig two-man slit trenches for foxholes. We are still along the front lines."

Off we went up the long hill to the very top. The whole 2nd Platoon, what was left of it, dug under the trees in a thinly wooded area. We paired off because it takes two shelter-halves to make one pup-tent. It was Bird and Holly, Folley and Cahoon, Black and Howard and so on. The six of us I just named all dug in close together and under the biggest old shade tree I was to see in all of France. It was going to rain any time now, and that big old tree would serve as an umbrella for us. Or so we thought.

Private Rennie Howard and I had dug only six inches deep when we ran into tree roots. They were too big and too many for us to overcome. It was too late for us to move to another spot because the rain had started falling—a full-blown summer storm. Lightning was sharp around the hillside, so sharp I was sorry I was under a big tree. I'd seen cattle killed by lightning back on the farm while they were standing under a tree in a big storm.

I stood the first two-hour guard watch in the rain in a real downpour.

The good Lord had taken care of me so far. I mean the jump, the night that followed, the Battle of Carentan and all the days and nights in between. Even that "Hopalong" Cassidy excursion behind enemy lines. Since I was going to get wet any way, I might as well be out in the open getting good and wet. I was sure that the Lord was taking out his wrath on friend and foe alike that night.

Lightning struck that big old tree while I was standing guard several yards away. Nobody got hurt, but Bird and Holly, Folly and Cahoon and Rennie Howard came out from under those three tents without opening the flaps! Tent poles flew. When Rennie Howard came out from under our tent he tore the whole damned thing down.

They wanted to know what happened. I told them that the Lord was just showing us that He was still in charge. I told them they'd better say their prayers if they hadn't already.

By the time Private Rennie Howard got our tent set back up, it was his turn to pull the next two-hour hitch. Man, it felt good to come in out of that rainstorm. With my raincoat plus my jump-boots and my steel helmet I was not as wet as you might think. But when I went into that tent looking forward to a good night's sleep, I got a rude awakening.

Our tent was slightly downhill from Bird and Holly's, and the water from their tent's roof had run in a stream straight down under our tent and into our foxhole bed. The little ditch Howard and I dug had washed out, and now our six-inch dugout under the tent was full of water. Both of our army blankets, which we had put down first, were water soaked and covered with mud. My bed was a hell of a mess. But I was too damned tired to stand up the rest of that night. I just lay down in that mud and water without even taking off my raincoat.

With the coming of dawn the storm passed on, and the sun came out. We were to march back to where the trucks were waiting for us to take us on a round-about ride across the Douve River and back again. We drove through the city of St. Sauveur-le-Vicomte, which our friends of the 82nd Airborne Division had captured. From there we moved into a bivouac area southwest of the city along the main highway to La Haye Du Puits where we would stay for the next three days.

It was still a tactical position, and we were still involved in combat. I felt we were there to back up something big that was underway. The sounds of war were close, artillery fire from both sides. The long afternoon wait was anything but easy. I was learning the real stress that builds up in a trooper's heart when he has to stand by and wait for the call to "move up."

Just before dark we were told to dig in where we were. At that point we saw a terrific explosion in front of us. It had to be an ammunition dump—ours or the Germans'—but I never found out for sure. It was a spectacular sight.

The next day was more of the same, waiting around not knowing what was going on or about to take place. At last the problem here at St. Sauver-le-Vicomte was to end. On Thursday, June 29 (D plus 23), the 101st Airborne Division was on the move again. This time we were heading north up the narrow peninsula to an area near Cherbourg, the biggest seaport of Normandy.

Our assignment was to settle in at a big bivouac area near Tollevast, four miles south of Cherbourg. We would then take over the defense of the entire Cherbourg Peninsula all the way to Montebourg, south of Valognes.

Back for a few days at Camp Denford in England, it was great being able to see many of our wounded 502 buddies. Many had returned to duty; others were on their way to the States. Sergeant Junior Nutter was back on duty as our 2nd Platoon Sergeant. Lieutenant Cahill was not so lucky; he was headed home with only one good hand. It was a shame to lose good men like Lieutenant Cahill. No other officer could ever take his place. Other troopers I talked to agreed with my assessment.

We enlisted men didn't know how the whole war was going. Later we learned that at this time our leaders such as Eisenhower, Marshall, and Patton didn't think we were doing well at all. General Patton blamed one man. "The British Field Marshall Montgomery has not done his job, and I told you so!" he said. The British and Canadian forces had fallen short of their assigned objectives for D-day. Montgomery was blamed for not using a blitz attack. Now, over a month later, Caen had still not been taken by the British. Neither had St. Lo been taken by the Yanks. The word was that some of the old-timers feared the prospect of trench warfare and hesitated to make bold moves.

My opinion is that Montgomery should be praised, not blamed, for going slowly the first month of the invasion. A million men with half a million tons of supplies and 175,000 motorized.

10

The Corridor Fight

In England, sometime in August of 1944, the prospects of a second "big jump" reached a fever pitch. To those of us who had made the first jump, the waiting wasn't easy. How could we prepare mentally for this second combat jump? Would the next jump be even worse than the one at Normandy?

These were great years for me. I was in my early twenties, and these were history-making times. Above all, I was a part of the action. A paratrooper! A 502nd paratrooper! A 101st Airborne paratrooper! That's about the best there is!

I had been prepared well for my twenties by my mother, by her religious teachings, and by my Dad with his common-sense approach to everything, regardless of its danger. So I walked right through those days of August and September, looking straight ahead and never back, right out the door and over Holland.

It was Sunday, 1300 hours (1 p.m.), on September 17, 1944. The sun was glorious all the way from Welford Airfield just northwest of London to our drop zone in big open fields in the center of a triangle with borders from Best to Zon to St.

Oedenrode, Holland. We had learned over the summer to trust the driving to the "fly boys" up front. After all, we did not go to work until the red light came on. Since we had a lot of new equipment on this jump and more weight to carry around, it was uncomfortable to move around. The best thing to do was to sit back and enjoy the ride. Another source of peace of mind was a new type of single-action, push-button opener for the chute. You just had to bump it hard with the heel of your hand, and it opened in a flash. For too many paratroopers at Normandy, the process of releasing the chute was too slow, and they drowned or got caught in trees and could not get out of their chute harness quickly enough to keep from getting killed.

I was "acting" corporal all summer in England, as "Buck" Sergeant Edwin Metz's assistant squad leader. Now I was promoted from Private First Class to "Buck" Sergeant in pay grade. That was a big jump back then. In less than two weeks from the Holland jump I would take Metz's place as the leader of my squad. By the end of the month I would be acting Staff Sergeant. I was in big money, but I had no place to spend it.

At a place called Bourg-Leopold about forty miles east of Antwerp and just north of the Alber Canal, our plane turned left and headed north across the front lines. At that point German flak began to fly up at us. From Bourg-Leopold it was some forty air miles to our drop zone and no more than fifteen miles to the front line where the British Second Army would soon be racing to reach Eindhoven, Holland, where the "airborne corridor" (known as "Hell's Highway") began. The British Second "Land" Army was across the Escant-Canal with a bridgehead. As we of the "First Allied Airborne Army" passed over the front lines of the British, another big invasion was under way by the Allies. With the code name, Market Garden, this invasion would be linked with the British Second Army that would spearhead the tanks of its Guards Armored Division straight for Eindhoven, Holland, over a single road.

Back on my plane, some eight hundred feet in the air, the flak was so thick you could have walked on it.

The Holland Jump was as different as night and day from the Normandy Jump. I was never one to look out the door or windows

The Corridor Fight

even when I went out the door on a jump. I always shut my eyes. But once the chute opened I looked around and enjoyed the view. I never knew if our plane had been hit, but it was tossing and rolling from side to side. Men fell down all along the line back through the plane as they tried to hook onto the plane's cable. It was like trying to get on a bucking horse. In a mass jump you are supposed to check the trooper's equipment in front of you. Our equipment check was almost impossible to carry out now.

Sergeant Nutter, our jump master, yelled up to the pilot, "Hold this bucking horse steady when you turn the green light on, captain, or we'll never make it out this door."

That's all it took. The "fly-boys" leveled that baby off like a feather, and the green light came on. I don't know how they did it. That was all we needed, just a few moments. Sergeant Nutter yelled, "Let's go!" Out we went.

Of the whole division of 428 planeloads of paratroopers, only three planes failed to reach the drop zone. From these 425 planes, a total of 6,760 troopers jumped in just one half hour. The casualty rate was under two percent, and the loss of equipment less than five percent.

For the second time in my ten jumps I was glad to leave that plane in the air. There was no need to worry about pulling my reserve chute, as my main chute snapped open, leaving the usual two burns on my shoulders. From that point on, what a beautiful sight! The sun was shining just as it had been in England. I do not remember a shot being fired. The entire Regiment came down in full view ahead of me. So did the 506th Parachute Regiment, since we both used the same drop zone area.

We landed at a place called Bourg-Leopold about forty miles east of Antwerp, just north of the Albert Canal. Holland was like no other place I had ever seen. The land was flat, and there were few trees and no hedgerows as in Normandy. As I floated down to earth it seemed like a training jump to me, like the whole Screaming Eagle Division was landing here in my full view. As our history book says (TSE, Division History, R.W.D., page 260), "It was a parade ground jump."

As I floated to earth I realized all of a sudden that I would have to slip my chute hard to keep from landing on top of one of my own company troopers below me. As I slipped the chute I seemed to stop in mid air, and then I just stepped onto the ground. It was that easy!

Paratroopers were on their feet everywhere. There wasn't a sign of a German anywhere. I stood up and hit my new chute release and felt my harness fall away. Absolute joy radiated from our faces when we realized we were safely on the ground.

Here in Holland in broad daylight it did not seem I was back in combat. No Germans in sight, no rifles firing, no machine guns, no big gun noise. The awful flak up there in the sky was far off now. "This is going to be easy," I found myself thinking.

All around me were my own squad. Over there was T/Sergeant Junior Nutter calling, "This way, 'C' Company, 2nd Platoon, fall in on me!"

Out loud I said, "Can you beat that? Two combat jumps and each time the first guy I see is Sarge." I yelled over to Nutter, "Hey, Sarge! What did you break this time?"

"I broke my ass, and if you don't get your machine gun over here I'll have yours," the sergeant yelled back. Sergeant Junior Nutter was a great guy, the best platoon sergeant in "C" Company that I was ever to know.

Our Second Squad settled in around Sergeant Nutter. All of us were there. Not a single scratch on the whole bunch. Squad leader Edwin Metz and myself, plus Privates James Flanagan, Wayne Dickerson, Irvine Goodwin and George Blackburn were the only survivors from Normandy. The rest of the Second Squad were new troopers who had joined up this past summer. My two machine gunners were Privates Leopold Martin and Jerry Domiguce, both little guys but with plenty of guts. The new firemen were Privates Edward Kessler and John Harigal.

I looked over and there was W. O. Bird's First Squad, with "Big" Holly bringing up the rear as the machine gun corporal. Next was Sergeant V. J. Folley with his Third Squad of old-timers leading the way: Privates First Class Bob Cahoon, William Blue and Marvin Milligan. Last to land was Sergeant James Colon's Fourth Squad with the 60 millimeter mortar gun. In less than five minutes we had assembled.

The Corridor Fight

The fourth squad of an airborne platoon in combat is actually the headquarters for the platoon. Within it are the key people needed for us to function as a strong unit. We had lost heavily at Carentan. Not a single leader from Normandy was in place. Only Privates Rennie Howard, Bernard Korst and Albert Hamerlind remained of the mortar men. All the rest were new to the platoon.

The 2nd Platoon jumped from two C-47 planes and landed together on the drop zone.

"Man, look at all the troopers that made it to Holland," Private Wayne Dickerson said.

Sergeant Metz had to spoil the moment. "Hell," he said, "it was easy getting here. The hard part will be to get back out. You know, all of you guys that are going to get killed will be buried here."

"What a rotten thing to say," I said.

"Knock it off!" yelled Sergeant Nutter. "We are moving out. Head for that smoke over there."

We started out just like we had done many times before working on "field problems" back in England, marching in a column of twos right off the drop zone. "Big" Holly was next to me, and he loved to kid me every chance he got. "Hey, Corporal Black," he said, "we're going the wrong way again."

I answered, "What makes you so smart about where we're going in Holland? You been here before?"

"W. O. told me that Nutter saw Colonel Cassidy head out this way."

"Well? He's our Battalion C.O., isn't he? Where he goes, we go, trooper!"

Holly kept at me. "I'll bet you your last chocolate bar that we are going the wrong way."

"No bet," I said. "I plan on having that last bar for myself, you hillbilly!"

Up front was Colonel Cassidy. Now he was heading back the other way. "Turn 'em around, Sergeant," he said to Sergeant Nutter. "That smoke signal belongs to the 506. Ours is back the other way."

With a big grin on his face, Holly said, "About face!"

"OK, OK. Don't give me a lecture, dammit! But how the hell did you know?" I asked Holly.

"You know how easy it is for Colonel Cassidy to get lost. You haven't forgotten about Normandy have you?" He meant the four-thousand-yard march of Cassidy's behind German lines outside Carentan. "When W. O. Bird said he saw the colonel going to the smoke down here I was sure he was already lost," Holly explained. "I could see the same kind of smoke off to the north just before I hit the ground."

We made it to the right smoke signal and joined our company along with the other three companies ("A," "B" and HQ) in the First Battalion. Our mission was to take and hold St. Oedenrode, a small Dutch town on the north edge of our drop zone.

Market Garden was the code name of the bold plan British Field Marshal Sir Bernard Montgomery proposed to General Eisenhower as an all-out attempt to end the war in 1944. With Ike's reluctant OK went the full use of the First Allied Airborne Army under Monty's command. Montgomery's plan called for airborne help to reach across the Rhine River by way of Holland and to launch an all-out drive to Berlin. General Eisenhower was in favor of the first part of Monty's plan, the securing of a bridgehead over the Rhine River by way of Holland with the use of the newly formed Airborne Army. His reluctance dealt with the overall depth of Monty's plan. He felt it was far too broad.

On September 7 Eisenhower gave his OK, and three days later the airborne began to work on the "Market" part of the plan. The objective of this part of the plan was the capture and holding open of a single road reaching from the Belgium-Dutch border in the south, near Eindhoven, to the Zuider Zee across the Rhine River in the north, at Arnhem. We of the airborne were to jump all along the roadway, taking all the bridges and towns and leaving them intact. We would have a 64-mile narrow corridor and would use 35,000 men and 4,700 aircraft. The concept, as General Browning put it (*A Bridge Too Far*, page 25), "... is to lay a carpet of airborne troops down over which our ground forces can pass."

The other half of the code name, "Garden" would then come into play—the ground forces of Field Marshal Montgomery's 21st (British) Army Group. The task would fall to General Dempsy's

The Corridor Fight

(British) Second Army, and, more specifically, to the armored units of General Brian Horrocks's (British) XXX Corps. The lead tanks of the Irish Guards directed by Lieutenant Colonel Joe Vandeleur would begin their breakout with a twenty-minute artillery attack starting at 1435 hours (2:35 p.m.).

The vast air armada would be off the ground back in England Sunday noon and would land in Holland starting an hour later. After that the first contact between the ground forces and airborne soldiers (where "Garden" meets "Market") was to take place in Eindhoven, Holland. The lead tanks were expected to link up with us troopers of the 101st before nightfall, a distance of fifteen miles for "Garden" to cover in six hours.

The airborne part of "Market-Garden" was divided into three parts: first, second, and third. I always thought of them as, "the bottom," "the middle," and "the top." All three were to take place at the same time, and each part was to carry the "element of surprise."

By studying the big map here in St. Oedenrode, it was easy to see that the 101st was the "bottom" part of the program. Speed in carrying out our assignments was paramount to the total success of the effort.

So delicate, so precarious was the "Market Garden" plan and so bold in every degree that it did not allow room for setback, let alone failure. Not one paratrooper I have ever talked to—American, British or Polish—gave a single thought to failure.

Each part of "Market" was divided among the three airborne divisions. We each had fifteen to twenty miles of corridor to secure. All bridges must be taken intact. The "plum" would surely be the big bridge at Arnhem over the Rhine River. Another big bridge two thousand feet long spanned the Waal River eleven miles to the south at Nijmegen, a city of 90,000. At Grave, ten miles south of Nijmegan, a fifteen-hundred-foot bridge crossed the Maas River.

The "top" part went to the First Airborne (British) Division, the "plum." Since it was their "pudding," that was fair. The "middle" part went to the 82nd Airborne (American). They had ten miles of corridor, a city of 90,000, another fair-sized town, a large river to cross and two huge bridges over a small canal to capture.

My outfit, the "Screaming Eagles" of the 101st Airborne, got the call to take the "bottom" or first part of the plan. It sounded hard as we compared our part with the other two. We had sixteen miles of corridor that included a sharp bend, two big cities, four small towns and eleven bridges to take and hold intact.

Our main drop zone was at the center of our area near the small town of Saint Oedenrode, Holland. Two parachute regiments, including my own 502nd, and one glider regiment used it. The other drop zone was four miles north at the city of Bechel.

The 501st Regiment had four bridges to take and hold at Vechel plus two road bridges and two railroad bridges. Then they had to take and hold the city of Bechel, a main point along the 64-mile corridor. The 506th Regiment had a tougher assignment: walking several miles from the drop zone to Eindenhoven, the biggest city in our 16-mile corridor sector. There were four bridges to take at Eiendehoven. Their challenge was to get the four bridges, liberate the city, and then hold the corridor road open at all cost until the British column of the Guard Armored Divisions tanks came through. On the way to Eindenhoven they had to take the small town of Zon with its highway bridge over the Wilhemina Canal.

Our division leaders must have thought that my regiment, 502, had the easiest assignment of the three. Our task was to secure the drop zone and the area around it, since it would soon become a landing zone for our gliders. The drop zone was bounded by three small Dutch towns: Saint Oedenrode to the north, Best to the west; and Zon to the south. Since the corridor road ran straight through Zon and St. Oedenrode, their capture was vital. Each had a waterway with a bridge, and we had to take those as well.

It was felt that only one of the 502nd's battalions was needed in the attack on the town of Saint Oedenrode. The rest of our regiment was assigned in a holding pattern around the drop zone.

11

Defending St. Oedenrode

We men of "C" Company drew the lead in our battalion and started our attack on the highway bridge in the center of St. Oedenrode by going straight down the main highway and launching a frontal attack on the bridge. Meanwhile "B" Company was going to the far right side of town to come in from the east on Vechel Road.

Here we go again—the 2nd Platoon leading the "C" Company. Remember, I said that Colonel Cassidy liked the "C" Company! We left the assembly area at the edge of the drop zone by moving down a narrow roadway about a thousand yards off the main highway.

At the point where my 2nd Platoon came upon the highway the Germans opened up on us with small arms fire. We crossed over the highway and went down the Dommel River bank, or dike, as they were called here in Holland, which happened to meet the highway, but the river did not cross the road until the center of town some five hundred yards north.

With the gun fire we were pinned down on the side of the dike, which was built up clean and neat with a path on top where one could walk or ride a bike with ease. There were no trees on the dike.

Our maps showed that the road was about two thousand yards away from the bridge, but by going along the dike the bridge was only about five hundred yards off.

The call went out from our platoon leader, Lieutenant Wall, for Captain Hancock to come forward and take a look at the landmarks. Both Captain Hancock and Lieutenant Bercherot, who was now the "C" Company's executive officer, did so at once. They saw the same thing that Lieutenant Wall and Sargent Nutter had seen: the quickest way to the bridge was the shortest and best way. Just rush it from here along the dike, get the bridge, and then clean out the town.

While the captain was coming forward, all three of our squads set up our machine guns and fired into St. Oedenrode. We fired across the Dommel River and down the river toward the bridge. My machine gun was manned by two new troopers, Privates Dominguce and Martin. They were small and very young, and both would get hit and captured—but not here in Holland. (I don't know if Private Martin survived the war, but Jerry Dominguce did and wrote me a nice letter after the war.)

With German steel cracking overhead, every trooper had his head down behind the Dommel dike waiting for Platoon Sergeant Nutter to give an order. He told his squad leaders what Lieutenant Wall wanted to do and said he was waiting for an order from the captain. In the meantime, he said, "Set up the machine guns and open fire."

"Big" Holly, O'Neil and I—the three assistant squad leaders—knew what was up and what to do about it. All three squad sergeants—Metz, Bird and Folley—had been with us on the machine guns since the States, so all we needed was something that looked like an order. Now we had it, and act we did. We were ready with all three of our guns by the time our squad leaders got back. Our two young machine gunners were down on the dike's bank as low as they could get, face down in the dirt. Every time a German burst of MG fire went kicking into the dirt at the top of the dike or sailed by overhead cracking the air with the deadly

Defending St. Oedenrode

sound one learns is "way too close," they would both take a bite of good old Dutch earth!

Someone had to take a look. For less than a dollar a day more, a sum I won't get unless I'm alive in the morning, I had the job.

I immediately saw the reason for our holdup and the call for Captain Hancock to come forward. I called out, "Hey, you two machine gunners!" They were lying across their gun. Neither one of them made a move, so I slid down the bank next to them. I tapped each one on his steel helmet with my rifle barrel. It got their attention. The look on each man's face was the same. I could have laughed, but I didn't.

Have you ever been so scared your mouth was dry? A surefire way to get scared is the baptism of fire. When this happens, I don't know why, but you usually try to lick your lips. If you have your face in the dirt, it is a sight! I said, "Bring the MG up here and set it on the bridge straight down this stream. Keep your heads low. One of you feed, and the other fire."

One of them said, "You mean—"

"You're damn right," I said. "We're going to shoot back at them. Fire on order!"

Within five or six minutes we had all three machine guns in action, firing at the bridge.

Captain Hancock walked by. "Let 'em have it!" he said. "Give 'em hell, men! We must take that bridge!"

It took the officers just one look up front to give Lieutenant Wall the OK. With that, Sergeant Nutter came down to tell us to keep our machine guns going but to fire across the Dommel into St. Oedenrode, not on the bridge. He led the platoon on the river by way of the dike to a point about two hundred yards short of the bridge. There the river split into two streams. The left stream went under the bridge we had been shooting at. The 2nd Platoon was supposed to jump up and run down the footpath on top of the dike all the way to the bridge. We followed Sergeant Junior Nutter in single file. The machine guns brought up the rear.

The rest of the platoon moved out, keeping low along the dike's bank with the two lead scouts—Jerry Johnston and Howard Crotts—out in front. Then came Sergeant Junior Nutter, the real platoon leader. By now our machine guns had taken some of the fight out of the Germans, or else they hadn't figured out whether to stay and fight or hit and run. When they saw 6,700 paratroopers coming down out of the sky at them, it probably wasn't hard for them to make up their minds about what to do.

We decided to leapfrog our three machine guns forward since we had three or four hundred yards to move up before the head of the platoon would start the mad dash for the bridge. In this way we could keep close to the main body and allow the rest of the "C" Company to move up in the advance. Since there was no artillery fire as yet and not one trooper had been hit, we moved quickly toward our jumping off point.

Just as at Carentan, we were totally out in the open for two hundred yards, with room for only one at a time on the footpath. Each man had to get up and follow as fast as he can go. No stopping, even if some are hit. Sheer numbers makes this work. Everyone must pass the order, "Go!" "Go!" "Go!"

Lieutenant Bercherdt, who had led us in Normandy, fell back along the 2nd Platoon, telling each trooper to get ready to run. "It's follow the leader, men," he said. "Fan out on both sides of the street when you cross that bridge. Sergeant Metz, keep to the right side. Sergeant Bird, take your men to the left. Sergeant Folley, go behind Bird. Sergeant Colon, follow Metz. Here we go. Go get 'em, Sergeant! Give 'em hell, Nutter!"

Two lead scouts took off first in plain view of all of us. One of them, Johnston, was hit by rifle fire and knocked to the ground within the first steps of the run. Sergeant Nutter, following the scouts, had already started to run when the scout fell right in front of him. Nutter never broke stride; he just leapt over the top of Johnston and kept going. He never looked back.

The next trooper froze. He could not get up for his turn. The next one behind him took too much time trying to talk him into moving forward. The guy behind him was a new man, and he made the mistake of calling out, "Hold up!" By the time the delay ended and the line moved up onto the path, Sergeant Nutter was a hundred and fifty yards ahead of the platoon. Germans still at the bridge started firing at Nutter. By the time he made it to the bridge the rest of us in the platoon had just reached the path.

Defending St. Oedenrode

Sergeant Nutter carried a Thompson submachine gun and held his fire until near the bridge. There he made a 90-degree turn onto the bridge. As he ran across he fired in spray bursts off in three directions. When he reached the far side he dropped to one knee, put in a new clip of ammo and looked back for the first time. What he saw must have stunned him, for his whole platoon was some one hundred yards behind him, stopped in our tracks to watch him. Everyone had quit running, and even the German firing had stopped.

Sergeant Nutter had just begun to fight. Remembering how Nutter had broken his ankle on the jump in Normandy and had missed all the fighting, I realized this jump was different. Those of us in his platoon, men who knew him and loved him so well, stood spellbound while he put on a one-man act that would have shamed John Wayne in any of his US marine movies.

His submachine gun reloaded and aware now that he stood alone in the town of St. Oedenrode, Sergeant Nutter stood up and started firing in short bursts, spraying lead in every direction. At the far end of the bridge he ran up the street shooting up buildings on both sides—into doorways and windows, upstairs and downstairs. Back to the bridge he came on a dead run, still firing. At the center of the bridge he ran out of ammo again. Once more he knelt on one knee, put in another clip, jumped to his feet and started shooting up this end of the main street of St. Oedendrode the same way he'd done at the other end. Then he came back to the center of the bridge and backed up to the rail nearest to us. With his back to us, he held his submachine in his right hand at the ready position, his left hand supporting his body weight on the bridge's railing. For a time he stood there as if waiting to see if the Germans wanted to answer him. They did not. There wasn't a shot fired after that.

Sergeant Nutter gave a head motion and without even looking toward the Platoon yelled, "Bring the 2nd Platoon into St. Oedenrode, Lieutenant!"

With that everyone began to move slowly onto the bridge, fanning out on both sides of the streets to head east, followed by the rest of the "C" Company. One platoon went west of the bridge to clean out the town. The rest of us joined "B" Company coming down the main street from the east. Just like that, St. Oedenrode was ours.

Still on the bridge, the sergeant stood there as we passed by him, watching doors and windows for Germans. He did not speak to anyone. Each man walking by spoke to the sergeant with great honor in his voice. "Great job, Sergeant!" "That's givin' 'em hell, Sarge!" "Those damned Krauts know now they can't mess around with the 2nd Platoon's Sergeant!" "He was great, wasn't he?" I said, "Thanks, Sarge! You OK?"

One of the new men said, "Hey, they've stopped shooting. Where did all the Germans go?"

Another new man piped in, "They're all dead, dummy. Didn't you see Sergeant Nutter shoot 'em?"

Sergeant Hollingsworth put the record straight and brought everybody back to the job at hand. "Sonny," he said, "take that rifle off your shoulder and keep your finger on the trigger, ya hear? Sergeant Nutter didn't kill all the Germans around here by any means. He just scared the hell out of those that were around this St. Oedenrode bridge!" Hollingsworth knew the Germans weren't gone and that they were up the street somewhere waiting for us. Maybe they were sandwiched between "B" Company and us.

His words brought Nutter off the bridge in a hurry. "Holly's right, men," he said. "Be ready! Keep a sharp eye open! They're down this street somewhere. Check every house as we go."

We did. And suddenly it was over—the capture of St. Oedenrode by the First Battalion of the 502nd Parachute Regiment. We ran into "B" Company coming down the main street from a point that was really the center of town at a second bridge we had not known about here in the city. Several German soldiers were caught between our two companies and gave up. Others came in during our fast cleanup of the city.

The enemy count was 20 killed and 58 captured. St. Oedenrode had been easy. Our Division's history book says, "But, to be fair, only rear area troops had been encountered, so far." I would like to throw in here that whenever high-ranking leaders try to tell me, an ordinary GI, that all I have to do is fight against some rear area troops or big military people have written this in their books and I come across that kind of a remark, I get mad.

Defending St. Oedenrode

I have read that we paratroopers were hindered wherever we landed in Holland by thankful and joyful people. Writers have implied that crowds of Dutch people gathered around us troopers as soon as we moved into their towns and cities, lending a "holiday feeling" to the occasion rather than a sense that this was really war.

This undoubtedly was true in key places such as Arnhem, Nijmegin and Eindhoven, but it was *not* true at St. Oedenrode. Not in Colonel "Hopalong" Cassidy's First Battalion. "Dig in!" "Stay on the ball!" "Be ready for anything!" "Set up roadblocks on every street!" "Every trooper, dig in!" "Man those foxholes!" "Goddammit, this is war!" "Keep your helmet on, soldier!"

The front lines is no place to celebrate. I give the colonel credit for our well-trained battalion. Always first things first with our leader. The Dutch people at St. Oedenrode were as glad to be free of German rule as people were anywhere. I'm sure they would like to have demonstrated their joy if we had given them the slightest chance.

Now that St. Oedenrode had been captured, our attention turned to its defense—holding the bridges and keeping the main road open as a corridor for the British.

My company was assigned the road to the Dutch town of Schindel as our defense area. My 2nd Platoon started digging in about fifty yards north of "Hell's Highway," the town's main street. Sergeant Nutter put the whole Platoon in support of the company holding that road. We soon learned that he had put all of our machine guns, bazookas and mortars covering the one road down which the Germans would surely come.

My machine gun was supposed to cover the right side of the street facing north. I chose an ideal spot for my foxhole, with good cover behind some bushes off the street in front of some Dutchman's front yard. Not just any Dutchman's front yard, I soon learned. It was the town doctor's. His home was new and had a beautiful front yard with flowers and shrubs and a little walkway leading up to the front door.

I hated digging holes in that front yard. I tried to figure out where not to dig. Every time I looked at the house someone was looking out the window. At last Sergeant Nutter came by and asked me why I hadn't started to dig in my gun. I told him I couldn't make up my mind where to dig.

Nutter said to me, "I just came down from Battalion CP, and Colonel Cassidy says that the Dutch Underground has reported that the Germans are moving in force into the town of Schijndel. That's about four miles out on this street, and they're getting set up for an attack down this road before dark!"

That did it. I said to my men, "Hey, what the hell are you waiting on? Dig that gun right in there, and fast. Dickerson, you dig over by the house, and I'll dig by this walkway near the gun crew."

The dirt had begun to fly as Sergeant Nutter walked across the street. "Big" Holly was well along in his foxhole digging. I heard Sergeant Nutter say, a little too loudly, "Sergeant Metz's squad is sure messing up that Dutchman's front yard!"

About halfway through digging my foxhole a small boy came out of the house and over to my foxhole. He started talking to me in English, as plainly as any young boy would in the US. He was very talkative and asked me a lot of questions. We became friends right on the spot. (I heard from him after the war.)

A few minutes later the father of the boy, the town doctor, came out into his front yard and introduced himself to me as Dr. Cooymans. He begged me to forgive his son for interfering with my duties. He assured me I was not to worry in the least about his front yard. "I am deeply honored to have the Americans fight for the freedom of my small town from my very own front yard," he said. As he walked away, he added, "Feel free to use anything you need, Sergeant." Then, turning back to me as if in afterthought, "Oh, Sergeant. I have one of your chaps in my house. He is severely wounded in the head. I have done all I can for him. You would do him no more harm by looking in on him. It might help him go to his Maker a little easier, sergeant."

I climbed out of my foxhole and followed the Dutch doctor into the house. The door opened straight into his office. At first I could not see anything. The doctor had to pull me along until my eyes adjusted to the darkness. Then I saw Private Crotts lying on the floor.

Defending St. Oedenrode

The soldier had a neat round hole in the center of his forehead. There was no bandage over it. At the side of his head the bullet had torn a much larger hole coming out. How had he lived this long?

The Dutch doctor spoke to Private Crotts. "I have one of your American friends here in the office with me now," he said. Private Crotts was lying flat on his back with his head propped up. He leaned forward on both elbows and said, "Come closer. I can't see you!"

I took two or three steps nearer. He was straining with both arms, as if to sit up. "Well, if it isn't Corporal Black," he said. "Did we get the bridge OK?"

"We sure did," I said, "thanks to troopers like you."

"How about the town?"

"It's all ours," I told him. "You'd better lie back and take it easy. If you need anything at all, tell the Doc here. He'll let me know right away, because I have my machine gun dug in just outside his front door."

"That's what I call real service," he said.

I started to go back out into the yard. As I opened the door Crotts said, "Thanks, Blackie! See you in London in about a week. If you don't make it I'll drink a mild bitter for you. Same goes for 'Big' Holly!"

Back in my foxhole I thought to myself, "Crotts is dying and doesn't know it." The Dutch doctor said so, and I had seen that terrible hole in the center of his forehead.

Soon our First Battalion medics came and took Private Crotts out of the house on a stretcher. As they passed by me headed down the street to the first aid station I could see he was covered over with a blanket. The Dutch doctor helped them down the front walkway and on his way back he stopped by at my foxhole. "I'm sorry, Sergeant," he said. "I may have been too harsh in my judgment. Your friend has real grit. If anyone can make it, he can!"

He did! Two weeks later he went AWOL from an English base hospital and was drinking beer in a London pub when they found him. By a quirk of fate the bullet had turned inside his head and had followed the side of his skull over his brain and out.

I finished my foxhole and had my machine gun crew set for any action the Germans might have planned for our street. Our whole platoon was dug in by now, and the Germans would have to use tanks to root us out of St. Oedenrode. The element of surprise had worked for us. The Germans had given us the luxury of plenty of time to prepare for their arrival.

It was about 1700 hours (5 p.m.). I was finishing my coffee after chow. Dutch men and women began to gather down our street at the center of town. People were coming out of every house. Some were running toward the town square. The town doctor headed that way, too, and I yelled at him, "What's going on down there, Doctor?" He said something about a town meeting that had just been called. I stood and watched for a while and then called to my friend "Big" Holly to join me in finding out what was up. "After all," I told myself, "isn't that part of a Corporal's job—find out what's going on around you? Check everything out in your area."

As we walked toward the city center I kidded Holly. "What's the matter, Holly? Curiosity killed the cat? I notice you're not lagging behind me going down there."

"That's right," Holly said. "Give me hell for trying to help you out. Sergeant Bird told me I'd better go with you because he's afraid you might get killed sticking your neck where it doesn't belong. He wants to see you get your sergeant's stripes in the morning!"

In the center of the townspeople was a chair with a pretty young girl seated on it. A man, apparently the town mayor, was giving her a haircut with a pair of sheep shears. Not a haircut befitting a pretty girl. More like a shave. She wasn't alone. By now she was the fourth one to undergo a head shave, and there were two more to go. We were told they had been a little too friendly with the German soldiers. The Dutch people called them "collaborators" with the enemy.

We learned that as soon as it looked like the U.S. forces were there to stay, the Dutch underground had gone to work rounding up their fellow countrymen and women who had collaborated with the Germans over the years. The six girls were

Defending St. Oedenrode

young, about eighteen to twenty-two years old, and pretty—until their heads were shaved.

Holly and I stood there seeing the agony of defeat in the face of those girls. We walked back to our machine guns without talking and stood for a while in the middle of the street. At last Holly spoke.

"How do those girls live that down, Blackie?" he said.

"I don't know. Maybe they don't. You know, most of us are just plain lucky. But once in a while some of us make mistakes that we pay for the rest of our lives."

I told my two gunners, Privates Martin and Dominguce, to go take a look for themselves, that I would man the gun until they came back. That's how D-day of the Invasion of Holland ended on September 17, 1944.

Sleep came easy for me, and the Germans left me alone to enjoy it. Any jump takes a lot out of a soldier, but when it's a combat jump you're so keyed up that when you do unwind, sleep takes over fast. Nevertheless, the Holland jump was a picnic for my platoon compared to the Normandy jump.

The word the next morning was "all quiet" here at St. Oedenrode, and it would remain so throughout the day. Still no sign of the British, and no word about what was holding them up.

We spent the day trying to improve our defensive outposts around the northern part of St. Oedenrode. Our main job was guarding the roadway from Schijndel. I moved my foxhole and Private Dickerson's to the rear of the doctor's house in order to cover a deep open ditch that ran behind his house. The ditch opened into a large town park about two hundred yards north and would have given the enemy a great way to sneak into the center of town. Later in the day our learned that our company's command post had moved into the park area, so the Germans would have had to deal them as well as with us if they chose that route.

Because of the move by "C" Company's headquarters unit in front of the 2nd Platoon, we were in what amounted to a "reserve" position by late afternoon. Colonel Cassidy took the liberty of sending half the platoon on a little "mission of mercy." He dispatched two squads—Sergeant W. O. Bird's and Sergeant Edwin

Metz's—to correct a "small mistake" made by a Colonel Cartwright from Division Headquarters.

The story is that the colonel had headed in a seven-jeep caravan from headquarters at Zon toward St. Oedenrode. For some reason Colonel Cartwright and his seven jeeps had turned north in St. Oedenrode and had gone right on past our "C" Company outpost on out the Schijndel road up the corridor highway to the 501st Regiment at Vechel. Our 3rd Platoon roadblock troopers tried to stop them because they were headed straight for the German-held Dutch town of Schnijndel four miles away.

Our official Division's history says, "Who's at fault is still in dispute! All seven jeeps took the road to Schijndel rather than turning right toward Vechel!" (R.W.D. page 292). What doesn't add up is the fact that there is no right turn for Vechel after you enter St. Oedenrode. You just keep going through town on the main corridor road. Every trooper in the 101st Airborne could read a map. Every officer knew every town and city from bottom to top on the map of the main corridor road. Why the order to make a turn off the main road in the center of St. Oedenroad and head for Schijndel when you're in a hurry to get to Vechtel?

Late afternoon our two squads started down the center of the road out of St. Oedenrode north toward Schijndel. We met a Lieutenant Joshua A. Newborn and three of his men from our 3rd Platoon: Privates Culverhouse, Leafty and Duval. They were on patrol on the Schjndel highway. We went north with them about three miles to a railroad crossing just this side of Schijndel. Our mission was to rescue Colonel Cartwright's men, who were pinned down by German fire. The colonel himself had somehow gotten away from the Germans and had made it in his jeep back to the safety of Oedenrode. The other six jeeps were still here, held by the Germans.

I didn't know who was in charge until I read in our division history that we were supposed to be under the leadership of Lieutenant Newborn. As so many times happened in hurry-up makeshift patrols, our success was in jeopardy.

When we got within sight of the six jeeps, possibly half a mile away, we met Lieutenant Newborn with three of his troopers. He

Defending St. Oedenrode 115

told us to take cover in the ditches. He said the Germans were just up ahead. That was the only orders I received from the lieutenant.

We moved into the ditches—First Squad on the left with Lieutenant Wall and W. O. Bird leading the way, and the Second Squad in the right ditch with Sergeant Nutter and Sergeant Metz in front. The rest of us men were strung out one by one five yards apart in back of the two ditches. I was last on the right, and "Big" Holly was last on the left. When the Germans opened fire on us, we were sitting ducks for them. They got Sergeant Nutter first. Then, across the road, they got W. O. Bird. Just like that, two of our best leaders were out of the battle.

Both Nutter and Bird were able to crawl past all of us out of the line of fire to the first aid station in the rear in time to be saved. Both had serious wounds. Sergeant Nutter later returned to the "C" Company from England, but not to our platoon. He served the rest of the war as a "field" First Sergeant. Sergeant W. O. Bird had a very bad head wound. As it turned out, his headstrong stand refusing to let the British operate on him at their field hospital saved his left eye. The British doctors wanted to remove his eye for fear that otherwise he would die before he made it back to the American hospital in England.

Miraculously, we did not lose any men. One reason was no doubt that Nutter and Bird moved on their own through us. Soldiers are reluctant to walk over their wounded, and doing so can slow down the advance. A more obvious reason was the heroic show our two leaders put on for those of us still in the ditch.

Lieutenant Newborn and his men ran forward down the ditch, firing as they ran, all the way to the jeeps. As they ran through German fire, somehow without being hit, they drew the fire away from us. That gave Lieutenant Wall and Sergeant Metz the chance to move both squads near the jeeps to lay down a good base of fire power.

The trick turned when Private Culverhouse jumped out of the ditch and ran for one of the jeeps, and Private Duval climbed into another. They turned the jeeps around and raced back to St. Oedenrode. While under cover of our gunfire from both ditches, Lieutenant Newborn and Private Leaty along with two of our medics were able to rescue all of the wounded jeep personnel. We then headed back down the ditches toward St. Oedenrode, leaving four jeeps standing on the road. I've never understood that. We were all the way up to the jeeps. Why didn't some of us jump in the remaining jeeps and ride them back to town? Sure would have beat walking! The jeep drivers were not hurt and walked back to town with us. Maybe they knew the four jeeps were disabled.

So began the fight for "Schijndel Road." Before leaving this assignment I would walk up and down that road seven times; not once would I ride. I'd had my chance and muffed it. But the guy who really muffed it that day was Colonel Cartwright.

12

The British Are Here

Sometime around noon in St. Oedenrode the word came down, passed along from foxhole to foxhole, "Cole is dead! Cole is dead!"

I'd played football under Cole in England my first year overseas. Lieutenant Colonel Robert Cole was our Regimental Coach. V. J. Folley and I both liked him because he was more than a good coach; he was a great leader. He proved that over and over to the men of the 3rd Battalion. We knew Cole was up for the Medal of Honor for his charge at the Battle of Carentan.

After returning from our "mission of mercy" for our Division Colonel, "Big" Holly and I were standing in the street near the Dutch doctor's house talking about losing Nutter and Bird. Someone from the 3rd Battalion came along and told us that Colonel Cole had died from a single rifle bullet while standing out in the middle of a bridge. After the war I learned that Colonel Cole was trying to capture the bridge and was actually out in an open field looking up at our planes when he was shot by a German.

As I drifted to sleep that night two things bothered me. First, we weren't doing so well here in St. Oedenrode and, second, "Where in hell are the British?"

We had lost the best soldier of the regiment, Colonel Cole. My platoon had lost its two scouts and two of its top leaders. We heard that Colonel Cole's 3rd Battalion had been "stopped cold." That meant great losses. And what about the report that our Second Battalion had been "cut to pieces"? And reports of up to twenty-five percent casualties in the "best" fight so far? Eight officers were dead in one wheat field. Colonel Steve Chappuis stopped the fight because the losses were just too great.

There was some good news. While we were after the jeeps, our "Glider-Rider" buddies of the 317th Regiment along with several other units from the 101st Airborne Division began gliding in to the landing zone here in St. Oedenrode.

It was quite a sight, but we were too busy at the time to enjoy it. Another air show just before dark the day of the jeep mission was put on by the 121 Eighth Air Force (British) bombers as they parachuted more supplies down to us. Unfortunately, over half the chutes dropped into enemy territory.

At 0730 hours (7:30 a.m.) I had just finished my breakfast of K-ration, ham and eggs, a fig bar and coffee. I was milling about in the street in front of the doctor's house when I heard that noise. It was unmistakable. The sound of half-tracks and tanks, followed by truck after truck after truck. And motorcycles. It was a sweet sound to our ears. The call went up, "The British are coming! The British are coming!"

As far as eye could see, nothing but British soldiers. "Hip-hip Hooray!" "Hip-Hip Hooray!" "God Save the Queen!" we shouted. The whole First Battalion must have left their posts to stand along the main corridor road cheering the British on. The Germans could have walked in and taken the town. Maybe they were watching, too.

The Dutch people lined the road that was to be called "Hell's Highway." I don't know how long we all stood there, but it was long enough for us to notice that two grooves were starting to show up on the highway. Over the next several days the tracks would become very deep, requiring road repair in some cases.

The British Are Here

A big Sherman tank captured by the "B" Company came up to the bridge, slowing to a crawl behind an MP (military police) on motorcycle, to save wear and tear on the bridge. Once across the bridge, the driver gunned that tank. With a tremendous roar it stood up on its tracks and scooted through the rest of the town. The earth under the whole town shook. The highway moved up and down as the tank passed by.

It was a great moment, like watching a parade.

The British Land Army led by the Guards Armored Division raced up the narrow corridor through Bechel, which our 501st Paratrooper Regiment held open all the way to Uden. On and on they went, pouring tank after tank and Englishmen by the hundreds. All were riding on something—infantrymen, artillerymen, medics, radiomen, engineers, and even some news reporters. The British were using every piece of equipment they had in this arena of the war.

North of Uden the British entered the sector held by the 82nd Airborne Division, with the big city of Nijmegen at its center. The 82nd had by now taken most of their objectives, but not their most important one. The capture of the huge bridge over the Waal River was crucial to the British Airborne at Arnhem. They needed armored help.

The bridge was finally taken after a heroic effort that afternoon by the 82nd Airborne Division. The British Guards Armored division, however, did not cross over the Waal River until the next morning (D plus 4).

Around noon I learned that my company had run into more trouble up the Schijndel Road. The Dutch underground warned Captain Hancock that the Germans were set to start an attack on the road. Captain Hancock sent out a patrol under the leadership of Lieutenant Harry Larson to check it out. The 1st Platoon's patrol was able to push an enemy outpost back from its advance position. But around 1100 hours (11 a.m.) the Germans made it too hot for them, and they had to fall back. By then Captain Hancock had already sent in Lieutenant Newborn's 3rd Platoon to help out. They were not enough to hold the enemy, so in went the rest of "C" Company.

Once again "Big" Holly and I went up the Schijndel Road, this time at the head of our respective squads. We brought up the rear of the company. Later in the afternoon the fight grew intense, and "C" Company was hard pressed to keep from being flanked. Holly and I took our two squads off the road to the left and spread out on a line across the field. We did not have time to dig in but were able to hold off the Germans from turning our flank. We spent the rest of the day flat on our bellies in that field.

From that position we missed seeing up close some great tank action led by one tank commander, "Paddy" McCrory.

"Hell yes!" was Paddy's reply when Colonel Cassidy asked him to help "C" Company out of the jam they were in. For some reason Paddy's tank had encountered mechanical problems on the way through St. Oedenrode that morning and would run at only five miles an hour. He pulled out of the line of march of British soldiers racing for Arnhem and brought his Sherman tank to a stop right beside the command post of our First Battalion.

Sergeant "Paddy" McCrory was also short on crew. In the airborne we could solve a little problem like that in a hurry because of our training working alongside English tanks back in England, preparing for just this type of warfare. Without any hesitation, our battalion's operations sergeant, Roy W. Nickrent, and Private Jack J. O'Brien Jr. of Sergeant Hollingsworth's First Squad, jumped on Paddy's tank and headed north out of the city toward Schijndel.

That tank arrived just in time to save the day. Paddy the Irishman knocked out a battery of three 20 millimeter guns, one 88 millimeter gun and hit one of Jerry's ammunition trucks as it tried to make a get-away. His tank fired box upon box of machine gun ammo into German positions along the highway. We were able to move Jerry some five hundred yards back by nightfall. At that time Colonel Cassidy pulled us back to St. Oedenrode to man our main line of defense through the hours of darkness.

The ammo truck that Paddy hit was just ahead of us in the field where "Big" Holly and I had our squads. It went up like a Fourth of July display, exploding all over the landscape. It was the high point of the day, and Holly and I thought it might mean a quiet night out of the line of fire.

The British Are Here

William T. Kelley of the 1st Platoon made the trip all the way from the battalion's first aid station at the center of town to give Sergeant Hollingsworth bad news. "Jack O'Brien is dead!" Sergeant Kelley began. "He died in my arms at the battalion aid station. Jack was riding in that Irishman's tank that just helped save our ass. I don't know if you guys over there in that field could see him or not, but Jack made like some kind of a hero. That's for sure."

"Big" Holly had wondered where O'Brien had been all afternoon. Now he remembered that Cassidy had sent him on the run back into town to get help from an English tanker. That was while we were still bringing up the rear in the attack.

Sergeant Kelley went on, "So, that's how he got in that tank. You wouldn't have believed it. Jack was clear down inside that big Sherman tank—the Irishman's—the guy called Paddy. He went past us, and I saw Sergeant Nickrent slide down off the hull of the tank and run for the ditch. It was getting hot around that tank." Kelley took his breath before continuing. "Then, right before my eyes, there was Jack O'Brien sticking his head out of the turret. He had a British Sten gun in his hands, and he sprayed lead down both ditches. What a sight that was! He just plain kept his head stuck up too long, Holly." Again Kelley stopped. "It must have been a German bullet from way up ahead somewhere," he said, puzzling it out as he spoke. "It was a lucky shot. He didn't have a chance. He didn't say a word the whole time I was with him. I was with him until he died back at the aid station. I talked to him like a father and, you know something? He understood what I was saying to him. The last thing he did was look at me and squeeze my hand. We're Catholics, Holly. I know he knew what I said to him!" Kelley was finished with his story.

"Sure he did, Kelley. Sure he did," Holly answered.

Now "C" Company had lost our first paratrooper killed in Holland, and the fifth casualty of our 2nd Platoon in three days. Great as the loss of Private Jack O'Brien was to the 2nd Platoon, it was even a greater loss to Sergeant William T. Kelley. He and Jack O'Brien had lived as neighbors back in Pittsburgh, Pennsylvania, and knew each other's parents. That made it tough.

Before he left us, Sergeant Kelley told us that Colonel Cassidy had assured him that Jack O'Brien had not died in vain, that the damned Germans had really paid and that with "C" Company's help, Jerry had been stopped cold from coming down from Schijndel. They lost over ninety soldiers, fifty-three captured and over thirty paying with their lives. The odds would have pleased Jack O'Brien.

By now nightfall was setting in. Even though we had stopped the Germans, we had not defeated them. I was pretty sure that we had just begun to fight. My platoon was dug in for the first time at the northern edge of St. Oedenrode as a regular line platoon. Sergeant Hollingsworth's First Squad dug in next to mine. We dug in tight to keep Jerry from sneaking in between our foxholes after dark. Holly and I dug our foxholes side by side.

We were dug in along with Olland Road just off the Schijndel highway. The road went due west for about a mile, then turned northwest through Olland, Holland, about three miles away, and on past single railroad tracks, coming to a dead end at the east-west road from Boxtel to Schijndel. At this road line, the Dutch underground told us, the enemy was waiting for us in large numbers. Maybe in full force.

Historians told us after the war that General Student's First (German) Parachute Army was in the area then with headquarters at Vught, due north of Boxtel on the same highway. We also know now that General Student held the entire "Market-Garden" plan in his hands from the first day of the operation. (See *A Bridge Too Far*.)

We didn't have the details, but we knew we were trapped behind the lines.

Word went around the Regiment that a man called Joe from "H" Company had given his own life to save the rest of the men in his dugout by diving on top of a live German grenade.

13

What's in a German Musette Bag?

Jerry's artillery opened the next dawn with a bang. If we wanted St. Oedenrode that bad, Jerry wanted to make sure we paid for it. Artillery was the order of the day, a steady diet of 88 millimeter shells. With this kind of shelling pounding all around, a soldier is always on the alert for a new enemy attack to start if there are any pauses in the gunfire.

Around noon four troopers were killed and two men wounded back in the center of town at the command post. With that news, Colonel Cassidy moved into the basement of an old factory in town. Also, the Germans found the range of the 101st new command post that was on the move into St. Oedenrode on this day. The Germans opened up on them with direct fire from their self-propelled 88s. Men in an advance detail got caught taking over an old castle for General Taylor and his staff.

Old "Hopalong" thought that was going a little too far. Since he was the one who had given St. Oedenrode to its new guests, "Hopalong" Cassidy took some of his boys with him to put a stop to it. This time he called on "A" Company. They took two British tanks along with them to help drive the bad guys back up the Schijndel Road. By afternoon we had some help from the 377th Parachute Field Artillery and Battery "C" of the 81st. As darkness fell over St. Oedenrode on the fourth day, we knew we were going to be there a while.

Late in the afternoon Sergeants Folley and Jimmy Colon stopped by to chat with me and "Big" Holly. For some reason, the two of them had just come back from town, maybe to pick up supplies for our platoon.

I said, "OK. What's the bad news?"

Sergeant Folley said, "There isn't any good news!" He added, "If you think we caught hell out here today, you ought to see it back in town." We knew they had caught it back there. Hell, a lot of that stuff was just over the tops of our heads. It wasn't that big of a town.

"Who got it back there today?" I asked.

"Both of our top company people were hit at the CP!" said Sergeant Colon.

"Yep," said Folley. "We lost the captain and the first Sergeant. Plus a new man from our platoon, Private Lee Master."

"You don't mean Captain Jay B. Shenk is gone? Hell, he is too tough for the damned Krauts to kill. Not Captain Hancock, too?" "Big" Holly didn't want to believe.

"No. Neither of them is dead—at least they made it to the battalion aid station alive," Sergeant V. J. Folley said. "Robert Hale got it, too," he added.

"What happened?" I asked.

James Colon said to me, "Blackie, can you remember when we marched past the CP yesterday and you joked to Jay B., 'You'd better move out from under that big elm tree before lightning strikes and kills everybody under it'? Well, they should've listened to you. An 88 millimeter tree burst shell hit just above them. That's all she wrote."

The two 2nd Platoon Sergeants told us about losses in the battalion and the regiment. But what hurt the most as far as Holly and I were concerned was the fact that "old" Jay B. Shenk would never come back to "C" Company again. We both seemed to know

What's in a German Musette Bag?

it that day. I never saw him again, although he did return to the Regiment as the "I" Company's First Sergeant during the Battle of the Bulge.

(Captain Hancock, we learned later, was sent back to England and returned to Regimental headquarters on December 18, 1944, but not to the "C" Company. Kent Lee Master rejoined us in Austria. Robert Hale headed for the States. I heard from all of these men after the war, including several letters from Jay B. Shenk)

Late that evening after both sergeants had settled in with us, Jerry hit us with a large patrol along the Olland road. They came at us head on through the fields. We turned them back after a sharp fire fight, losing only one trooper from the 2nd Platoon.

Private First Class George A. Hash, a rifleman in Sergeant Hollingsworth's First Squad, decided on his own to go on a one-man patrol after the Germans. He simply got up out of his foxhole and started walking straight toward the Germans heading back to their own lines—the ones whose dead bodies weren't lying out in the field in front of us.

After a while "Big" Holly became concerned about Hash and decided to go look for him. I tried to talk Holly out of going out on his own. He went anyway. And that's how it was that Sergeant William T. Hollingsworth was out in front of our lines, in no-man land, where he stumbled onto a dead German soldier stretched out spread-eagle on the ground. Still in his hand, in a death grip, was the handle of a large pack, or, as I shall call it, a "musette bag."

Holly had but one thought when he saw that bag, fully packed and held by a dead man: he had to have what was in that bag!

We were well trained, Holly as well as any of us. "Watch out for German booby traps planted on dead bodies," had been a quote repeated many times in our training. No one knew this better than me.

Holly knows this, and he tries everything to get the contents of the bag. He finds a long stick and tries to pry the bag open. That doesn't work. He finds a long wire, but that is no use. As a last resort, "Big" Holly decides to shoot the "musette bag" out of the dead soldier's hands. He backs off about twenty yards, stretches out in a spread-eagle position on the ground, takes aim and squeezes off three shots.

I heard the rifle shots and passed the word to the squad men, "Be ready for anything! Sergeant Hollingsworth is still out there, men. Maybe he's in trouble!" I even said, "Hold your fire! Don't hit Pfc. Hash or the sergeant as they come in. Keep your eyes and ears open."

"Big" Holly is as good a marksman as anyone in the 502nd, and even though it is almost dark, he cuts the handle in two with three M-1 rifle shots. Still there is no explosion, and time is running out for Holly. The Germans have surely heard his shots; maybe they have seen him. There is only one thing left to do. Jump off on a dead run. Head in a straight line for the musette bag and head for our lines yelling, "Don't shoot! Don't shoot! It's me! 'Big' Holly! I'm coming in! I'm coming in!"

As he heads for the bag he must be sure to get his toe into it, like the old pigskin, to set it flying in the air toward our lines and then on a dead run reach down and take it on the first bounce right off his shoe tops. Then, if Sergeant Hollingsworth is lucky enough to do all of that, he has only fifty yards left to run for a touchdown!

Well, here he comes. I see him. And so does Jerry!

Get ready! Holly hits that old "pigskin" perfectly, with his toe. He even has his head down just like a good kicker should. But it isn't a football; it's a musette bag! It doesn't rise off the ground an inch. It might roll six feet, which is about as far as Holly goes.

When his toe hits that damned bag he yells, "Ouch!" skips on his left foot, grabs his right foot and falls to the ground, probably saving his life, because fire had already begun from the German end of the field.

Since "Big" Holly was rolling on the ground holding his toe, I ordered "open fire" on Jerry. Our fire pinned them down somewhat, and Holly came hopping back to our lines, bringing that damned musette bag with him.

I can still see him crawling through the line of brush that helped protect our foxhole positions along the Olland Road ditch and gave us a strong advantage over the Germans in that location. He was holding the musette bag with both hands, his rifle slung over his back.

What's in a German Musette Bag?

The first thing I said to him was, "What kept you out there so long?" I couldn't help myself from adding, "What in hell is so damned important about that bag? It got all of us in another fire fight with Jerry!" I was mad. We had just run Jerry off, and now Hash and Holly had stirred them up again. It was like stirring up a nest of "eyebungers" (bumble bees). The first time you hit them with a stick, they aren't sure what hit them. The second time, they're all mad at you and come after you from everywhere.

Before Holly could answer me I said, "Where's George?"

"George who?" he said.

I was really mad at him now. I said something like, "Damn it, Holly, that's the trooper you went out after. Private First Class George Hash. Don't you remember? Hell! He's one of your men, Holly!"

Like a little kid caught in a prank, Holly was really sorry. In a soft voice he said, "Private First-Class George Hash. Of course. You are right to be mad at me, Sergeant Black. I almost forgot why I was out there. I'm telling you the truth. I looked everywhere for him. He isn't out there anywhere, Black." Holly was convincing me. "I looked into the faces of every dead man out there. Not a one of them was American. They are all Germans." He ended by saying, "You know what I think, Sergeant Black? I think they captured Pfc. Hash and took him back to their lines alive."

As Sergeant Hollingsworth sat on the edge of his foxhole telling me this, I noticed he was starting to take off one of his jump boots. The German musette bag lay next to his other foot. It might have caused a broken toe. It was stuffed full of something, and you couldn't put any more into it.

Now aware of the bag, I remembered that Holly had not answered my second question. So I repeated it. "What is so damned important about that bag there by your foot? What the hell is in it?" I said.

Holly picked it up and handed it to me. "Lift that," he said. "See how heavy it is? No! Don't open it! Give it back to me, Sergeant Black! Don't you remember any of your training? I don't know how you will make it through this war if anything ever happens to me." Holly was scolding me. "Hell, Blackie," he said.

"This could be a German booby trap. It might blow both our heads off if I don't open it slowly."

"Well, for God's sake," I said, "I've heard it all now. Have you forgotten that you kicked that bag like a football? If it had been booby-trapped you would be on your way to kingdom come by now. Since it isn't booby-trapped, what is it?"

"Any fool can see that it is a German musette bag," "Big" Holly said to me in disgust.

"But what's in it?" I wanted to know.

Holly was in no hurry now. He was going to have some fun with me.

"Take a guess. I'll tell you what, Sergeant Black," he said. "You can have three guesses. If you guess what's in this German musette bag, you can have half of it!"

I said, "How the hell do I know what the Germans carry around the battlefield on their backs in their damned musette bags!" I was starting to get burned up again, because I really wanted to know what was in there. But I had to play his little game. "OK," I said. "My first guess is—let me see—I'm hungry and since we are very short on American food I will guess it is something to eat. I will say that the dead soldier got greedy when he found one of our supply parachute bundles and filled his musette bag full of our K rations."

Holly opened his mouth to speak, but I cut him off.

"Wait a minute. I'm not through with my first guess yet," I said. "If that dead German was a smart NCO, those K rations will all be breakfasts. But they will be all dinners if he was a dumb officer."

"That's a good guess for a farm boy," Holly said, "but let me point out that you don't have to get that technical. At this rate we'll be here all night. I would like to see what's in here before it gets pitch dark."

"You mean to tell me you don't know?"

"What is your second guess, Sergeant? Hurry up!" Holly shot back at me.

"OK. How about me saying it's full of cartons of Lucky Strikes (cigarettes)?"

What's in a German Musette Bag?

"Hey, that's another good guess, Sergeant Black. Now for your last chance!"

I thought for a while and then said, "How about if I said there was a million dollars in that bag?"

"Now you're talking hillbilly talk, Sergeant. Damn! Black, you're a good guesser. Bring your flashlight over here, and I'll get down in my foxhole where no one else can see what we have here." Sergeant Hollingsworth was as excited as a little kid, and it had built up in myself as well.

"What do you guess is in there?" I asked Holly. He already had one of the straps undone.

"You know what I think?" he said. "I think this musette bag is full of secret plans. It has all kinds of maps that Hitler himself drew up. He was sending them on to the Russian front, but we got them before they were dropped off."

I looked at him, spellbound. "Are you kidding?" I said.

"No," he said. "Honest to God. That's what I think is in here!"

He let the other strap fall loose, lifted the flap and whatever was in there could be seen wrapped in strong brown paper. He shook the bag upside down, and it all fell out in a lump. He cut the paper with his jump knife, and the contents spilled all over the bottom of his foxhole.

It was money. New Dutch money, all tied up in neat packs like money that had just come from a bank. It was the payroll for a German battalion. Even though neither Holly nor I knew one piece of paper from the other, it looked good. If that package was good, there was more money in the bottom of Holly's foxhole than he or I had ever seen before. (It turned out to be equal to about $40,000 in American money!)

"You'd better hide that stuff for tonight," I said to Holly. "Those damned Germans are bound to look for it. Tomorrow we can figure out what to do with it."

"You're right, Black. Go ahead and kick some dirt down here on me, and I'll cover it over all this money."

I did.

"More dirt, Black."

I did.

"More dirt, Black."
I did.
"More."
"Hell's fire! That's enough!" I jumped into my own foxhole next to his. I was ready for sleep. The last thing I remember hearing on that day was, "More dirt, Black. More."

The next morning I saw that the dirt I'd kicked in covered all that Dutch money as well as Holly himself up to his belt line. I couldn't believe I'd kicked that much dirt on him. Maybe I hadn't. He might have done that himself sometime during the night. He didn't get much sleep. He must have spent the whole night thinking about what to do with all that money.

One thing was obvious. Holly was planning on putting up a doggone good fight to keep that money. His M-1 rifle with the bayonet was already in place, lying at port arms. He had six (I counted them) hand grenades in a neat row across his legs in the fresh dirt. His trench knife was stuck at eye level in the dirt wall of his foxhole. In his right hand, by his side, he held his army 45 rifle. And last, but equally effective, he had two bandoliers of rifle ammo hung loosely around his neck. Oh, yes. I almost forgot. He had his helmet on. That isn't unusual in itself. All 502nd troopers kept their helmets on at night because they made good pillows. But not with both chin straps fastened!

I thought better of awakening him while standing over him. I backed off several feet and called him. He came awake on my first call. He dug himself out of his foxhole and checked his Dutch money. No question about it. It was Holland's good Dutch money.

We had been told on the D-day jump into France as well as in the Holland jump that no regular French or Dutch money would be made good by the military. "So don't take any!"

Now I informed Holly that his work and the chances he'd taken to get the money into his foxhole and his sleepless night to guard it were all in vain. "Holly," I said to him in plain English, "it isn't worth a damn!" I believed that, and I had just ruined his whole day, maybe the whole war.

Sergeant Hollingsworth mumbled to me that most of the time I knew what I was talking about, and that he, too, had heard Jay B. Shenk say, "Damn it, no other monies will be any good, so

What's in a German Musette Bag?

don't bother with them." Nevertheless, Holly continued, "all of that Dutch money done up in neat little packs looked too good not to be any good at all. If you would do me a big favor," he said, "and guard my foxhole while I go talk to Lieutenant Wall about my find, you will be my friend for life."

I never knew what Lieutenant Wall told Holly to do with the money. Within minutes we received word that our whole Regiment was to prepare for a big attack at noon today. We in the First Battalion were to strike back on the Schijndel highway once more, the third time for me. We were to jump off at 1400 hours (2 p.m.) with my "C" company centered on the highway. My platoon would use a squad in each ditch, the same procedure we had followed on the other two attacks.

This time Sergeant Hollingsworth's First Squad drew the left ditch, and my Second Squad was on the right. Sergeant Folley's Third Squad was behind me, and Sergeant Colon's Mortar Squad followed Holly. Lieutenant Lake, our assistant platoon leader, was in the lead on the attack just in front of Holly. The "B" Company was attacking down the Olland Road, far to the left, while "A" Company was attacking up "Hell's Highway" toward Koevering, far to our right. The rest of our Regiment was to take the offensive as well. The Second Battalion was to attack due south all the way back to our drop zone area. The 3rd Battalion was moving west down the highway to Donderonk that led back to the town of Best.

Once again, it seemed to me, Colonel Mike was about to make the same mistake again: spreading our regiment too far away from our main objective, the corridor road.

For an attack like this on the scale of a battalion with the leadership not sure when or where we might return, or even if we would return, we always packed up our bedrolls and left them with our S-4 supply people. Sergeant Hollingsworth's bedroll took on an odd shape. Try sometime to pack $40,000 in small bills into your regular army bedroll so it will pass a GI inspection! Holly did about as good a job as anybody could. I watched him try about ten different ways, and he made sure his bedroll was at the bottom of the pile in the supply trailer. He told Sergeant Anderson that he had a few German helmets wrapped up in his bedroll. It looked like it, and Sergeant Anderson believed him.

I can't remember eating before going into battle early that afternoon, but I do remember Sergeant Hollingsworth taking off his jump boot and showing me the big toe of his right foot. He'd banged it up good, but I had no intention of letting him get out of this attack. Not if I had to go! So I used "Doctor Black's psychology treatment" on him.

I said, "A guy bangs up his toe a lot playing football. The best thing for it is to walk on it a lot. It is not broken, I'm sure of that." I told him that if he went on sick call those medics back at battalion in town would start him on shots for lockjaw. At least twice a day. I said, "Hell. If that happens, Holly, you won't be able to sit down." And then the clincher. "Anyway, it isn't safe back there. You know how many troopers got killed yesterday, don't you?"

That did it. Sergeant Hollingsworth put his boot back on and said, "Come on, men! Let's go get those damned Jerrys."

For Holly and me this meant moving up the Schijndel Road for the third time to push the Germans back the shortest distance and the toughest to achieve of the three attacks. The other two times we had made it past the old monastery, but each time we ran into more soldiers, and they were better dug in the second time than the first. The monastery was off the road a hundred yards to the east. It was a beautiful old place with large park-like grounds around it and big shade trees everywhere. A terrible setting for a war.

My "C" Company was halted about five hundred yards short of the monastery, where we dug in for the night. Some of us made it up to the grounds of the Monastery, and those of us who advanced that far were part of some of the bravest fighting I saw in the whole war.

A British tank squadron had been attached to our regiment for the next few days. Two of their tanks had been sent up the Schijndel Road with us and were supposed to stay behind us, the parachute rifle men, and help out against the self-propelled German 88s and strong points in Dutch farm houses along this road.

All of a sudden, for no apparent reason, the lead tanker decided to move out in front of us. I think the reason he made this brave move forward was in angry response to the killing of our

What's in a German Musette Bag?

assistant platoon leader, Lieutenant Lake, by machine gun fire. He was shot in the ditch up front. The British tanker up on the road must have seen it happen and felt that the Jerrys had the rest of the ditch zeroed in. So after him he went, to draw fire away from Holly. When the tanker passed me he had his head sticking out of the open hatch. He looked at me and yelled, "We'll get those bloody bastards, Yank!" They were sitting ducks once they passed Holly's and my squad.

Jerry let both tanks go on up the road about fifty yards past them. Then "Bang!" Jerry hit them with rockets. Both tanks were gone, and so were the British soldiers in them. I don't remember anyone getting out. One tanker tried to crawl out, but halfway out he died as he helplessly hung there in plain view of soldiers on both sides of the road.

There was nothing we could do. The Germans had both ditches zeroed in, and they were dug in on the road better than anywhere else where we would meet them in the whole war.

Colonel Cassidy asked Paddy McCrory if he would help out his company, which was having trouble with Jerry up the Schijndel highway near the old monastery. "Sure," said Paddy. Sergeant Czarniak of the First Battalion headquarters company filled out the crew.

Tank Commander McCrory (British) and his crippled Sherman tank started down the highway in our direction from St. Oedenrode. We could hear it coming, and we could tell by the sound of the engine that it was our friend Paddy and his tank. There were tank drivers in the war, and there were tank commanders. We knew that Paddy was a commander. As he came alongside of us, both of our squads from the ditches stood up. By firing our rifles we were able to move forward, keeping to each side ditch and keeping pace with Paddy's crippled tank. So far all of the tank action in our area had been on the road itself.

When Paddy caught up to two British Sherman tanks that had been smashed, he stopped and got out of his tank to look into the two tanks that were blocking his path. He wanted to be sure none of his own countrymen were still alive inside. "Big" Holly and I stopped our squads to watch. I remember thinking how brave a man this Irishman was, and wondering why none of us American paratroopers would do the same. I felt ashamed of myself.

Suddenly, with no warning, Paddy McCrory drew his six-shooter revolver, which all British tankers carried as sidearms. He jumped down from the second smashed tank and ran up to the center of the road straight toward the Germans. Still with his 38 revolver drawn, he slid to a stop by the side of the road, pointed the barrel down into the ditch on my side and fired all six shots point blank. I thought Paddy had gone berserk seeing his mutilated countrymen in those two tanks.

Then he made another sudden move. He jumped down in the ditch on all fours, picked something up and then came on the dead run toward me. In one hand he was carrying a small, squealing, squirming suckling pig by the feet. He threw the pig up to Sergeant Czarniak, still in his tank. "Tonight we eat!" he said. He crawled back into his tank, pushed the two disabled tanks out of his way, and forward into battle we all went.

Jerry's fire from the small arms let up after that, or so it seemed to me. We stopped at a Dutch farmhouse very near the roadway. A Jerry machine gun nest was set up inside it, and Jerry raised hell with us all afternoon into the early evening from that house. But now Paddy had given us something we needed to reach our objective: new life. If Colonel Cassidy let us, we would have walked through hell with Paddy that afternoon. In fact, we did!

Paddy pulled his tank slowly right up in front of that house, with us alongside him. His machine guns ripped into the house while Jerry with 88 millimeter guns just behind the house in the garden did their damnedest to knock him off. Paddy put three canon shots point blank into that house. What a sight that was! Walls went flying everywhere, and we all cheered. That was the end of the machine gun nest. Paddy moved his crippled tank just past the farmhouse and skip-fired three more rounds into the garden at the rear to get Jerry's self-propelled 88 gun! He got it! No more 88s. The enemy strong point went deathly silent.

We moved slowly up the Schijndel Road with "Paddy" moving straight down the center of the road. All of "C" Company was coming behind us. When "Paddy" saw an armored car up ahead,

What's in a German Musette Bag?

he got it with one shot. By now "Paddy" and our two front squads had reached the old monastery. He was in for trouble here.

Behind the old monastery the Germans were dug in very well. They opened up on us as soon as Paddy's big Sherman tank came into view. From their well dug-in anti-tank gun they sent three rounds at Paddy. No hits! But that was too damned close. With a crippled tank low on ammo now and darkness near, there was only one thing to do: withdraw. Colonel Cassidy stopped the advance and ordered the "C" Company to pull back five hundred yards from the monastery. We set up a line running east and west from the Olland Road, where "B" Company was halted in its attack, all the way over to "A" Company, which had been called back from their march toward Koevering to join us on our right flank. We all dug in for the night.

I dug in just off the Schijndel Road, maybe fifty yards to the right in a field alongside a wooded area. Just after we finished our attack a British tank squad pulled in beside me. They were using the wooded area as cover.

14

The Big Battle on the Road to Schijndel

Sometime before daylight a company runner woke me up. "Join me and Sergeants Metz, Hollingsworth, Folley and Colon at the CP. First Lieutenant Jack Bercherdt (our acting CO) has called a meeting of all NCOs from the rank of squad leader and up. Grab your rifle and helmet," he said. "Come on! There's no time to waste."

Just like that, the most disastrous day of the war began.

In the pitch darkness of early morning I walk up the road. My mind is awake, but my body doesn't seem to be. I stumble on almost every step. I'm thinking about last night's heavy artillery attack we carried out, and now this early morning rush to a big company meeting. What else could it mean than a big attack coming up?

Our company runner found our command post near the spot where we had entered this field the previous night. We were in the ditch along Schijndel Road. Lieutenant Bercherdt did not waste any time telling us what was going on. "Men," he said, "our plan is simple. We are going to attack with a two-battalion line, advancing as skirmishers. We've used this many times on dry runs back in England. We will have British tanks on line with us today. They will not get ahead of us. Our job is that of an infantry. Remember that. The tanks are here to help out against Jerry's tanks and any big stuff. Keep up! Keep your men on line! That's damned important. We are to be on line ready to move out at 0630 hours (6:30 a.m.) sharp! An artillery barrage by our 377 boys will start the pre-attack. Any questions, sergeants?" Then as an afterthought he added, "Oh, yes. I might as well tell you. We expect Jerry to be well dug in and out in front of us in full force. The Dutch underground told regiment headquarters last evening of a large number of enemy trucks stopping in Schijndel and unloading over two thousand infantry troops. Our artillery barrage last night was aimed at those trucks. We got several of them, but the bad news is that Jerry had already gotten off the trucks we hit. Good luck, men!"

The next thing I can remember we were all standing in a line on both sides of the road running through fields. At 0600 hours (6 a.m.) when the day began to show light, the fog was with us as always in Holland. It felt eery, and it seemed to me as I stood there before the shelling started that something about this was wrong.

I put that feeling out of my mind. Then it happened. Our artillery guns began to fire the first barrage that we wanted to land at the very door of the enemy's front lines, the foxholes we would first encounter on our attack. Our two front lines were only a hundred yards apart. This meant that our 377 parachute artillery boys would be cutting it close.

The 377 boys must not be short today with their aim because of the stand-up skirmishing line of advance we were using. We were hidden by the dense morning fog. The first rounds were short, and they all landed on the "C" Company!

Just like that, eight of our paratroopers were hit. We had not taken the first step forward and already had eight casualties.

The morale of our company could have been destroyed, but we regarded the firing as an unfortunate mistake and went on with the attack. At the set time, we went forward standing straight up and firing our rifles as we walked straight into the German lines.

The Big Battle on the Road to Schijndel 139

Although enemy resistance was present, for some reason small arms fire was erratic. By 0700 hours we had covered the five hundred yards we had lost the previous night. We were back at the old monastery and had not lost another man.

Our machine guns leapfrogged forward with the advancing regiment. Ten Sherman tanks on our line of advance moved across the fields. The two tanks with "C" Company were positioned in the fields a few yards off the Schijndel highway. Guns on our tanks blazed away, laying down a heavy volume of fire.

Jerry almost always put the main line of resistance several yards behind a line they gambled we would mistake as their front line. Often they would place some of their worst soldiers on this phony front line. They would fire erratically and then surrender. We would be lulled into thinking that the campaign was going to be easy. Then, when we did hit their main line of defense, they had their best men waiting for us.

That's how it happened that day. The German soldiers on Germany's primary defense line were the best in the area—General Student's paratroopers!

Jerry made his stand on the north side of the old monastery behind a wooded area, watched us walk right up on top of them and then opened fire.

The 3rd Platoon had the job of clearing the grounds at the monastery and a thick wooded area north of it. The Germans had put barbed wire all around the big building, apparently planning to use it as a headquarters building later on. The 3rd Platoon came out of the wooded area and all the rest of "C" Company came on line with them. Across the fields as far as I could see were 502nd paratroopers.

All hell broke loose. This time Jerry didn't miss.

Across the road from me in the 3rd Platoon the word went up and down the line: "Sergeant Clyde Featherstone has been hit!" Then, as if a correction, the word came down the line, "Featherstone's dead! Sergeant Clyde Featherstone has been killed!" Featherstone was well liked by everyone in the company, a handsome man with a good build and beautiful blond hair.

Jerry was really letting us have it now, but the entire regimental line continued moving forward. Again, a devastating cry rang out and traveled the entire line of the "C" Company. "Lieutenant Baker has been killed over in the 3rd Platoon!" Then on my left, "Private First Class John Kern is killed!" My fellow soldiers of "C" Company were dropping like flies.

I pulled my squad over to the side of Schijndel road to once again, taking cover in the ditch. Private First Class James Flanagan, my scout, went ahead several yards down the ditch. An explosion of German mortar shells flashed in the ditch near Flanagan. Although he was hit, he was not knocked down.

He jumped out of the ditch and started to run down the center of the road. His jumpsuit was torn in many places, and he was bleeding from shell wounds all over his body. "Corporal Black, I'm hit!" he shouted. Now he was running in a circle on the highway, with rifle and machine gun fire everywhere.

I jumped out of the ditch and ran after Flanagan. With his arm around my neck I got him back down into the ditch and helped him walk until we reached the monastery and back toward St. Oedenrode until we met a regimental aid jeep that stopped and took him the rest of the way to the aid station.

I was glad I'd been able to calm him down, but Flanagan had been hit hard and it looked like he was headed for the States and out of this war. He had been one hell of a combat soldier, seeming to thrive on the dangers and living a charmed life. (I was wrong about the severity of his injuries. Later James Flanagan rejoined me in the Second Squad.)

At the point on the highway where I put Flanagan on the regimental aid jeep, I noticed several other jeeps standing by were being loaded with wounded 502nd paratroopers on stretchers. It looked to me that they were high-ranking officers being carried from a ditch on the east side, evidently from a command post.

Suddenly I realized it was our 502nd command post that had been hit! The last officer loaded on an aid jeep was Colonel Michaelis, the Commanding Officer for the Regiment. He had led us since the first days of Normandy! (Later Colonel "Mike" came back to the 502nd Parachute Regiment.)

"What happened to all of our officers?" I asked.

The Big Battle on the Road to Schijndel

"A German 88 shell, a tree-burst, exploded above the ditch that was being used as a command post," a soldier said. "It got the entire group in one burst by spraying steel fragments all over them." It was the heaviest single blow our division would take in the whole war in terms of losing high-ranking officers—a total of fourteen casualties from one shell.

On my way back to my squad up the Schijndel highway I heard the call go out for Colonel Steve Chappuis, the Commanding Officer of the Second Battalion. He was needed back at the Regimental command post as the new Commanding Officer for the 502nd.

As I walked down the center of that damned highway, my thoughts were of the terrible losses we'd taken only a little distance past the point we'd reached the day before. We'd been further along the day before that, and still further two days earlier. When I reached our machine gun crew I learned that our whole company was pinned down and our line of advance was stopped. Jerry's self-propelled guns were doing their job on us.

Our British friends in Sherman tanks saved the day for us. They just kept firing at the German guns until they knocked them out. Once more we moved forward until we were halted by our new Commanding Officer, Colonel Chappuis.

Shortly after fighting resumed we ran into a German strong point just off the highway at a Dutch farmhouse and other buildings. Jerry was well dug in, not only in and around the farmhouse but in the small fields around it as well.

The plan was for British tankers to soften up the buildings, and then for the paratroopers to rush in. The German soldiers fought well at their strong point near the buildings, but we ended up killing or capturing them.

Once the British tankers had hit the strong point, Sergeant Metz pulled the whole platoon to the road ditch in an all-out rush on the farm house and another main building close to the highway from Schijndel to St. Oedenrode.

Sergeant Metz and Private First Class Blackburn led us out of the farm yard into the open fields, followed by Sergeant Hollingsworth's First Squad, Sergeant Colon's Fourth Squad, Sergeant Folley's Third Squad and my Second Squad. I was just coming into the farm house driveway with my squad when the quiet ended with the "Br-up! Br-up!" of German machine guns. I didn't see the firing start because the house was in my way, but as I came around the corner of the house, lead and steel were flying everywhere.

I halted my men and called to Sergeant Folley to hold up until we could find out what we had run into. Then I yelled over to some of "Big" Holly's men lying on the ground beside a huge mound of dirt a few feet away. They called back that Sergeant Hollingsworth was inside the mound of dirt and that someone was hit in there. I decided to see for myself. Sergeant Folley had the same idea. We met each other when our steel helmets bumped at the big mound of dirt in a hail of bullets.

We found out it wasn't just a mound of dirt. It was a Dutch farmer's air raid shelter, and a damned good one at that. It looked like an old-fashioned storm cellar or root cellar common on US farms in the Midwest in the 1930s. The inside dimensions were about five feet high, six feet wide and twelve feet long. There were two bunk beds on each side against the wall with an aisle between and two doorways, one at each end of the room. Other items included a table and chairs and miscellaneous items a family might want on hand to last out an air raid attack.

The Dutch farmer and his family had tried to cut the odds of being hit by bombs or shells by building a shelter just a few yards from the back door of their farm home.

In this flat country a pile of dirt seemed to be a safe place. With enemy bullets cracking overhead, Sergeant Folley and I were less concerned about ourselves than we were about Holly's men. Who had been hit? Where was Holly? What about Sergeant Metz? Where was Lieutenant Wall, our platoon leader?

Sergeant William T. Hollingsworth heard us talking and came out the doorway. He looked beaten. The fight had gone out of him. His face was white, and he didn't have his helmet on. His blue-black hair was matted across his forehead from sweat. I asked the question that was on both of our minds. "What the hell happened, Holly?"

Holly sat with his back against the mound of dirt that was the roof of the shelter. He began speaking slowly in a soft whisper. "Jimmy Colon—is dying in there on that cot—and, Black, that should be me—not that good-looking boy in there. That should be me—I tell you. That should be me!"

Holly continued, "There is a doorway on the other end of this bomb shelter that leads out the north side. We saw Blackburn and Sergeant Metz get hit just after they jumped across the ditch over in the next field. So I said to Colon, 'Let's try this bomb shelter.' Once inside we saw the other doorway. We figured that if Jerry didn't see us go in, how would they know we had gone out? We told all our men to come through this bomb shelter behind us."

Holly paused to think again about how such a good plan could have failed. Then he went on. "You know, they must have had that other door zeroed in by a sniper. Anyway, it should have been me, Black. My squad should have been first. When we got inside, Jimmy wanted to be the first out. But it should have been me!"

"Where was Jimmy hit?" Sargent Folley asked.

"Dead center in the forehead, with one rifle bullet. It had to be a sniper. Must have seen us go in somehow. He must have seen us! When Jimmy got hit I was right behind him. The force of the bullet drove him back into my arms. I kept him from falling to the ground. I've been in there holding him in my arms ever since. He asked me to take his pocketbook and to promise him I would send it home after he died. Jimmy knew he was going to die from the moment he was hit. He made me promise I would hold his head until he was dead. He kept saying to me, 'Hold my head.' 'Hold my head.' 'Hold my head.' God, Black! It was awful. Come in and take a look. See if we can do anything to help Jimmy. Folley, you and he were great friends. Help me! Help me!"

We three troopers went inside. Holly was down on the cot where Staff Sergeant James Colon lay, barely alive. Holly sat down on the cot, put Colon's head in his lap, and with water from his canteen and using a piece of green parachute silk, tried to make James Colon's last minutes a little easier.

Standing there looking down at the tragic scene, V. J. Folley was the first to speak. "Jim," he said, "can you hear me? This is Folley talking to you. We want you to hang on, Jim. Corporal Hollingsworth has got hold of you, and he won't let go. You hear me? Jim! Hang on! Corporal Black has gone to get a doctor, and he'll be back in a shake! This is Folley talking to you. Jimmy, we are all going to help you get out of here. So hang on a little longer, Jim. We'll make it!"

With Folley's words, I took off on the run toward the house and onto the road. As I ran for help I could hear the cries of Sergeant Metz and Private First Class Blackburn, who lay helplessly wounded some forty yards out in an open field that was now no-man's land. The Germans had the back of this farmyard zeroed in.

Someone heard my desperate call as I kept yelling, "Hey! 'C' Company 2nd Platoon. We have to have a doctor. Not a medic. We need a doctor! A doctor!" I'll never know who heard me. Maybe it was one of the British tankers who were near the farmhouse. Or a radio man somewhere in my own company. Whoever it was, the word got back to Regiment, and the message returned to me, "Two jeeps, a doctor, and two medics are on their way!" Somewhere along the road someone said, "Hang on! They're on the way. Hang on!"

I knew it would take time to get back to us. Back in the air raid shelter with the news that a doctor was on his way, I could hear Jerry shelling us with mortars. Sergeant Folley and I decided we'd better have our men dig in right where they were. Folley and I had not seen another noncommissioned officer of any kind for some time. Even Corporal Hollingsworth was going to be occupied for a while.

After checking on our squads, the two of us met back in the bomb shelter. Sergeant Colon was still alive, by not by much. Folley and I were sure it was a matter of time, that no doctor could help Jim now. My thoughts turned to Hollingsworth and how he would take this terrible tragedy. "What happens when Colon dies in his arms?" I took care of his squad for the time being.

Just forty yards away from the shelter's north door we could see three of our men lying wounded in the field. We figured the third one was a platoon medic. By now it had been a good fifteen minutes since they had been hit. All were moaning that terrible sound that comes before one is about to pass out from loss of blood or shock from pain and exposure. Even though they were all in no-man's land, we had to go out there and try to save them. Somehow!

The Big Battle on the Road to Schijndel

I asked Sergeant Folley to try to find a blanket in the house that would be strong enough to carry a soldier as big as Metz. Meanwhile, I said, I would try to get some of our men to volunteer to go out in no-man's land under heavy enemy fire and pull them back.

I went to the oldest trooper in our 2nd Platoon, Private First Class Wayne Dickson. He did not want to volunteer. He said, "I will go if you order me, Corporal Black. But please don't make me go!" By now all of our men knew about the wounded men. The shock of it was settling into the whole 2nd Platoon. It just seemed like too much to ask of anyone. So I went back to the bomb shelter, where Sergeant Folley was waiting with a blanket.

I told Folley I couldn't ask anyone to do what I thought was impossible. Then I said, "But you and I, we have to try!"

Folley said, "Which way do we go?"

I said, "How about down that ditch right there?"

"Follow me," Folley said.

We took a route down two water-filled ditches. The ditches gave us the cover we needed, but that route was the longest way out and the hardest way back. The ditches were so narrow that only one of us could walk in it at a time, and the water reached our hips.

All the way out Jerry was shooting at us. The dirt around us spat in our faces, and at times the whine of ricochets overhead kept us from getting careless. Once in the water of the ditches we were barely able to bend over far enough to stay under enemy fire. All three of the wounded men were five or ten yards beyond the last ditch into the field. For the last few yards we had to crawl on our bellies out to them.

The first man we reached was Private First Class George Blackburn. A machine gun had caught him across both legs above the knees. We could see bone in both legs. "They are surely gone by now," I thought. "If he lives, he'll have two stumps."

We rolled him onto the blanket. Then, with Folley on one end of the blanket and me on the other, we dragged him to the ditch before we could ease the pain by carrying him.

He was still alive when Folley and I laid him safely down beside the farmhouse in the driveway. His forty-yard ride in a blanket had not been a pleasure trip, and certainly not gentle. Somehow, though, I thought I saw a faint smile for just a moment that to me meant he knew what we had just done.

Our next trip was harder, for Sergeant Edwin Metz was possibly the biggest man in "C" Company! He'd been a corporal in the 2nd Platoon back when I joined the outfit in the spring of 1943. He probably went back to the Alabama days at Phoenix City with "Big" Holly, Junior Nutter and Jay B. Shenk. Metz had been Nutter's assistant all those years and they were, in fact, from the same state, Virginia.

Charles O'Neil said, "I'll help you, Corporal Black. I'll help you bring Sergeant Metz back. He's a big man! Let Sergeant Folley go check on his friend, Jimmy Colon."

We found Sergeant Metz about ten yards on down the second ditch past the one where we had picked up Blackburn. The task of getting to Metz from the ditch was the same as with Blackburn, but it was harder to roll him onto the blanket and even harder to drag him back to the ditch. Somehow we did it, and brought the sergeant next to the place where George Blackburn was lying. They had both been hit in the same way. Their legs were gone.

During the rescue the thought crossed my mind that Edwin Metz was one of the few men I'd ever met whom I really disliked. There was nothing I could find to like in him. I'm sure Metz never knew that. He may have thought just the opposite. But I helped save his life anyway, simply because it needed to be done.

A medic, a new man in "C" Company, was lying wounded in no-man's land, too. Or in what had been no-man's land earlier that day. By now the Germans were in the process of giving up. They had ceased firing and were surrendering to our troops on both ditches. We were exhausted by now, but on our third trip we stood up and marched out of the ditch straight to where the medic lay. He, too, was in bad shape.

By now two jeeps had pulled up alongside the farmhouse. We called for someone to run a stretcher out to us. As we placed the stretcher onto its mount in the first jeep, I noticed that each jeep had several stretcher mounts. The second jeep also had a two-wheel trailer behind it. The doctor had already gone into the bomb shelter, where Corporal Hollingsworth was holding onto what was

The Big Battle on the Road to Schijndel

left of life in James Colon. I was so tired by now that I could not stand up any longer. I sat down against an apple tree in the yard and did not move from that spot while the medics loaded our wounded and dead. With the help of the doctor, they strapped down each wounded paratrooper and suspended each one's blood bottle in the air on a stand of some sort to give them blood transfusions.

The medics said nothing as they worked to save lives. The doctor spoke now and then. I sat spellbound watching them work.

On the jeep nearest me I watched them load our Company Commander, Lieutenant Jack Bercherdt and Sergeant Folley's Third Squad machine gunner, Private First Class Robert Cahoon. Bob had been a dear friend of mine and Folley's. I learned that our Platoon Leader, Lieutenant Wall, had been hit by early shelling and was out. When the 3rd Platoon men brought the body of Sergeant Featherstone up and laid him in the trailer, I heard the doctor say, "We're ready to take off! How about you medics back there?"

The medic closest to me was walking toward the bomb shelter. He called over his shoulder, "Just as soon as we load the body that is in the shelter, Captain!"

I watched while Sergeant Folley helped the medics carry the body of Sergeant James Colon on a stretcher to the trailer, where the body of another dead U.S. paratrooper also lay.

Corporal Hollingsworth walked by, and I got up and followed him and Folley to the trailer. "Big" Holly had Colon's helmet and rifle, and he laid them beside him in the trailer. Just then a GI came up to the trailer with two German prisoners who were carrying the body of a German soldier.

"Put him in the trailer with the other dead," someone said.

Tears streamed down Holly's face. Without raising his voice, he said, "Don't let them dare, Captain, or I'll kill both of them where they stand!" In his right hand he held his drawn 45.

The doctor spoke up. "You're damned right, Corporal," he said. "And I'll help you. We're not hauling any dead Germans anywhere. Let's get to the aid station on the double!"

"Don't forget to stop and pick up your mess kit on your way back home," Sergeant Folley said to Sergeant Metz. "Wouldn't want you to forget any of our names, Metz!"

As the jeeps rolled back down the Schijndel Highway toward St. Oedenrode I said to the men who were left, "There goes another part of 'C' Company we will never see again!"

Finally someone of higher rank—I think it was Colonel Cassidy—came by and told us to move the men forward several hundred yards into an apple orchard.

Now we were back to the spot where we had tried to save the seven jeeps.

15

The Steel Helmet Is Part of Your Head

The time was 1230 hours (12:30 p.m.) when we started to dig in at the apple orchard. The orders were, "Regroup the company, put out a defense and dig in! Take charge until you get further orders from Battalion headquarters people!"

As far as Folley knew, the 2nd Platoon *was* the company. All that was left of the noncommissioned officers were four corporals: Black, Holly, O'Neil and Charron. There were no officers in that orchard.

Since the "C" Company had centered on the Schijndel Road all along, we were the center of the battalion as well as the regiment. I could see Colonels Cassidy and Chappuis now.

Colonel Chappuis halted the whole regiment along this advance line. The colonel suspected that the 501st troopers had been delayed in their fight at Schijndel, now just a quarter mile north of us, so this was as far north as we would go. The fighting officially stopped for the day, but there were still German soldiers to round up as they continued to surrender to us. Also, Jerry left field pieces standing, and many of them were still loaded. A patrol from "C" Company led by Corporal Ray Charron went around and blew them up.

Later that afternoon a huge German Tiger tank cut across in front of those of us in "C" Company along the highway. That caused some stirring and rapid heartbeats. A gun crew from our 81st boys fired one shot at it and hit the front end, causing it to turn around and come back after us. From our perspective in the foxholes in the apple orchard, it just looked like our gun-crew boys had made them mad. "Leave a ferocious dog alone," Holly said.

Fortunately, one of our British friends with a Sherman tank saw the big Tiger and let three rounds go into its rear end as the machine was turning around to come down after us. "Bang!" The Tiger exploded and burned up on the highway in front of us.

The rest of the day was quiet. At 1630 hours (4:30 p.m.) Colonel Chappuis had us all pull back into St. Oedenrode once more. Many of the men from "C" Company made their way over into the bare open field across the road from the orchard. The German First Parachute Regiment had dug into single stand-up foxholes in that field. The field was a meadow that had been grazed so short by cattle that it looked like a lawn. Jerry had cut neat, round holes in the sod and laid lumber in the holes with sod on top to cover the foxholes. Then they hauled away the dirt they dug up to make the foxholes. Our men could not see where the enemy was firing from. They were the best enemy foxholes I encountered in battle any time during the war.

I walked up the highway to look at the jeeps the colonel had lost at the beginning of this damned "Schijndel Highway Battle." They had been destroyed and pushed into the ditches. There were several self-propelled 88s in the ditches near the railroad trucks, also destroyed.

We never did meet up with our sister outfit, the 501st Parachute Regiment. By the time we reached St. Oedenrode word was out that "C" Company would be restaffed the next day with new officers. In the meantime we would be digging in around the fence lines of this field.

Even though we were on a reserve status until we could be restaffed, our company was on alert through the night. We

The Steel Helmet Is Part of Your Head 151

received new information, that Jerry had cut the corridor road north of Vechel on this side of Uden around 11 a.m. that day. This had been done after part of the 506th Parachute Regiment had started moving into Uden. For the first time in the war, part of our division was cut off from the main body.

We also learned that the 501st Parachute Regiment, under Colonel Johnson, was preparing to meet up with us to launch an attack from Schijindel. They had started moving about 1330 hours (1:30 p.m.) but were halted an hour later when Colonel Johnson learned that the corridor road had been cut. He sent his men from his two battalions on a hasty retreat to Vechel. Meanwhile two thirds of the men under a full colonel whose main mission was to hold Vechel and its bridges as well as the main highway we called the "corridor," were four miles away engaged in an attack for another road.

As I sat on the edge of my foxhole at the end of that day, I reflected on the thought that no one in charge seemed to give a damn about the main reason we were here—to keep the corridor open as a single road all the way to Arnhem. Had they forgotten about those ten thousand troopers up there?

I was so tired after what I had been through that I couldn't finish my K-ration supper and simply fell asleep. At the front, some positions are better than others. On this day the position for "C" Company was to remain in regimental reserves, rebuilding our company on this, the seventh day of the Holland invasion.

The call went out for all remaining noncommissioned officers from each platoon to stand by and meet with our new First Sergeant before noon.

Robert Grotjan had been a Staff Sergeant in the Headquarters Company, First Battalion. He became the "C" Company's fourth First Sergeant in the war. He would lead us all the way to Austria.

Sergeant Grotjan introduced us to our new Company Commander, Captain George R. Cody. He, too, was from the Headquarters Company, First Battalion. We were told that First Lieutenant William O. Dwyer, Jr. would be joining us from Special Troops in the 82nd in a few days. Our Platoon Sergeant would be Staff Sergeant Curtis DeWitt, coming from the rank of T/Sergeant from the 3rd Platoon of our own Company. We old-timers knew Sergeant DeWitt from back in the States where he had been part of our 2nd Platoon. From now on Williams T. Hollingsworth and I could sign our letters as "Sergeant." We were now squad leaders of the first and second squads. Sergeant DeWitt let "Big" Holly and I pick our own Assistant Squad Leaders. I picked Private First Class Wayne Dickerson; Holly named Private First Class Steve Gromac. They were old-timers and damned good in combat. Dickerson was hit shortly after this and left the war for the States. I then named Private First Class Marvin Milligan as my Assistant Squad Leader, and he finished out the war into Austria with me.

We spent the whole day getting our Company squared away.

For a 97-hour period starting at 1100 hours (11 a.m.) on D + 5 (the fifth day after the Holland Invasion) and running until 1200 hours on D plus 10, the corridor road was closed for all but twenty hours.

The British land forces reached Driel on the Lower Rhine River on D plus 5, about the time that the road was blocked at Vechel. The British met with the Polish Paratroopers of the Allied Airborne Army at Driel, just across the river from Arnhem. However, the British regular army units of armored tanks and infantry had not reached their own paratroopers at Arnhem. It ended up taking the British another 72 hours to reach their own troops.

With all the delays, we failed to take the bridge at Zon before it blew up. As a result, tanks from General Dempsey's Second British Army were held up twelve hours while they rebuilt the bridge. When those tanks finally reached the City of Nijmegen they had to stop and wait for the 82nd Airborne Division, which had been unable to take the river bridge over the Wide Wall.

These delays early in the Holland Invasion cost our side precious time and lives.

I put in a lot of nights in the war without a shot fired and no sight of a single Jerry. On that kind of a night a squad sergeant has to stay on his toes, keep awake at all times, see in the dark, hear a pin drop at fifty yards and smell a Jerry twice that far away.

With Holland's rain and fog, I had to use every trick I knew. I learned how to pick up the smell of Germans near by. I think it was either their tobacco or coffee that gave them a recognizable odor. It certainly wasn't that they were dirtier than we GIs were; we had them beat hands down on that score.

On this night, as on others like it, I made up my mind before dark that my men were going to do their job no matter what. I stayed awake all night, straining my eyes for ten hours until they felt like they were budding out of my head. No matter how dark it is, I learned, you can see everything that is in front of you. By working hard at it, you can see a full 180 degrees at one time. Before it got dark I memorized everything in front of me. I knew how far it was from that post to the next one, from that little tree on the left to that big one way back on the right, from the barn to the house down the lane to my foxhole. I counted the steps of my walking guards and knew how long it would take Corporal Dickerson to come from his foxhole to the clearing of the first building along the lane. After a count of 25 I knew I would see him on the skyline.

After a quiet night, I sighed in relief that I had made it through another night with all my men. All night long I had thought about eating, but I didn't dare. Now I could eat but was too tired. There was only one thing I wanted in the growing light of this day, and that was sleep. I didn't even ask the Platoon Sergeant for permission. I just went to sleep. Even if only for three hours, I knew sleep would help.

I woke up. Someone was kicking dirt down on my face. "Damn it, watch where you're going!" I said. More dirt in my face. "Who in the hell did that?" I said. "Oh. That you, Sergeant DeWitt? Sorry. I didn't see you standing there."

"No, I'm sure you didn't. You were asleep, Sergeant. But that's OK. You earned it. You did a damned good job pulling guard last night. Battalion told us this morning that Jerry was all around us but didn't come through to 'C' Company. Nice work, Black!"

By now Hollingsworth, Folley and Howard were all standing by my foxhole. "What a tough-looking bunch," I thought as I looked up at them from my position lying on my back at the bottom of my foxhole. "I'd hate to be the German waking up to see those men standing over me."

Without getting up I said, "What's up? Give me the bad news."

Sergeant DeWitt began. "We are to be in battle dress, ready to move out in one hour. 'C' Company and 'D' Company of the Second Battalion have the job today of helping to open up the corridor highway that is now cut off at Koevering. Get the hell up, Sergeant Black! Drop off your bed rolls! Re-check your ammunition! Stand by to en-truck! We in 'C' Company are going to move over and come back at them from the other side. Tell your men we will be fighting alongside the Limeys today, the bloody Queen's guards. So look alive! Ya hear!"

"Hey, now. This Captain is all right," said V. J. Folley with a big grin. "We get to ride into battle for a change."

"Beware of strangers bearing gifts," said "Big" Holly.

We were working under a new leader, Captain Cody, and many of us were new in our noncommissioned officer jobs. In addition, we would be working with the British in the road-clearing effort. I wondered whose orders we would follow. The only thing I was sure of was that I didn't know what was going on.

My squad dug in at another Dutch farm site near Koevering, a few hundred yards north of the corridor highway. We spent the night around the farm buildings, walking guard duty from one outpost to another. It was the same as the previous night except now we were guarding British tanks parked here.

Two men were killed the next day, both from the 3rd Platoon: Private First Class John Suski and Private First Class William McClimate.

It was Tuesday, September 16, 1944, our tenth day in the Battle of Holland. Jerry was still holding onto a very small section of the corridor road at Koevering.

On that day I learned two things from the British that would make living during the rest of the war a little more bearable. First, don't spend every second in an underground foxhole. Move into houses and other buildings. Put a roof over your head once in a while. Second, don't be in such a damned hurry to win the war all by yourself.

The Steel Helmet Is Part of Your Head

By noon we had pushed Jerry off the corridor highway once more, and the corridor was open all the way to Arnhem—with the exception of a three-mile stretch from Elst to Driel, Holland.

On the previous night, September 25, the British First Airborne Division had successfully carried out an after-dark withdrawal at a place near Driel. British paratroopers who survived the evacuation passed by us in one open truck after another. We learned from them that out of 10,005 paratroopers who jumped over the road, only 2,163 troopers got back across the Rhine that night. The evacuation continued into the day and even into the next night.

As they rode by us down "hell's highway," I thought they were the saddest sight I'd seen in the war. It was as if they were "passing in review" for us Yankees to get an idea what was waiting for us ahead.

We stood there, stunned. "Holly," I said. "This damned war's not over, and by the looks of those men if we keep this up, by God, we may not win!"

We couldn't stand to watch any longer and moved off the highway to dig in for the night. I knew we were in for a hell of a fight.

My 2nd Platoon dug in next to a unit of British Artillery. If there is strength in numbers, we had it. The British Second Army moved into a large house nearby and made it their headquarters. We had high-ranking British officers all over the place. Word came down from our Company's First Sergeant to shape up and stay on the ball throughout the night, not because of Jerry but because of the "English Rank" nearby.

The night was uneventful, one of my easiest nights in Holland. The high-ranking British officers turned out to be great guys. Many of them came by our foxholes to chat with us. They told us what a great job we had done holding the corridor open as long as we had.

The British officers also filled us in on what had happened to the Red Devils, our paratrooper brothers, at Arnhem. Everything went wrong for them from the start. The British troopers landed in a hornets' nest, and Jerry never let up on them. They fought against unbelievable odds, holding out for four days without any help from the ground or air. They fought off everything the Germans threw at them for four more days, the longest they could possibly last without support.

We were up bright and early the morning of Saturday, September 30, 1944, the fourteenth day of the Holland Invasion. We moved out in a column of twos on a company march straight north to Earde, onto a side road just off "hell's highway" where trucks were waiting for us.

As we climbed on board, Holly said to me, "This place looks like one I've been to before! How about you, Sergeant Black?"

We moved slowly down the side road toward the main corridor road, all of us standing up and looking for landmarks. We could see plenty of evidence that there had been a big fight here a few days back. We saw several burned-out tanks, and not all of them Jerry's. All of the Dutch buildings had been hit hard.

We came to a halt just before the last turn onto "hell's highway" while a British column of trucks passed by. "Hey, Blackie," Holly said, "Isn't that the windmill we played poker in a while back?"

"You're right," I said. "Look over there in that field. See all those foxholes. That's where we were dug in. Remember?"

Some of our Division Artillery troopers were still dug in along this side road. Sergeant Howard, who had played poker with us in the windmill, yelled down, "What the hell happened around here after we left? Who shot up the old windmill?"

An artillery sergeant from the 377th Parachute Field Artillery Battalion yelled up to us, "Jerry cut the corridor road here and put a sniper in the top of the windmill. The limeys used their tanks to get him out! The Dutchmen around here are mad as hell at the British because that windmill was the oldest one in Holland."

At last our column of trucks began to move up "hell's highway" on our way to Veghel. At the first big bridge we turned off the main road to the right just beyond the canal. The trucks of the whole First Battalion were unloading in a very large field where we bivouacked for the next three days and nights. In one corner of the field, which was three or four hundred acres in size, were the farmhouse and other buildings.

The Steel Helmet Is Part of Your Head

First Sergeant Grotjan wasted no time passing out orders. "We are here in this big field," he said, "back together with the whole First Battalion for the first time since the jump because Colonel Cassidy wants to inspect each one of us personally. Gentlemen, that means just one thing. For the next few days you will spend all your time cleaning up everything—most important, yourselves! Need I tell you, that rifle is only an extension of your arm!"

After a few words with Captain Cody, Sergeant Grotjan continued, "Some more good news, men. That steel helmet, like your rifle, is part of your head. Don't be caught with it off! Not one of you got this far without digging a foxhole. So dig another one. And, gentlemen, I really do have some good news for you. Everyone of us will get to take a hot shower within the next few days, and that's a promise!"

The troopers of the 2nd Platoon missed a chance at a Saturday night bath and did a lot of kidding about it among ourselves. It had been two weeks since the jump into Holland, and none of us had taken a bath in that time. In fact, I didn't know anyone who'd taken his clothes off. The word late Saturday night was that Holly's and my squads would be first in line Sunday morning for the showers truck. Every man was waiting in line long before the truck pulled up.

We rode into the City of Veghel to a large dairy plant where showers had been installed in one of the buildings. The dairy used a lot of hot water, and this made it easy to set up the showers. It was an unbelievable treat for Holly and me because we had come from poor backgrounds without the luxury of running water in our homes.

We were like a couple of kids. Sergeant DeWitt had to make us get out, but only after a long time. Talk about clean! We were so clean we squeaked. We used up a bar of soap between us. That shower came the closest to being a real thrill as anything else in the war. Then we were issued a clean jumpsuit to put on after our shower. As we came out of the shower an old Dutchman gave each of us a cup of whole cow's milk. After fourteen days on nothing but K-rations, that cup of milk was a luxury as fine as it ever got in combat in the ETO (European Theatre of Operations).

Back at our camp site we got word that church call was off for us Protestants in the 502nd. The message said, "Due to the 'bare' fact that Jerry has captured Chaplain Hall, there will be no church today."

We church-going paratroopers of the 502nd Parachute Regiment could not believe this and wanted to know more. The Commanding Officer for the 501st Parachute Regiment, Colonel Johnson, said that the Germans had offered to trade our captured chaplain for one of their captured Battalion Commanders and that he had turned the offer down.

That didn't set well with us 502nd "Protestant boys." We were sure that "Chappie Hall" was worth three of any German Battalion COs. He was one of the best liked of all men in the 502nd Parachute Regiment, including the Catholics. (Chaplain Hall lived out most of the war as a prisoner, although he escaped to the east near the war's end and was freed by the Russians.)

On Monday, October 2, we turned the corner into our third week. By now "Market Garden" had come to an end. We in the First Battalion were damn sure of that now as we stood by our equipment in a single row running all the way around this huge three-sided field along the Auid Williams Vaart Canal outside Veghel. Colonel Cassidy was there, checking us out, and the process took a full day.

For someone at the bottom of the command chain, a day like that seemed a waste of time. As a buck sergeant, however, I was learning that it wasn't. Colonel Cassidy asked a lot of questions as he went around on his inspection. Whenever he asked a soldier what he thought needed improving, he got a straightforward answer. "The chow!" one private said. "You know, Colonel, sir, we're getting damned tired of K-rations. How about some ten and ones? Better still, how about some hot cooked meals once in a while?"

Our fare actually improved for a while, until it got worse again.

The first order on Tuesday, October 3, was "Pack your bedrolls. We are moving out!"

"Where to, Sergeant?"

"We are moving up to Nijmegen."

In combat the words, "moving up," almost always meant bad news, but not today. For the next two days at Nijmegen the 502nd Parachute Regiment would serve as the reserve of the 82nd Airborne Division.

We made the move on Wednesday, October 4, on GI trucks going up the corridor road. Sergeant DeWitt called it our "sightseeing tour" because it was a first-hand look at what the other guys had fought for. "Enjoy it, Gentlemen," Sergeant Rennie Howard said. "It is conducted by the British and paid for by Uncle Sam!"

First on the tour was Uden, the last stronghold of the 101st in the corridor. After that we were into 82nd Airborne country.

We had nothing big to worry about in that area. We ended up going through only the outskirts of Uden and de-trucked on Groesbeck heights, an evergreen wooded area.

Wherever men have gathered, sooner or later there have been women. In the airborne it was no different. Holly set me up this time. I bought his whole story, hook, line and sinker.

We were farm boys, but we knew something about "purebred" and had read stories about the "master race." We knew those SS guys were big, tough and handsome, at least the ones we'd seen up close. I'd even read that Hitler had hand picked women to "serve" him.

"Holly," I said, "are you telling me that this camp we are in was the main base for the master race women of all Germany? Did you say you saw a baby factory with your own eyes? A baby factory? What the hell is a baby factory?"

Holly answered, nonchalantly, "A place where they make babies."

"Now, Holly," I said, "you've gone too far. But since you brought it up, where are all those women now?"

Holly played his little game all the way out. "Someone told me," he said, "but I don't remember who it was, that they were sent out to an SS camp back in Germany. You know, Sergeant Black. For a little hanky panky and for breeding purposes only!"

"But you said you've seen some of those women," I reminded him.

"I sure did," Holly said. "Black, let me be the first to tell you. Those girls are beautiful. There's no doubt about it. They're the master race all right."

"Where?"

"There are several barracks full of them down the hill at the other end of the camp."

"Beautiful, you say! How far down the hill? Damn! I sure would like to see them." I pressed him on.

"Come on. I'll show you. It's only about a mile away." Holly was already on his way down the hill. I caught up with him on the run. Since he knew he had me set up, he poured it on as we walked along. By the time we reached the area where the women were, he had me feeling like a young bull. It reminded me of the story of the young bull and the old bull looking down from a field at the next field full of cows. The young bull said, "Let's run down there, jump the fence into that field and screw one of those cows." "No," the old bull said, "Not that way. Let's walk around to the other side, go through the gate and screw all of them."

On the way to the barracks Holly said, "I heard Colonel Cassidy tell someone that he was going to turn the whole First Battalion loose inside the women's master race compound after dark tonight so we could foul up the next batch for sure!"

One point Holly had not covered was staring me in the face at that moment. A ten-foot high barbed wire fence went all the way around an area enclosing several barracks buildings. These barracks were full of women—that we could see. Standing guard around the fence was a detail of 82nd Division paratroopers. In big English letters a sign declared, "STAY OUT—THIS MEANS YOU."

Another point Holly had not bothered to tell me about. After walking half way around the barbed wire compound, in full view, appeared the biggest-bellied woman I've ever seen before or since. Every woman in sight was as pregnant as she could get.

"Big" Holly said, "That's what I call a baby factory!"

I couldn't believe it. I stood there with my mouth open, looking through the fence at all those German "brood mares" from Hitler's "master race." It must have been time for their morning walk, because all the women were outside just walking around.

I looked Holly in the eye and said, "OK, Holly. Where in hell are all the non-pregnant girls?"

"Why don't you ask that big sergeant from the 82nd Airborne standing over there by the gate?"

So I did.

The sergeant said to me, loud enough for everyone standing around to hear, "Sergeant, when are you troopers from the 101st going to get it through your heads? This is a baby factory, not a whorehouse!"

When I recovered from the sergeant's loud remark, I turned to Holly for some kind of verbal support. He was just turning the corner at the end of this fenced compound on his way back to our barracks.

Sergeant Hollingsworth had put one over on me again. This one cut deep. He hadn't broken the knife off, but neither had he pulled it out. I just left it where it was. We didn't talk about it for days, and when I mentioned it after I caught up with Holly a few weeks later, all I got was his big hillbilly smile.

Thoughts of "back to London by the weekend" to enjoy pretty English girls and all the "mild and bitters" we could drink had been building in our hearts. Those thoughts crashed down the hillside south of Nijmegen, Holland, early on Thursday, October 5, the eighteenth day after the Holland Invasion.

Sergeant Grotjan called a company formation and announced, "Men of 'C' Company, now hear this. The battle for the corridor has ended. Market Garden is over!" Smiles broke out on every face in front of him.

He went on. "But the fight for this tiny country has just begun. The good British need our help a little longer. General Taylor has 'volunteered' all of us in the 101st to help them. Since he knew none of us would mind—"

"Booooh!"

The First Sergeant dismissed all of us except the noncommissioned officers, who were to meet with Captain Cody and the other officers in one of the buildings.

Combat had not ended for "C" Company here in Holland. Not by a long ways. "Hell," I said to Holly and Folley, "by the looks of that big map of the captain's there, we are going from the frying pan into the fire!"

Captain Cody pointed out to the noncommissioned officers that we were moving into an "island-like" area that morning. We would cross over the Waal River and go north of Nijmegen to a small Dutch town called Elst on the corridor road about halfway between Nijmegan and Arnhem. From that point it was only five miles to the Lower Rhine River at Arnhem, where Jerry still held the big bridge. However, if we took the double railroad tracks, it was only four miles to the banks of the river at Oosterbeek, the west end of Arnhem.

At this briefing session we noncommissioned officers got the American view of what had happened at Arnhem to the "Red Devils," our British friends.

"They had the hell kicked right out of them," is the way Captain Cody put it. "Make no mistake about it, troopers," he said, "the British paratroopers fought brilliantly without any help for eight full days and nights. Their own ground troops let them down six full days." He paused a moment. "Not even we, the great Screaming Eagles, could have held out much longer."

On the large map in front of us Captain Cody pointed out the British front lines as of October 5, our nineteenth day in Holland. The map did not show one place where the British had crossed the Lower Rhine. They were, however, up against the south bank at the double railroad tracks near where the railroad bridge had been blown up at Oosterbeek.

The British front lines bent sharply southeast from the place where the railroad bridge had been and crossed the corridor highway about two miles north of Elst.

The lines ran due east about a mile out of Elst, then almost due south all the way to Bemmel and on to the Waal River at a point two miles upstream from Nijmegen.

Looking at the map we could see at once the island-like appearance of the area where we were to advance our lines. For that reason we of the 101st Airborne Division named the next 54 days in Holland "the fight on the island."

Captain Cody pointed out that the 101st would be under the British command in every way; in some cases such as when spelling them at their front lines we would even use their foxholes.

This new chapter of my life in the 2nd Platoon was anything but airborne. Except for my Screaming Eagle shoulder patch, there was no way to tell that I was a paratrooper. I arrived on the "island" by truck, like everyone else, and rumbled across the huge "Waal River Bridge" at Nijmegen. My ride through town was my first look at the city and the first big city I had seen up close in Europe so far, not counting the time I spent on the British Isles.

Signs of war were everywhere. In places whole buildings of brick and masonry had tumbled. Yet in this city just two miles from the front, the Dutch people were at work everywhere cleaning it up. They swept the streets clean of all debris. They pushed bricks back to the sidewalks. Wherever they could, they restored and opened at least one lane of all the main streets to our trucks.

I never crossed that bridge again because in the end Jerry bombed it.

16

Stuck in a Two-Man Foxhole

We moved onto the "island" about noon on Thursday, October 5. Jerry had this place zeroed in. The feeling I had crossing this bridge was the forerunner of the fear that would stalk me the whole time I was there.

Our trucks stopped and let us off on the Nijmegen side of Elst. "That's as far as you better go, Yanks!" the British artillery boys told our drivers. We went on foot the rest of the way—on through the town of Elst along the main highway to an area next to a man-made ditch draining the center of the "island" and running east and west between the two rivers. We dug in there for the next two days.

There was no front-line fighting for two days, just small patrols and a few incoming German shells. Off to the east and north in front of us, however, where the lines were still manned by the British, we could hear a steady roar of gunfire.

German guns were firing from the Arnhem area from the advance of higher ground across the Lower Rhine River. We soon learned that Jerry held all the high ground to the north across the Rhine, along the whole front. No matter where we might go on the front lines, Jerry would see every move we made.

"No moving around in daylight. Stay in your foxholes, and I mean *stay* in your foxholes. Don't even try to take a shit in the daytime. Those Germans can see you. You hear? They will throw everything on top of you. And I mean you! Any questions?" A British Sergeant Major is talking to my 2nd Platoon, telling them what it will be like the next morning when daylight arrives on the front lines and we of the "C" Company will be replacing the British infantry in front-line combat.

As always, there is one guy with a question. In this case the soldier isn't asking the British sergeant. He means to ask his own American paratrooper buddy standing next to him. But he speaks too loudly. "What the hell do you do if you have to 'go' in the daytime?" he says.

The British sergeant hears him, as do the rest of us. He says, "Well, Yank, you just shit in your mess kit and throw it out after dark. I said, after dark! If you throw it out in the daylight those damned Germans will shoot a hole in your mess kit. They're that mean!"

The "island" area between the two rivers was not only flat; it was also further below sea level than anywhere I had been so far. When we took over the foxholes the British used, we learned that we could not dig more than about two feet deep into the ground or water would seep in. The depth to the water level changed from time to time, depending on how much rain we were having. Sometimes I got lucky and dug my foxhole in dry ground along the sides of road dikes that rose some six or eight feet above the lay of the land.

If foxhole digging was a major problem, it was not our worst worry. The biggest fear, although it never became my personal concern, was that at any time the Germans might flood the area and drown us like rats! (They did this later in the war and caught the British after we of the 101st had gone south to France.)

Our company's preparation for replacing the British infantry soldiers began before noon on Friday, October 6. We should have been in place by midnight, but the process dragged on throughout

Stuck in a Two-Man Foxhole

the early morning hours of darkness. My squad was not in place until the first light of day, and I was the last in our company to come on line in the whole maneuver. We had spent ten hours out in the open trying to come on line. That's too damned long even if it's dark.

Although the Germans had been sending in artillery shells all night long, they had been guessing about our location. Since they had the British foxholes already zeroed in, they were just firing at the noise on the front lines. We didn't know that and spent too much time with the details of the transition from British to American troops.

By the time we were moving into the foxholes, Jerry's 88s found us. I lost one trooper before we could start, my Assistant Squad Leader, Corporal Wayne Dickerson. The war ended for him; he headed for the States. The British also lost men while we were making the change-over.

We had been informed that all the foxholes in our area would be two-man foxholes. Before we moved out, Sergeant DeWitt made a strong pitch for us squad leaders to pair our men to be as compatible as possible. "Let close friends stay together as much as you can within your squads," he said. "For the most part you will spend the next three days underground. That in itself will be bad enough even if you're friends. It will be sheer hell if you're stuck with someone you dislike!" It was damned good advice.

In the process of pairing my squad men up to take over the British foxholes in front of Arnhem, I overlooked myself.

I dropped the first two troopers on the 30-caliber machine gun, Private Domingues and Private Martin, off at the first foxhole. Two by two my men dropped off as we crawled down a small drainage ditch behind our new underground homes. The ditch was at least three feet deep and had more than a foot of water in it. We started out all wet!

The British foxholes were about fifty feet apart and ran almost straight west down the "DeLinge." When I came to a foxhole, I would drop off my men, and only then would the two English "Tommies" take their leave. They would hurry back past me down the same ditch we had taken to their foxhole, never saying a word. Now and then one of the British soldiers would pat me on my back as he went by and smile. I think that meant they were glad to be alive.

I could not recall anything about Private Irvine D. Goodwin since the jump in Normandy. He was just "there" all the time. He did his job, whatever he was told. I liked Goodwin, and when I realized that he was a true loner, I decided to ask him to join me in my foxhole for the next three days.

Before we had a chance to get to know each other, we had one thing in mind—to get the hell underground as fast as we could. The two of us entered the front door of our new home at the same moment, head first, on the double, with a belly slide that would have made Pete Rose proud.

The shells were on top of us. The earth shook, and then fine dirt sifted down our necks as we lay there without breathing. The fear was that our next breath might be our last. "How many rounds were there? Ten? Or was it twenty? Woooh! Were they ever close! God! What a way to start a day! Better wait a second longer, then check on my men." These thoughts ran through my mind.

There was a short wait with no more shells. I started to raise myself up and turn over on my back so that I could crawl out of the foxhole. "Bang!" My head inside that steel helmet rebounded back to the floor of the foxhole with such force that my nose started to bleed. I lay there stunned, seeing stars of all sizes. I tried once more to turn over on my back and found there wasn't that much room between the floor and the ceiling. So I slid back out the same way I went in, on my belly.

I sat up, leaning on my knees and called to my men down the line. All answered, "OK!" I could barely hear them for all the ringing in my ears.

Jerry must have seen the top of my helmet because more than incoming mail was headed my way. With that unmistakable sound and the onrush of air, you know it's on top of you.

"Wahooooooo-Baaaaaaam!" Once more, on my belly, head first, back into my new home. That was enough proof for me that the British Sergeant knew what he was talking about. Private Goodwin and I spent the rest of that Saturday's daylight hours out of sight.

This foxhole was like none other I saw in the war. I never did figure out how the British soldiers dug it. Once inside, you spent all of your time either on your back or on your belly, and, you

Stuck in a Two-Man Foxhole 169

made that decision before you went underground! I doubt if it was more than twelve inches from the floor to the ceiling and no more than forty inches wide. It was just five feet long; our feet stuck outside into the open ditch area.

All the foxholes in this open-ditch area went straight back into the ditch bank parallel to the ground and had at least twenty-four inches of dirt on top of them. The dirt dug out of the foxhole was piled in a semi-circle around the open end closest to the ditch to divert water coming that way from the ditch.

The two of us started out the night trying to pull guard duty. I used two hours on and two off, with the man on duty stint outside our foxhole at the other man's feet. Jerry didn't like that idea; they kept their guns busy even after dark. The soldier on guard spent most of his time diving back into his foxhole. In turn, the "protected" man got very little sleep. It was one helluva day!

Sometime near daylight on Sunday, October 8, as I was pulling my hitch at the foot of our foxhole, the "urge" hit me. When nature calls on a poor soldier on the front lines there can be some trying moments. Some are painful; others are downright embarrassing. You always take an awful chance of getting caught with your pants down. I thought at the time that I had a break since it was still dark. The British Sergeant had made a strong point about the hazards of the daylight hours, and all day long Jerry seemed to prove the sergeant right.

Since Private Goodwin was asleep, I decided not to bother him. I just stepped across the water in the ditch, up on the far bank, and proceeded to relieve myself. As I squatted there, maybe twenty feet from the lip of my foxhole, I became aware of the beautiful bright, moonlight in the early morning. What a silhouette I must be making, facing straight toward Arnhem!

At that moment of thought I saw them—flashing lights—straight ahead, from Arnhem! It can't be lightning! Not in all this moonlight without a cloud in the sky! I realized I had been caught up in hell, yes! hell! just as I was starting to enjoy one of nature's few pleasures still left for man to enjoy alone! In the place of that fleeting thought, instinct and training took over. The words of the British Sergeant rushed forward into my brain. "Those are flashes of the German guns! They've seen me—my bare ass shining in the moonlight. They're damned near—here!"

Somewhere between "bare ass" and "in the moonlight," I started to uncoil my great spring back to the inside of my foxhole in one leap. Keep in mind, it was from the squatting position at least twenty-six feet to full safety. An "Olympic" try.

I struck the ground to the entrance of my foxhole at the very same moment that incoming German shells exploded around me. They landed on the bank, in front of me, in back of me, up and down that ditch. It was the closest yet, but they didn't get me! I cleared the ditch like a champion swimmer reaching out as far as he can in his dive off the edge of the pool to start the hundred-yard free-style race, and I landed on my belly with my head and shoulders inside my foxhole. But I was two feet short, and the rest of me was still sticking outside in the bright moonlight.

I lay there without moving, waiting for more shells, I guess, when I heard a voice say, "What happened?" There was a long pause, and then laughter. Right next to me. Of course, it was Private Goodwin, who else? He had slept through the first part of the show, but now he was wide awake for the tail end of it.

What Private Goodwin had been looking at since he woke up was my bare ass shining in the moonlight. There hadn't been time for me to pull my pants up yet, nor time for me to think about not pulling them up. Once again I wanted to know what was so damned funny.

By now I was getting as mad at him as I was at the Germans. Private Goodwin tried hard to be polite. He said, "Well, Sergeant, if you were me lying where I am, looking out of this foxhole and seeing what I see, you would laugh, too!" Then he asked, "What happened to your pants?"

For the first time I became aware of the fact that my pants were at my ankles. I jerked back out of the foxhole and found that I had jumped straight through my pant legs, turning them inside out. I had a bit of good luck. We paratroopers in the airborne blouse our pants by putting the bottoms into the tops of our boots. Because of this my pants followed me across the ditch all the way to my foxhole. I didn't have to go back to that far bank across the ditch and look for them. Jerry would surely have seen me and sent

Stuck in a Two-Man Foxhole

another round of shells my way. I admit, it wasn't easy pulling my pants back over my big jump boots, right side out, but I did it.

Jerry kept laying up big stuff on us. There was no way you could stick your head out, let alone get out of your foxhole and stretch. They kept it up all day and into the night. Whether 88s or mortars, they kept something coming at us. They were now using a new gun we called the "Screaming Meemie." There was no use trying to stand guard even at night. When darkness came Sunday night we both stayed underground. Although we did not pull any guard duty, per se, we did not sleep, either.

As the third day's sun came up on Monday, October 9, at this "hell hole," two things were starting to get to Private Goodwin and me: the terrible noise and the closed-in feeling of our living quarters. In addition, the constant exposure to gun powder was making us sick.

Our food was the worst of the war. Since the jump, twenty-three days earlier, we had eaten bully-beef, English stew and K-rations. Along with a shortage of water and no exercise at all for three days, we were in bad shape.

As hard as it is for me to believe now, in my foxhole we were living mostly on cigarettes. A few short months back on June 5, when I made the Normandy jump, the only cigarettes I had were the ones that came with my K-rations. In a day or two I'd smoked all of them, and a few days later I was begging for more. After the big battle of Carentan I started to inhale the cigarette smoke.

By noon on the third day here at the front on this island, Private Goodwin and Sergeant Black were about to run out of smokes.

Our British chow was terrible. Rations were just as bad. Rations were the "PX" type of items we were used to in combat: American cigarettes, candy, soap, toothpaste and so on. Now we were getting British-issue rations. As a GI, I wouldn't have named anything British as the best. As the day wore on my feelings for the British grew worse, and worst of all was their damned cigarettes.

I did everything I could to conserve my American cigarettes. I smoked three English to one of our American cigarettes. With every K-ration meal we got four cigarettes, a total of twelve a day. In addition, I got thirty-six English cigarettes a day. That was more than two packs, and I thought that would carry me through those three days. I hadn't been smoking even a pack a day before that.

Every once in a while the British rations would have a tin of sweets in them. That tin box was just the right size to hold two packs of cigarettes, and some of the boxes had a hinged lid. This was the perfect place to carry cigarettes on the front lines because they would stay dry, and the tin box would keep them from crushing. That little tin box fit perfectly in the breast pocket of my jumpsuit. It was also a great place to carry a snapshot of my "best" girl. That way, every time I took out a smoke I saw my girl's picture.

So far Private Goodwin had not caught on to my cigarette case habit. But every time I opened mine and took out a cigarette he would say, "Sarge, that's a good idea. I'll have to get one of those for myself." I was getting tired of hearing that same thing over and over. In fact, I was tired of a lot of things about Private Goodwin by now, and he was just as tired of me!

For one thing, Goodwin didn't like the way I inhaled my cigarettes. Every now and then I would take a deep breath and suck in a big puff of smoke that I could feel clear down to my toes. I would hold it there a while and then rapidly force smoke out of my mouth. What Goodwin objected to was all the noise I made, the "huffing and puffing" that went along with the inhaling.

"Damn it, Sarge," he would say, "you don't need to make that awful sucking noise when you inhale. And when you exhale, just breathe normally. There's no need for you to whistle every time!"

Even though it made me mad when he said that, I'd been able to keep still. But now I'd had enough. I let him have it. "Goddamn it, Goodwin!" I said. "If you don't like the way I smoke you can get the hell out of this foxhole and go dig one of your own—or shut up!"

For the first time I had pulled rank on him, evidence that the situation was getting to me. After that outburst we stopped talking to each other altogether. It was 1400 hours (2 p.m.), and German shells were still coming in.

Stuck in a Two-Man Foxhole

After a while I was down to my last Chesterfield. I had four English cigarettes and one American cigarette. I smoked that last Chesterfield in style—no noise! My roommate did not say a word. I'd tried to talk Private Goodwin into rationing his supply of cigarettes the night before, since by then he had fewer than I did. I figured he was out of cigarettes by now, and I hadn't offered him any of mine.

At 1500 hours (3 p.m.), I lit up my hourly cigarette. This time I took out an English cigarette. It was awful! Now I had only four left. Once more, there was no comment from the soldier next to me.

About an hour later Jerry decided to give us hell again. This time they shelled us for twenty minutes straight, hitting us with everything they had. Three mortar shells landed almost on top of us. Shells landed on top of the bank within ten feet of our hole. Those Screaming Meemies were terrible!

We were both lying on our backs head first into the foxhole. Dirt fell in our faces and all over us each time those shells hit close by. I was sure the dirt above our heads would fall on top of us and bury us alive. In my mind I could see one of those shells hitting dead center on top of us and driving Goodwin and me to kingdom come.

Then it stopped! Five minutes passed. No shelling. Ten full minutes passed. You could hear a pin drop. For the first time since the heavy shelling began Private Goodwin spoke. "Sergeant Black," he said, "could I have one of your cigarettes, please? I'll pay you back if I ever get out of here alive."

I reached for my tin cigarette case, took it slowly out of my breast pocket, set it on my chest in front of my nose so I could see into it. I brushed loose dirt off my chest so the little tin box would sit level. Very slowly I opened the lid. Private Goodwin watched me as if caught in a trance. It was the single most deliberate act I carried out in the entire war. I opened the lid as if it contained jewels. Stuck to the lid was the picture of my "best" girl friend. For a while we both just lay there looking at her picture.

Then the Private spoke. "Boy, Sarge. She sure is good looking."

"Damned if she isn't!" I replied. Slowly I took my big finger and rolled each cigarette so I could read its name: "Player, Player, Chelsea, Player." (Only the Chelsea was an American brand.) I rolled each cigarette so that the Private could not read the brand name. I then set the tin case on his chest and said, "Help yourself to one of my cigarettes, if you please."

Goodwin took his finger and slowly rolled each of those four cigarettes so their names were visible. Then he read aloud, "Player, Player, Chelsea, Player." He picked up the Chelsea, put it in his mouth, struck a match to it, took a deep puff and then two more puffs.

The tin case with the lid still open sat boldly before my eyes on the Private's chest. I grabbed my case, shut the lid, jammed it into my breast pocket and began to speak, slowly at first but increasing the tempo as I went along.

"You godamned ungrateful New England, Rhode Island, United States of American, Yankee-Doodle Sapsucker," I began. I continued for five minutes without using the same word twice. I had never been that mad at anyone in the Army before.

If Jerry hadn't resumed shelling about then I believe I would have ordered Private Goodwin out of that foxhole, and we would have fought some sort of a duel until one of us had died. I was absolutely certain that Private Goodwin had taken my very best cigarette with utter disregard for the kindness of my heart, the very one I was saving for my last smoke! I was furious.

When I finally stopped speaking, Private Goodwin said, "What did I do that was so wrong, Sergeant Black?"

I was dumbfounded. "Well, goddamn it! You cheated! You deliberately took my last American cigarette," I said.

"I did? What one was that?" The private seemed puzzled.

"That Chelsea you've half smoked up by now, damn it!"

Goodwin held the cigarette in his hand, looked at it and said, "Well, I'll be damned if I didn't." He paused for a long time between puffs and said, "Sergeant Black, if you wanted that last Chelsea for yourself, why didn't you just take it out of the case?"

"Because I wanted to give you a sporting chance! You saw me roll all the names down!"

Stuck in a Two-Man Foxhole

Another long pause between puffs while the private figured it out. "You know, I wondered why you did that at the time. That sure was clever, Sarge! I'm sorry."

"Oh, shut up! It's over and done with," I said. After sulking for a while I took out an English Player and started to smoke it in dead silence. Halfway through the cigarette a sharp belly cramp hit me. It was the "GI shits" that anyone in the service of his or her country in that war knew well.

You have to act fast when this happens, or you can have real trouble on your hands—and everywhere else. I needed a bedpan! The British sergeant had said, "Use your mess kit." But I hadn't listened. I didn't have my mess kit with me. "Hey, Goodwin," I said. "Let me try that K-ration box next to you. Hand it here. Hurry it up—before I—"

On Tuesday morning, October 10, Sergeant DeWitt asked me to name a replacement for my assistant squad leader I'd lost near Elst. The man I chose was Private First Class Marvin Milligan in Sergeant Folley's Third Squad. Milligan was from Tennessee and was an old-timer in our 2nd Platoon, all the way back to Alabama days. He knew the 30-caliber machine gun and its job in a paratrooper squad for the well-being of the whole platoon.

I told Sergeant DeWitt that I wanted an old-timer because my squad was short on them. He pointed out that the whole platoon was short on old-timers. I asked Milligan to help me run the Second Squad, and he agreed. Sergeant DeWitt approved of my selection, as did First Sergeant Grotjan and, in the end, the captain. It was the beginning of a partnership that would last out the war.

Sometime around noon that day, three squads—Holly's, Folley's and mine—moved off the Andelst road into the open fields west of the town. About three hundred yards into the fields we dug down "slit trenches" for our foxholes and faced them toward the west. From these trenches we were prepared to fight in a kneeling fashion with only our head and shoulders sticking out, and loose dirt piled on three sides. We squad leaders felt that if we had to fight back here it would be tonight. So we dug each squad's foxholes in two clusters of four holes each and spread out the clusters about fifty yards apart.

The 2nd Platoon's command post was in an apple orchard several hundred yards behind us. The Company's command post was back in the town of Andelst. We took turns going all the way back to Company in Andelst for a hot meal in the evening. Chow took place early so that all of the company's front-line squads would be settled in before dark.

"We expect trouble tonight," was the word from the "big boys." Our squad's section was on the railroad's side of Andelst out in the open. I knew we would have to pull an all-night watch. I talked it over with all the other noncommissioned officers: Hollingsworth, Folley, Milligan, O'Neil and Gromac after we were back from chow.

I was most concerned about the point where the 327th Regiment was positioned along the railroad tracks a mile west of Hemmen-Dodewaard Station. If the Germans broke through the 327th at the railroad tracks, it would be clear sailing for them all the way to us! Jerry had been pounding at the 327th for days now with infantry, armored and artillery attacks. They had hammered away all night and were at it again today.

Short of a breakthrough by the Germans, I was concerned about infiltrating patrols threatening our position. We agreed to keep two men awake at all times in each of the four clustered positions. A noncommissioned officer would be at each cluster, and every other cluster would have a noncommissioned officer on duty at all times.

We expected to see Jerry before daylight came again. At about 2200 hours (10 p.m.) our platoon runner arrived with news that Jerry had been seen at Hemmen-Dodewaard Station along the tracks and were heading our way.

I asked the runner, "Has there been a breakthrough? When were the troops seen? How many Germans were there? Where did the word come from?"

He knew the answer to only one of my questions. "The word came from the Platoon Sergeant."

He must have felt really bad not having more information, so he tried to fill us in. "I think there's been a breakthrough," he said. "It must have been around 2100 or 2130 hours (9 or 9:30 p.m.), and there were several Germans!"

"Was it a squad?"

"Well, uh, there were many Germans."

"Did they say it was platoon size? Or was it the size of a Company breakthrough?"

Our runner was sure now. "There were lots of them, Sergeant," said the runner as he left for the rear.

The word was passed on down the line to all the 2nd Platoon troopers, who were already on edge. "It's just a matter of time until someone pulls the trigger," I said. "I hope it's not one of our machine gunners."

Maybe a half hour later we heard the "Rat-a-tat-tat, Rat-a-tat-tat" of a machine gun.

On my right, somewhere in the 1st Platoon area by the railroad tracks, a machine gun opened up. Then one in my platoon cut loose on my left. Maybe it was Sergeant Folley's gun. Then a few riflemen fired away. It was my squad's turn, and my machine gun crew under Sergeant Milligan opened up. The whole line around me in "C" Company came alive and kept firing for about five minutes, but I could not see anything moving in front of me.

Maybe forty yards in front of my foxhole a wire farm fence ran in a straight line. Round wood posts stuck up about five feet out of the ground every twenty yards. The fence was the only thing that showed in front of me on the skyline. I noticed that not all of those wood posts was standing straight. Some leaned to the right, others to the left. Still others had a bend in them.

They made a weird silhouette in the moonlight. As the night dragged on and patches of fog drifted in front of me, I finally began to see things moving in front of me. I fired a few rounds. The longer I looked at those fence posts and the harder I tried to make out everything in between, the more certain I was that they were not all fence posts.

They changed shapes on me. I saw two or three posts where I thought there had been only one. Then the ones on the right seemed much closer now than they were at my last look. Wait a minute. Over there on the left. That "post" wasn't standing there!

You son-of-a-bitch. Take that! "Bang! Bang! Bang!" All hell broke loose. Machine guns, rifles and even a few hand grenades. After firing traveled up and down our lines, dead silence set in.

"What were you firing at, Sergeant?" one of my men asked.

"The same damn thing you were," I said. "Nothing!"

This happened three times before daybreak. As daylight increased to the full dawn of a new day, nothing moved in front of us anywhere. We slowly became aware of the fact that the magnification of our imagination had played tricks on us through the night, although we would search all day for evidence to prove to ourselves it wasn't so!

After a fine breakfast of "10-in-1" American rations, we set out in search-patrol teams. We walked back and forth, covering every inch of ground between Zetten-Andelst Station and Hemmen-Dodewaard Station. We started along the railroad tracks on the north and worked our way south toward the main highway along the Waal River running from Andelst to Hien.

We were hunting for those Germans someone had reported seeing last night at Hemmen-Dodewaard Station. With our display of fireworks, the "C" Company had acted as if we had seen them, too. Colonel Cassidy decided we should go and help find them. I had a feeling that old "Hopalong" Cassidy was teaching my "C" Company a lesson.

We didn't find any Germans. There hadn't been a breakthrough, not even a German patrol. Someone had seen a few German soldiers who had been hiding out since the early day of the Opheusden Fight when they were cut off from their own outfits.

We made two full trips up and back on each of the two days, a round trip of about eight miles. After being cramped in those two-man foxholes, daily marches were a welcome task.

Besides the exercise, we were able to supplement our hot chow that day. We came across a wounded cow or two. When we found one alive and in good shape, we marked the spot, finished the kill and set about "field butchering." A runner was sent back to our mess sergeant and soon the company supply jeep was on the way.

Supply Sergeant Anderson was always the driver. He wouldn't trust anybody else to an important task like this. Word about our feast passed along through the First Battalion. For the next several days we all ate well!

17

A Box From Home

The next day (Thursday, October 12) "Big" Holly, V. J. Folley and I took off with our squads on an all-day walking tour of this "island." Captain Cody called it "search-out" patrol duty.

As we walked around on our sight-seeing tour, I realized what a great farm area this "island" was. This island area created by the Waal and Rhine Rivers was the fruit-growing area of Holland. There were fruit orchards everywhere, and apples in abundance. We had been in Holland nearly a month, and the apple crop had ripened. Apples hung on trees ready to eat, ours for the taking.

In the afternoon we came upon a modern Dutch farm, as nice as any I had seen in the U.S. Several old Dutchmen and their women were plowing out sugarbeets just like we harvested potatoes. Then they de-topped them, gave the tops to their livestock to eat, cleaned the dirt off the sugar beets and left them to dry in the sun. After they were dry they were loaded on single horse-drawn carts.

This farmer had somehow been able to save his livestock from the ravages of war. Each two-wheeled cart, or wagon, was pulled by a beautiful big horse. How they kept those wagons in perfect balance when loaded down with heavy sugar beets was a mystery to us. We three sergeants stood around watching for some time.

Since we hadn't found any Jerrys and knew by now that we wouldn't, we were more or less killing time with our squads until time to return to our outposts. Not one of us Yanks could speak a word of the Dutch language. By sign language Holly and I were able to get a point across to an old farmer that we wanted to look in all the buildings. He was absolutely delighted to show us around. He took us to every building and showed us every crack in them.

The main barn was long and wide. It was made of brick and designed for milk cows and draft horses. Running water was piped into each stall. The barn and all the stalls were clean to a point of disbelief.

The Belgian and Clydesdale horses in the barn looked like our show horses in the U.S. They were beauties.

In a smaller brick building they were feeding pigs in total confinement until they were fat and ready to butcher. The hog barn was also equipped with underground pipes supplying running water. "These pigs have it better than I did back on the farm in Ohio," I commented. "Hell, we didn't even have running water in our house!"

When we returned to our outpost late that afternoon, we were treated to another outstanding meal. For the past several days our company cooks had been outdoing themselves with one meal after another.

Friday morning Sergeant DeWitt sent word that we were to prepare to move up. All squad leaders were to report back to the platoon command post as soon as we were packed and ready to move. At that time, the message said, he would explain a new regimental policy to us.

Sergeant DeWitt sent a runner twice to our outposts, trying to hurry us around. Finally Folley, Hollingsworth and I headed back to the apple orchard to hear the latest from the regiment.

"I'll bet you my next turn on guard duty it has something to do with the chow!" Corporal Milligan said to me as we started

A Box from Home

back. "We've been eating too good to please our Colonel." He thought about that a while and then said, "Hell, Sergeant Black, the colonel is so skinny he can't stand to see anyone get fat. I'll bet he doesn't eat as much as a killdeer does!"

"Let's don't cry before we get hurt," I said.

When we reached the meeting site in the orchard, Sergeant DeWitt let us know he didn't appreciate the amount of time we'd taken to get there. Sergeant Hollingsworth cooled him off a bit by pointing out that we squad leaders were never in a hurry to pass on bad news to our men.

Sergeant DeWitt began his little talk. "As of now this will be the new regimental policy," he said. "Our regiment is taking over a section of the front-line defense tonight. It will be a battalion-sized front with three companies on line at once and reinforced strong points of heavy weapons from our Headquarters Company. All three battalions will rotate every four days.

"The regiment is setting up three phase lines in the sector. That is to say, we will have three main lines of resistance. Since we are all on the defensive, all of us on this island, everything will lend itself to that end. That will be the case until the 101st is relieved."

He paused to catch his breath and then began again. "Phase I, of course, will be the very front lines. Phase II will be about one mile back, and Phase III will be four miles back. That means that Phase III will be just about where we are now, here, at this north-south Andelst road line.

"Now look at your maps, and I'll point out 502nd's sector," DeWitt said. "It covers the sector we are already in, here on the extreme southwest corner of the island, starting at the Waal River just west of Dodewaard..." and he continued showing us on the map exactly where we would be positioned.

"See that on the map there, Holly?" Sergeant DeWitt asked.

"Hell, yes!" Holly said. The big hillbilly was never caught off guard. "I studied Dutch map reading just before I quit school in the sixth grade. I'm following you."

Sergeant DeWitt concluded his talk by saying, "Our Second Battalion moves up to Phase I tonight. We move up to Phase II this morning and will spend the next four days there and then move to

Phase I to replace the Second Battalion for four days. Thus, eight days from now we will be back here around Andelst for four days of rest. Any questions?"

"Yes! What about cigarette rations? American, that is," said "Big" Holly.

Sergeant DeWitt stormed back. "Just keep your GI shirt on, Sergeant! I'll get to that." He paused to puff on his Lucky Strike as did everybody else seated around that command post. Then Corporal Hartman stood up and passed his pack of Lucky Strike cigarettes around to each of us noncommissioned officers as Sergeant DeWitt resumed his talk.

"Now, men," he said, "we are going to have to start thinking in terms of bad weather before long. So, from now on we have the OK from Division Headquarters to use any buildings that are in the immediate battle zone area. That will include houses. But! And let me say it again—But! Clear it with me first!"

DeWitt explained that one house would be set up as the platoon command post where the men could come in to clean up, cook hot chow and just get warm.

He reminded us to keep dry, and to have our men pitch their pup tents over the foxholes and make sure they were camouflaged from the air. "Every squad shall keep one trooper on duty, fully on the alert, with live ammunition in the chamber! We expect to see German patrols. So stay on the ball! Oh, yes. When it is raining, make sure your guards wear raincoats. We are too damned short of men for any sickness."

This time there were no questions, so Sergeant went on. "OK," he said. "Let me see. What else? All right. As to our rations and chow!" He gained a smile for just a moment. Speaking more rapidly he told us that our rations would be flown in from England along with our mail and that our Christmas packages would be in Holland in a day or two. "As to chow," he said, "well, that is going to be another story, I'm afraid."

Gaining speed as he went along, he said, "Now hear this, you squad sergeants! Pass it along to your men so they understand it properly. Up until now no one is going to blame anybody for the non-regulation chow we have been eating the past few days. From now on we will be eating K, 10 in 1, 14 in 1, or some other Gov-

A Box from Home

ernment Issue. More than likely it will be British issue as long as we stay under them here in Holland. In other words, sergeants, no more of this living off the fat of the land! Ya hear? Hell, men! If we ever win this country back for the Dutch people, they would like to have something left to eat for themselves, don't you think?" He looked each one of us in the eye.

Almost under his breath Sergeant Howard said, "By God, I'm not going to go hungry with apples falling down and hitting me on top of my head!"

"That's fine!" DeWitt said. "Eat any apple that hits you on the head—in fact, any apple lying on the ground. But I don't want to catch anybody climbing a tree! The point is this: The Dutch people are our friends, not our enemies. We do not loot our friends!"

Then he said, "I have just one other point to make. Everybody will be clean shaven, in clean clothes, with clean equipment, and will keep his individual foxhole area policed up at all times that he is at Phases II and III. The Colonel himself will inspect from time to time.

"That, troopers, is the new Regimental Policy. Any questions? None! Be ready to move out, on foot, at 1200 hours (noon). Sergeants, dismissed!"

All things considered, this was the way it should be. But for the time being there were four stunned squad leaders walking back to their squads in the 2nd Platoon. We knew that all buck passing stopped with us. Whatever we asked our men to do, we would do likewise. We were the backbone of this army, no question about it. All the way back we walked in silence, taking the time we needed to put aside our own disappointments.

Finally I spoke up. "You all know as well as I what we have to do. It is not for us to question why, but to do or die!"

I was trying to be funny, but Rennie Howard didn't care much for poetry. He said, "Who in hell was the guy that ever said that dumb thing?"

Then I became more serious. "You know," I said, "I think it would be better to wait and tell our men the whole story until we have moved up and are all dug in this afternoon. What do you men think?"

On Saturday, October 14, we spread the word around to our men. They seemed to take it a lot better than we sergeants had.

Corporal Milligan had to say, "Didn't I tell you, Sergeant?" since he had predicted that the policy on chow would change. "Colonel Chappuis hasn't changed a bit."

He was referring back to the previous April while we were in Denford, England, when Colonel Chappuis had cut our rations because he believed we were wasting too much food.

At Phase II, our secondary line of defense, my squad dug in just off the north-south road to Hemmen-Dodewaard Station in an apple orchard. We dug two-man, lay-down foxholes (slit trenches) and then pitched our pup tents over them. We were glad to have the pup tents when it started to rain Saturday afternoon.

We dug our foxholes under apple trees, as ordered by Sergeant DeWitt, so that the trees would conceal our tents from Jerry's aircraft. Every tree was loaded with big ripe apples. My tree was so full of apples that some of the branches touched the ground. I had to fit my tent among the apples. At one point I could reach up and pick an apple from the bottom of my foxhole. It was wonderful at first, but there are just so many apples a soldier can eat before he gets sick of them.

I spent all afternoon digging and weather-proofing my living quarters for our four-day stay here in the orchard. The next morning I found I had not wasted my time. My new home was warm and dry. However, I did get wet during my turn at guard duty. It rained all night. Because of that and all the mud from the freshly dug dirt around my tent area, I spent Sunday drying out my clothes and cleaning up.

Some men used the 2nd Platoon's command post house in Hien, but I felt no need to leave the orchard since headquarters sent everything we needed out to us.

Tragic news from our 3rd Platoon reached us that morning. In this same orchard Private James "Dutch" Slaysman left his foxhole and went back into the orchard. He must have gotten turned around and confused. When he came back he did not answer the password challenge of his close friend, T-F Clarence "Red" Kell (Headquarters Platoon). Slaysman just kept walking toward Kell, ignoring his call to halt. He didn't even speak. Kell fired his rifle,

A Box from Home

and his friend died. It was the second time in the war that a "C" Company man had shot and killed one of his own buddies. Both happened after the trooper who died did not give the password when challenged.

It was a sad reminder for me to constantly harp on the need for safety day and night. More than once I had said, "Hell, men, be sure! Use the butt of your rifle! What's wrong with your trench knife? Don't give your position away! Only fire at night when you have to!"

Word got out that some of the Christmas packages from our base camp in England were on their way to us. Some of us guys had mothers who loved to send us "Christmas packs." My mother was one. She sent me a package every two weeks throughout September and October. Besides that, I had a few girlfriends back in the States and a lot of relatives. All of them kept me well remembered.

When "mail call" rolled around, Sergeant Black's name was almost always called out. Today was no exception. The mail clerk passed the word that Sergeant Black had hit the jackpot. I had eight letters, four of them perfumed and one of those with a lipstick kiss imprinted on it, and a big, heavy, Christmas box!

The mail clerk drove up in the company jeep along the road in front of our orchard. He stopped in front of my foxhole and called out a few names of soldiers that had letters. Then in a very loud voice he yelled, "Package for Sergeant Black! A Christmas package for Black!"

I was thrilled. A package delivered to me in combat! That hadn't happened before.

Men gathered around my foxhole. I said, "It has to be something to eat. Cake or cookies? Maybe candy?"

I was drawing a crowd, so I poured it on. "I know exactly what is in this Christmas box that has come all the way from Ohio to brighten my day," I said. "Cake and a bunch of overnight sugar cookies, and plenty of candy. I mean candy from a store like Clark Bars, Milky Ways, Mounds Bars, and there has to be Tootsie Rolls!"

The men were all talking at once. Martin liked Clark Bars the best; Jerry Dominguee wanted a Mound Bar. Sergeants Howard and Folley wanted some homemade cake and cookies. Holly hadn't made up his mind yet. He just wanted me to open the box. "Hell, Black," he said. "What are you waiting for—Christmas?"

"That's right, Holly," I said. "It says right here on the box, Christmas. Maybe I'm not supposed to open until then."

That brought on, "Oh, come on, Sergeant, that's not fair!"

Just then Sergeant DeWitt walked up. "I came all the way out here to see something from the States," he said. "Open up, or, by God, I'll put you on patrol!"

"OK," I said. "Gather around. Here goes." I cut the heavy twine and tore open the box. Everybody jammed in close looking down into the open box.

For at least a minute you could hear a pin drop. Then one guy said, "What the hell is it?"

I sat stunned at the sight before me in that box. Then I said, "Damn it! Can't you see? It's apples!"

The wind went out of everyone at the same time. I dumped the whole box on the ground. There must have been two dozen apples, and every one of them was rotten.

As the soldiers walked away, including those from my own squad, I heard Holly say to Sergeant DeWitt, "The kind of punishment you should give Sergeant Black is to send him on patrol to deliver that box of rotten apples to Jerry."

The letters I received occupied my afternoon. For some of the guys from the platoon who hadn't received any mail and were disappointed by my box of rotten apples, adventure was the name of their game. Private Martin from my squad along with soldiers from other squads decided to go on a "scouting patrol" under Corporal O'Neill's leadership to check out a report of an abandoned factory.

That might sound like a lot of fun, but when you have to go into no-man's land to a place called Dodewaard to reach the factory, it also sounds like anyone who goes isn't too smart. I changed my mind later that afternoon when Private Martin brought back samples of the factory's wares for our squad to enjoy.

It turned out that it was a Dutch jam factory packed full of that summer's stock. The jam was packed in small, wooden boxes lined with paper. Each box held a gallon or so of the sweet stuff. That jam gave the crackers the British gave us the taste of a jelly-roll cake. We had more jam than we could eat.

18

"Get in and Shut Up!"

We were facing west for the first time. That meant we looked into the sun in the afternoon when it was clear. Another advantage going to Jerry.

For now my main problem was making the change-over as smooth as possible. I had some questions to ask the outgoing Sergeant for the Second Battalion. He seemed in a hurry to get the hell out of there.

I asked him, "How far are the Germans over there?"
He replied, "Not very far."
"Can they see us?"
"Yes!"
"How about night-time movement?"
"Don't!"
"How bad is the enemy artillery?"
"Bad!"
"How far apart are my foxholes?"
"Too far!"
"Would you answer just one more question for me?"
"Make it short!"

"Could you tell me how I can get in the Air Force?"

"Yes. Follow me!"

We all took off marching along the back side of the road dike. The plan was to drop off one of my men at each hole as we went along, while the Second Battalion Sergeant picked up each of his men.

He told me there was a trick to it, and there was. "Don't make any noise or be seen while doing it. The only cover along this road is darkness. If caught out of a foxhole when a shell lands, as the British would say, 'You've had it, Yank!' Those coming in, get in and shut up! Those leaving, do so on the double without comment."

By doing just that we made it in, every man safe and sound in spite of Jerry's Screaming Meemies.

The Germans pounded away at us for the next two hours, and then all was quiet until daylight. Once Jerry had planted the seed of fear we had to sweat out the whole night under the threat of attack.

War was hard work. I slept sitting up. That is, almost sitting up. When not on guard I would take off the outer steel part of my helmet and put it under me for a seat at the bottom of my foxhole. Then I would slouch down until I was seated on it. My back and knees were pressed hard against the sides of my foxhole. At first the only thing that went to sleep was my rear end and my feet. By the third night all of me was able to sleep.

Sleep was never an unbroken thing of six hours or so, or even the two hours we were off guard. It was always a cat-nap type of thing. During the daytime shelling from both sides kept me awake; at night it was the fear of German attacks plus the coming and going of our patrols.

Jerry made a big withdrawal, pulling back some two thousand yards in front of our two regiments (502nd and 327th) to a point just east of the town of Kesteren. The main German strong point there was their defense at the railroad bridge over the Lower Rhine at Rehenen and the high ground surrounding it. All they gave up in their withdrawal was an impossible stretch of marshland that neither side could expect to hold.

"Get in and Shut Up!" 189

By this time I'd learned several things about artillery attacks. One was the art of listening for "incoming mail" (shells). Another was the ability to pass time in a useful manner.

Starting my second day here, October 18, I made up my mind that it was going to take a direct hit to get me out of my foxhole and that I was going to enjoy myself on this beautiful day watching the clouds go by from the bottom of my foxhole.

That's how I happened to see one of our airplanes, a B-17, high in the sky. It was on its way towards Germany. Then I saw three more—and three more—with a loud, steady roar. Hell, the sky was full of our bombers, all headed east!

As if by prearranged signal I let out a loud cheer, "Go get 'em! Give 'em hell! Get that bastard Hitler for me!" By now I was standing straight up, out of my foxhole, waving my arms and yelling at the top of my lungs, and so was everyone else up and down the line.

For several minutes we stood there yelling and waving back and forth to each other in total disregard for our safety. The only reason I can think of why Jerry didn't shell us while we were standing there was that they were standing up looking at the air show, too.

Finally I settled back into my foxhole and started to count the planes passing over in my view. Every time I reached a hundred I made a mark on the wall of my foxhole. There would be nine marks on the wall that day.

A sight like that, and we foxhole soldiers felt great. After having the hell kicked out of us and putting up with bad weather, now we had beautiful weather and a new team taking over. Someone else would catch hell for a change, and we would get to sit back and watch.

To tell the truth, those of us on the ground were jealous of the "glamour boys" in the Air Force with their high IQs, white shirts, and meals served on cloth-covered tables. They were driven to their planes and fought the war sitting down.

But on that day, looking up from my foxhole, the Air Force was the greatest bunch of guys since they dropped us off here in Holland back on September 17.

Another feeling crowded my heart that day—pure hate for the German people who had made this war possible. On the front we had to kill the enemy, usually at close range. Those Germans were human beings, the same size and color as we were. In order to hate them enough to kill them, we had to believe that we were right and they were wrong and that it was our duty to wipe them out. More than that, we had to have a sense of revenge.

So I sat in my foxhole and watched our planes above, hoping that the people of Germany would have to spend the night sleeping on the ground like me. No, worse than that. I hoped their homes and their factories would be blown to bits. I wanted our big planes to destroy whole towns. Somewhere in all my hate I'd been taught that these German people would fight us until the death, that after reaching their homeland we would have to kill everybody in order to win. "Everybody" meant old men, women, and even young boys, in some cases.

Now it was time for me to show the incoming 3rd Battalion's Sergeant his new home for the next four days. My men were looking forward to getting off this front-line dike and back to the rear area for the next eight days. The strain was showing in their faces because Jerry was still sending in plenty of mail at the least sound.

It was well after dark when I made my way to the command post where I would meet the incoming Battalion Sergeant. I took time to stop at each one of my men's foxholes. I made sure they knew this night's new password and told them exactly how we would carry out the change-over. The main thing to remember as we moved off the line, I told them, was "make no noise whatsoever!"

The last thing each of my men said to me was something like, "Tell that guy taking my place to keep his mouth shut!"

The war-torn dirt road leading to the command post ran along a large wooded area. It was not a pleasant walk. Once at platoon headquarters I met the sergeant and his squad from the 3rd Battalion. I made up my mind I wouldn't treat the incoming sergeant the way I had been treated when I was bringing my squad in. I wanted to give him and his men a nice little talk and answer their questions.

I did that. My last point was to ask the sergeant and his men to stay on the ball! I told them that my men had earned a rest for the next few days and the last thing we wanted was to have to hunt Jerry down in the rear.

Sergeant DeWitt asked me to hurry it up since mine was the last squad making the change-over. We set out for the front lines, and once more I told the squad sergeant, "No talking from now on." As we walked along the wooded area I had a feeling that I was leading them to their slaughter. It was an eerie feeling in the darkness of that scary place.

The walk by myself past these same woods had not been easy, but the fear I felt on that walk had been for myself. Now my fear as I led the 3rd Battalion Squad was for their safety. I'd seen fear in each man's eyes back at our command post. Now, in the pitch dark of these spooky woods I felt their fear in the back of my neck. The worst moments of war are when you don't know what to expect. The men marching behind me were having such a moment.

We reached the road dike without a shot being fired. All quiet. So far, so good. One by one I dropped off the sergeant's men, and one by one my men took off for the rear. It was working just as slick as any field problem back in England ever did. At last, my foxhole. The sergeant dropped off. I took his two machine gunners to the last hole. My two gunners took off with me behind them. We had to go past each foxhole to the road by the woods before we could head for the rear. That would take extra time.

Then it happened. As we reached my former foxhole, now the foxhole of the 3rd Battalion Sergeant, he stopped us and started to talk. I told my men to keep going. I would catch up. The sergeant had not yet gotten into his foxhole. He wanted to know what time it was. I held my wristwatch out for him to see for himself.

He walked up beside me, looked at the watch, and then called to one of his gunners to come over to check his watch. This sergeant was consumed by the fear of not having the correct time. I started to leave in a hurry. Maybe I took two steps, no more.

"Bang! Bang!"

Hell, there wasn't a chance for anybody. They were on top of us. They got the gunner, bad. The sergeant who had been standing right beside me a moment or two before was hit bad in the face and eyes. They were German phosphorous shells. The phosphorus landed on my shoulders and back. Luckily, I was wearing leather gloves. In a flash I swept off the phosphorus, stripped my jump jacket off and beat out the phosphorus, but not before holes were starting to appear.

Once again luck had been on my side, but not with the 3rd Battalion Sergeant and machine gunner. I never knew how badly they had been hurt. Their medic asked me how badly I was burned, and I told him I felt no pain. "Well, Sergeant, that's good," he said, "but you have your own medic check you out when you get back. You have holes all over your jump jacket!"

I turned onto the dirt road and once more went along that eerie woods all by myself. I kept thinking, this was the worst one yet. How many close calls had I had? How many more would there be? How much luck does any one man have? Damn! I was shaking like a leaf. I had to think about something else, but I could not. I kept comparing this experience to other close calls, hoping to find one that was a little worse.

"Hell's fire!" I said out loud. "That was a lucky shot. Those damned Jerrys never would have fired if our 3rd Battalion Sergeant had kept still." The more I talked to myself, the madder I got. Somehow it helped. My head cleared, but I was still shaking all over.

I reached my command post just in time to find my platoon moving out for the rear area some five miles away at Andelst. As I turned into the CP area I heard Sergeant Hollingsworth say, "Hold up, Sergeant DeWitt! Someone is coming back from the front. It might be Sergeant Black!"

My two machine gunners had beat me back by several minutes. They were close enough to see the two shells land but too far away to tell how bad it was. They had simply passed the word on to DeWitt that I'd been hit.

"Big" Holly was the first to speak. "Sergeant Black! You OK? Need any help? Here, let me carry that. Orr, take this other box of ammunition while I help Sergeant Black for a while."

Holly put his arm around me in a gesture of brotherly love that was genuine. "Damn it, Blackie," he said, "you're shaking like a leaf. You sure you're OK?"

My teeth were chattering so fast I could barely speak. Somehow I got the words out. "I'm just cold. If I keep walking I'll soon warm up, and then I'll be OK. I'll be OK!"

Holly took a piece of silk parachute from one of his big jump pockets and put it around my neck to use as a scarf. That big guy was really concerned about me.

It took the whole five miles for me to lick those shakes.

It was good to be off the front lines if for no other reason than the good rest I had that night. Since my platoon had been the last off the lines, we were given the morning off. Long before noon I was awake and on the go again.

They called it a "rest" back here at Andelst, but it seemed there was always something to do. First off, we had to pick up our heavy equipment and pitch pup tents. Heavy equipment meant that our duffle bags had come in by sea from England. We pitched our tents in open fields. I didn't like that after being under heavy artillery fire, but they became our homes for the next four days.

"Now hear this! Clean up everything!" That was our next order. We enjoyed hot showers on this day (Saturday, October 21, 1944). Somehow they had a way in the airborne of spoiling even a good day. How could anybody but a paratrooper colonel dream up "close-order drill" as the last order on the menu for our first day of "rest"? And we were still in range of German guns.

Close-order drill, calisthenics and sports so near the front lines were a bit hard to get used to. But in the airborne things were never quite what you expected, and we were prepared to try anything. Try we did, and I'm sure it was good for us. But it seemed so British!

Four days at Phase III straightened out all of our kinks and toned us up somewhat, but every man in my 2nd Platoon was ready to move up to Phase II. We knew that in Phase II we would be closer to the front lines and more apt to be shelled by the enemy. But there would be a lot less "rank" breathing down our necks. At or near the front lines high-ranking officers didn't do a lot of moving around checking on the welfare of the enlisted men.

When we moved to Hein we were told that our whole company would be under a roof of some kind. The 2nd Platoon was to be together in a big dairy barn that was not in use. It had been a working barn a few days back and was still in good condition. With the changing weather and the knowledge that the Germans had withdrawn by two thousand yards, our Phase II reserve activities were based on a strong point with heavy patrol action during daylight hours. We would still be on the alert here at Phase II, but on a much smaller scale than when we manned a full-secondary line.

We posted one of our three machine guns at the corner of the big barn nearest the road that ran near the barn on its way along the Waal River west toward Dodewaard. The top of road bed was level with the eave or the spout line of the dairy barn. A sharp ramp-like driveway led off the road bed down to the barn. At the high point of this ramp we set up our second platoon machine gun. It was a beautiful spot in the daytime for an outpost to command the main roadway, but I would not have liked it so well at night. As it happened, I was able to avoid night-time guard at Hein.

There were more goodies for me here at Phase II—letters and two Christmas boxes. This time the boxes contained cookies and candy as well as a picture of that certain girl in school back at Ohio State. Her picture was all done up in a beautiful leather frame. It made a big hit with my fellow troopers. I never met a GI overseas who didn't like to take a good, long look at a beautiful American girl!

On our first day at Hein the call came down from the company for Sergeant DeWitt to send one squad out from our second platoon on a daytime patrol. A squad sergeant would lead the patrol.

It seemed to be another dumb, damned patrol that was of no use whatsoever. A bad waste of time and maybe men, serving no useful purpose. It was the kind of order you hated to carry out, but carry it out you will. Daytime patrol duty in no-man's land, in mine-infested territory makes the sergeant's job that much harder.

I felt real lucky when Sergeant DeWitt called out Sergeant Hollingsworth's name and told him to report with his squad to the company command post and see First Sergeant Grotjan.

I'll never know why DeWitt sent Holly's squad instead of Folley's or mine, but Holly let me know that the next "bad deal order" for the second platoon would go to my squad!

Sergeant William T. Hollingsworth and his first squad made that patrol, and it was a memorable one. For one thing, Platoon Sergeant DeWitt and a couple of the company headquarters men went along. Maybe that was so that the squad would have twelve men, including a radio man and a medic trooper, just in case. I never could figure out why Sergeant DeWitt went along, unless our platoon leader made him go just for the hell of it.

Private Frank Orr found a big St. Bernard dog out in no-man's land, abandoned and half scared to death. Orr had a real love for dogs and befriended this poor critter to the point that the dog followed him back to our dairy barn. We soon found out that this huge dog was scared of his own shadow and even more so of the sound of gunfire!

The first event of the patrol was a tragedy. One of the men in the patrol stepped on a German land mine and was killed. This was Private Junior E. Leafty, a hero from the jeep rescue patrol.

Men getting hurt was something that you might be able to get used to. Death was different; you never got used to it no matter what.

Back in camp after the patrol Holly was upset. To him it was a damned useless patrol that had harassed the whole squad at a time when they were about due to go back on line.

I thought I had Holly all figured out and knew when to believe him and when he was playing games. After telling me about the land mine tragedy and how he felt about the patrol, he told me that soon he would be a famous sergeant. "I will be seen all over the world," he said, "in movie houses, on billboards, and in newspapers and magazines. They will show me leading the great patrol!"

"What...great...patrol?" I said through clenched teeth. "I thought you just told me how bad this one stunk!"

"You know that, Black, and I know that," Holly said, "but nobody else will believe what you and I say."

I was lost now. "What in hell are you talking about?"

Once again he had me hooked. I had walked right into the old setup, same as always. No sense backing out now. So I said, "OK, OK. What happened to make you so damned famous? Did you run into Ernie Pyle? Or maybe that war correspondent that jumped with us in Normandy—Walter Cornpipe (Cronkite)?"

"No!" Holly shot back at me. "No! Nothing like that, damn it, Black! You always get carried away. It was just a photographer from *Life Magazine*, that's all. I'll let you know when they send me back to the States for a Savings Bond tour!" (Years later, back in Ohio I was visiting an old "C" Company friend, William T. Kelly. As we were looking at a copy of *101st Epic,* a pictorial book on World War II, Kelly pointed out a picture of Sergeant Hollingsworth. There he was, big as life, leading his First Squad on the Holland patrol. Holly died without seeing that picture of himself, but I'll make a bet he was looking down from up above on my face the day that Kelly pointed it out to me!)

On Sunday, October 29, we moved up to Phase I. That was good news, moving up to the front lines in broad daylight. It was the first time we had taken that kind of a chance at the front since coming to this island area. It didn't mean that Jerry couldn't see us, only that it was not easy for them any more. Besides, this time we would use a squad-sized stronghold as a listening post and would have a telephone wire running around the platoon and back to Company.

Our "C" Company would have four listening posts, and the 2nd Platoon would be responsible for two of them—each one from eight hundred to a thousand yards out in no-man's land. The posts did not run in a straight line but were set up in areas of some kind of cover, always where we could see at least three sides.

There was no way I could miss drawing one of the two outposts. The sad part of it was that Sergeant Hollingsworth and his squad drew an outpost, too.

Late that Saturday afternoon we two second platoon squad sergeants along with two from the third platoon were briefed. We were told that our task was simply to keep our eyes and ears open and report everything back to our platoons by telephone. A company runner would supply us with everything we needed.

"Get in and Shut Up!" 197

I felt a bit sorry for Sergeant Hollingsworth and his first squad. They'd just completed a tough job, and I felt they should not have to go right back into no-man's land. I wasn't sorry to the point of coming right out and volunteering to take over the worst of our two outposts, but that's what appeared to take place.

One of the posts was to be set up at a road junction where there were several buildings in fairly good shape, or so we were told. On the map the name of this place was De Hofstede. Our other outpost was in an apple orchard in the direction of the railroad. We were using a single underground emplacement under the trees there because there were no buildings nearby. The lay of the land was better at this point than at any we had seen so far on the island.

My map study showed me which one of the two posts I would like to man. But how do I get my choice? I was sure "Big" Holly would have first crack from Sergeant Curtis DeWitt, so I started laying some plans.

I'd already made up my mind that my best chance was to tell Holly what I thought was good and bad at each point without telling him which one I wanted. I was counting on Holly to make his own choice. If I could make him believe I was telling the truth, he would surely take the one I didn't want.

Whenever I had a choice between digging in at a set of buildings or out in the open, I always chose the latter because there was less likely to be artillery fire, and there was much better vision and therefore less chance of the enemy getting behind me.

It was late fall now, and we had cold nights to contend with. A building of any kind—farm houses, village crossroads or small towns—meant a good chance of keeping warm and dry. Out in the open you had only your own body heat to keep you warm, and a lot of work was required to make your space livable.

All of this must have been running through Sergeant Hollingsworth mind. Should he go for the possibility of an easier time with the Germans or play it safe with the weather? Saturday night's rain may have had some influence on Holly's decision.

On Sunday when Sergeant DeWitt asked which outposts we would be manning, Holly looked me straight in the eye and said, "First squad, second platoon will man the crossroads at De Hofstede!" I saw the victory smile he was wearing.

My squad had a long, daring march to reach our spot at the apple orchard. There was only one clear-cut way to go: straight out through the countryside where Jerry could see us all the way. For some reason the Germans weren't watching, and we made it without a shot being fired.

Because we were taking a "bee line," our radio man, Corporal Hartman, went along with me to set up my telephone line first. He left a telephone with me and set out for the crossroads. Hartman was a great guy with guts to spare, always smiling and full of fun. He was careful but did not show fear.

I decided to place my outpost on the west edge of the orchard facing the German lines and set about the task of putting together a strong, weatherproof outpost. As I worked on the site, I noticed Corporal Hartman from time to time as he made his way the three-quarters of a mile across open fields to Holly's outpost.

Holly's outpost was much closer to the platoon command post than mine, so he was dug in before I was.

Although Jerry had missed seeing me come into the orchard, I was sure they would see the corporal as he strung wire toward the crossroads. Sure enough. As he reached the first house, they opened up. Jerry sent at least four rounds to start the battle. I sat on the edge of my dugout and watched. Huge pieces of roof and walls flew into the air. I was right. Jerry was more concerned with the crossroads than with the orchard.

My telephone line was open back to the platoon's command post, so I reported to Sergeant DeWitt what I had seen, adding that I had not seen any movement at the crossroads since the gunfire.

I continued guiding my men in their "home-making" activities, taking time every now and then to check the crossroads with my field glasses for any sign of movement by Holly's squad.

We were through digging and settled in when a whistling noise came over the telephone line, loud and clear. "Charley Two to Black Two, Charley Two to Black Two. Come in, Black Two. Do you read me?"

It was Corporal Hartman calling me from Hollingsworth outpost at De Hofstede. I picked up the phone and said, "This is Black Two. Everybody is OK here."

"Those 88s tore up hell around the crossroads here," Hartman said. "Sergeant Hollingsworth has everybody out digging their foxholes deeper. I'm starting now for the platoon command post. Will call back from there. Over and out!"

Jerry probably saw Corporal Hartman leave the crossroads area and concluded that something was going on around there. Their thinking was apparently bent more on keeping Holly's first squad out of those buildings than anything else. Maybe they figured we would use those buildings for an artillery base. Every time one of Hollingsworth's men set foot in one of those buildings, four rounds of 88s landed nearby, followed by more. "Bang! Bang! Bang! Bang!"

Sergeant Hollingsworth set up his headquarters in the main house and kept one man on guard duty watching out the upstairs window throughout the daylight hours. I'm sure it was his dream come true. He was looking forward to four days in a real house, keeping warm and dry. He and his men would be able to clean up and sleep in the building. They would cook hot meals and eat them there. They would have four wonderful days.

Holly set up his machine gun to cover the crossroads on the west side, in case he needed delaying action to get his men out. The rest of the men dug foxholes in the yard of the main house in case there might be some stray shelling. The closest foxhole to the doorway into the house was Sergeant Hollingsworth's.

By 1100 hours Corporal Hartman had returned safely to the command post and had reported, "Charley Two, reporting everything working A-OK. Over and out." Suddenly out of my phone came, "Hey over there in the land of the apple! This is Holly Two to Black Two. From the one and only 'Big' Holly. Do you read me? Come in, Black Two!"

Holly was speaking in a deep, hoarse whisper with no sign of despair. He and I exchanged comments about the day, the weather and other things two old paratroopers might talk about. I was careful not to say a word about the shelling he was drawing at his crossroads. Better for him to say something first.

As I got set to report back to platoon headquarters, the sounds of shells exploding came through my receiver. This is what I heard:

"Oooops! What the hell...?" (Holly's voice)
"Aaarf! Aaarf! Aaarf!"
"Bang! Bang! Bang!"
"Get off of me!"
"Aaarf! Aaarf Aaarf!"
"Come on now! Get the hell off of me!"
"Bang! Bang! Bang!"
"Aaarf! Aaarf! Aaarf!"
"You dumb dog. Get off of me!"
"Bang! Bang! Bang!"
"Aaarf! Aaarf! Aaarf!"
"Private Orr!" (louder) "Private Orr!"
"Did you call me, Sergeant?"
"Yes! Where are you?"
"Right on top of you, now."
"Well, get the hell off of me! And take that damned dog to your own foxhole! Ya hear?"
"Grrr! Grrr! Grrr!"
"Watch out, Orr! He's going to bite me! Don't! Don't touch him! Look out! He has hold of my leg! Let go! Let go! You sonofabitch! Don't pull on his tail, Orr. Let go! Let him stay. I'm getting the hell out of here!"

A short time later I could hear Holly breathing hard again. The shelling had stopped, so I felt I should talk to him. But each time I tried to whistle into the phone I started to laugh.

Finally Holly came on the line and said, "OK, Black! What is so damned funny? Tell me so I can laugh, too."

"How did you know I was about to call you?" I said. "I haven't had a chance to whistle up your number yet." (Holly's call was one whistle, mine was two, and Sergeant DeWitt's was three.)

"By the way," I said, "since I have you on the phone, what's going on over there? What are you guys doing to make Jerry so damned mad at you? Sounds like the Germans are trying to kill all of you! Has anyone been hit?"

"No one so far, but they are getting close every time."

"How many dog bites have you had to treat over there so far?" I asked.

Holly pretended he couldn't hear me. "Say again, say again! You're not coming in clear! Do you read me? Do you read me? Black Two, this is Holly Two!"

I bypassed the dog bite for now and went on to tell him how peaceful and quiet it was here in my orchard. I told him that all my men were sitting around my beautiful, weather-proofed foxhole sunning themselves. "How does that song go?" I said. I sang out, "In the shade of the old apple tree."

With the pause in the shelling, Holly had regained his composure and was back to normal spirits.

I heard him yell out for Private Orr. "Hey, Orr! Go into the house and see how soon the cherry pie will be ready to eat."

Private Orr must have been sitting right next to him because I heard him say, "What are you talking about, Sergeant?"

"Dammit, Private Orr, can't you understand English?" Holly barked over the telephone line for my benefit.

That comment brought Sergeant Curtis DeWitt to the forefront. Apparently he'd been listening all the time. "Hey, Sergeant Hollingsworth. This is Sergeant DeWitt talking. You will have to cut your fires up there at the crossroads. Your smoke is drawing too much enemy artillery."

"Cut the fires?" Holly yelled.

"That's too bad," I said. "Now you city people will have to live like we do here in the country." Then I signed off. "This is Black Two to Holly Two. Over and Out."

After taking a drumming from the Germans, Holly and his men experienced bad weather. Just before dark it started to rain.

I made a point to talk to Holly after every shelling outburst throughout the afternoon. They caught hell all day long. All day not one shell landed anywhere near my orchard. At Holly's place every time a shell popped, it was run for your foxhole or someone else's. And hope that damn dog didn't choose you to land on.

No matter how hard Private Orr tried to contain him, the St. Bernard broke away from wherever Orr put him. Twice Holly made Private Orr take him all the way back to the platoon's command post in the rear. The dog always found his way back. At night the dog was still with them at the crossroads.

There was nothing left to do but shoot the dog or give up. Holly didn't have the heart to shoot him, so he gave up. By nightfall and the start of a cold rain and that dog jumping on his back along with Sergeant Black laughing over the telephone—pneumonia set in. Holly had had it!

Corporal Hartman told me about it later. "We had to call the meat wagon and take Sergeant Hollingsworth all the way back to the main hospital at Nijmegan," he said. "He was in bad shape when I picked him up at the crossroads. The Platoon Sergeant ordered me to bring him back to the command post. I'm no medic, Sergeant Black. I'm just carrying the medic's bag to fill in. But it didn't take a doctor to tell me that he's a very sick man. Holly's in the third stage of pneumonia; I'll bet on it! He may not make it."

I heard all of this from Hartman when I called in at 2400 hours (midnight) at the start of my turn on guard. I'd been asleep all evening. I was sure it was an act of Holly's. "Dammit, Hartman!" I yelled. "He hasn't got pneumonia any more than I've got spring fever!"

"You're being too hard on him," Hartman said. "You'll be sorry if he doesn't make it."

"Doesn't make it? Well, damn him," I said. "He sure has pulled the wool over your eyes at command post. All he wants is to sleep under clean sheets for one night. He'll be back tomorrow."

"You're being too rough on him," Hartman said.

On Monday, October 30, a German shell cut the telephone wire at De Hofstede crossroads. Corporal Hartman found and repaired the cut wire and then went into the first squad's outpost to see if Corporal Gromac, now in charge, needed anything. He also wanted to call me to tell me he was on his way over to see me in the orchard. When he got to the outpost, to his great surprise, there was Sergeant William T. Hollingsworth manning the main foxhole.

"Sergeant Black," Hartman said to me later, "you could have knocked me over with a feather. He looked great! When he said 'hello' to me, he didn't sound a bit like he had pneumonia. Dammit, Sergeant! I must have been drunk last night!"

"Hell, no! You were as sober as a judge," I said.

"I tell you, Corporal. I thought he was dying of pneumonia for sure. How did you know he didn't have it?"

I could see my answer called for some thought. I waited for a time before I said, "There is a thing called instinct, Corporal. No one can teach it to you. You can't learn it if you want to. For some reason a few of us have it."

Corporal Hartman wanted me to call Holly on the phone and ask him what happened at the Nijmegan Hospital for him to come back so soon.

"No," I said, "I've gone about as far as I dare go. I've rubbed his nose in that crossroads thing almost as much as Jerry has. I've got to let him get something on me for a change." I explained I didn't want Holly ever to get ahead of me but that I didn't want to be too far ahead of him, either.

We both had nearly three days left at our outposts and had to talk back and forth from time to time. I let on as if nothing had happened and before long he told me all about it.

Jerry bombed the hell out of Nijmegan Hospital soon after he arrived and before the hospital people had a chance to know who he was or what was wrong with him.

"Hell, Blackie!" Holly said. "It was awful! Beds were flying every way! It may be bad up here, but back at the hospital it was downright terrible."

"How did you get out of there alive?" I asked.

"After the first bomb I ran out and jumped in the same ambulance as the one I came in. The first driver was dead, but another paratrooper from 502nd jumped in the driver's seat and away we went."

Somehow they found their way back to their companies without a scratch—and absent the threat of pneumonia.

The St. Bernard was hit at last by a piece of flying shrapnel and received the "purple heart" for his bravery. He was not killed outright, so the task of dispatching him fell to Sergeant Hollingsworth. After befriending him, Private Orr could not bring himself to do it. The dog's trouble was, first, that he couldn't stay away from Private Orr and, second, that he did not understand the meaning of the "swishing" sound made by the first incoming shell. That's why the humans always won the race to the foxholes. Private Orr buried the dog at De Hofstede

19

My Last Fast Draw

The day of October 31 dawned clear and sunny with not a cloud in the sky. In the sky we saw for the first time Hitler's new jet planes. I watched two of them flying overhead for quite some time, but no USAF or RAF planes went after them. These were Messerchmidt 262 jet fighters. They had been developed in 1944, but Hitler insisted on having them modified to carry bombs. As a result, the development of these planes was delayed one full year. This was a serious mistake by Hitler. He made the decision in spite of objections by all of the Luftwaffe generals, even Goering himself, who tried in vain to point out the desperate need for fast fighter planes to hold off the increasing numbers of bomber planes from the British Royal Air Force. Compounding the delay, Hitler never had more than one hundred jets at any one time that were ready to fly.

We saw several German "rocket" firings that afternoon. We were familiar with the V-1 rockets from Normandy days, but none of us had seen a launching up close.

The V-1 was first used on London on June 13, 1944, one week after D-day. The British people named it the "Buss Bomb" because of the sound it made. It was unmanned, had a speed of 400 miles per hour and was loaded with explosives. When the motor of the V-1 cut off, the rocket headed down and exploded on whatever happened to be under it when it hit the ground.

Starting in June of 1944 more than eight thousand V-1s were shot toward London from ramps in the Pas de Callais area on the coast, but only about twenty-four hundred reached their target area. A total of seventy-seven "Buss Bombs" and one thousand V-2s hit London, killing nearly nine thousand British civilians and seriously injuring twenty-four thousand more.

The V-2s were much faster and were a true rocket as we have come to know them today. The V-2 was a forerunner of long-range ballistic missiles. It carried a tank of liquid oxygen so that it could fly above the earth's atmosphere. It was fired from a fixed position and reached a speed four times the speed of sound by the time it hit the ground. At its top arch it reached sixty miles above earth. Its total weight was fourteen tons with a one-ton bomb load packed in its forty-six-foot length.

When the V-2 hit the ground it was devastating in every sense of the word. It first hit England, September 1, 1944, and quickly became the greatest fear of the whole war for the English people. They could not see or hear the rocket until it was too late to escape its impact. There was no way to stop the V-2 once it was in the air; the only chance of stopping the V-2 was at its launching site.

British civilians caught up in the terror of Hitler's revenge weapons began to see a trend by America's leaders leading into France straight for Paris and the heart of Europe. These civilians felt they had been bypassed, left behind to suffer a worse fate from Hitler's revenge weapons.

Hitler became obsessed with desire to bomb English civilians and gave top priority to the manufacture of V-1 rocket and the jet plane as a bomber.

It was easy for me to understand the feelings of the British people the summer of 1944. I had lived among them, talked to them, drank beer with them in their pubs, talked to their girls, rode their trains and buses and taxicabs. I knew their soldiers here in Holland.

My Last Fast Draw

After a year in Europe, I thought it only fair once we had gained a solid foothold in France and had made good progress in our long-planned second front, for the British and Canadian armies to drive north up the coast across from the Straits of Dover all the way along the North Sea until they were past Amsterdam. Moreover, it seemed fair to me to assume that the Allied Airborne Army would help them. British, American and even Polish paratroopers were working together in the Allied Airborne Army. I felt that if a big effort was needed by the Allied Airborne Army, it would at Antwerp or Amsterdam, the big seaports, or at Paris, the big capital city.

Then came the British General Montgomery's "Market-Garden" plan, a bold effort to slash all the way to the Zuider Zee. If successful, the effort would result in the easing up of Hitler's revenge weapons that were being fired from this coastal area.

Hitler was losing the war and could no longer afford to be obsessed by revenge. The plan of bombing the British into submission didn't work when he was winning; it made even less sense now that he was losing.

The first day of November, 1944, was my last day at Phase I at the orchard outpost. We had not received one German artillery shell in the four days and nights we spent in the orchard and walked out without being noticed.

We made the change-over with incoming troops in daylight and then started the long march back to the Phase III line in the Andelst area. For some reason my 2nd Platoon stopped off at a large dairy farm and spent the night in the barn. It was almost dark when we moved into that barn, which was full of milk cows that the Dutch farmers were in the process of milking.

By the time we finished eating it was dark. Front line duty is always a strain, and for "Big" Holly and his men the pounding they'd taken had left them dog tired. Sleep was on everyone's mind. Holly's first squad and Folley's third squad took the west hay mow. My second squad and Sergeant Howard's fourth squad took the east hay mow. Sergeant DeWitt and Lieutenant Dwyer, our platoon leader, along with the other members of the headquarters group, stayed on the ground floor in the driveway into the barn.

When we moved into the barn we were told to drop our field packs and other equipment and get ready for hot chow. I unloaded my side arm but kept my pistol belt on and put the bullets in my pocket. I was carrying an English 38 western-style six-shooter pistol that I had picked up here in Holland. I liked that gun and always kept it loaded after dark.

The driveway opened all the way to the top of the rafts, so they could see into both hay mows from there. Dwyer and DeWitt rigged up a fire in the center of that long barn for heat and light. Somebody was assigned guard duty by the fire and the metal container of fuel oil.

Sergeant Hollingsworth and I were both on the north end of the barn, straight across from each other. I took some extra time getting into the hay mow. I stopped by the fire to chat and pass the time.

By the time I was ready to bed down in my squad's hay mow, Holly was already in his sleeping bag with his head against the north wall of whitewashed brick and masonry cement. Both hay mows were full of new summer hay. The troopers up here were in for a warm soft snooze in the hay.

I decided to take a few moments, as I often did, to practice my fast draw. It was a five-step thing: "Draw—twirl—pull (the hammer back and fire)—twirl (again)—sock (the pistol back in the holster). I did it best using numbers: "one, two, three, four, five!" Over and over I practiced this procedure while standing up at my spot in the hay mow.

The fire down in the driveway gave off more light than I expected, and the click of my pistol made more noise than I thought. Still, only one paratrooper seemed to be aware of what I was doing, but he said nothing.

When I grew tired, I put my "live" ammo back in my pistol, replaced the gun in its holster and started to get into bed. That meant pulling your blanket or sleeping bag up around you and lying down somewhere—anywhere—to sleep. I'd done all of the above except to lie down. My sleeping bag was zipped to my hips but not past the pistol holster.

As I stood there before bedding down, the urge hit me to try one more "fast draw." One, two, BANG!

It sounded like a canon going off.

For the next few seconds I was as scared as I've ever been. I knew I'd made a bad mistake. I wondered if anybody had been hit.

Even with my ears still ringing, I didn't think I'd heard anyone making a sound. When the words finally came, I said, "Did anybody get hit?" Nobody answered.

I stood frozen, the pistol still in my right hand pointing the same direction it had fired. Slowly I realized where that was. Damn! I had that gun pointed straight across the driveway at the wall in the hay mow near the spot where "Big" Holly must be lying.

Once more I asked, "Is anybody hurt?"

There was no mistaking the voice that replied. "No thanks to you!" said Holly. "I'm alive, but it's a miracle. Damn it, everybody is trying to kill me. But why you, Sergeant? I thought we were friends. I know you've turned against me ever since you made me Sergeant here in Holland. But I sure didn't think you would try to shoot me in my sleep!"

"Gee, I'm sorry, Holly," I said. "My damn pistol went off as I was zipping up my sleeping bag. I must have bumped the hammer in the holster somehow."

"Yeah, yeah! I know how that could happen, Sergeant Black," he said. "I've seen it in cowboy movies. Yes, sir! You get your hammer caught in the zipper of your sleeping bag. You hear that, men?"

There was dead silence.

I deserved everything Holly had given me so far. What I had done was a cardinal sin in my book of combat rules. I was always yapping about being careful to the men around me. There was nothing more to say. I put my pistol away and lay down in the hay.

Sleep came at last to me, to Holly, and everybody else.

The call went out for chow early the next morning. We could smell the powdered eggs, fried potatoes, cinnamon rolls and hot coffee above the smell of dairy cows being milked by the Dutch farmers.

As I stood in chow line next to Sergeant Hollingsworth, he said to me, "I'll give you, right now, thirty dollars for that English horse pistol."

"Oh, yeah?" I said. "Why's that?"

"To keep you from shooting me or one of my men!" Holly said loudly enough for everybody to hear. Corporal Hartman laughed out loud while Private Orr looked on with a puzzled look on his face.

"No!" I said. "Why only thirty dollars this morning?"

"Because that's the same offer I made you yesterday, and the day before that, and last week at that other dairy barn. Remember? Ten dollars a bullet. That's my offer. You and I both know that you are down to three bullets."

He was right about my having only three bullets left. Holly had been counting them all along and was hoping I would run out of ammo. What good would an English gun do me without any ammo? Come to think about it, I realized we hadn't seen a limey, let alone a tanker, since pulling back over at Elst on D plus 22.

To myself I thought, "Now is a good time as any to let him know." As we finished getting our chow, I said, "I've made up my mind to get rid of this weapon. I'll sell it to the highest bidder. I'll give you a chance if you still want it. By the way, Holly, I'm really sorry about last night. How close was it to you, really?"

Holly hadn't forgotten my laughing at him just a few days back, so he made a big deal out of his response. He didn't talk to me; he told everybody else within earshot. "Sergeant Black was practicing his cowboy routine hoping to make it to Hollywood after the war," he announced. "I can tell you this much. Sergeant Black is not a bad shot. He missed me by an inch. I thought for sure I'd been hit, but it turned out to be chips of brick. See there where a chip cut my chin, Hartman?"

Holly had gone one step too far. Private Orr was standing near by and butted in with, "I thought you cut your chin shaving this morning, Sergeant!"

The look Private Orr drew from Holly was a killer. Orr went to the back of the line without a word.

The best thing for me to do at that point was to shut up. But I had to go back up to that hay mow and see for myself where the bullet had hit the wall. I found the hole in the roof. It wasn't even close to Holly. Not even close! I stopped carrying a pistol after that.

My Last Fast Draw

Once more we pitched our pup tents at the Phase III area around Andelst. We spent the day cleaning up and did some calisthenics. In the afternoon we took a truck ride back to the city of Nijmegan where we enjoyed a hot shower. Our supply people laid out a bundle of fresh laundry for each trooper.

Things were becoming routine for us and running smoothly.

On Friday, November 3, Sergeant Grotjan passed the word that there would be a movie call for "C" Company after dark.

I met our new battalion Commanding Officer, Major John D. Hanlon, who had come to replace our long-time friend "Hopalong" Cassidy, who had been promoted to Executive Officer for the 502nd Regiment. I liked Major Hanlon from the start.

For the next twenty-one days war went on the same as in the past. Rain was plentiful, and the weather had a little more winter in it every day.

Our last day at Hein before moving back to the front lines was one of our worst days for weather. Winter set in, and the rain turned to snow. By the time I went on line the sun came out, and it was warmer.

Artillery battles continued, which meant that those of us on line had to keep our heads down. We had to keep alert, but about all we had to worry about was a direct hit.

For the high-ranking officers, another worry was growing with each passing day: the possible flooding of the "island" by Jerry.

Saturday, November 11, 1944, was Armistice Day, and at exactly 1100 hours (11 a.m.), every gun we British and Americans had on this island opened up on the Germans.

We all got into the act. We fired everything we had at Jerry—mortars, bazookas, rifles and machine guns. We even threw some hand grenades. It must have lasted five minutes and was more like the Fourth of July than Armistice Day! For their own reasons, Jerry answered back with a barrage of their own fire.

Thanksgiving Day was always a big day everywhere in the U.S. Army. In 1944 it came while I was on line at Phase I, the "C" Company's second day of our last four days on front line duty in Holland.

Rumors were hot and heavy that the Canadians would be taking over for the 101st in a few days. The word was that we would go south for the winter, but not to England. We also heard that the 501st Parachute Regiment would pull out the next day, and that we would follow a few days later.

All of this was good news, but there had to be some bad news, too. There would be *no* Thanksgiving dinner for us American chow hounds. The 101st Airborne Division was still under British control, and we were stuck with *their* rations. To Corporal Milligan and several other soldiers this was a terrible blow.

Then the word was passed down to the men of the 101st all the way from General Taylor himself: "We will have our Thanksgiving Day dinner with all the trimmings just as soon as we are back with our own people in command."

It was true. The Battle of Holland had come to an end for the 101st. We got ready to move south, to a place called "Camp Mourmelon" near Reims, France. Some dumb guy asked, "Where the hell is Reims, France?" and some smart guy answered, "It's near Paris!"

On Monday, November 27, the men of the "C" Company of the 502nd Parachute Regiment boarded trucks and rode slowly out of the island. We drove across the wide Waal River on an Army pontoon bridge. I remember looking up at the beautiful Nijmegan Bridge high above the water. One span was down in the river thanks to a German air raid.

As we were pulling out someone passed along the word to us that our Division had set a new record of continuous days on the front lines, a total of 72 days! And this was an airborne outfit!

There was nothing but pride among us as we rode on those open trucks down "hell's highway," through Nijmegan, Grave, Uden, Bechel, St. Oedenrode, Zon and Eindhoven.

Dutch people lined up along the road shouting as we passed by, "September 17! September 17!" To these people of Holland, the day the Allied Paratroopers fell from the skies was a day they would always remember. They were indeed grateful for what we were able to do for them. Ask me or any Dutchman who was there when we left Holland what we saw that day, and we will answer, "What we saw was victory."

20

Frolic in Paris

It was great to be out of combat. We ran into rain in Belgium or somewhere else along the way. Riding up front in an army truck is bad enough even on a short trip; a trip in the back across three countries is plain hell. The sound of rain beating down on the canvas and the zinging noise of the big truck's dual tires squeezing water from their path lulled many of us to sleep.

General Taylor gave all of us men of the battalions ten days off to rest and straighten ourselves out in Reims. Everyone who wanted to go to Paris got a two-day pass.

We continued training with close-order drill and calisthenics. On November 29, our second day back, we stood in retreat formation with cannon firing and a full inspection. The word "retreat" had real meaning to me now.

Someone had tried to get the camp ready for us, but we had to do it "our" way. We spent several hours a day cleaning our one-floor stucco barracks, repairing windows, tightening doors and getting ready for winter. It looked like we were getting set to spend a long time in our winter quarters, even more so when the call came down to organize football and boxing teams.

Reinforcements were pouring in to fill the gaping holes left by our early, heavy losses around St. Oedenrode and Best. Each day new men were sent up for a fast indoctrination in how to go about fighting the war with the 502nd. Most of these new men got only about ten days of this type of training.

On November 30, we celebrated a late Thanksgiving dinner just as General Taylor had promised. What a meal it was! One of my best in the army.

Pay call and 48-hour passes to Paris were handed out. After our turkey dinner "C" Company stood in formation as First Sergeant Grotjan explained "pay call." We would be drawing two months' pay at one time. "Keep enough money out, those of you who are going on pass," the sergeant said. "And, oh, yes! Those of you who have some English money left, change it to French money here in my office. Also, if you have any Dutch money you may have come across while we were in Holland, exchange it for French currency."

"Uh-oh!" said Sergeant Hollingsworth. "They're still looking for those bank robbers!"

Sergeant Grotjan heard that and said, "Oh, they caught those guys. We forgot to pass that word along to you. Don't be afraid to turn in any Dutch money you may have. Captain Cody rescinded his order on Dutch money in the 'C' Company several days back."

Someone in the 1st Platoon yelled out, "How in hell would anybody get any Dutch money if he didn't rob a bank or something?"

Holly looked stunned when he heard the First Sergeant's answer. "Well, gentlemen, the word going the rounds in the Battalion, in case you haven't heard, is that someone found a German musette bag while we were in Holland that was full of new Dutch money for a Jerry payroll. Since it was Dutch guilders it's as good as gold," he said.

He paused and continued, "Now the word also is that whoever it was who found it was a very kind soul and passed it out to everyone. However, I didn't get any. I would rather think, knowing paratroopers, that he lost it playing poker. Now if any of you just happen to have some of this Dutch money, turn it in. It's good. Fall out!"

Frolic in Paris   215

I looked over at the big guy standing next to me and said, "Holly, did that kind soul give you any of that good Dutch money?"

Holly didn't look at me. He just put his head down and started walking down the company street. He looked like a big old St. Bernard dog with his tail between his legs. I don't remember seeing Holly for several days after that. He didn't go on pass, and I don't think he even drew his pay that day.

In mid afternoon W. O. Bird and I reported to the First Sergeant and were told to be ready to go on a two-day pass to Paris in the morning. Sometimes it paid to be in the right alphabetical order.

In the true technical sense, W. O. Bird came back to us in the 2nd Platoon in the Battle of the Bulge. But in a physical sense, here he was with all of us at Camp Mourmelen. He and the other returning wounded were at the camp waiting for us when we arrived.

When Holly and I saw W. O. Bird we were delighted. He had no visual signs of his head wound or any apparent ill effects with the exception of a loss of peripheral vision in his left eye.

It was a three-hour ride to Paris by way of Reims, the home of the Reims Cathedral. On the way Bird told me about his ordeal with the British medics. He refused to let them remove his left eye to get the piece of metal shrapnel located there. They warned him that he might die if he waited until he was back at an American hospital in England. He took the gamble and was glad for that now.

I doubt if anyone ever had as much fun as two guys with the last names of Bird and Black from the farming area of the U.S. Midwest cutting a wide swath through the city of Paris.

"Hey, watch where you're stepping! Are you blind, sir?" I said to a First Lieutenant on the truck to Paris as I jerked my feet out of his way.

"Sorry, Sergeant," said the officer. "I was blinded by the shine on your boots. Those can't be the jump boots you wore in Holland!"

"No, sir! These are my dancing boots that I save for special times like this. Sir!" I said.

Bird asked me, "When are we going to find time to do any dancing, Blackie?"

The other troopers on the truck chuckled at Bird's question. I didn't know, but I did have an extra pair of jump boots for going on pass, and that meant I would probably be doing some dancing. In England dancing was popular in all of the cities and towns. I assumed France would be the same.

The most important thing to every paratrooper going on pass was his jump boots. They had to shine. Bird and I had spent half the night getting ready to go on pass, and most of that time we spent shining our boots. They weren't the only things that had to shine. Our jump wings were a close second. And now we were to wear "stars" on our wings for combat jumps. Both Bird and I had two stars on our jump wings now, and Bird had a purple heart (a medal for soldiers wounded in combat) for each of his.

We were a happy bunch of troopers jumping off the back of the army trucks on December 1, 1944. We stopped first at a hotel the American Red Cross had taken over for us GIs to use while on pass. Bird and I were there only long enough to be assigned to a room with a bath. We used that bath once.

Once again, I was so clean I squeaked. But now I was on my own with someplace to go and the greatest town on earth to enjoy. Bird and I had planned how we would spend our time in Paris. The first thing we did was "reconnoiter" the area to get as far away from the hotel as necessary to find an area where there would not be any other paratroopers for the time being.

We walked along with the mainstream of paratroopers for a time. When I felt we had gone far enough we made a "by the right flank, march!" turn. It took another three blocks to get away from all the other paratroopers. At that point, Bird and I made a "left flank" and headed more or less in the direction of downtown Paris.

Along the way were several sidewalk cafes. We walked along until we came to a cafe we liked on the corner of the street. We got a table for two. I ordered a cognac for each of us and then we tried to act like two run-of-the-mill GIs who came to Paris every weekend. I know we failed miserably because everyone kept staring at us. By their looks I was sure we were the first paratroopers they had ever seen. Since our French was limited to a word or

Frolic in Paris

two, we would stare back at them from time to time. Then they would smile at us and nod, as if saying "hello" to us. We started saying "hello" back. Every time we did that some Frenchman would smile, nod, then stand up and raise his wineglass to us and say something.

It gave us a "real hero" feeling because we knew that the welcome these French people gave us came from the heart.

Once our "reconnoitring" had put us on the right track, Bird and I stopped at a French barbershop for a haircut, a facial and a fingernail job, all administered by a pretty French girl. We felt the "eyes of Paris" on us as we received the royal treatment.

From the barbershop we were ready to head up town and see Paris at its core. It was a beautiful sunny day. Paris was a wonderful sight with its wide streets and sidewalks. Unlike London, this city did not show the devastation of an air war.

Our stroll downtown had a calculated purpose planned into it. We were headed for the main American PX, where each trooper had only to show his pass papers to buy anything in the place—if he had the money.

Our goal was to stretch our money, open doors, win friends and influence people—that is, girls. We weren't headed for the black market of French women, but we were going to play the grab-bag game. You choose the best-looking girl and she gets to take her pick of goodies in your musette bag. We bought soap, candy and cigarettes—all American.

Every French girl I ever met loved to smoke an American-made cigarette. It was something to come up with a full pack in the early days of the war. But to be given a whole carton of Lucky Strikes or Camels! "Merci beaucoup!" "Oui, oui. Jeune se plait. Yanky Dandy!" "Anywhere you say, soldier!" "I'm in love with you, big boy!"

Add to that a candy bar and you could forget the war. With enough goodies, Bird and I could own the whole town by morning.

Back at the PX we did not overlook the perfume counter and came away the second time with a good supply of the latest fragrance.

On the street again, we two staff Sergeants from "C" Company of the Screaming Eagles were ready. We picked up a bottle of cognac and flagged a horse-drawn open-air carriage with two seats. Bird opened the flap on his musette bag and told the driver he could have his pick if he would take us to where the action was. I said, "That means the very prettiest girls in Paris, or all you'll get is cab fare!"

The driver spoke English. "You GI jumpers," he said. "I take you to 42 Blondel. You like, OK!"

On the way Bird and I began to wonder if we were being taken for a real ride. Finally our driver brought his horse to a stop at a street named "Blondel." He pointed down the street to a big sign that read "42 Blondel" in front of a cafe about halfway down the block. "Plenty the girls," he said.

I jumped out first and looked the cab driver right in the eye. "Are you sure that they are pretty French girls?" I said.

"Beaucoup jolie mademoiselles. Oui! Oui!"

Bird was still in the back seat holding the musette bag in his lap with the flap wide open. "Blackie," he said. "Go check it out. I'll wait here in the cab."

"Oh, hell, Bird," I said. "Give him something and come on. See all those girls looking out the windows. Come on! Hurry it up!" I started down the street.

The cab driver took something, probably cigarettes. Bird yelled, "Wait for me!" and came on the run. We reached the door to the cafe. It opened into a short hallway ended with closed doors. On both doors and all over each wall were signs in English saying "OFF LIMITS!" But Bird and I had just enough drinks for those signs to read, "COME ON IN!"

Bird opened the door, and I stepped in. Neither of us said a word. We just looked around.

A big Amazon of a woman, fully dressed, suddenly had a big hand on each of our chests and pushed us out into the vestibule. She pointed to the signs and shook her head, "No!" In very good English she said, "I know what you boys want." Still manhandling us, she backed us out the last door into the street. There in the street she pointed us to a small hotel down at the end of the street.

Frolic in Paris

Looking out the front window were four French girls. We walked to the hotel and tried to talk to the girls using sign language. One signal was clear. Everyone was all smiles, and they wanted us to come in.

"Those girls are pretty!" I said to W.O. "Let's go in. This looks easy!"

Once in the hotel we knew why. These French gals were all prostitutes, and damn good-looking ones at that.

I cannot speak for W. O. Bird, but the last time I had even been close to any girl was at St. Oedenrode on September 17 when those six Dutch girls were getting a haircut and a shave.

Sometime later, back in the street, Bird and I stood talking.

"Did you see what I saw there in 42 Blondel?" he said.

I nodded my head. "What the hell goes on in that place?"

"Let's go back and check it out again," Bird said.

This time our plan of attack would start with Bird opening the main door. I would run inside as far as I could. Then he would move off to one side to get time to look around. That Amazon would have to throw us out one at a time.

In the vestibule, W. O. Bird said, "Are you ready, Sergeant! Geronimo!"

I put my head down like a fullback and took off on the run down through that French cafe clear to the far end. Only one person noticed me. It was that Amazon. The rest didn't give a damn. Out of the corner of my eye I could see her behind the bar. She was on her way after me. Now was my chance to look the place over.

What a fabulous place! Everything was plush and in the latest style. Wall-to-wall carpet, a leather-covered bar, bar stools with short back supports. There were mirrors everywhere, with people looking back at every angle. French people were dressed to kill, and it was still in the afternoon

The cafe's bar seemed a mile long. There must have been at least fifty barstools in one row. There was one row of tables and chairs along the back wall, leaving a wide aisle between the bar and tables. Then I saw the main attraction of the place—an open stairway leading up to the second floor. The stairway was covered with mirrors, even the steps. When two beautiful girls walked down those steps it looked like twenty. How about if they were stark, raving naked?

The big Amazon had reached me by now and had me by the arm. "I'm sorry, Sergeant," she said, "but no Yanks can come in here. Come along, now. We don't want any trouble with the USA, now do we?"

As we were walking out I said, "Do I have to shut my eyes, or can I look?"

For the first time she smiled. "Drink it in, trooper," she said. "I hear you Yanks still have to jump the Rhine."

At least ten of those beautiful gals, naked from the shoes up, gave Bird and me big smiles. By now we had reached Bird at the front of the cafe where he stood, totally occupied with the view of the stairway. I tried to delay our departure for a longer look at it. What a view those mirrors gave of a red-headed beauty on her way up. I followed her every ripple until my eyes caught a French-Algerian brunette coming down. All they were wearing were high heel shoes and a head dress.

The big Amazon gave me a jerk and said, "Come on soldiers, before you go blind!"

Just like that, Bird and I were standing in the street again. The Amazon pointed to the little hotel down the street again. "Those are your kind of girls, Yanks," she said. "These 42 Blondel girls belong to the black market of Paris!" She put her strong arms around both of us and said, "Now boys, be good and stay out of 42 Blondel. I don't want to have to get rough with you! Go on back over there and have yourself a fling!"

Darkness was not far off, so we quickened our pace to beat the blackout. We signaled to two French girls that we would pay for their dinner if they would take us to a restaurant. They skipped along arm and arm beside us, singing French songs.

"I'll bet we've passed a dozen restaurants," I said to Bird after we had passed row upon row of houses and turned corner after corner.

"We'll end up at some high-priced place is my guess," said Bird. He was right. We came out on a big boulevard with a fancy restaurant in front of us.

We were hungry by now so went in with the girls, all smiles. They had a big time, eating and laughing at our expense. They told us the way to "Place Pigalle" and said good-bye.

We had wanted to see the world-famous Folies Berger but were told at the Pigalle restaurant that it was sold out. Instead, we were told, we should go to the Casino De Paris, which had a "girlie" show that some in Paris thought was even better than the "follies."

Boldly we walked up to the doorkeeper. Bird made sure that a carton of Lucky Strikes was exposed in his musette bag of goodies.

"Hey, Monsieur," I said. "We just got back from the front in Holland, and we need to meet two pretty young girls to go dancing with after the show. Can you fix us up?"

He was ready for us. "What's in it for me?" he said.

W. O. started to open up the musette bag right there in front of everyone, including many American military officers. The doorkeeper took us both in arm and walked us away from the crowd down near the street.

In English he said, "I fix you dates with two of the best girls in the show tonight. They main actors. Very pretty. You Yanks like very much. Oui! Oui! What you give me?"

I said, "You're kidding us. Two of the main actors? Hell, we're only staff sergeants!"

"You airborne," he said. "You 101st Airborne. You jump in Normandy. You deserve the best. I get for you the main actors. They like you. They have fun with you. You wait. You see. You trust me! What you give to me?"

W. O. and I looked at each other trying to read each other's minds. I was thinking there could be a Hedy Lamarr or a Rita Hayworth in this show. Maybe at least a Linda Darnell. "Hell, Bird," I said. "Give him his pick."

Bird's sights weren't set that high. "Not so fast, Blackie," he said. "This guy hasn't delivered yet. Hey, Frenchie, tell you what we'll do. Here's a pack of American Luckys. You deliver us two god-looking gals after the show, and you can have your pick. Take a look and see what you can pick from!"

He opened the musette bag, and the doorkeeper's eyes bulged as he looked in. A big smile came to his face. Bird shut the flap and started walking into the theater, saying, "See you right after the show."

I said, "Beautiful well-built girls or nothing."

At intermission we checked out the doorkeeper to be sure he had not forgotten us. He had been looking for us to tell us that the girls were all set to see us after the show. Bird and I went back to our seats in great spirits. Here we were watching our dates dance and caper before our eyes in every state of dress—and undress—and they were beautiful, every one of them.

The show ended sometime before midnight, and people cleared out in a hurry. We went outside the theater where we could keep an eye on our new friend. He was busy at his job, but from time to time he would look over at us and smile. After the audience had left he asked Bird and me to come back into the lobby. One by one, and then in groups of two or three, the people in the show began to leave. They came from back stage to the center aisle, to the lobby and then out the doorway. The doorkeeper spoke to each one personally as he let them out the main doorway.

All the show people gave Bird and me a big smile as they passed by. "Everybody in the show must know about our dates," I said. "Maybe they are playing us for the sucker! What do you think, Bird?"

Never in a hurry to push the panic button, Bird said. "We don't have to be back to camp until Sunday night. Relax. Let's play the doorkeeper's little game on out. We've got nothing to lose and everything to gain. Hang in there!"

So we did, down to the last three show people. Then out onto the stage and down the aisle came a man and two women. They were the three main people in the show. The doorkeeper came straight over to us and announced, "Your dates, Paratroopers!"

We stood spellbound as the three show people walked up to us. The doorkeeper introduced us to them. I don't remember their names any more, but I do remember their friendliness. They overwhelmed us with their appreciation for ridding their homeland of the Germans.

We gave the doorkeeper an extra grab from our musette bag, and we both shook hands with him to say our thanks.

Frolic in Paris

Our two Paris girls now took over and set the course for the rest of the evening.

"Now we show you two jumpers our Paris at night," said one.

"We take you to our favorite night clubs. You like, I bet," said the other.

These two beautiful French showgirls gave W.O. and me a whirlwind of show people's favorite night spots. Everywhere we went the girls knew other people. We received the royal French treatment at every spot. We saw few Americans at any of the spots, and nobody from the airborne. I'm sure many of the places were off limits to GIs.

W. O. Bird was the typical American tourist with a camera around his neck, ready to swing into action at the first sight of a landmark.

For any soldier in the world who got to Paris the first place to see was the Arc de Triomphe (now called Place de Charles deGuale). Haussman Boulevard went straight to the Arc de Triomphe, but that was at least fifteen blocks away. We went to an underground station and took the underground to the Arc de Triomphe.

We stood in awe at the Arc de Triomph standing as a massive gateway arch far out in front of us. No autos, jeeps, trucks or buses were anywhere in sight. We started walking toward it. Bird stopped twice to take pictures at long range. The huge structure stood in the middle of a giant circle of streets running off in every direction. Once under the arch, my feelings changed upon seeing the Eternal Flame. This was the Tomb of the Unknown Soldier for France, our ally in the great wars. I had jumped into Normandy to help free her of four years under Hitler. We stood there, each in our own thoughts for many minutes, feeling kinship to these unknown soldiers.

After a while we walked away and just kept walking. We walked to the Place de Troacadero where the great Palais de Chaillot stood, a vast structure of marble and stone. We climbed the Eiffel Tower and looked at Paris from a paratrooper's view. We could see the Seine make its big bend as it went through the center. Down river on an island lay Notre Dame, the great French cathedral.

Back down to earth we walked along the Seine toward Notre Dame. We crossed over bridges, passed from the left bank and then to the right bank. We stopped on a bench along the river and just relaxed.

After that wonderful evening, W. O. and I immediately laid plans to spend our last night in Paris beginning on the street of Pigalle. Where would two 24-year-old single men rather be? The night began with a fine restaurant.

From dinner we stumbled into a place called "Eve," a large night club with a big floor show. As many as twelve dancing girls were on stage at one time.

W. O. Bird and I spent the rest of Saturday night right there, drinking wine, cognac and champagne all night long. We had showgirls at our table by the dozen. The night closed when several of them escorted two staff sergeants back to the American Red Cross Hotel just in time to catch the 101st Airborne trucks back to Rheims on Sunday morning.

21

How I Heard about the German Breakthrough

As a boy on the farm I'd spent untold hours passing a football back and forth through an old rubber tire hanging from a limb of a giant elm tree. Times were tough in those days, and our small country high school couldn't afford football, so I grew up without any experience playing a real football game.

Now here I was in Nancy, France, getting ready to play in my first real football game on the strength of my ability to pass the football. Our teams were made of lieutenants, sergeants, corporals and other military officers as well as rank-and-file soldiers. I played my heart out, and the game was going fast and furiously when suddenly the loudspeaker system we were using for our game would blast out a call for "Major so-and-so," "Captain so-and-so," "Lieutenant this," and "Corporal that," saying, "You are to report to your squadron at once. On the double!"

Looking across the line from us we saw four of their first-line players walk away from the game. Four substitute players ran onto the field, and we continued to play. Several plays later,

"Colonel this," "Major that," plus two captains and two more lieutenants were called out of the game. As before, "You are to report to your squadrons at once, on the double!"

Two of those officers were on the field when they were called, and two subs ran into the game to take their place. "What the hell is up over at headquarters?" I heard the players on the other side ask the subs. They didn't seem to know, and the game went on.

After a few more plays we could hear the roaring of one after another P-47 plane soaring into the sky. More names were called out, and player after player left the game as the P-47 divebombers flew out in a steady stream and the evening went on.

Something big was up. That was easy to see. Finally the word came out into the field that there was a big push on and that our side had called for air support. We knew who was doing the pushing—General Patton! The news didn't stop the game, and we kept playing to the end.

About halfway through the last quarter, I came out of the game. Coach Swanson called me over to him so he could tell me something. I knelt on one knee next to the coach, who was squatting along by the sideline on our side of the field. He started to show me something on his clipboard when suddenly the lights went out for me! I heard a noise like thundering hooves and then nothing. I vaguely remember seeing Captain Swanson stand up and a surge of humanity moving backwards.

The next thing I remember was the faint sound of my name being called. I heard that call a long time before I could see, and when I could see, the only thing I could make sense of was the blue, blue sky above and a lot of people's legs in front of me.

Slowly I came to my senses and started to crawl through that mass of legs on my hands and knees, saying out loud, "Here I am, captain. Down here. Let me through here, please. Pardon me, please. I got to get through. The captain's calling to me. Hey, up there! He wants me back in the game. Hey! Open up!"

And then I made it.

"Where in the Sam hill have you been, Sergeant Black?" Captain Swanson said to me. "What the devil happened to you anyway. Medic! Someone get the medic over here."

How I Heard about the German Breakthrough

My face was covered with blood, my nose was broken and cut pretty bad. My cheek and forehead had the signs of a pretty good raspberry on them. I looked like hell and felt worse.

Talking with the captain back in the game, I had my helmet off, and I must have caught someone's shoulder pad as he was going full tilt down the side of the field. I was patched up, but I didn't get a chance to have my broken nose set at the field hospital. The Air Force was wining and dining us paratroopers in their style, which is tops for any of the services, and the celebration was under way.

We ate off of a clean white tablecloth and used regular table silverware, plus white china cups for our coffee. We had cake and ice cream as well. Then it was off to the service clubs for beer and dancing. The Air Force even furnished the girls, local French ladies from Nancy. By 8 o'clock my nose didn't hurt any more, and I was having the best day I'd ever spent in this man's army.

Just before I fell asleep I heard loud talking downstairs. I could hear the Air Force people going around putting the base on alert. Their words were clear. "There has been a breakthrough, and paratroopers have been dropped."

"Hey down there!" I yelled. "What's going on? Anything we ought to know about up here?" I woke up everyone.

"Who in hell are those guys upstairs?" I heard someone say.

"They are those football players from the 101st Airborne, our paratroopers," someone said.

"Paratroopers? 101st Airborne? They have been put on alert. Haven't they left yet? Go wake them up! They have got to get back to their camp!"

That's how I heard about the German breakthrough.

It was just after midnight on Monday, December 18, 1944. None of our own officers had come by yet to tell us NCOs what had happened, let alone what we were supposed to do. After talking it over among ourselves, we sent the ranking officer among us over to the Officers Club to find out what the hot poop really was. Back came our fellow soldier with the order. "We NCOs are to stay where we are for the night. Yes, there has been a German breakthrough. But it is way up north in a place called the

Ardennes. Go back to sleep because we are to move out early in the morning for Camp Mourmelon."

What about German paratroopers being dropped in the area? We wanted to know about that rumor. "Yes, there's an alert along the whole ETO front," our messenger said. "Someone said they were dressed like American GIs, and some even thought they might be trying to capture General Ike!"

The next morning we were informed that our key officers were racing back to Camp Mourmelon in a three-jeep caravan and that we were to follow them by truck after breakfast.

Captain Swanson stopped to say a few words to us before he took off in the caravan. "The 101st Division has been alerted to move up," he said. "Somewhere to the north in the Ardennes there has been a breakthrough. It is big enough to cause Ike to send in his reserves. And, just in case you didn't know it, that's what the 101st and 82nd Divisions have been since we left Holland, the ETO Reserve."

Before we could ask why, he said, "Because our two divisions are the *only* reserve. Everyone else is on line!"

When we pulled up in front of our regimental headquarters, there lining all the streets of each company were big semi trucks, the open cattle tractor-trailer type that held half a company on each trailer. The trucks were already loaded down with the entire regiment of 502 paratroopers less the football team. Their engines were running.

It looked like the whole regiment had just been waiting for our football team to get back. My own platoon people even brought me my battle dress, rifle and everything they thought I might want with me. They laid it out for me on the ground beside our company truck.

I changed into my uniform right there beside the truck, all the way down to my bare ass. The orders said it was cold where we were going. "Put on your long johns," was the word, and "Hurry up! We are pulling out in fifteen minutes!" And, by God, we did.

At noon we left Camp Mourmelon for somewhere in Belgium and the Battle of the Bulge.

How I Heard about the German Breakthrough 229

For some reason General Eisenhower took the chance of not having reserves behind each army in a ready-reserve posture for the fight for Bastogne.

The two airbornes divisions (82nd and 101st) were far below their normal strength because of the long time on line in Holland. We were just back from taking great losses and had hardly started to regroup. I thought we would be spending the winter here at Mourmelon, preparing for a jump over the Rhine River into Germany.

The German command at the division level knew they were creating chaos, and that was their goal. Hitler mixed a clever bag of tricks, and Allied intelligence fell for all of them. Far from being a fanatical maniac or a military fool, Hitler showed by his offensive plans for the "Watch on the Rhine" (the Battle of the Bulge) that he was a genius at confusing the enemy and striking at the peak of chaos. The Germans launched a major offensive at 0500 hours (5 a.m.) on Sunday, December 16, 1944. It was forty hours before word came down to us from the Supreme Command's staff that the 82nd and 101st Airborne Divisions would be on our way to the new front.

The Germans rammed straight into the 28th Division and advanced almost five miles the first day and four miles the second. By nightfall they were within eleven miles of Bastogne. Everywhere along the front, Jerry had forced a withdrawal by the VIII Corps of four to six miles.

The mission of the VIII Corps had been to hold in place a line running about 85 miles north and south along "Our River" and the Belgium-Luxembourg-German border. The countryside was called the "Ardennes" and was made up of rugged hills very much like southern Ohio. The terrain and a restricted road network restricted tank warfare.

Six enemy divisions hit the 28th Infantry Division. Two Panzers, three infantry and one paratrooper divisions in an infantry tank attack with ten thousand men to our two thousand and twice as many tanks as we had.

On the third day of Jerry's big offensive, he increased the momentum on the center of the VIII Corps. The push was so overwhelming that their thin lines disintegrated, and Jerry had a major breakthrough.

Now it was only a matter of time. Enemy forces encircled small companies and strong points, wiping them out or capturing them one by one. The command post of the 28th Division was attacked. Stragglers found their way back into Bastogne by late afternoon and evening. Sometime after dark the enemy was within three miles of Bastogne.

At this critical time, probably about 1630 hours (4:30 p.m.), the "C" Company moved into Bastogne. We rode into the area past the aimless drifting of men who once were soldiers. All the mechanized equipment seemed to us to be headed in the wrong direction.

General McAuliffe's party arrived at VIII Corps Headquarters in the Bastogne at the same time that my "C" Company reached our strong point. General McAuliffe had just enough time before dark to take a quick swing in his jeep over the area west of Bastogne to pick out where he wanted to place his division.

Another miracle man rode into town at the same time that McAuliffe landed at the 8th Corps' command post in Bastogne. He was Colonel William Roberts, the head of "Combat Command B" of the 10th Armored Division. He had been on the move since early that morning.

Colonel Roberts' tanks raced to beat darkness. Jerry's troops were pouring down from Houffalize and in from St. Vith and up from Wiltz. In front of them was the staggering tragedy of an American army in defeat. By the next day, Tuesday, December 19, they surrendered what was left to the Germans. In all some eight thousand men were lost, the worst loss of American arms in the war.

Down these same roads came men of the 28th Division. Some say manpower was six to one against our side. Jerry's tanks outnumbered ours four to one. How long can you fight against odds like that?

The 99th Infantry Division gave up several thousand yards of ground and then were combined into the veteran Second Infantry Division under General Robertson's command. They were to stand together making a solid anchor for the north flank. They

How I Heard about the German Breakthrough 231

withstood all the German onslaughts for the remainder of the Battle of the Bulge.

Soldiers from the 14th Cavalry Group attached to the 106th Division also fell back. Many of these men were able to fall back fast enough to keep ahead of the charging elite *Liebenstandart*, the first SS Panzer Division of General Dietrich's. They were then able to join new divisions rushing into the breach, to regroup and fight again in the Bulge. They did so without their group commander, who was "relieved" for withdrawing his troops without an order from the 106th Division.

All roads leading away from the path of the Germans were clogged over a sixty-mile front when darkness fell at the end of the third day. Not just beaten men on foot, but truck after truck hogged the roads and filled the streets of the little towns around Bastogne as our 101st raced against time to deploy their troops and equipment here in defense of Bastogne.

I could see frustration on the faces of our leaders and felt sympathy for them.

Big semi-trucks carrying our First Battalion troopers were trying to work us west of the town of Bastogne by using a bypass. They were using every road they could find. Some were too narrow, contributing to more chaos because there was no advance party waiting for us.

Somewhere on a narrow road just outside of "Long Champs" we came to a standstill at 1600 hours (4 p.m.). Some trucks were stuck after pulling too far off on the side to pass. Groups of battalion and company officers clustered here and there by the side of the road. Regimental officers came by in their jeeps, trying hard to deploy the whole regiment.

I saw General McAuliffe and Colonel Kinnard drive up in their jeeps. While the General was stopped near our truck talking to a group of our officers, someone yelled down from our truck, "Better get these men out of the hot sun and let them dig in before Jerry sends over their Luftwaffe!" The voice was "Big" Holly's, and came across as a plea for our leaders to give us something to do to protect ourselves.

The general must have heard him and agreed with his suggestion. The officers came to attention and gave a snappy salute while old General "Mac" drove on down the line waving to us troopers. Soon the call rang out from our officers, "Off the trucks and into the fields, men! Dig in!"

In nothing flat we were spread out in our platoon units in the bare fields next to the road, all digging foxholes. We spent the night on a hillside at "Long Champs" a few miles northwest of Bastogne. That was the 502nd Parachute Regiment's start in the Battle of the Bulge.

Since they drew the lead in the division's order of march, the 502nd Parachute Regiment was scheduled to be the first into Bastogne and the first to defend it.

General McAuliffe gave the order to Colonel Julian Ewell, the 501st Regiment Commander: "Move out on the attack at 0600 hours (6 a.m.) December 19, down the east road out of Bastogne leading to St. Vith, pass on through the town of Longvilly to a road junction to Noville. Seize that road junction and hold it." The junction was almost ten miles from their assembly area in Bastogne. They started out in darkness with a misty rain falling, but it was not cold. They encountered fog at daylight, which either hurt or helped them, depending on who was talking.

At 2030 hours (8:30 p.m.) Tuesday Lieutenant Colonel Clifford D. Templeton somehow rode into town with his 705th Tank Destroyer Battalion. Now we had the major elements needed to withstand that German seizure until the end and win at Bastogne!

Colonel Templeton and his battalion were situated to the northeast of Bastogne when they got the orders at 1800 hours (6 p.m.) the previous day to march to Bastogne. Within five hours they were rolling. But by then Jerry had closed in on Houffalize, Belgium, in his line of march. The 705th had to swing far to the west and fight their way into Bastogne. By then the Germans had completed their breakthrough in the area called the Bulge.

American units in semi-shock along the roads were falling back everywhere, according to Colonel Templeton, Colonel Ewell and Colonel Roberts. Colonel Ewell tried to find out something about the enemy and his whereabouts from these straggling American soldiers. It was hopeless. They didn't know where they had been or where they were going. Most of them said, "We have been wiped out." They were done fighting. Colonel Ewell knew he was

How I Heard about the German Breakthrough 233

just wasting his time, so he gave up. The retreating Americans stumbled away in the dark.

Colonel Roberts had more trouble with the motorized units of the VIII Corps than with men on foot. He could not get them to give up their motor parks so he could get his vehicles off the streets in the city of Bastogne.

There was no attempt to stop and hold any of these retreating men and their equipment. I don't know why we didn't do that because sooner or later we were going to need all the men we could get. The attitude seemed to be, "We are here now. Get out of our way and let us do our job. This is what we are trained for!"

We were experiencing high morale. We believed that Bastogne was our cup of tea and that it was a job for the airborne (even though we did not jump). "Don't take any kind of a chance by infecting it with those of defeat," was the policy.

By Tuesday afternoon we had all we were going to need, although it would be close a few times. They did not come any better than the men who stood with us in the stand of Bastogne.

The stage for the great showdown at Bastogne had been set as the sole responsibility of Brigadier General Anthony C. McAuliffe. The 101st Airborne Division came under the command of the VIII Corps and would contain the road net in and around Bastogne. The VIII Corps Headquarters moved to safer place in the rear.

This left General Ridgeway with the 18th Airborne Corps intact, less the 101st Airborne. He took the 82nd Airborne Division under his command and moved them to fight on the north side of the Bulge at Webomont.

Commanding officers had the task of placing units in a methodical manner, free of panic, while preserving a strong reserve on the move until we were at last surrounded by our own men.

My regiment, my battalion, and my company, was the last one put on line; we plugged the last hole. My lot on the first day was to walk my legs off from one end of the circle to the other as a "reserve." When I woke up in the morning in a slit-trench foxhole, water was already settling in. The day started with rain and remained foggy and misty most of the day.

It seemed to me that nothing had changed from the way things were three weeks earlier! Only the terrain was different; now there were hills. Same Germans, same noise of war, the same dirty foxhole for a home. We were back in combat.

One thing I knew—it was getting tougher and tougher to go back into combat. The war wasn't so bad; it was fascinating. What got to us GIs who had survived without a scratch was the starting of combat and knowing that sooner or later your luck is bound to run out.

I hadn't been hurt in combat, but my broken nose from that football game in Reims on Christmas Day hurt me worse than I let on. After the game it seemed best to wait until I was back at Camp Mourmelon to see about my nose. But back at the camp it didn't seem like a good time to ask for sick call. Captain Cody took one look at me and said, "You'd better go on sick call in the morning, sergeant. Your nose looks broken."

My two hillbilly friends, Hollingsworth and Milligan, had less respect for my injury. They felt that anyone dumb enough to spend the afternoon down on all fours lined up like a bunch of billy goats across from each other got his fair pay with a broken nose.

The Germans became so obsessed with taking the town of Bastogne that they lost sight of their main objective in the Battle of the Bulge.

The 501st Regiment, led by Colonel Ewell, started the 101st fight. It spread like wildfire from east to north, then to the south and west until the Germans completed the circle. General McAuliffe waited until just the right moment to move his regiments one by one into line. His strategy was to move in the same direction around the circle as the Germans were fighting with us.

As each regiment became fully engaged with the enemy, they established their own reserve. In every case they used their reserve troops to deny the enemy a full breakthrough in their sector.

My regiment established a line of defense near a hill just south of "Long Champs" that overlooked the town. My battalion

How I Heard about the German Breakthrough 235

moved in and spent an uneventful night. The entire regiment was in division reserve and saw no action the second night.

The sounds of war were muffled and far off, but growing closer and closer in the east. We were waiting.

I soon learned what we were waiting on—a call for help by someone else in the division. The 506th Parachute Regiment fighting around Noville and Foy were the first to call on 502nd for support, and the 3rd Battalion responded.

The 3rd Battalion attacked east through Recogne to link with Colonel Sink's 506th troopers at Foy. Our plan was to withdraw back through Foy to high ground where we had a better chance to defend Bastogne. Hit-and-run action like this was costly to both sides, but we were locating the best spots to hold and growing more confident in each other. All of us who would hold Bastogne from the Germans—people with armored tanks, tank destroyer people, artillery people, and infantry men—had to mesh well with each other.

Our first few lessons came hard. The First Battalion of the 506th lost thirteen officers and one hundred ninety-nine enlisted men in support of the armored units at Noville. Another team lost eleven out of fifteen tanks. Jerry lost approximately thirty tanks of all sizes and half a regiment of soldiers (at least eight hundred).

By the third day my First Battalion of the 502nd Regiment had not seen any action. We moved to the edge of a town west of Foy late in the afternoon so that we could provide support to some of our division people under threat of attack by German tanks.

The road into this little town led down a winding hillside with deep cut banks on each side. The town sat in a sunken depression. Darkness took over, and our "C" Company halted on the road for the entire night. My squad dug in on the back side of the last big bend. Fog settled in heavy long before morning. I never could see enough to know what that town looked like in daylight.

We were hit by tank fire off and on all night. It was our first sleepless night on the Bulge. Corporal Charles O'Neill was hit in his foxhole straight across from mine.

At 0730 hours (7:30 a.m.) we marched out of that hot spot—which had cooled down by morning—and went on another forced march down the road, through the fields and over the hills to help Colonel Sink's "G" Company hold on to Recogne.

I walked all over hell that day and personally dug four round, deep foxholes with a small army hand shovel on a wooded hillside where I had to contend with tree roots and rocks. Those of us in the 2nd Platoon did not fire a shot, did not make it to the front lines, did not see a single German and did not lose one trooper to shell fire on that day.

It was like a play. I was waiting to go on stage but for some reason I never quite made it.

The front lines of "G" Company of 506th that we had come to support were drawn over and beyond a large, long, sloping hill. The top of the hill was covered with tall hardwood trees forming a woods at least two hundred yards down the slope of the hill. From that point evergreen trees had been planted in rows running east and west for another hundred yards or so. After that it was bare, farm and pasture land. I remember thinking that any farmer would be proud to own that grass-covered land.

At the point where we would be committed to actual fighting the "G" Company was still holding out. With a long day of waiting and heavy German shelling from time to time, we needed to do some foxhole digging.

I dug a very deep round foxhole, up to my neck. I had a chance to dive head first into it several times before I was finished digging it. I had just settled into it when the call came from ahead to move to another spot several yards away. I dug another foxhole there.

Three times I repeated this procedure while moving up the hill. With each foxhole I had time to stand inside and look around me. The beauty of that hillside outshone the ugliness of war on the other side.

Sometime in late afternoon, maybe about 1700 hours (5 p.m.), we were told that the 506th troopers were going to hold on through the night. Captain Cody pulled "C" Company back down that beautiful hillside to an area just inside the evergreen tree line.

We dug single close-together foxholes among young spruce evergreens that were no more than fifteen feet tall but had a wide branch spread at the bottom. It was easy digging under those

How I Heard about the German Breakthrough 237

branches, and they protected us from the weather. We knew that Jerry wouldn't stumble into our holes during the darkness of night while on patrol.

My fifth day in the "Bulge" began at 0200 hours (2 a.m.) when I took my turn on a two-hour hitch of guard duty along the treeline. While on guard we stood outside our foxholes, making sure that the guard next to you, on both sides, can hear you. It was very dark, so we talked to keep posted.

"OK here in the second position," I said. Both men answered me.

As I stood out in the open away from the tree branches, something brushed against my face. A paratrooper's heavy jumpsuit plus the big steel helmet keeps the weather at bay, and I was concentrating on my duty at hand, so it was a while before I realized what it was.

It was cold, but we were used to living like this and didn't notice the cold that much. Not yet anyway. No one said anything for a long time about the fact that it was snowing. It was the second time in our whole army experience that we had seen snow for most of us.

About 0300 hours (3 a.m.) it came to me that the snow was really putting down. We could actually *hear* snowflakes falling!

I started the word that kept up until daylight. "Everything OK! Snowing up here in 2nd Platoon." All over the hillside could be heard a guard's call ending with, "Snowing here, too!"

What a beautiful sight was waiting for us when we woke up in the morning! We just stood around and gazed in awe. There must have been four or five inches of wet snow hanging on everything. Everywhere you looked it was white.

The whole First Battalion began marching off the hill, through the valley, winding slowly off in the distance heading for the far hill. It was black on white, with the battalion moving in single file. I was the last trooper to leave the hill, so I had time to sit and watch. Three companies of paratroopers—at least 500 of us—all moving in single file as if playing a game of follow-the-leader.

"C" Company moved into a wooded area on a hillside along a main road two miles east of Champs. My Second Squad and

Holly's First Squad went to the far high side of this little woods and dug in as the outer defense for the night.

Just as it was growing dark in the Grosse Hez woods, we heard chow call from our company mess people. It was our first hot chow since landing in the Bulge five days earlier.

We sat on the edges of our foxhole eating our hot chow in this beautiful snow-draped woodland. We ate in silence as we listened to the Germans pound away at Bastogne from four sides.

I think it was Rennie Howard who said, "I don't know what you guys think, but I have a damned funny feeling we're stuck in here!"

"What the hell do you mean by that shit?" snorted Milligan.

"Damn it, can't you hear those 88s?" said Howard.

"Hell yes! I can hear the sons-of-bitches! And I'm getting damned tired of it," Milligan shot back.

"Hear that?" Howard pointed his GI spoon toward the east. "Hear that? And that?" He moved his spoon to the north and then to the west. Then he pointed to the south as if queuing in the Germans. He waited, spoon in air. No sound of guns in the south. Then we heard them. "There!" he said. "What did I tell you? Hell, men! We're surrounded!"

Nobody said a word after that. We all got up and checked foxholes. We had a long lonely night in a pitch dark woods to think about what Howard had said. As we tried to sleep we could hear the guns pounding away.

That night German Luftwaffe began bombing attacks on the city of Bastogne. It was close enough that I bounced off the ground every time the bombs exploded. After each bombing run the planes circled over my head, adding to the stress.

In the morning we were told to pack up our gear and prepare to move out as the division's reserves. We moved without breakfast, not even a K-ration to a place called Hemroulle about two miles west of Bastogne.

As we fell into formation ready for the line of march, we could hear our company officers talking about being surrounded. No one was saying it for sure, just that it was probable. When I looked at Sergeant Howard, he gave me a faint smile that said, "I told you so!"

How I Heard about the German Breakthrough 239

"C" Company moved into the little farming village of Hemroulle, Belgium. My 2nd Platoon moved to a bare hillside on the outskirts of the village. We dug in a line of defense in case of a breakthrough in the 327th Glider Regiment, now under heavy attack by both tanks and infantry.

Added to the frustration of walking our legs off, digging one foxhole after another, not really knowing what's going on except that the circle around us was growing smaller was the news that food and ammunition supplies were growing short. How could that be? We hadn't eaten much. Only one hot meal in six days and no food at all today, and it was almost noon. Short of ammo? We hadn't fired a shot yet in the whole damned company!

Word was sent to our foxholes, "Send a few men at a time to come in with their mess kit. Make sure no one misses." It was our only meal of the whole day, at 1100 hours (11 a.m.), and what we had to eat was one pancake apiece. The First Sergeant told us we were out of food. "At least," he said, "until our planes can get through." He added, "We are mighty low on gas for the tanks and ammo for our big guns. Our medical supplies are in desperate shape. Our wounded are in dire straits. They're short of blankets back in Bastogne. Hell! We're not bad off out here in "C" Company, men! Look at all those cows down the street we can eat."

Then Sergeant Grotjan got mad. "Would you believe, men, that those bastard Krauts think they've got us surrounded? They had the damnedest nerve yesterday to ask General Mac to surrender us. He told them, 'Nuts!' We got a bunch of troopers out there in 'C' Company that haven't fired a shot yet!'"

At 1200 hours (noon) the sun began to shine. I saw my shadow first and then looked up and saw the sun. A big cheer went up from everybody. People in Bastogne ran out into the streets, into the fields, out into the open, all over that "bulge." Within two minutes a giant roar filled the sky above us. It was the roar of 241 C-47 planes dropping 144 tons of supplies. For the next two days the fighter planes of the USAF tore hell out of the German armored troops. We hadn't seen our fighter planes for six days since we drove in here from France.

It was warm in the sun, and we stood outside our foxholes watching those brightly colored parachutes fall softly to the ground. None of them fell near my area at Hemroulle.

On Sunday we were in the same spot, still in reserve for the regiment. We did not fire a single shot. The first of the supplies to come in were ammo, medical supplies, gas and other essentials. Winter clothing was still in short supply in all of our front-line companies, and the weather had turned cold and windy.

Captain Cody called the whole company to come out of the wind and allowed us to start fires at the barns on the edge of the small farm village of Hemroulle even with Jerry still hammering away in the west at the 327th Regiment's lines.

To keep warm, we burned up all of a Belgian farmer's pile of twigs he'd tied in neat little bundles and piled under a lean-to. When he came home that night and saw the big fire, he had a fit. We were sorry!

22

Christmas in Bastogne

Since it had become bitter cold for the first time in the Bulge, Sergeant DeWitt moved the 2nd Platoon into an old barn with a hayloft. We bedded down with the darkness, except for those who were on guard. We crawled up into the hayloft, got into our sleeping bags and covered ourselves with loose hay. I was never that warm again in the Bulge.

Bastogne was surrounded, and we sensed that trouble was about to break out here at Hemroulle. We knew that "C" Company was overdue for action on the front lines. We lay there in the dark in the rickety barn, nobody asleep, just thinking.

Someone from that soft hayloft bed called out, "Sergeant Black! Are you asleep yet?"

"No, not yet!"

"When do you think we are going up?"

"Maybe tonight. Better get some sleep." I tried to sound calm.

"Sergeant Bird," somebody else called out. "Are you asleep yet? They won't fight on Christmas Eve, will they?" I don't remember Bird's answer.

I thought about home, about Christmas in the States, about Mom and Dad, about my best girl, my three brothers and my sister. Also, I thought about the very first Christmas, the barn, the hayloft, in a far-off time. What did it all mean?

One thing I didn't think about was of the 101st ever giving up, of us losing here in Bastogne.

Maybe it was 2000 hours (8 p.m.) when someone came into the barn, yelled, "Santa Claus is here!" and passed out a box of cookies to each of us. They just might have been the best cookies I ever ate.

Sometime after that I fell asleep. What woke me up was the terrible shaking of our old barn and the noise of German bombs falling nearby. Some men went outside to have a look.

Our guards told us that the Germans had bombed Bastogne at midnight and that fires could be seen from outside our hayloft. We fell back asleep only to be awakened at 0330 hours (3:30 a.m.). This time there were orders: "Get ready to move up and back up our Regiment's front lines." Our "C" Company was in a real dog fight with Jerry, and it looked like they needed help for sure.

We got ready in a hurry with few words. Everyone knew it was coming—the fighting. What upset me the most was that Jerry wasn't going to take Christmas off!

We moved out onto the road out of Hemroulle at 0400 hours (4 a.m.). Our "B" Company, which was also in reserve still and not yet on line, had moved ahead of us into the lead. They had been ordered to go to the very edge of Champs and await daylight before moving in to help "A" Company hold the line. By now Jerry had broken through on the east side of them in the area of our Second Battalion.

Our "C" Company moved about halfway up the road. My 2nd Platoon, in close-order marching formation, held up on the road next to the farm house that was the command post of the 327th Glider Regiment.

It had taken us three hours, until 7 a.m., to move half a mile up the road. There we were halted and stood in full battle dress, loaded down with heavy ammo, machine guns, mortars and bazookas. We had our heavy overcoats on but still had not received winter boots,

Christmas in Bastogne 243

sweaters, hoods and other winter clothing. It was cold, and everything was covered with snow. We were jumpy.

While I was standing there with my fellow troopers, not seeing or knowing the meaning of what was going on, a dogfight took place in the black sky above. A German plane shot down one of our big planes. I saw it go down in flames just behind German lines. No one got out. But maybe it was dark, and I just couldn't see them jump. Damn the Germans, I'm cold! Let's move off this road! It's colder than hell! Start a fire. It's getting daylight anyway. Damn those Germans! I hope those bastards do see us and come on the run. "C" Company hasn't fired a shot yet.

We moved off the road and into the courtyard of the farmhouse. About thirty troopers, the whole platoon at this point, moved in and started a fire to warm up by. Somebody started to heat up coffee. I took my time setting up my squad's machine gun at the corner of the courtyard gate. I faced it due west with a line of fire to the open field on top of a hill some eight hundred yards away. I told a gunner to keep an eye open and to take turns with the other gunners coming over to the fire.

It was just starting to get daylight when we moved off the road. I remarked to "Big" Holly that it was going to be a foggy Christmas morning. I realized my whole 2nd Platoon was standing around a fire in the center of some else's command post. This battalion command post was leaving. We hadn't started the fire. They had, to burn maps and papers. I saw the colonel. He was leaving on foot for somewhere else.

At the command post of the 327th Glider Regiment's 3rd Battalion. The cry, "German tanks!" rang out. All hell broke loose.

The first thing you do when you're being fired at in battle is to look for the biggest gun you have. But as "Big" Holly and I reached the gate, my 30-caliber machine gun was flying through the air in pieces. The first round from a German tank had caught that gun as we stood on the cold road near Hemroulle.

Enemy tanks have a way of freezing men in their tracks. Eighteen of them topping the hill ahead was a devastating sight.

Survival was my only thought. Surrender was never one of them. "Every man for himself!" I called out the order. "Get the hell out of here! Head for the trees!" The saying goes, "He who turns and runs away may live to return and fight another day!"

Not everyone in the 2nd Platoon in that area of the farm quadrangle heard me or was able to react. The rest of the "C" Company was standing out in the road.

I learned later that the German Armored had made a big breakthrough in the 327th Glider Regiment's 3rd Battalion area at 0715 hours (7:15 a.m.) on Christmas Day. This was due west of their battalion's command post, where my 2nd Platoon was trying to get warm.

Eighteen enemy M-IV tanks came straight at us until they reached the top of the long hill. Then with infantrymen riding and walking alongside the tanks, they fanned out left and right. Some headed for Hemroulle to the south; others cut north to swing into Champs and catch our "A" Company from the rear.

They were firing their rifles and tank guns as they came our way. Seven of the tanks came on straight at us. If you were going north you could have walked on steel.

This farm was a split-level with the house over the horse and cow stables. We could not run out of the courtyard, through the stables and straight out on the level to the Hemroulle-Champs road.

I took a trip in among the big Belgium draft horses, calling for my squad to follow me. I knew time was running out on us if I couldn't find a way out through there. Horses eat hay, I reasoned, and you put hay in a mow over the horses. "Find the hay chute," I said. Once in the hay mow, I found a door to a hallway leading into the house and out the front door onto a roadway on the east side.

We could muster all the guts we had or we could stay and surrender. As I came down the hall, Colonel Allen, Commanding Officer of the 3rd Battalion, 327th Glider Regiment, was going out the front door running straight for the young fir thicket with low-hanging branches just east of the front door. I could see German tracer bullets all over his head.

I didn't wait to see if he made it (he did). The Colonel's run was at least two hundred yards to the first cover of any kind. I decided to take a shorter route, maybe half as far, but I would lose the cover of the house much quicker.

Christmas in Bastogne

The first cover was a man-made mound of dirt about four and a half feet high and a hundred feet long. It was a typical European storage place for potatoes. Jerry fired too high, and I made it. At the end of the potato pile I took off my heavy GI coat because I knew I would have to do some real running. I was only a third of the way to the trees. As I lay on my back taking my coat off, I could see 30-caliber bullets above me. They were about seven feet in the air above ground.

Just then the 2nd Platoon Mortar Sergeant, Gene Griffith, ran up and hit the ground by me. He was OK. Then another trooper. Then another. Then it was time for me to move on again. I took off, and the rest came one by one.

Halfway up this long hillside, already in the open past the tree line, I looked up. There stood Captain Cody with his arms raised high. "Hold up right there!" he said. "This is as far as we're going to run. Turn around! We are going back and fight the bastards!

From where we stopped we could see over the treetops below. The Germans had halted and had not followed us. Four noncommissioned officers—Sergeant Holly, Sergeant Bird, Sergeant Griffith, and me—set about checking to see what men and equipment we could find. We found half the platoon, but no machine guns, mortars or bazookas. Captain Cody started us back for a counter attack. We did not have a platoon leader or a platoon sergeant. No radio man. No medic. We had a mortar sergeant, but no mortar. The same was true with machine gunner.

The thought of the other men—were they killed or captured?—spurred us on. Then we met up with other "C" Company men from the First and 3rd Platoons. They were scattered, too, but in good shape.

Halfway back to the farmhouse command post, we were cocky about our chances of taking on all those German tanks. Out of nowhere appeared two 704th U.S. T.D.'s (tank destroyers) showed up in the woods. When we were within two hundred yards of the farmhouse, we could see four of Jerry's tanks sitting there with their infantry milling around the house.

Some of the Jerrys were cooking their breakfast. They had made the mistake of not coming after us or not being ready for a counter attack.

We opened up at the same time. We poured all our rifle fire into that old farm house. All four tanks took off north, headed down the road toward Champs, one right behind the other, as if the only thing that mattered was saving the tanks.

German infantrymen rushed out of the farm house to catch a ride on the tanks. Many of them were cut down by our rifle fire, now crossfire of the Second, First and 3rd Platoons of "C" Company.

I walked along near the edge of the potato pile next to Staff Sergeant Don Williams, from Connecticut. He was a platoon sergeant for the "C" Company's 705th T.D. Battalion. Two of his T.D.'s were following us at a slow pace. Williams asked me to hold up my men while he taught the Germans a small lesson in tank warfare.

Sergeant Tony D'Angelo was the tank commander of the T.D. nearest me. He was out of his T.D. walking in front to lead his tank around the big trees. He stopped his driver beside me. I heard him say to his gunner inside, "Take the last tank first, and then one at a time on up the line. Fire when ready!"

The gunner fired point blank into the side of each M-IV enemy tank. The last tank and so on down the road was hit and caught fire. The T.D. next to me fired six shots. Two hit big trees, four hit tanks, and four were knocked out. It was the best hit I ever saw.

As for the German infantry, not a man got away.

Some of our men were pouring rifle fire into the farmhouse when a white flag began to wave back and forth at the front door. We stopped firing and out stepped Corporal Milligan from my squad. The fighting ended, and all of the 2nd Platoon troops Jerry had captured came running out of that old farm house. They were a happy bunch of troopers. They knew the victory had come just in time. That old house was on fire, blazing to the sky.

We got everyone back in my platoon but one. Private First Class Bernard Korst, from Sergeant Griffith's mortar squad, was badly wounded and ended up leaving the war for the States. Also, Lieutenant Porter C. Little from the 2nd Platoon was killed in action on this Christmas Day.

Our "C" Company took thirty-five prisoners and killed sixty-seven Germans for our part in that Christmas morning fight. The

Christmas in Bastogne 247

real glory to save the front lines and prevent a major German breakthrough belongs to our "A" Company, which captured eighty-one Germans and killed ninety-eight. Private John Ballard knocked out a tank with his bazooka. Our Regimental Headquarters from 502nd got credit for knocking out a tank. The other twelve German tanks were finished off by the 327th Gliders. Most shooting was at point blank.

After the fight we "mopped up" the battleground area—the thick trees, hillside, farm house, barn and yard. Now freed, our 2nd Platoon men who had been captured and held by Jerry wanted some sort of revenge. Our round-up was like a fox drive, where you drive all the foxes into a small circle and then capture or kill them. W. O. Bird, "Big" Holly and I went hunting together. We found a badly wounded German soldier at the edge of the fir trees. He was wounded too badly to speak or move. Seated with him in the snow was a soldier that couldn't have been more than fourteen years old. He was half frozen and scared to death. We saw that the boy was not going to be able to move his wounded friend, so I went for help.

By now a small circle of prisoners had developed at the edge of the woods near the road. A truck was waiting to load the prisoners. I took one of the prisoners back with me to have him help carry his countrymen to the circle. He talked the boy into helping him, but it was a long walk, and the boy wasn't much help. The more he yelled at the boy, the worse it got.

We made them drag the wounded man the last few yards into the circle of prisoners. The prisoners who had watched from the circle began to yell at the boy to the effect that because of him the wounded German might die.

At this moment one of our own troopers walked out of nowhere, moved into the circle and dropped to one knee. He took aim with his rifle and fired point blank, shooting the boy through the head. He was dead before he hit the ground.

We rounded up thirty-five prisoners. I enjoyed a feeling of success as they were put on that truck like cattle. Even the dead boy was thrown onto the truck. The sick and disgusted feeling I had was only for the way our officer had killed the boy, not that he had done so.

On that truck was living proof of a great "C" Company victory. Even General George C. Patton came to look upon it in a few days.

It must have been 1600 hours (4 p.m.) when we settled back in our newly furnished homes. We enjoyed winter-time combat comfort, eating K rations and drinking hot coffee by the canteen cup. We had been resupplied after the fight. Now we had all the ammo we needed. Machine guns, mortars and bazookas were brought up to us. Behind us, well dug in, were our American TDs. We were in a strong position.

It was still daylight when a division runner appeared out of nowhere. He was delivering a Christmas card from General McAuliffe to each man. Part of it said,

> Merry Christmas! What's merry about all this, you ask? We're fighting—it's cold—and we aren't home. All true, but what has the proud Eagle division accomplished with its worthy comrades? Just this: we have stopped cold everything that has been thrown us from north, east, south and west. How effectively this was done will be written in history; not alone in our division's glorious history, but in world history. Well Done
>
> A. C. McAuliffe

Christmas night was quiet, but we pulled guard duty in two-man shifts of two hours on and two off. As the day after Christmas unfolded, we stood in place and by noon we were moving back across the road into the thick wooded area of fir trees. We dug in as the reserve for our own regiment but we were still behind the 327th Glider Regiment. I dug a slit-trench foxhole to lie stretched out under the low-hanging branches by a young fir tree. I had a warm bed even though it snowed.

Our next move took us north of the regiment's command post at Rolle into a wooded area of hardwood trees thinly placed along a hillside overlooking a brook that wound its way through the valley far below us on into Rolle.

My squad and the mortar squad dug in on the southeast corner at the top of the hill. We built a pit fire and dug slit trenches close around the fire. We put hay and straw in our trenches for bedding and covered the top to keep the snow out. We stayed in that spot for

Christmas in Bastogne 249

three days, as quiet as any I spent in the Bulge. It was cold but sunny. This made for good flying weather, and our boys were flying and keeping the German Panzers hidden from sight.

We got the good word that the 4th Armored Division had finally broken through to us from the south late the previous night. With them came our Commanding General, Maxwell D. Taylor, who had missed the show so far. All of the good news made little difference as far as we were concerned. The bitterest days in the battle were yet to come.

Sergeant Griffith and his mortar squad were down to three men; one of them was Sergeant Rennie Howard. Howard had been in the mortar squad as long as I could remember and led his squad in Holland after Sergeant Colon was killed. For some reason, Sergeant Griffith had taken over the squad once he joined us just before the Bulge. Now Sergeant Howard held an enviable position in the 2nd Platoon. He was an extra noncommissioned officer and had no one to command. He could do as he damned well pleased.

One thing Sergeant Howard liked to do was go out on a one-man scouting mission when things were quiet. We called it "snooping and pooping." He was a one-man "field problem" looking for something to eat.

The 502nd had been famous for field problems all the way back to the States. Back in Tennessee we went "snooping and pooping" for water. In Normandy it was wine. In Holland, meat and fruit jam. Here in the Bulge it was food of any kind.

Sergeant Howard hit the jackpot—three hams! "I was only saving them from a burning smokehouse," he said. Plus we had bread and a sack of potatoes from our supplies. With our pit fire going full blast all day long, we ate hot ham all hours of the day and night. The smell brought sightseers up to our hill for three days. We ate well the last days of 1944. As W. O. Bird put it one day after paying me his third visit that afternoon, "Sergeant Black, you sure have a great view from your patio! What a place for a cookout!"

We didn't do any shooting, but there was still fighting around Bastogne. There was always artillery along the front, and small company-sized attacks sprang up here and there every day. A few German JU-88s slipped in at night and bombed Bastogne.

History tells us that Hitler ordered a new concentrated attack on Bastogne. On December 28, at a meeting in Hitler's Berlin headquarters, Hitler was persuaded by General Jodl, his chief of operations, to abandon the campaign to cross the Meuse River. This change in strategy marked the end of Germany's success in the Bulge. It was, however, by no means the end of their effort to hold onto the ground they had won east of the Meuse River.

Before noon we moved up in a push to get into the front lines at Champs on the southwest side of "A" Company. A German patrol caught us on the way and pinned us down. They had a machine gun set up at the crossroad and fired a "delay action" to get their men out first.

A single machine gun can pin a whole company down if it is in the right spot. We had just walked out of the wooded area, down across and open field and up to the crossroads. All of a sudden, the "Rat-a-tat-tat" of a German machine gun put us flat out and face down in the snow.

Since my platoon was in the lead, I was right up front when their gunner opened up. As we all lay there in the road, we could hear the sound of a vehicle approaching. It came straight down the road headed for the crossroads in front of me. I looked up and saw an American jeep coming like a bat out of hell straight into the line of fire of the German machine gun. The top of the jeep was down and, standing with both hands on top of the windshield, was General George S. Patton. There was no mistaking him. His dress, that helmet, those pearl-handled pistols identified him. Above all else, what general would be out in the front lines but old "blood-and-guts" Patton?

Patton's jeep pulled up in front of me and slid to a stop. Not a shot was fired. (Jerry had run when they heard the jeep coming.) General Patton did not understand any of this. He said, "Your Colonel (Chappuis) brought me out here to show me the brave paratroopers who knocked out all those tanks on Christmas morning. I find you all lying face down in the snow. Get the hell up out of there before you all catch pneumonia and die!"

We got up and crossed the road. No more Germans the rest of the day. I've always said, "You have to be lucky to be good!" General George S. Patton was both.

23

"Where the Hell Did that Shell Hit?"

I dug in on a thick evergreen hillside just outside the small village of Champs. For the first time in the "Bulge" we of the 2nd Platoon were finally on the front lines. As I dug in it started to snow—big, flaky, heavy, wet snow.

It was cold now and would stay that way the rest of the time in the Bulge. War was bad enough; the cold weather and the snow made it that much worse.

Before I could use my foxhole, the call rang out over the hillside, "Send Sergeant Black down here." It was the Platoon Sergeant, Curtis DeWitt. When I got to him, he said, "See the lieutenant over in the next foxhole."

First Lieutenant Wall had special orders for me. "Sergeant Black," he said, "take your squad over there to the top of that big hill. It's just fifteen hundred yards west of Champs. Move down the far slope about two hundred yards into a small patch of thick, young pine trees. Dig in deep. You'll be out there on a point all by yourself. You are to be a listening post at night and in the daytime you will be an artillery outpost. Regiment is stringing up a private line up there for you. It will go back to Company and on to Regiment. The Division will also be able to hook in. They know there's a buildup in front of you, and they want to know what is going on at all times. The Germans are down the hill about a mile from you in a little town. You'll be able to see the town from up there. Report everything you see and hear. Everything. Is that clear, Sergeant?"

"Too damned clear," I said.

First Lieutenant Wall went on, "Pick out your own foxholes and set up your machine guns to defend yourselves. Remember, you're on your own! Keep the line open on your end. You'll have twelve men with yourself. That's ten rifles plus two machine guns and two bazookas. Take all the ammo you can carry. Get up there and get set before dark!"

"You said two machine guns?"

"Yes, I did. You will have Sergeant Bird and his gun crew with you, giving you twelve men all together."

W. O. Bird had just come onto the scene. I looked at him; he smiled undaunted approval that we were going to be together.

"Is that all I need to know?" I asked Lieutenant Wall.

"Not quite. Watch your step going in there, Sergeant, and hold the noise down when you get there. Jerry can see you all the way, and they can hear you after you are there. Oh, yes! One other point I should tell you about. Sergeant Hollingsworth's squad will be three hundred yards to your left, dug in on a line running to your rear. On your right Private First Class William Haddick will have his machine gun crew from the 1st Platoon. Straight behind you will be the mortar squad with Sergeants Howard and Griffith. They will dig in on the crest of your hill. Whatever you do, hang in there and keep 'em posted! Remember that! We're back in town backing you up!"

Those last words rang in my ears for the next several days. To my men I said, "Spread out, and keep it down, men. We are going over there where that patch of trees is, and Jerry can see us coming all the way!"

It was 1500 hours (3 p.m.) when we moved out. We made that long march through the deep snow, carrying all of our equip-

Where the Hell Did that Shell Hit? 253

ment in one trip in dead silence. That in itself was something; to do it without a single shot from Jerry was even better.

Standing in the tree patch I laid out for my squad what we were going to do. I laid out our field of fire—straight ahead, down that long hill for at least a mile, due west to the bottom. For 180 degrees in front of that patch of trees it was all downhill to a small valley. Over in the northwest corner lay the small town of Gievry, which was full of Germans. It was the biggest field of fire I had ever seen.

The tree patch canceled our movement in the daylight, but it stuck out like a sore thumb on that hillside. The patch was only thirty yards deep and maybe six yards long. The trees were evergreen spruce at least twenty-five feet tall, planted in straight rows about fifteen feet apart.

On our left flank as we looked down the hill at our Germans, it was three hundred yards to a point where the hill fell sharply off to the south. Sergeant Hollingsworth had his men dug into two-man foxholes at that point for a hundred yards. He had eight men in four holes thirty yards apart. He was my cover for my left flank.

But there was a gap of three hundred yards. Holly was on the south slope, and we could not see each other. The same was true for my right flank to the north where the 1st Platoon started on a line with Pfc William Haddick's machine gun.

Our 2nd Platoon mortar squad (Sergeants Griffith and Howard) were dug in off the crest of the hill to the rear slope. They overlooked the town of Champs to the east and could not see a single one of the foxholes of our three squads.

It seemed to me from the top of that hill where our 2nd Platoon had dug in that we had built an underground stronghold like the one Jerry used when he went on the defensive in January. I believe we could have held that hill forever.

I called Sergeant Bird aside and asked him to come with me to look our tree patch over. We decided together where to put the men. Our main concern was the two machine guns. We decided to place my machine gun in the center of tree patch on a line with the second row of trees in from the edge nearest the Germans. We put

Bird's machine gun on the same line but thirty to forty yards to the left of the tree patch.

I had my riflemen dig single stand-up foxholes that were eye-level deep on the same line as the machine guns. All my men were inside the tree patch but one. I moved one trooper further out on the left flank because of a haystack that cut our line of vision to the south.

Sergeant W. O. Bird and I knew that our main problem would be German shelling. Once we started to dig in they would lay the big stuff on us. I felt sure Jerry would try to knock me out first with artillery and then send up a patrol after dark to capture what was left. Their concern would be to deny us the use of this patch of trees as an outpost in our daylight shelling of them. We both agreed that the snow was helping us and that we should keep pushing the men.

We were mostly right in our thinking, but Jerry gave us too much time. It seemed easier digging in that little woods. Or maybe we just dug in faster. We had time to put hay in our foxholes and get all set in place before dark. This gave me time to visit each of my men at their holes. I told them what I thought we could look for and warned them to stay ready. "We should eat now," I said, "and plan for a long night ahead." Everyone was to stay awake; this whole tree patch was to be on guard all night.

I dug my foxhole just a few feet away from the machine gun in order to be in the center of my squad. Our radio man ran the telephone line in under cover of darkness. That did it. Our "incoming mail" started to arrive. First it was small mortars, one at a time, but they kept it up steady. Then the big stuff—88s. They let us have it! I don't know how long it kept up, at least into overtime.

We lost only one man, but he was my first machine gunner. He could still walk, so I sent him to the rear after telling company headquarters over the telephone that he was on his way back.

Since I had been a machine gunner, I decided to move in with Milligan on the gun and take the telephone along. I felt that was better than weakening any point in the dark. I was sure the Germans were coming after us with a good-sized patrol at least. I knew the value of my men working as a team. As long as each trooper is sure the trooper on his right and left is still there and knows him, he will be dependable and tough as hell to root out of his hole.

I passed the word to everyone to be ready for attack. "Don't shoot at the first thing that moves. We don't want to give away our positions until we have to." Once more I said, "Throw a hand grenade first! Above all, don't leave your foxhole. You could get shot by one of us! From now on—no talking. Keep still!"

That's how it began at 2200 hours (10 p.m.), according to the glowing numbers on my GI watch.

As the last day of the year came upon us it was still snowing, and Jerry's big stuff (88s) kept going back over our heads, landing somewhere in Champs. I knew the Germans were on foot in front of us now, at least a patrol.

I was sure the Germans wanted only our tree patch now, in the darkness, but with daylight they would attack in full strength with tanks and everything else. I could hear them building up in the small town in front of me all evening and into the night.

Corporal Milligan and I were concerned about a German patrol that we wouldn't be able to see until they were on top of us. I was sure Jerry would come straight up the hill and into our tree patch rather than try to flank us. I didn't think they knew about our 300-yard gap on each flank that they could use to bypass us and take us from the rear. I was so sure of this that Milligan and I didn't spend any time watching our rear.

From the time I jumped in with Corporal Milligan to help on the machine gun, I reported everything by telephone that I could see and hear. There was plenty to report: Noises from tanks, trucks and horse-drawn wagons as the Germans moved in the small town of Gievry straight down in front of us.

At about 2300 hours (11 p.m.) Jerry lifted his 88 fire over our heads to Champs. For their rest of the night they kept up with harassing fire and succeeded 100 percent. They sent two to four rounds of 88s at a time off and on until morning. Always the shells went over our heads at the tree patch outpost.

I stopped talking non-stop when the shelling picked up and for the next two hours only answered questions in a whisper. At that point Milligan took over phone duty and tried to keep up with the incessant questions Captain Cody asked. He had set up our "C" Company's command post in one of the better buildings in Champs and was determined that our tree patch outpost would be his listening post. For at least an hour Milligan did his best sending information back to Cody. By the time the shelling of Champs passed the three-hour mark, the captain had boiled things down to one question: "Where did that one hit?"

It went something like this: Jerry would send up to four 88s in a row over our heads. We would hear a "Powww!" way down in the valley below us. Then a loud "S-s-s-s-s-s-s-s-s-s-s!" over our heads just missing the top of the hill behind us. A short pause, then "Bang! Bang!" behind us somewhere in or near the town of Champs. As soon as the last one landed, over our telephone wire from "C" Company's command post: "Where did that one hit?"

Corporal Milligan whispered, "One thousand yards to our rear, two hundred yards to our right," or "Fourteen hundred yards to our rear, one hundred yards to our left," or "Twelve hundred yards to our rear, dead behind us." And so it went into the last day of 1944.

I often wondered why our CP in Champs bothered to ask us where we thought the shells were landing since no one from there had bothered to come out to see where we were in the first place.

We could control the noise when we were whispering, but the fact that the phone was always on gave us more problems than our whispering. If anyone wanted to talk to us at our end, they would give a loud, shrill whistle into their end of the phone. That sound could be heard several feet away. At night, on the front lines, it was like yelling to the Germans, "Here we are, down in this foxhole!"

Milligan and I were sure we saw something moving out in front of us. The words, "Open fire," were only a breath away from my lips. The only thing that held me back was the fact that we didn't see it at the same time. It was more like Milligan saying, "Black, did you see that?"

"No, where?"

"There!"

"What was it?"

Where the Hell Did that Shell Hit?

"Something moved!"
"I didn't see anything. Can you still see it?"
"No!"
Then it was my turn.
"Hey, Milligan, what was that?"
"Where?"
"Over there!"
"You mean, right there?"
"No! Over more to my left."
"Oh! That's that bush again, I think!"
"Did you hear it or did you see it, Sergeant?"
"I thought I saw something. It must have been that bush. Yeah, that's what it was. Man, I almost pulled the trigger on this air-cooled baby that time!"

Time went on for a while without either of us saying anything. At last Corporal Milligan broke the silence. "Boy, Sergeant," he said, "it's snowing harder than ever now."

"How can you tell?" I asked.

"Water is running off my face and dripping down my neck."

"Hell, Milligan. That's not water; that's sweat."

Just as we had talked ourselves out of seeing things, Jerry sat down to play another tune on his 88s. "Powww! Powww! Powww! Powww! S-s-s-s-s-s-s-s! Bang! Bang! Bang! Bang!" Total silence.

Wow! What a tune that was! Best of the night so far. You could reach out and touch those shells. They scratched the ground getting over the hill behind us. I was sure they were hitting downtown Champs by now.

Suddenly out of the dead silence the damnedest whistling noise I have ever heard blared out of our foxhole. The hair stood up on the back of my neck. I was sure the Germans heard that clear to Gievry. All of my men out to the haystack heard it.

That was the straw that did it. Milligan held the phone receiver in his right hand as he waited for the question. Captain Cody's words came in a mad rush, "Where did that one hit?" And again, "Where did that one hit?" And once more, "What did that one hit?" Finally, as if he realized his voice might not be clear, he asked once more, "Where in hell did those shells hit?"

Milligan stared straight ahead, sitting as stiff as a board. Waiting to be sure there were no more questions he said, slowly and clearly as I've ever heard anyone talk, "Right on top of the damned Company CP!"

Dead silence followed. Then at the top of his lungs Captain Cody cried out, "Don't get smart with me! I'm the company Commander of 'C' Company, Captain Cody! To whom am I speaking?"

At that, Milligan must have forgotten where he was because he stood straight up out of our foxhole, came to attention and said loud and clear, "Corporal Marvin Roundhead Jumpknife Milligan! Haven't you ever heard of him?"

Captain Cody was yelling out of the phone now, "What company are you from, Corporal? What company are you from, Corporal?"

I pulled Milligan down inside the foxhole and yelled, "Open fire!" I held the trigger down on the machine gun. As as I did, everybody else opened up, too. I threw several hand grenades, and so did everybody else.

I don't know how long we had firing when Corporal Milligan came to himself. "What in hell happened?" he asked me.

I said, "That last batch of 88s hit the company command post, so I opened up on these damned Germans!"

Milligan said, "Are you shittin' me, Sergeant? The Germans hit our Company CP?"

"Hell yes! I'm sure," I said.

"How do you know?" he said.

"By God, because you said so!"

Then I started to laugh. I laughed until tears ran down my face.

In between our laughing, firing and throwing hand grenades, no Germans got through to us in our tree patch all night. We kept firing for half an hour of so, using up two boxes of machine gun ammo, all of our hand grenades and half of our rifle ammo. We had yet to fire our bazooka.

Where the Hell Did that Shell Hit? 259

We'd made it through the Germans' attempt to capture us, but I was sure daylight would bring us trouble.

My men and I really needed the next two hours of quiet. Milligan and I finally brought quiet to the telephone, but only for a little peace in the storm. We didn't get any sleep as we strained our eyes into the darkest night I could remember.

Sleep might have come if it hadn't been for the sound of a German soldier's moan a short distance in front of us. He was dying, but slowly. He was the only proof we had that Germans had been out there that night.

Before I knew it the quiet was over as Jerry's artillery opened up from everywhere on our whole battalion front. They used 88s, mortars and nebelwerfers to hit us first along the front lines and then back in the town of Champs. I said to Milligan, "This is the start of Jerry's daylight attack." I passed the word on to the rest of my men to be alert to any movement of any kind, even from the rear. I called into the company's command post and told them to look out for an attack that could come at them through our tree patch outpost. I also said I thought it would start as soon as they stopped shelling us.

It was after 0530 hours (5:30 a.m.) when shelling stopped, and machine gun fire began. Small mortars continued coming in on our tree patch for a while longer. I tried to call the company command post, but the line was dead. For the first time in this long night we really needed that damned telephone in the tree patch, and it had been knocked out.

We opened fire with machine guns and rifles firing at our field of fire from the tree patch. We did not see the enemy. By a stroke of luck, a phosphorus or mortar shell hit a haystack and set it on fire. It was better than any flare. It was like the sun coming out. That haystack burned until daylight and influenced Jerry to swing both right and left of us since we could now see everything in front of us. It did cost us two troopers, however: one at the haystack foxhole and one on my right flank at the far end of the tree patch.

As daylight came on us, firing was coming from our right rear flank in the 1st Platoon's area as well as back in town. There was no firing on our left flank where Sergeant Hollingsworth's squad was dug in.

German soldiers had been around us all night, but we hadn't seen a single one. At 7:30 the haystack was still smoking, and it was still snowing a little. I decided it was time for me to make a move.

I asked Corporal Milligan to back up to our hillside to Sergeants Griffith's and Howard's mortar squad position to find out about them, and then to check on Sergeant Hollingsworth's squad to our left. He didn't want to go, said it would be better if I went. Someone had to go. We needed a medic and our telephone line needed to be repaired. Also, I needed to know what was going on in my right rear flank.

I knew it was my job as the squad leader to let the Platoon Sergeant know what was happening. Since we needed ammo as well, somebody had to climb out of his foxhole and risk being seen on that bare hillside.

I passed the word to each of my men by stopping at their foxholes and telling them I was going to go straight behind the trees and up the bare hillside to Sergeants Griffith's and Howard's position at the top of the hill overlooking Champs.

I forgot to tell Corporal Milligan the route I would take out of the trees. After going from hole to hole talking to each trooper, I ended up at the far right (north) end of the tree patch. I started running straight up the hill from that corner of the trees and then changed my mind. I came back toward Milligan's machine gun position on the rear of the tree patch to tell him I was leaving and to ask him to cover me from the rear. Fifteen yards away from him I stopped to catch my breath. At that moment I saw Corporal Milligan's rifle pointed straight at my head.

I dropped to the ground like I'd been shot. I yelled, "It's me! Sergeant Black! Milligan! It's me! Sergeant Black!"

It scared him half to death. I came back through the trees to his foxhole, and he was shaking like a leaf. "Sergeant Black," he said, "you don't know how close I came to killing you!"

"Yes, I do," I said, "and it would have been my own fault. Forget about it, and cover me up this hill." With that I took off on a dead run, zig-zagging up the hill to the mortar squad's foxhole.

Where the Hell Did that Shell Hit? 261

I hit the ground at the spot where a German shell had cut our telephone line. The break was big and would require more wire to repair it. I looked around and caught my breath, feeling that small arms fire had almost come to a stop—at least here around our hillside.

I went on up the hill to the top, not running, but being careful about walking in on my own people uninvited. I started calling out Sergeant Howard's name because I knew his voice better than Sergeant Griffith's. I called out my name, "This is Sergeant Black! This is Sergeant Black!"

Once over the top of the hill I could see Champs plainly down in the valley. There was still some machine gun fire on the north edge of town. I heard Howard's voice calling out, "Come on in with your hands up!"

As I walked up to their big dugout, I realized that our mortar squad was behind the hill.

"Hell's fire! We can't see anybody or talk to anybody," Sergeant Howard said when I asked him about Holly's and Haddick's positions. Corporal Hartman had told them just before dark the night before that our 2nd Platoon Command post was located in the north end of town. "Right there," Sergeant Howard said, pointing, "in one of those houses where all that shooting is still taking place."

"We have yet to fire a mortar round," Sergeant Griffith said, "but we did have some rifle practice a while ago."

"Yeah," said Sergeant Howard. "Three of those Jerrys got a little too darn close. That one there damned near got in bed with us!"

I looked over to their left where the bodies of three dead German soldiers lay. One was only three yards from the lip of their foxhole dugout. Now I knew why Milligan and the rest of us in the tree patch hadn't seen the Germans. They were dressed in white uniforms from head to toe. I hadn't seen the soldiers lying there dead in the snow even in the daylight as I'd walked up.

I learned that they had started their breakfast when the three German soldiers walked in on them. Now they were calmly back enjoying their meal. They gave me some coffee and said they would check on Sergeant Hollingsworth's squad while I went down into Champs to our platoon's command post.

I went straight down the sloping hill into the town of Champs. By the time I reached the edge of town it had stopped snowing and the sun was shining brightly. All small arms fire had come to a halt. Looking back up the hill to where the mortar squad stood I thought, "What a beautiful winter scene here at Champs!" How beauty could so quickly replace the ugliness of war was something only God could do. To me it meant that this fight had ended.

I found the 2nd Platoon command post in one of the houses at the north edge of town. The Germans had not taken that house in this morning's fight but had made it to the house next to it. Headquarters people had fought a fire fight, and the "C" Company, with the help of our First Battalion reserve troops, had pushed the last of the enemy out and had retaken all the lost houses. All was quiet now.

I told the Platoon Sergeant my story and got the help I needed. The radio wire man, Corporal Hartman, and the medic, Doc Garner, and myself loaded up with ammo, wire, food and water as we set out for the tree patch outpost.

24

Holly's Great Escape

As I was walking out the door of the command post word came down that three of our troopers had been killed and four were wounded. The death of any paratrooper hurt. But in every company there was always one man everybody loved. In my company that was Pfc William F. Haddick, from the 1st Platoon. The word was that Haddick, the machine gunner on my right, was dead.

The news of Haddick's death triggered in my memory the time back in May 1944 when five "C" Company troopers, including Haddick and myself, were on a committee to organize a company dance in the city of Swindon about twenty miles northwest of Denford Camp in England.

We rode over to Swindon in Army trucks just like we were on some kind of a "field problem." There were no girls when we got there, and nobody seemed to know whose job it had been to get them. The band was set to play, and the English "mild and bitters" (beer) was on hand. But no girls for dancing. The dance was about to be a big flop.

That's when Pfc "Fritz" Haddick called me over to one side and said, "Blackie, get out there in the street and bring some girls in here. Any kind will do, but get some!"

Out in the street I saw four girls coming by. Well, they were older than "girls," but they were females. They had heard our band music and were wondering what was going on. That broke the ice, and I improvised with a little story of my own. I told them we were having an American dance in honor of all the ladies of Swindon and that we had refreshments for the taking—all the American Coca-Cola and English beer you could drink and all the ice cream and cake you could eat.

In they came.

William F. Haddick took over. He was on the bandstand with the mike as the M.C. for the evening. "Hey gang!" he yelled out. "Look what Blackie has found. Four of the loveliest ladies of Swindon. Hey, Blazick. You, too, 'Big' Holly. Get these beautiful dolls some of our best champagne. Who wants to be first to dance with these gorgeous gals? OK! OK! Let's line up over here. No fighting for the first dance. Stay in line, Steinfield. You, too, Kelley. Watch it or I'll make you go to the end of the line!"

He went on like this for a while, and then with his hand over the mike, he yelled in my ear as the band played, "Where did you get these dogs?" Back into the mike, he said, "Blackie, you have saved the day with these lovely ladies. Let's everybody dance!"

The whole Company came to life. All were on their feet and smiling. Some of the troopers were dancing with each other. The band played another dance tune, and everyone cut in. The ladies seemed to be on top of the world. There was only one problem. None of those four women could dance worth a damn, and everybody knew it!

Fritz said to me, "This won't last, Blackie."

"Maybe they can sing," I said.

"Great! Stop the music!" he shouted to the band. "Ladies and Gentlemen! I have just heard that one of these ladies is a great English singer. Bring her up on the bandstand."

"Hey," I said to Haddick. "I said *maybe* one of them could sing." That didn't slow him down.

"Blazick!" he called out. "That one there with the beer. Bring her up here!"

Believe it or not, she did want to sing. I asked her what she wanted to sing so I could get the band ready. I thought she said, "I'm Forever Blowing Bubbles." I checked with one of the other girls to make sure I was right. "Yes, that's her favorite song," they said. So I told the band leader.

Haddick walked to center stage, took the mike and as everyone became quiet he said, "Ladies and Gentlemen, Miss Bubbles will now sing for us. Her first song will be dedicated to Private Wilfred E. Blazick of Richmond, California, now stationed somewhere in old England. The name of her first song is, 'I'm Forever Blowing Bubbles—and Bubbles is Forever Blowing Me!' Take it away, Bubbles!"

Everyone roared with laughter. As she tried to sing and the band tried to keep up with her, out in the street buses were pulling up in front. Beautiful young English girls, all of them fine dancers, it turned out, streamed into the auditorium. William F. Haddick's 1st Platoon had come through in the nick of time, and Haddick had saved a Company dance.

Back at Champs...Before we left for the tree patch, the Platoon Sergeant told me to pick up Lieutenant James Robinson from the division artillery to go to the tree patch as the official observer for the 377th Parachute Field Artillery Battalion.

On my way to the command post to pick up the lieutenant I saw the First Sergeant, Robert Grotjan.

"I heard Jerry landed a direct hit in here last night," I said.

"How the hell do you know about that?" was all he said.

On the way up the hill I kept thinking about Haddick's death and was becoming more concerned about the safety of "Big" Holly and his squad. Sergeant Howard hadn't heard from any of them since the previous night. I quickened my steps as the thought of the three dead German soldiers came to mind. I remembered, too, the last news about our losses. One officer and two enlisted men dead, four wounded. I wondered if Holly had run into any trouble. Try as hard as I could, I could not remember hearing small arms firing from my left flank. By now I was almost running up that long hill west of Champs. I heard someone behind me say, "What's the big hurry, Sergeant?"

When I reached Sergeant Griffith's mortar dugout, Sergeant Howard said that "Big" Holly and his whole squad were gone! "Damn it, Blackie, they ain't there!" he said. He had taken a look and had found no one in their foxholes.

I was stunned. No one left! I would have to look out for myself.

Everything was still in place around each foxhole, even machine guns and rifles, all the ammo plus their bedding. It looked as though they'd just crawled out of their beds. Hell! They had all been captured in their sleep!

Coming back from Holly's position to my tree patch outpost, I stopped by Sergeant Bird's gun crew to see how he was doing. They'd had a close call sometime after the haystack had burned out, about the time I'd reached Sergeant Howard's foxhole on my way out.

As near as Bird and I could put the pieces together the Germans had slipped to the far left of my tree patch because of the haystack fire and then had come upon "Big" Holly's squad. Finding them easy to capture, Jerry became even bolder. But they found that Griffith and Howard were not so easy. Three Germans were dead just like that. That must have forced them to think about saving their prisoner catch. They started back down the hill toward their lines, but one Jerry came too close to Bird's gun crew.

Over in the tree patch Corporal "Jumpknife" Milligan was standing alone. He saw the German soldier the same time Bird did. He ran and jumped into Bird's foxhole to help out. Sergeant W. O. Bird yelled to his machine gunner to swing his gun to the rear and open fire. The boy, a new trooper named Kelley, turned in time to see the German soldier coming straight for him. Kelley froze, and both Bird and Milligan fired. Kelley was wounded, and Jerry hurried off with their prisoners.

At work in the tree patch, Corporal Hartman was putting in my new telephone wire. He was also running new wire from

Holly's Great Escape

Sergeant Griffith's foxhole down to our Platoon command post in Champs. Still coming over my head was our good stuff from the 377th. Lieutenant Robinson was giving the Germans hell all over the valley in front of me. He had them on the run and was paying them back double for last night.

Sometime after 1030 hours (10:30 a.m.) the artillery officer called for me from to come up to where he was. As I reached the top of the hill I heard rifle fire to the south. It seemed closer to Sergeant Hollingsworth's area than mine—or the area where he had been. It was a single rifle firing, "Pow! Pow! Pow! Pow!" followed by the cling of the ammo clip jumping out empty. After a pause it began again. "Pow! Pow! Pow! Pow!" until the ring of another empty clip.

"What in hell is going on?" I asked the lieutenant.

"Take a look," he said.

He pointed to a lone GI trooper seated in the snow down the hill. There before my eyes was an unbelievable sight. I laughed until I cried because there, in the best sitting firing position you will ever see on a firing range, was Sergeant William T. Hollingsworth.

"Big" Holly had no coat or helmet on and no gloves. The sling of his rifle was fastened around his arm as is customary when firing from that position. The officer handed me his powerful field glasses, and I saw clearly what Holly was shooting at. He was firing at a German soldier at least six hundred yards away.

I watched five shots hit on either side of the German, who was down in the snow. One of Holly's shots would land to the left, and the German would roll over to his right. The next shot landed to the right, and the German rolled left. So it went for the five shots.

I handed the glasses back to Lieutenant Robinson. He put them up to his eyes and began to call out, "Left—right—left—right—left! He got him! He got him, men!" A cheer went up from everyone on our hillside.

Robinson said, "That is a brave trooper over there sitting on the hillside all alone where Jerry can see him."

"Yeah, and a hell of a shot, too," I said as I started walking toward Holly. "Get the hell back here before the Germans start laying in mortars on all of us!" I yelled.

With the sound of my voice Holly stood up. "That you, Black? I thought they got you, too." As he came near me I saw right away what was wrong. Holly had been drinking! I knew Holly better than anyone else. For him to take that kind of a chance with his own life, he had to be drunk.

Holly wasn't totally drunk. He was at that "don't give a damn" stage. I got him to go with me to the foxhole area furthest away from the office. "OK," I said. "What happened? Sit down here and tell me. Before you do, give me a drink out of your bottle."

"I haven't got any bottle, Sergeant Black," he said.

"Don't pull that Sergeant shit on me now," I said. "You know what I mean. Where did you find that stuff out here?"

Holly said, "Blackie, I never can fool you. How did you ever get so damned smart?"

"Come on," I said, "What happened? Where are the rest of your men?"

That did it. I had gotten through to him. I liked this big North Carolina hillbilly best when he turned serious and needed my help because most of the time I needed his help.

"Where the hell are the rest of your men?" I repeated.

"They captured us this morning," he said.

"How? Who? When? Why didn't they get you?"

"Shut up," Holly said, "and give me a chance to tell you."

He started to talk, slowly. "Those damned Germans walked right up to each one of my foxholes and stuck their bayonets in on us. We didn't have a chance, Sergeant Black. We couldn't see them. They were all wearing white uniforms. You know it was still snowing, not quite daylight."

"You guys must have been asleep. Couldn't you hear them coming?"

"No, sir! They did not make a sound. It's damn scary the way they can creep up!"

"Well, why didn't they take you?" I asked.

"They did!" he said.

"Well?" I said. "Damn it! Go on and tell me the whole story. I'll shut up."

Holly continued with his story. A squad of big German SS soldiers started to take them back down the hill toward their lines. "For some reason," Holly said, "they stopped for a while." He couldn't remember how long they were stopped, maybe until the haystack fire burned out.

After they moved out again under the control of their German captors and were part way down the long hill, they were stopped by our 101st Artillery. Holly said it came right in on top of them, and everybody hit the ground. Holly dived under a bush for protection. The shelling was devastating and seemed to last a long time.

"When our guns let up, the Germans all jumped up and started to hurry off down the hill. One of them could speak good English and told us GIs to get up and go down the hill before more shells came in. Everyone but me got up and ran on down the hill with the Germans. I guess they never missed me, for some reason," Holly said. "Maybe they couldn't count too good."

When Holly was sure there were no Jerrys anywhere around, he got up and walked back to the tree patch.

"You sure were lucky," I said. "You must have stopped at a bar on the way back!"

"Yeah," he said, "in a way I did. Here! Have a drink!" He handed me a German canteen full of Schnapps, a very strong German drink made of potatoes.

As I took a drink I asked Holly, "Where did you find this?"

"Over in front of your tree patch outpost!" the big sergeant said. He kept talking. "Those dead German soldiers lying out there had their canteens filled with Schnapps! They sure weren't going to need it, and it seemed a shame to see it go to waste, Blackie. I brought back three full canteens. See them down there in my foxhole?"

I took another drink from Holly's canteen and said, "Well, it's no damn wonder Jerry came up that long hill straight at us and into Bird's and my great field of fire. A few drinks as strong as that and a soldier wouldn't care if he lives or dies."

Holly told me that while the German attack was still in progress with a stray Jerry here and there on the hillside, he made his way back to his foxhole for his rifle. He then worked his way back to the tree patch area. As he came by a mound of dirt Holly ran smack into a German soldier with his rifle aimed at a fellow trooper. Sergeant Hollingsworth fired first, and the German fell dead.

(I didn't learn until forty-two years later that the American whose life Holly saved was Captain James Robinson of the 377th Paratrooper F. Artillery Battalion, the same officer I came up the hill with that day.)

"Holly, I'm truly glad you made it back to our lines," I said, "and sorry your men didn't. With all the old timers gone, this war isn't going to be any fun."

I was thinking about the loss of William Haddick, and I knew he hadn't heard about that yet. I sat on the edge of the big Sergeant's foxhole, wondering if now would be the time to tell him. The two men were great friends and had been together as far back as basic training. They'd both come into the 502nd back in "Alabama" days, both as machine gunners, and two of the Regiment's best. Besides that, they were two of the best-liked men in the whole outfit.

I began, "We in 'C' Company lost two of our best men today—one from the 'first' and one from the 'second' platoon. We here in the 'second' lucked out. We got you back. The boys over in the 'first' were not so lucky. They didn't get a second chance. William Haddick died today, Holly. Shot straight through the head. He didn't know what hit him. It was a clean shot, they said. We can thank God for that."

It was a terrible blow to "Big" Holly. Tears streamed down his face. All he said was, "Not Haddick, Black. Not Haddick! Not William Haddick! Oh, God! Not Haddick!"

I got up and walked back to my foxhole in the tree patch outpost.

Around noon the aftermath of the battle settled down. The milling around my tree patch came to an end. W. O. Bird, "Jumpknife" Milligan, and I regrouped. We even talked "Big" Holly into joining us. He moved in with Sergeant Bird in the place where the haystack had been. Later in the afternoon we sent a few of our men into Champs to dry out and warm up.

The news of our "C" Company's losses trickled up to us. Corporal George C. Dagres of the 3rd Platoon had died in early-morning fighting as did Second Lieutenant George W. Manhardt, a new officer. A total of six troopers had been wounded, counting the three at our tree patch. We lost only five by enemy capture, MIA.

(All five survived the German imprisonment, although one of them, John Lesko, was in such bad condition from prison starvation that he died in our hospital overseas. Edmond Lozano escaped from Stalag #12 in March 1945, and made his way back to the Rhine River and our lines before the war's end. Although Lozano was down to only one hundred pounds from prison starvation plus a bad arm wound from the Holland jump, he recovered. Ed Kessler, Leopold Martin and Barnard Orr all survived.)

The New Year of 1945 here at Champs came in with a bang. Lieutenant Robinson and the men of the Division Artillery joined every gun on the Third Army front at midnight.

On this day my squad people took turns going down into Champs. Sergeant DeWitt gave us the use of one of the few houses still standing in the north end of town. German soldiers had moved in and out of it many times in the fight for Bastogne, and I will never forget the distinctive smell the Germans left behind them in that house. It had been hit many times, but still had one room standing—the one with a stove in it. That was what all we wanted—to warm up!

The enemy now was not just men with guns. Our new foe was "trench foot" or "frostbite," and it was showing up in alarming numbers. We troopers who had stayed too long in foxholes here on the front lines of the Bulge were the hardest hit. At this point no one in the 101st had yet been refitted with winter gear or even fully refitted from our last combat campaign. That changed today, but not soon enough for James Flanagan. He had been with me in the tree patch and had frozen his feet. He was struggling to hang on.

This day brought the good news of several old Screaming Eagles returning to duty. With them came winter gear—new heavy socks and "long-john" underwear, tops and bottoms, plus gloves, sweaters and wool scarves. They also brought heavy overshoes and a new knit cap to fit under that cold, steel helmet and give us something to pull over our ears.

All of these supplies came up from Camp Mourmelon by the road that Patton's Army had opened to the south.

On Tuesday, January 2, 1945, I heard the bad news that two more men of "C" Company had been killed in action—Private First Class Woodrow W. Atchison and Private Frederick E. Leisner, both of the 1st Platoon. Jerry Johnston joined us for the first time since he was hit at Saint Oedenrode. A new kid we all called "Rabbit" (his name was Frank Hare) came to us straight from jump school in England.

That night as darkness came and with it time for changeover at the tree patch outpost, I could hear noise in front of us. The Germans were up to something. The official division history records that the Germans hit the 327th Regiment's First Battalion with eleven tanks and a regiment of infantry. They drove their tanks, in spite of the dark, along our outpost and main firing line, firing their cannon directly into our foxholes. They quickly killed or captured most of the 327th men in the line. When daylight came, the dead lay along a patch of ground they had never seen. The First Battalion of the 327th Regiment did not give up without a fight. It has been said by men who know that "the First Battalion never had a fiercer fight than during the first fifteen minutes of that night!"

"Remember Christmas morning?" I said to the men replacing me. "Stay on the ball! The word is out the Jerry is under way with a big attack! They may strike here again." I was glad to get off that hill.

We pulled back to a wooded hill near our regimental command post and in the same place we had spent December 27, 28 and 29. Once again it started snowing hard.

The First Battalion of the 217th Gliders started moving into our position, but relief for the "C" Company on the main line of resistance was not completed until nearly midnight. By then it was too dark for the glider boys to see their fields of fire. They chose to dig new foxholes instead of using the ones

Holly's Great Escape 273

already there. Most of the men dug only shallow holes. By then it was so cold that the ground was frozen solid. What a terrible beating they took in an area that had been "ours" only a short time before!

We in the First Battalion (502nd) were alerted early in the morning just as we thought. However, "B" Company got the call to move out first. Since they were able to do the job, we were not needed. The "B" Company lost three of their officers and three of their enlisted men as they helped First Battalion Gliders turn Jerry back at Champs. We in "C" Company lost only one trooper, but it was my best friend, Sergeant W. O. Bird, who got hit.

Sergeant Bird was standing nearby as Captain Cody gave the order to Lieutenant Wall: "Place ground-to-air warning panels out there in that open field, Lieutenant. Division has called in the dive-bombers for an air strike on those Jerry tanks at Champs. We sure don't want those fly boys to mistake this wood full of our 'C' Company for the damned Jerrys." Lieutenant Wall turned to Sergeant Bird and said, "You heard the captain, Sergeant. Get those air warning panels out there in the open—on the double!"

"Buck passing" was not Sergeant W. O. Bird's nature. He grabbed the panels and ran out from the cover of the woods into the open field. On his way back a mortar shell landed near him, and he was hit by a piece of shrapnel from it. Once more Bird was on his way to the rear. It was "Purple Heart" Number 3 for him! Damn it! Holly and I felt bad.

About dark the need for "C" Company was greater at Long Champs than at Champs, so we moved into Long Champs and spent the night in houses on the alert. We were there to back up our Second Battalion, who had lost heavily on Wednesday, January 3. That's where I heard that our "C" Company's First Lieutenant William O. Dwyer had been killed in action. He had led the 2nd Platoon in the latter part of the Holland campaign in October and November. He was a wonderful man, a fine paratrooper officer.

Back at Long Champs, we enjoyed the real comforts of living in town—in houses! These were the quiet days for us in the

Battle of the Bulge at Bastogne. That does not mean that the division would not lose any men. Each day we took some losses due to German artillery, including the worse loss from artillery by a single round in the whole war. Twelve troopers were unloading a truckload of land mines at the 501st Parachute Regimental Headquarters when a German shell apparently hit, and the whole truck exploded at once. The twelve men simply disappeared. Not a trace of any of their bodies was ever found.

The price was beginning to mount as the 101st Airborne hung on to Bastogne. The cuts hurt the deepest in the leadership ranks at both the noncommissioned and commissioned officer levels.

25

Mad as Hell

Saturday, January 6, 1945, was a big day for me. It was my twenty-third birthday, and the U.S. Army had a present for me. Along with everyone else in "C" Company, I was to get my first bath in twenty days!

We had one more day in regimental reserves, and my squad and I were still in the same house in Long Champs. I spent the day lying around and waiting my turn to clean up. The division brought a portable hot shower for us. That was something wonderful, a great feeling on my birthday!

Jerry tried to spoil my day by playing a tune on the old 88, but I thought the risk was worth it to take the chance of being caught with only my "birthday suit" on. The feeling of being clean, even a clean uniform to put on, made it a happy birthday for me. We even had a chance to wash our other uniforms that day. To add to my birthday joy, it was one of the few bright sunshiny days in the "Bulge."

That afternoon several of us were sitting in the back yard at our house sunning ourselves. We were used to being outdoors in the snow and cold weather, and the sun felt warm and refreshing.

"Big" Holly, V. J. Folley, "Jumpknife" Milligan, Rennie Howard, Corporal Hartman and "Doc" Garner were there with me.

That winter the ETO (European Theatre of Operations) was hosting a contest to see which soldier could grow the longest handlebar mustache. We all tried, but one of the front runners in our "C" Company was Sergeant Bob Marohn of the 1st Platoon. He stopped by our back yard that afternoon to show off. His handlebars put us all to shame.

The next day the damned German artillery boys fired a last round for no reason at all. They caught four troopers from our company who were out in the open gathering hay at the town's haystack to winterize their foxholes. Two of them, including "Doc" Garner, from my platoon, were hit bad enough to leave the war for the States. ("Doc" had been my platoon medic since the Holland jump. I saw him next in 1989; he had paid a price, but made it back to a useful life.)

The other trooper hit hard that day was an old-timer from Alabama days, Sergeant William T. Kelley. Kelley had been the best friend of William Haddick; now they were both gone within a week, leaving a gaping hole in the 1st Platoon. (Sergeant Kelley also survived; I saw him at his home in Hamilton, Ohio, in 1980. He was still a great guy, but he'd had to put up a real battle to make it.)

From the day back in December when the Germans closed the circle around us, the 101st had not given up one foot of ground. We had bent in the heat of attack, but in every case we won it back by the end of the day.

Word came down to our house early Sunday morning that there would be no church call today. Instead, our 2nd Platoon was to get set to move up on the front lines sometime today.

Our Platoon command post was located in a house out of the town of Champs. Foxhole digging by now had become a real chore with bitter cold each day freezing the ground deeper and deeper. Our Supply Sergeant, Cam Anderson, somehow came up with big picks and shovels, and we took turns using them.

Our 2nd Platoon had an excellent field of fire this time. We could see a long distance ahead of us, and there were no blind spots. It seemed we could see forever on a clear day.

We all helped winterize our dugouts from the town haystack. We dug a rectangular hole two feet deep and large enough for three men to lie down and sleep in at the same time, with a fourth man sitting up at our feet across the front opening to keep watch. We covered our outpost foxhole with wood posts, fence boards and anything else we could find. Then we put dirt on top of that and snow over the dirt. We left an opening of only about a foot and a half at the front so we could see out or send fire if and when we needed to. Our foxhole was so well constructed that a tank could have run over it without hurting any of us.

Our outpost line was just in front of a wood picket fence that ran across the crest of the hill from east to west. We dug our holes facing north about ten yards in front of it so we could use the fence as a wind break. Instead, it turned into a big snowdrift that covered our outpost!

I had the last watch before daylight on Monday morning. The snow had been falling heavily all night and was deep by now. The wind was starting to blow hard. The open end of the dugout was full of snow, and my "underground home" was a huge snowdrift. When it became full light we could see that we had been caught in a blizzard. It lasted all day and night. We couldn't see or hear anything but the wind, and neither could the Germans. We closed the entrance with a GI blanket and lasted out the storm underground. Some men didn't leave their foxholes for over forty-eight hours.

As Tuesday dawned, snowing had stopped but not the blowing. Snow continued to drift all day. The sun came out and made matters worse, causing snow blindness. The best place to be was underground.

In the afternoon a call came for Sergeants Folley, Hollingsworth and Black to report to the platoon command post. "Man," I thought to myself, "that's good news. Now I'll have a chance to dry off and get warm. I'll eat, drink and smoke good cigarettes back at the command post. Being a squad leader has its advantages!"

When I climbed out of my underground home everything was white. Everywhere I looked, everything was covered. I knew I had to cross the fence somehow and go back a hundred yards, turn right, go down hill into the sun for two hundred yards or more. There should be a lone house standing there. The picket fence was hell to get across. I was already tired by the time I got over it and away from the four-foot snowdrifts.

I looked around to see where I was headed but was snow-blinded by the bright sun and the blowing snow. Everything looked the same. My tracks were barely visible behind me. Still, I made up my mind to go on as I'd planned. It was a mistake. I should have gone back while I could still see my tracks.

I moved away from the fence to snow that was three feet deep until I reached a point on the hillside where I guessed I should turn right. I still could not see anything but white. I turned into the sun and started to walk toward it. At that moment Jerry decided to blow the snow out of the barrels of two of their nebelwerfer guns.

I heard the shells coming and started to run for cover. There was none anywhere. I dived headlong into the snow. How many were there? Eight or ten in a bunch? They were all on top of me! The smell of gun powder, the whine of steel all around me—the noise was deafening when they struck the ground. And that was just from the first gun.

Then the screams all over again. I dug with my hands to the bare ground. There wasn't time to look up. I didn't want to anyway; I was too scared. The second bunch hit. The ground shook and bounced—or was it me? I was certain one of those shells would land in the middle of my back. I tried to make myself smaller. Suddenly I couldn't hear. I felt as if I was falling, like I was jumping out of a plane. I started counting out loud. At twenty I raised up to look around me. Well, I didn't actually raise up; it was more like turning over on my back.

I lay there with my eyes closed for a long time. I was afraid I would see blood-stained snow if I took a look. When I did open my eyes the air around me was filled with smoke. The smell of gun powder made me feel sick. I waited for more shells. None came.

At last I sat up. No blood anywhere. But all around me were straight lines cutting across the snow in every direction. Some were thin lines a small boy might make dragging his sled home from play. Others were large lines like farmers will leave when plowing a furrow. There must have been twenty shell holes around me on that hill, kicking the dirt out in a neat, round circle.

As I stood up to move on, there straight ahead in front of me was my Platoon command post. "Just another close call," I told myself, "but damn it, I'll bet there'll be more!"

That scare cleared up my snow blindness, and I could see the town down the valley to my left. I was walking into a stiff wind in snow over three feet deep some two hundred yards to the house. By the time I reached the front door I was pooped out.

The first words to reach my ears were the wrong ones to say to me, and they came from the Platoon Sergeant, Curtis DeWitt. "Where in hell have you been all day, Sergeant Black? I called you over an hour ago. Everyone else has been here and gone long ago. What the hell kept you?"

I stood in the warm room spellbound. The look on my face must have reflected what I was thinking. As I looked around that warm, comfortable room into the face of each of the other 2nd Platoon troopers, I suddenly blew up. "Why you ungrateful bastard!" I said.

It was our twenty-third day in the Bulge, and I had yet to shave. My beard was covered with frozen snow and ice plus dirt from having my face rammed in it. Snow covered me from head to foot. My outer uniform was frozen solid.

Looking at my fellow troopers I realized they were my friends, that they felt sorry for me and wanted me to speak out. So speak out I did. I slowly told them what had happened. I said I thought the Platoon Sergeant was being ungrateful and that he had no idea what his men were going through so that he could be warm and safe back here behind the lines. That this winter storm was terrible. That he had no idea or even seemed to care about my Second Squad back when we were in the tree patch over in Champs. The longer I talked the madder I got. I told him my men should each have a chance to come back here to the command post or some other house to get warm once in a while. If that didn't happen soon, I went on, I was going to go to the captain! Then I asked him what he wanted of me that he was in such a hurry about.

"Your squad's rations for today are ready for you," he said. They were on the floor—three K-rations per man plus two packs of cigarettes and two candy bars each and a large GI can of water for all eight of my men. I asked the sergeant how he thought I could carry all of that, and he answered, "You will have to make two trips!"

I told him that none of my men would leave that hill after dark. If he could not give me help from the command post now, I would take only what I could carry with me safely and send two men back in the morning. He said nothing.

Then I noticed that my ration of cigarettes were Reighleys and Old Golds. But my men smoked Camels and Lucky Strikes. Sergeant DeWitt was lighting up a Lucky Strike. That was too much. I began again.

"I notice, Sergeant, you're smoking Luckies," I said. "How about everybody else? How about Sergeant Folley and big Hollingsworth? What the hell are they smoking today?"

"Lucky Strikes and Camels," he shot back. "What about it, Sergeant?"

"OK, Sergeant, that's what I thought. But next time, my squad gets the breaks. I damned near got killed on my way down here for my squad, and I've got the farthest to come of anyone. Now I have to go back and tell them we got the shitty end of the stick."

With that Lieutenant Wall stood up and said, "Sergeant! Get the hell back up on that hill!"

Had it not been for two great guys, Sergeant Marquart (our medic) and our radio man Corporal Hartman, my spouting off probably would have cost me my rank.

Marquart and Hartman both jumped up, grabbed the water can and the K rations, took me by the arm and went out the door. Sergeant DeWitt yelled, "Where you two think you're going?"

Hartman yelled back, "To check out the telephone line after all that shelling."

Marquart said, "I want to see how the troopers' feet are holding up on the front lines!"

The door slammed behind us.

What I'd said had gotten to them. They knew they had to get me out of there. What I'd said got to Sergeant DeWitt, too. My squad never had to smoke Reighleys and Old Golds again!

Mad as Hell 281

There was a large scale American attack on my right flank that day. We of the First Battalion were standing in place at Long Champs. The attack involved two Corps in General Patton's Third Army. The 101st Division's assignment was to seize Noville, an objective of our division since December 18 when we landed here. From the 502nd Regiment, only the 3rd Battalion was participating, and they ended up losing 36 troopers that day. The 506th P.I. Regiment had 69 casualties, and the 501st lost 28 men. Another loss to the 101st Airborne was General McAuliffe, who left our division to command the 103rd Infantry Division (not airborne).

The main thing I remember about Wednesday, January 10, 1945, was all the movement going through my 2nd Platoon area. With the blowing snow, it had been tough sledding for our tanks and self-propelled guns. The roads were almost impassable. Nevertheless, the attack continued.

We stood in place at Long Champs for the second straight day of the attack. It was about 15 degrees with a wind chill much below zero. The sky was clear part of the day so our airplanes could fly air support, but for most of the day it was a bad winter day. The tanks slipping and sliding were a spectacular sight from my view on top of Long Champs Hill.

The 506th parachute troopers were still trying to take Noville just east of me. It was a bad day for the "Sixers." They were hit heavy by German artillery before they started their attack. They lost 126 paratroopers before the day was over. The 3rd Battalion of the 502nd succeeded in taking "Les Assins Woods" but suffered 43 casualties doing it.

In the far right flank the 3rd Battalion of the 320th Infantry Regiment from the 35th Infantry Division did not move. Our 501st paratroopers used the railroad as a natural boundary line between Corps, and they pushed ahead for 1,000 yards in the "Bois Jacques Woods." This left our right flank open for Jerry to attack, and they hit them with heavy fire along the railroad. Then the attack stopped on all fronts, and everybody pulled back to the lines held two days earlier.

With all the pulling back, my squad moved several hundred yards to our left. I moved into an old farm house right on the front lines. A German Mark IV tank standing next to the house. It had been hit and burned out at that spot a few days before. We dug our squad's outpost foxholes in back of that tank along the stone wall on the border of the farm. It gave us a grim reminder each time we passed by it going from the house to our outpost.

On Thursday there was no fighting at all in the northern part of Bastogne. More snow fell, and the temperature dropped to zero. We spent most of the day in our farm house by a wood-burning stove, except for our turns on guard duty out in the foxholes. A new job was added to our tasks: we kept a detail busy cutting wood for our stove.

The farm building was an old house built of masonry stone with very thick walls and thus able to take quite a beating. The house was also fairly easy to heat.

Late Thursday afternoon Private First Class James Flanagan rejoined our squad, returning from a field hospital after treatment for frostbite to his feet. I spent most of the evening around the stove talking to James. He brought some good news from the rear: "The 101st is to pull out of the Bulge in a day or two!" He went on, "We will all be sent on pass to Paris for at least a week. It will be just like the time after we came back from Normandy. We are all heroes back there to those guys in the rear," he said.

When the call came after dark for Sergeant Black to report to the command post, all the men in the 2nd Platoon gave a cheer. Flanagan said, "What did I tell you, Sergeant?"

At 1930 hours (7:30 p.m.) I started down the hill. When I walked in the door of the command post, Hollingsworth and Folley were already there. The Headquarters men had already packed their bedrolls. But we weren't going to Paris, that was for damn sure!

I said, "What the hell is the matter with you guys? Don't you like Paris?"

Sergeant DeWitt said, "You can forget about Paris!"

"Good!" I said. "I like the winters here at Bastogne better anyway. What's up?"

"Tell your men to dress warm. Clean socks, overcoats. Bring your bedrolls down here and take them on to Company CP See Supply Sergeant Anderson and pick up three K-rations per man.

Mad as Hell

Fill you canteens with water and draw two bandoliers of rifle ammo. Check the rest of your ammo, machine guns, bazookas and hand grenades. Once again, Sergeant, make sure each one of your men dresses warm!" That's the way Sergeant DeWitt put it to me.

I looked at Sergeant DeWitt first, then at "Big" Holly, and then at V. J. Folley. There were no smiles, just the grim look of knowing you are going over onto the attack—the real war!

I didn't even look at Sergeant DeWitt as I repeated, "What's up?"

Holly, Folley and I left the command post together. We each lit a cigarette and stood for a while. Holly spoke first.

"Those big shits back in the rear seem to know more than they can understand. Don't they understand it's too cold to fight?"

"Damn those Germans," I said.

Folley said, "They've made us all mad now."

Starting up the hill, I said, "That's war in the ETO, gentlemen, that's for damned sure!"

Folley's last words were, "Taylor told Ike, 'Hey, General! I missed the Christmas show. How 'bout me showing you what I can do?'"

How will my men, all but two new since Holland, take it when I tell them that Flanagan's rumor was just that, a damned rumor? Instead of going back, we were going to a "new" front! Instead of being on the defensive, we were going onto the attack at daybreak! We were to pack up, resupply and be in full battle dress in front of our Company CP, ready to move out at 2100 hours (9 p.m.) and join our First Battalion in an all-night cross-country forced march!

I knew these would be the hardest orders I ever had to pass on to my men. The biggest problem would be with Private First Class Flanagan. And maybe Milligan.

When I reached my billet I opened the door and called to Sergeant Milligan to come outside and go with me to get the men on outpost guard. As we left I yelled back to the other men that we would be back in a minute. As the door closed behind us I heard the men ask, "When do we leave?"

We walked around the house past the burned-out German Mark IV. I told Milligan the story, and then I said, "Remember the reason I picked you for my assistant squad leader? We are the only old 'C' Company men left in this squad and, by God, I need all the help I can get right now. Flanagan is going to raise all kinds of hell. Keep in mind, he just got back to the front."

I could see I had Milligan's full attention, so I went on. "Flanagan did not want to come up here to Bastogne. Now he has talked himself as well as all the other men into believing that rumor about Paris. Remember, he never got to go to Paris like we did! And," I continued, "he has been in the hospital. You never know about a big guy like that. He was a damned good trooper until he got hit in Holland. Now, who knows?"

My speech worked on Milligan. He knew I needed him, and he was a good assistant squad leader. I could count on him.

By now we had picked up the men at the outpost and were back to the door of the house. Inside, Sergeant Milligan chose a position where he could see Flanagan. I began with a command. "Everyone will shut up!" I said. "I will now tell you what's up. Yes! We are moving out. I am truly sorry to say it is not Reims or Paris. We are moving out of Long Champ, but not out of Bastogne! You will be ready to move in one hour, in full battle dress, ready to fight in an all-out attack that will begin at daybreak. Between now and then we must make a forced march all the way over to the east side. We have about ten thousand yards to cover. The whole ETO front goes on the attack at 0830 hours (8:30 a.m.). The sooner we get to our jumping off area, the more time we'll have to rest before the fighting starts. Any questions?"

There was dead silence. Everyone's face went from anticipation of a joke to absolute disbelieve. They were stunned. Then one question.

It came from Flanagan, sitting at the table. "Are you shitting me, Sergeant Black?" I'll never forget the look on his face. It was proof he knew the answer. I said nothing; I only slowly shook my head.

All hell broke loose. In one motion Flanagan kicked the big table upside down and knocked over his own chair before he got out of it. Backwards he fell, rolling over, kicking, arms flying, swearing with every breath. He struggled to get out of the chair he was now fastened in.

Everyone else stood up, backs against the wall out of his way, just watching him roll over and over. Finally he came to rest belly down on the floor. The chair was still stuck to his rear end, all bent out of shape. Three of the chair's legs were broken off.

At last dead silence, except for Flanagan's heavy breathing. Then softly he said, "Please, Sergeant Black, get this damned thing off of me!"

I made a snap decision. "OK, everybody!" I said. "You have five minutes to let off steam. You want to help Flanagan tear up this place? Get that chair off his ass and go ahead. I'll time you with my watch. Sergeant Milligan and I will step outside. OK. Start!" With that said, we stepped out. Once again, all hell broke loose.

After five minutes I fired a rifle shot into the air, opened the door and stepped back in. It was over! Sergeant Milligan took over. "Pack your bedrolls and take them down to the company CP," he said. "Get at it. We're already five minutes late!"

It is important to note here that on a cold still winter's night on the front lines, a single rifle shot will start—or stop—almost anything!

The griping died down as we headed out across country. By the time we reached the end of the first two thousand yards of following the leader in a zig-zag march through snow up to three feet deep, all talking had stopped.

There was no moonlight, so it was dark as hell. The battalion pathfinders used flares in the deepest snow drifts to mark the way. We were tired out after going only a fourth of the way.

The remaining eight thousand yards was more like sleep walking than marching. Men would fall down in front of you and lie there until you came by and gave them a hand. When too many were falling down, the leaders would give us a ten-minute break.

It took the 1st Battalion some five hours to cover the whole ten thousand yards. By 0300 hours (3 a.m.) we were walking in an evergreen thicket in the "Bois-Jacques Woods" on the west side of the railroad tracks. I put my men down a line of spruce trees, two to a tree and told them to crawl under the low-hanging branches that were weighted down with snow and touching the ground.

Under the branches near the trunks there was no snow, only soft, dry pine needles. We all fell asleep without thinking about digging foxholes.

It was not full light, maybe 0730 hours (7:30 a.m.) when they woke us up. Most of us had slept four full hours. While I was getting my men up and ready to move out of the evergreen trees so we could go into our company's assembly area, I noticed that the tops of the tall trees had been cut off. Branches lay scattered around everywhere. It was hard to walk among the rows of trees.

Down at a fire break where one of our battalion guides was standing, I asked if there had been any shelling since we'd come in.

"Hell, yes!" he said. "Where in the hell have you been? Two hours ago Jerry threw everything they had at us. Several of our troopers got hit here. They were tree bursts. Can't you tell, Sergeant?"

"Ya," I said. "I'm not blind. Just deaf, I guess."

I asked each of my men if they had heard any shelling. All were like me—not a sound. We were too damned tired.

In the next five days I remember eating only three meals, even though I carried K-rations in the big pockets of my jumpsuit just as everyone else did. I didn't feel really hungry, but was always glad to have something hot to eat. Most of the time fear replaced hunger.

The battle began with a bang! On our side, the Eighth and Third Corps gave Germans all hell with our artillery. At 0830 hours (8:30 a.m.) the First and 3rd Battalions of 502nd moved out, passing through a viaduct under the railroad over to the east side.

It wasn't easy crossing all that open ground. The Germans were well dug in up at the wood line with tanks, machine guns, 88 artillery, mortars and plenty of infantry. We used up at least half of our eight hours of good daylight to reach the trees. It was hell.

Get the picture. On top of the railroad tracks stood our Regimental Commander, Colonel Chappuis, with "whiphandle" in hand. His "handle" was made up of his two Battalion Commanders, Colonel John P. Stopka (3rd Battalion) and Major John D. Hanlon (First Battalion). The rest of his whip was made up of four companies of paratroopers snaking under the railroad, through the viaduct and out into the open fields. Five hundred yards away, up

Mad as Hell

on the high ground at the tree line, the German soldiers could see us all the way. For the major part of the four hours it took the colonel to crack the whip, artillery was the name of the game—theirs and ours.

The only thing about the arrangement that was nothing like a whip was the speed at which the tip end of it (me) cracked out there. In my case most of those 2,000 by 500 yards was spent face down in knee-deep snow with German 88 shells landing all around me. Throw in near-zero bitter cold and blowing wind. It was snowing most of the time. I got so wet from lying face down in the snow that my clothing frozen stiff. Worse than any of this were the noises of war: the screaming of the nebelwerfer guns, the whistling of the 88s, the cracking of rifles and machine gun fire overhead, all of the time. Then there was the sound of tanks revving up their motors and the steady "creak" of their tracks coming closer and closer. We were never sure whose they were, ours or theirs?

Then the worse sound of all: one of my own men has been hit. "Med-ic! Med-ic!" Then someone else, away up ahead. "Medic! Med-ic!" Still another. "Med-ic!" And another. "Med-ic!" Good God! That's four in a row. We've got to get moving! What in hell is the hold-up? Then the cry of my own trooper again. "Medic!" The call rings out everywhere.

"That you, Doc?" I asked.

"Yah. Sergeant Floyd Marquart. Who's that? Sounds like Sergeant Black! This one of your boys?"

"Yes. How bad is he?"

"He'll be OK. He can walk out. I'm sending him back. But he's done with this battle. Got it in the arm. Nothing you can do, Sergeant Black. Keep yourself down till they move again or I'll be patching you up next!"

With that, Sergeant Floyd Marquart crawled away toward the next wounded soldier. He was now on the Regiment's Medical Detachment after being our 2nd Platoon's medic on the jump into France. He was a great guy, dearly loved by all of us old-timers.

More shells came over, but at last the call came down the line, "Move up!" This time we moved more than a hundred yards. Maybe someone figured out we might have a better chance on the move than lying in the snow getting picked off one at a time or freezing to death. A few yards up I reached the point where a wounded paratrooper had called out for a medic's help. Only now, two dead figures lay in the blood-stained snow before my eyes. One was the body of the paratrooper; the other was Sergeant Floyd Marquart, my friend.

It was said that Sergeant Marquart had won a full scholarship to medical school and would be leaving at the end of the battle at Bastogne. What a loss to the human race if that was true. He would have made a great doctor. His death was an awful blow to me, and to Hollingsworth, Bird, Milligan, Flanagan, DeWitt, Folley, Howard and others who knew him so well.

The loss of a medic was the worst thing that could happen to a line company. The official history of our regiment noted that on this day two medics were killed while tending to casualties in the 502nd.

From time to time I moved forward until at last I came to the tree line. Our tanks came up across the open fields to help us. We stood up and walked behind the tanks, firing our rifles as we went. This arrangement always seemed to work when Jerry was well dug in and there was enough open ground for our tanks to move around.

The hardest part of our attack was to push the Germans out of these thick evergreen woods running down both sides of the railroad tracks for the next six thousand yards to the town of Bourcy. The woods ran over hills and dales, sometimes gently rolling, sometimes steep. Regardless of rank, everyone who went through those woods agrees that each of those six thousand yards was a stiff step with a high price.

The German officers were masters of defense. When they had time—and they'd had it now—they dug in their men and weapons and made us pay. We found they were dug in on a line every hundred yards all the way to Bourcy. They would fight until the last minute, then fall back one tree at a time until they reached their next dug-in line of defense. There were always more Germans to root out a hundred yards up ahead.

We carried out a constant frontal attack in the bitter cold in wet, frozen clothes that never thawed out. Lack of sleep built up each day. Our need for hot food grew. This was my lot for five days.

By following one of our Sherman tanks for a hundred yards, I reached the evergreen trees at a point where a fire break wide enough for only one tank ran straight through the woods. Once a tank started down the fire break, it couldn't turn around until it reached the next clearing, in this case some three hundred yards.

While we were standing around in the clearing waiting on the Airborne and Armored officers to decide who was going to go first, in came the German shells, small mortars. I was standing next to the first tank, which was parked with its motor running at the start of the fire break. I heard Jerry pop his shells into their mortar tubes and knew they were on their way to us. I yelled out, "Get down!" It was too late. I didn't have time to hit the ground. The shells landed all around us. A phosphorous shell hit the back part of the tank beside me. It must have been part dud because it hit within three feet of me and sprayed all over me, but I didn't get hurt. I was able to brush the phosphorous off without burning any of my skin. I did have a few holes in my uniform, however. Once more I had escaped serious injury from a direct mortar hit.

I was lucky, and so was everyone else. "Let's get the hell out of here!" we paratroopers cried.

"We don't have any tanks with us when we jump, men," Captain Cody said. "Let's go get those damn Germans. Move out! We don't need extra help!"

I yelled to my men, "Let's go! I've never liked tanks that near me anyway! They make too much noise!"

"Big" Holly said, "Tanks draw shelling like the stink around shit. Come on, let's move out."

I yelled over to the 320th Infantry soldier, "We're moving out! Keep in contact!"

We started moving up through that thick forest like we were hunting rabbits, yelling back and forth as if we were on a field problem back in England.

We had gone about 150 yards when I stopped, frozen in my tracks. I had been concerned with keeping contact with the soldier from the 320th and had been looking to the left and to the right rather than up ahead. Dead ahead of me, maybe thirty yards, I saw the barrel of a rifle pointing straight at me.

In one motion I leaned back and jumped sideways behind a tall pine tree about ten inches in diameter. I stood there without moving, just waiting for the splash of the enemy's bullet tearing into the bark of the tree. I held my breath. But there was no splash, no bullet. I raised my M-1 rifle, stepped out from behind the tree and took aim at the enemy.

Now it was his turn to duck behind a tree out of my sight. I stood there aiming at nothing for a moment and then stepped back behind my tree. My heart was in my throat. I knew the grim reaper had crossed our path. Bullets were flying in every direction from both sides, but between me and the Jerry behind that tree up ahead, we were part of a private action.

I thought I'd better let somebody else know what was going on. I called out softly, "Hold up over there!" Already several of my men had stopped and were watching me. They all had a puzzled look on their faces, as if they thought I had cracked from that mortar shell hit. I felt I needed to say something more. Softly again, I said, "I think it's a damned Jerry playing games."

When I reached that spot in the woods there were footprints to prove there had been a soldier behind that tree. They must have belonged to a German who felt as I did. Maybe he was a German squad leader.

By the time we of "C" Company reached the first small clearing, our "B" Company had pulled too far to their right and had worked themselves in front of us while we were making that fuss with the tankers. Our First Battalion lost more time as we straightened ourselves up again. We moved on forward for another 150 yards where we were stopped and told to dig in for the night.

Our officers wanted us in place before night. They knew that foxhole digging was hard, slow work since the ground had been frozen solid for some time now, and that daylight was in short supply this time of year, even more so in the Ardennes woods.

26

One Down, Four to Go

Today our 502nd Regiment had to slip to the left in order to mop up the Germans that had slipped in behind the 327th. We had to spread out more, and our 3rd Battalion crossed to the west side of the railroad tracks. By nightfall I had moved closer to the tracks. Before nightfall we had to undergo a nightmare of artillery fire. With shells everywhere, my men and I spent most of our second day out in the open. It was near zero, and the wind on the hillside made it at least thirty below.

About halfway across the two thousand yards we were mopping up, we came across a clump of old hardwood trees, maybe three or four acres in all. Jerry had dug in there last night and had held us up for a while with their stubborn fight. We rooted them out of their dugouts in that woods, but we had to use everything we had. Artillery, tanks and even our planes had bombed the hell out of them, but we still had to come in with mortars and machine guns to get them out of there to stay.

By the time I reached that patch of trees my "C" Company was trailing. We had spent five straight hours out in the open in the cold. Add to that the most devastating kind of German artillery, their 88s and Nebelwerfer guns, and it was no damned wonder I only wanted to get underground, to get away from flying steel. I also wanted to be out of the wind to get just a little bit warmer. Somehow.

When my squad reached the woods I told my men to find a hole, get in it and warm up. There was one problem. All of the German foxholes were occupied by other American soldiers, and not all paratroopers, either. The 320th Infantry Regiment next to me had pulled too far to the left, probably drawn to the tree patch that offered cover to them.

Given enough time, the Germans would always dig in as if to stay. We could tell how much time they had by their dugouts. In this patch of woods the German dugouts were something to see. They had tree logs over the top of them and dirt from the hole on the logs and snow covering the dirt. They left only a small opening to crawl in or out. The bigger dugouts even had oil stoves with metal stove pipes for venting chimneys. I never got to use one of those; only officers of higher rank from headquarters were allowed in them!

Some of the regular soldiers had been in the dugouts long enough to get plenty warm, but I knew it would take more rank than I had to make them move. With luck, I found a small hole that had only four men in it. I yelled, "Move over! One of my men and I are coming in to get warm." In we went, and they didn't move a muscle. We lay right on top of them until we were able to wiggle down beside them.

The soldiers in that hole were shell shocked. They didn't speak to us or move, not even when German shells landed straight ahead. They just lay there, staring straight ahead. It was like they were dead but didn't know it. I thank God that they were not really dead because the heat from their bodies helped us get warm. It didn't take long.

After I'd warmed up a bit I rounded up our "C" Company troopers, and we started to move again. The sun came out, and we could see our planes overhead. That always helped boost our spirits because we knew the tide was turning.

The Germans fell back and some of them surrendered. We moved across the open ground into another heavily wooded area

One Down, Four to Go

in the tall, thick evergreens of "Bois Jacques." We were near the railroad tracks. Just before dark we were halted and told to dig in for the night.

A roadway ran along one side of the railroad tracks, and an open field spread out on the other side. Along the edge of the trees my 2nd Platoon dug in for the night. The flat terrain made it possible to cover the open field with our machine guns.

Word came down to us as we were digging in before dark that we would have hot chow tonight. We were told to go two at a time two hundred yards through the woods to the roadway, turn right and go another two hundred yards. At that point our Company's "mess" people had brought in a jeep and set up a field kitchen on the roadway. They placed each pot of hot food down on the roadway several yards apart, just in case Jerry had ideas of spoiling our supper.

I was digging fast with night approaching, but when I saw the hot chow my men brought back and found out there was plenty of it, I wasn't going to miss out. I decided to take a shortcut through the evergreen trees, which were covered with a blanket of snow, their heavy branches hanging to the ground in a beautiful winter scene. No shells fell on either side, and I remember thinking, "I'll just follow my footprints back."

The smell of the food led me to the right place. Each trooper was to re-supply himself with water, ammo, K-rations and whatever for the next day's needs before eating. For that we had to walk over to a supply depot on the road a short distance away. While I was waiting for my supplies, Supply Sergeant Cam Anderson gave me bad news. Our own Air Force's P-47s had made another bad mistake and had bombed our 502nd's 3rd Battalion. In the process they killed the Battalion Commander, Lieutenant Colonel John P. Stopka, the officer who helped Colonel Cole lead his bayonet charge at Carentan.

After picking up my chow I went back to the supply depot to ask Anderson for more details about Colonel Stopka. At that moment Jerry let go with his Nebelwerfer guns, their last dirty act for the day. They had to know we were eating hot chow. If nothing else, they could smell it!

At least twenty-four shells hit the beautiful evergreen woods I had just come through. If I hadn't gone back to talk to Sergeant Anderson, I would have been in the middle of that forest on my way back. Every shell was a tree burst. Tree limbs fell for at least five full minutes.

I started back along the roadway looking for another place to cut through, but there was simply no way I could walk through that mess. I could not recognize any part of that once beautiful evergreen forest I had enjoyed just a short time back. This time I had to walk about two hundred yards on the roadway to a fire break running at right angles toward my 2nd Platoon's outpost on the edge of the woods. I knew it was the long way around, but it was the only way. By now it was total darkness. I was challenged at every single foxhole and had to give the password.

I had covered eight hundred yards for hot chow, and by the time I got back to my foxhole it was frozen!

Somehow we did not lose a trooper. Not one was hit, not even scratched. I ate all of that "hot" chow, ice and all in my foxhole. You want to know something? I didn't complain, either. Looking out there toward the forest when the moon came up I saw that all twenty-four shells landed in the trees. Hell, if I'd been in a hurry to eat I'd have been in the middle of that mess!

On the third day of this big attack they ran patrols in the daylight hours. I spent most of the day in my foxhole trying to keep warm. I took a walk around our devastated woods in the afternoon, not just for the exercise but to pick up my squad's daily supplies at the company command post.

There was good news for me—a letter from Mom and one from my best gal back in Ohio. I saved those two goodies to read over and over back in my foxhole.

On Tuesday, January 16, 1945, the call came for 502nd to move out on the attack at 0830 hours (8:30 a.m.) to size up the village of Bourcy and the high ground overlooking it.

We gained ground, with the Second and 3rd Battalions taking high ground south and west of Bourcy. When our two battalions tried to move into Bourcy, however, they ran into six "big tigers" dug in and waiting for us. Those tanks and the intense artillery fire stopped us short. We were ordered to dig in early in the afternoon.

Later we learned we had to stop because the 320th Infantry Regiment had moved too slowly and that a gap of at least a thousand yards had developed between our two regiments. Now it would take another day to capture Bourcy.

Another foxhole to dig before it got dark—on the highest hill with the roughest, meanest terrain of the whole area. We had to climb a steep hill by winding around it to reach its top. On top there was a cleared area of about two or three acres that might have been used as a pasture.

Our bedrolls weighted us down as we made our way through the deep snow. As I reached the top and went out into the clearing I saw an American jeep. I couldn't believe it. I said to the driver, "How did you get up that hill?"

"The same way you did," he said, adding that the jeep's four-wheel drive made it an easy drive. I could see that the jeep had replaced the mule!

That jeep had brought us hot chow for our supper. The kitchen people set up for chow call while we started digging.

I dug my foxhole just inside the tree line a few feet off the top of the hill and a few feet from a cliff-like drop-off. I could see toward Bourcy, just a thousand yards away. About halfway through my digging I heard the damnedest noise maybe two hundred yards below me. It was the unmistakable sound of tanks. I got up to take a look with my squad members following behind.

My common sense had told me a few minutes earlier that we had little to worry about up here. My feelings were confirmed when I looked into the biggest, finest German dugout I'd ever seen. It had just been built with pine logs a foot thick, branches piled on top. Jerry hadn't had time to put dirt and snow on yet before our 3rd Battalion took the hill.

Americans were already inside that dugout. My squad followed me down the steps that had been cut out of the frozen ground right into our First Battalion command post. The place was full of officers: Majors, Captains, and maybe a Colonel. There was more brass than on a parade ground.

Major John D. Hanlon, our Battalion Commanding Officer, barked out, "What the hell you doing in here, Sergeant? You lost?"

"No, Sir!" I said. "I just made a wrong turn. Sorry, Sir!"

My men had already gotten the message and were on their way out. How much nicer it would have been if my men had heard Major Hanlon say, "If your men are cold, Sergeant, bring them over here by our stove." That would have been real leadership. I wouldn't have let my men stay, and he would have won all our respect. Nevertheless, that was some dugout: lights, chairs, even a table of sorts, and a stove with a chimney. All the comforts of home.

My common sense told me again that no way was there any Germans near here. My squad and I kept on digging even with the noise of tanks down below us.

After finishing our foxholes, Private First Class Flanagan decided to take a look at the source of the noise. He had to go down our side of the hill around some trees and then hang out over the edge to see the bottom of our cliff.

I sat on the edge of my foxhole waiting for Flanagan to report back what he saw. Instead, I heard a yell from him for me to get the hell down there. When I got to him, Flanagan had made up his mind about what was going on. "Those are not our tanks, Sergeant!" he said. "They're Jerry's. Look down there!"

I did. Sure enough, they were the biggest they make. "They're Tiger tanks!" I said. One of the Tigers had been dug back into the bank of the hill below us, probably to hide from our aircraft, and had become stuck. For the past half hour the other Tiger tank had been pulling it loose.

Flanagan took off on a dead run up the hill, yelling "German Tiger tanks!" as loud as he could. I yelled after him, "Bring the bazooka!" But by then both tanks were free. One was pulling the other toward Bourcy, and we could see them in full view, but by the time we got the bazooka set up, they were too far away to reach.

With Flanagan's yelling, our hillside came to life and the Battalion's dugout command post was buzzing like a beehive hit with a stick. They put patrols out right away, but the tanks had pulled back to Bourcy from right under our feet!

One Down, Four to Go   297

All night long I kept seeing those two big Tiger tanks in my sleep. When daylight came they were still foremost in my mind. It was the same with everyone else, and our bazooka men became our key people on the attack we launched that morning.

My squad drew the area leading down and around the hill past the place where the tanks had been stuck. They had been so close to where we were digging our foxholes that we had damn near stepped on them.

Moving slowly over the high ground and through the woods, we occasionally ran into enemy infantry as we went along. We kept our eyes open for Tigers on this morning's hunt.

By noon we had reached the big highway north of Bourcy, a new two-lane blacktop road cutting straight through the hills. I came out onto the highway at a big, old house that had been hit by artillery or bombs within the past few days. The well-wooded grounds around it made me think it was some sort of an estate. Jerry must have used it as a headquarters of some sort or as a motorpark. I could see a lot of burned-out tanks and other ruined equipment near by.

We crossed the highway and climbed up the road bank to flat, open fields. Several hundred yards ahead of us we could see Germans on the run as they fell back. We broke into a run, firing at them as we ran. They would stop now and then and fire back at us, hoping to slow us down.

I saw four of our own "C" Company troopers get hit (but not killed) out in that open field chase. We kept on going, yelling back and forth to each other, "Get 'em! Get 'em! Keep going! Shoot the son-of-bitches! Shoot 'em!" All the time we sensed a great victory. We were gaining on them, and everyone was laughing and full of joy each time we saw a German get hit and fall.

I remember feeling joy shooting at one German soldier out in front of me. I don't know why I took my wrath out on him, but he didn't give up easy. Every time I fired my M-1 rifle at him, he would go down on the ground. Then all of a sudden he would jump up and run some more. He was still four hundred yards ahead of me, but I was gaining on him. No matter how many times he was hit—if he was hit—he always got up. The last time I saw him he was still on the run.

At this point our First Battalion officers realized we in the "C" Company were still on the attack, that we had not stopped at the highway that was supposed to be the end of our line of attack. Carried away with our success and the sight of Jerry in full flight as we reached the highway, we had not thought of letting them get away. It seemed the right thing to do. Keep going! Which we did—two thousand yards too far!

They finally got us all stopped, and we returned to the highway and dug in overlooking that big field we had just taken—all two thousand yards of it. Now we were giving it back to Jerry.

By noon it was raining more than snowing. With our foxhole digging finished, I decided to move all but two of my men inside the big old house just across the highway. I wanted to get my men out of the rain, and I was curious about that house. The war had ruined it, but once it was a beautiful house. I climbed its several staircases, even those that were badly damaged. From the attic above the third floor I could see a long way. What an artillery outpost this had been for Jerry, and now for us!

American units were starting to move in around the house and its grounds. By 1400 hours (2 p.m.) there were American jeeps and trucks and artillery pieces. "What the hell is going on around here?" I said, out loud. That much action is bound to bring on German shelling. Sure thing, here she comes! German 88s started tuning us in. My men and I ended up in the basement for the rest of the afternoon.

I had just started a fire in the fireplace when the good word came down by runner from my company command post. "Pack up everything but your mess kit. We are moving out of Bastogne. It's all over! We will have a hot turkey dinner with all the trimmings for chow tonight. This will be our Christmas dinner, ya hear?" It was the southern drawl of Sergeant Howard.

Howard was now back in charge of the mortar squad in our 2nd Platoon, since Sergeant Griffith had been wounded earlier today. "Our Company's chow line will be set up in that nice wooded area behind the buildings around this house, just five hun-

One Down, Four to Go

dred yards away. We'll eat just after dark, around 1800 hours (6 p.m.)," he said.

Just like that it was to end. Almost as strange as the way it began. At first it didn't sink in to me or to my men. Private Flanagan reminded me of the time five days earlier when we'd gotten our hopes too high.

I'd been too burned up all afternoon about those two thousand yards we gave back to the Germans to pay attention to the rumors flying around. The word was that "C" Company officers, not the Battalion, had made the mistake. We were supposed to stop at the highway line, where the Battle of the Bulge would end for the 502nd Parachute Regiment with the capture of Bourcy.

All around me were men of the 11th Armored Division. They were coming into this big estate all afternoon. All I could get out of any of them was that they were moving into this old estate and setting up a tank park.

We stopped thinking about the war and began anticipating chow. We had an hour to wait—time enough for real joy to set in.

German shells had been landing along the highway for the past hour. The Germans knew that we (now the 11th Armored Division) were dug in for the night. Once in a while they would try to hit the old house, but it was just harassing fire. We knew we'd be safe in the chow line that had been set up in the wooded area.

I hadn't talked to Sergeant Hollingsworth for the past five days because the fighting had been so intense. Now, as we lined up for chow, Holly, Milligan and Howard marched with our men to our feast. We all picked up the Christmas spirit at once, singing "Jingle Bells" and rattling our mess kits as we marched along.

Less than a hundred yards inside the pitch dark woods, someone came toward us on a dead run waving his flashlight in a frantic motion. He was acting like a mad man. We all stopped singing and rattling our mess kits and stopped in our tracks.

"Who in hell is this nut?" Holly said to me.

The soldier wasn't shining his flashlight in front to see where he was going. He was waving it in the air. About ten yards in front of us and still on a dead run, he aimed his light beam on the ground in front of him. We both saw it at the same time.

"Look out!" We yelled. We were too late.

"Black, whoever he was," Holly said, "He's killed himself. He ran right into the ground. I've never seen anything like that." In front of us was a deep shell hole or a bomb crater at least four feet deep. The soldier wasn't even looking down when he hit bottom. But he wasn't dead, not even hurt. He crawled up to the edge of the crater where we were all standing looking down at him. He still held the flashlight in his hand, and it was burning brightly.

His first words were, "Sergeant Hollingsworth? You, too, Sergeant Black? Why in hell were you guys *singing*?"

I said, "I'll be damned if it isn't Blazick!"

Holly said, "We were singing 'Jingle Bells.' Where have you been all this time?"

Blazick said, "I'm trying to stay alive. Don't any of you guys know there's a war going on? Hell! The Germans are just over there—back the way you all came!"

"We must have walked right past them!" Holly said.

"Hell, Blazick," Milligan said. "We asked Jerry to hold up the war until we have Christmas dinner."

Someone who was new to "C" Company said, "Who did the sergeant say he was?"

Flanagan answered, "That's Blazick from the 1st Platoon."

Another new man said, "Who the blazes is Blazick?"

A third new soldier said, "I think he is a Second Lieutenant from the way he acts."

By now *Private* Blazick was on his feet going from man to man. "Shut up. Keep it down. Spread out. What the hell is the matter with your troopers, anyway? This isn't the Tennessee Maneuvers! Don't any of you dummies realize this is a combat zone?" All the time he was talking in a stage whisper.

After making the rounds to all our men he came back to Holly and me. "Hey, you two Sergeants," he said. "Make your men hold it down. There's nothing to celebrate now! Christmas was over a month ago!"

"Maybe where you've been, but not for us," Holly said. "All of us here in Bastogne have earned a big Christmas dinner and a little fun with it. Come on, men. Let's enjoy it." Away we went singing at the top of our lungs headed for the chow line.

One Down, Four to Go

Blazick couldn't let go of it. As he dished up mashed potatoes and gravy he kept up a constant chatter in a loud whisper: "Keep it moving! Close that line back there! What's the holdup, Sergeant? Move on! What are you waiting on, trooper? More potatoes and gravy? Hell, trooper, you can't eat what I gave you. Hey, men. Remember, you've been eating a lot of K-rations. Your stomachs are all shrunk up. Don't eat too much. Hurry up! This is no place to get sick. Hey, over there! Shhhh! Keep it down!"

He never did stop talking, probably making more noise than any of the rest of us. We went back for seconds and thirds and kept the whole mess crew longer than we would have without Blazick.

Back in the basement of the big house after chow, we got the word, "Move back!" This time it was for real. We were pulling out of Bastogne.

Our orders were to march to the rear, taking all of our "C" Company back across the ground we had fought for the past five days—back away from Bourcy along the railroad tracks and under the viaduct where we had taken so long to "crack the whip" into place.

At the start of our march back we were laughing, talking and joking back and forth. We didn't know for sure where we were going. The Captain just said, "To the rear—march!" That was good enough at the start, but the going was hard work through deep snow, over hills, and through the dense wooded area. It stopped snowing, and the moon came out and helped light our way. The moonlight also showed us terrible reminders of war over the past five days.

"Look over there!" James Flanagan said. "That's where Colonel Stopka got killed!" A little later he said, "There is where Sergeant Folley went out." A few steps more, and "There's the spot where the three troopers were hit by the same shell!" And so it went. The worst place for those of us still left in the 2nd Platoon was the cold wind-swept open hillside where medic Floyd Marquart was killed helping a fellow trooper stay alive.

After that all talking stopped. We were struggling now, just walking—not marching. We looked like tired old men. The pride and joy of the "victory look" had faded.

We reached the first road, and it was easier walking from there on. We had to take many rest breaks. Other units passed us or caught up with us as the night went on.

About midnight we reached the "big" town of Bastogne. Our Company Commander, Captain Cody, drifted back from up front to tell each of us to be sure to take a good look walking through because we were not stopping. "This is what you fought so hard for, men!" he said. "This is the town of Bastogne. What you and the men we leave behind have done will be in the history books for your kids to read!"

It was too dark to see anything, and all war-torn towns look alike. I do remember taking a good look as we marched down the town's main street in a column of two. No one said a word as we marched along. We looked back and forth, up and down, all around at this beat-up town. We were walking so slowly that it seemed to me to be nothing but a town with a very long and a very wide main street.

"They'll rebuild it all someday," Captain Cody said to me at the end of that long street. "It doesn't matter what it looked like before. All that matters now is the name. They will never change that. You helped make sure of that, Sergeant!"

As we walked out of Bastogne, Sergeant Hollingsworth said to me, "Hey, Sergeant Black, how do you spell the name of this place?"

"B-A-S-T-O-G-N-E!" I said. It wasn't that I was such a good speller; I simply turned around and read it off the road sign we'd just passed at the south end of town.

27

Back to France

From the hayloft of a building in a town about six or eight miles southwest of Bastogne I woke up to the call, "Sergeant Black, report to the First Sergeant!" It was 1000 hours (10 a.m.), and we had been left to sleep in the morning after the "end" of the fighting at Bastogne. In a nearby building I found our Company command post with First Sergeant Grotjan on duty.

"How would you like to take a jeep ride this afternoon, Sergeant Black?" he said to me.

"Where to?"

"We don't know yet," the First Sergeant said. "I hope it is somewhere south where it's warm." Then he said, "I'm putting you on the advance party detail for the Division. You are to pack up and report over to Battalion, ready to move out at 1300 hours (1 p.m.) today. See Lieutenant Odom; he will be in charge."

At Battalion I learned that the Division was moving nearly two hundred miles, but more east than south. Lieutenant Odom showed us our route of travel, by way of Neufchateau and Arlon, Belgium, into France at Longway, ending up at the Province of Alsace just north of the City of Strasbourg. Once more our Division would be close to the Rhine River, and once more we would return to France.

On the big map of Europe you could almost draw a straight line from west to east across France to show where I had been and where I was going in this big country. It was from sea to border, and the border was Germany.

The Rhine crossing had been the talk in the 101st, and now we were moving up to it. Only maybe we wouldn't jump. After Bastogne, the big boys may have figured out we could just walk across and take the Rhine crossing.

It was my first jeep ride, and less than a joy because it was down to zero when we pulled out. We were in a caravan of at least twenty jeeps, but our line of march was difficult to maintain because the roads were ice coated, and it was still snowing. More important, I felt, was the hazard from all the heavy military traffic moving up the roads toward Bastogne.

Hitler was at it again. Now it was "Operation Nordwind" begun on New Year's Day, a plan to deal us a series of blows to keep us off balance. Hitler put Himmler in charge, and the Germans struck for the recapture of the city of Strassbourg, France. Hitler's plan called for regaining Alsace-Lorraine and destroying one Allied army at a time. By January 18 he was well under way, and Eisenhower gave the call for the "Screaming Eagles"!

A look at the battle lines on January 20, 1945, showed a huge bulge in our lines at a place called Colmar in the Vosges Mountains. To an old trooper like me, the town of Haguenau, the place where our lines cut almost straight northwest to Bastogne in a 90-degree bend, had the look of another Bastogne.

On the slow trek by jeep, hugging the clogged back roads near the front lines, I felt something different this time. Everything was moving "up" and nothing was moving back. I could see U.S. military hardware everywhere. More than once we passed our huge 240 millimeter gun emplacements. They weren't just parked by the road; they were firing away at Jerry.

On the way through a small town at lunch time (noon hour), we were crawling along the main street crowded with armored vehicles. Tanks and half-tracks were parked everywhere. We passed a line of tanker drivers going into a building to eat. Lieu-

Back to France

tenant Odom asked us Sergeants if we wanted a hot meal. "You're damned right," we said. So we stopped.

A tank officer was standing in the chow line. Lieutenant Odom walked over to him, saluted smartly and said, "We are the 101st Airborne, Sir!" Then he said, "My men are cold and hungry. It has been weeks since we had a good, hot meal. May we please join you for dinner? We will be very glad to pay you back if we ever fight alongside you."

The tank officer was a southern gentleman like Lieutenant Odom. "Indeed you may," he said without hesitation. He stepped out of line, and we three Sergeants and the Lieutenant followed him into the building, which had been turned into a mess hall. The officer stepped up to the head of the line where the Mess Sergeant was dishing up food. He said something to him, then turned to the rest of the men in the room.

"Gentlemen," he said, "we have four guests for dinner today. We are honored to have these four paratroopers from the 101st Airborne Division take chow with us. They have just come from the great battle at Bastogne."

Someone in the room stood up and said, "Three cheers for the 101st!" Then followed, "Hip! Hip! Hooray! Hip! Hip! Hooray! Hip! Hip! Hooray!"

Traveling east through France I observed that the farmer fared the worst with the war. The town of Sarrebourg was an old farm settlement in the traditional European style with the house and barn built together as a place of business and a dwelling with no grassy area, trees, shrubs, or fences between building like in America.

About 1630 hours (4:30 p.m.) I began banging on front doors with my French interpreter. Time after time I knocked and found no one at home. Damn! How could I take over someone's house and not even tell him I was doing it? Just as I was about to knock on yet another door, I saw a man come out of a barn I had passed by several doors back.

I went back to the barn. The front door was wide open, and inside all the people of the town were hard at work thrashing wheat. Wait a minute! In Ohio we would work out in the fields and on a good day we might thrash two thousand bushels, always in

July and August in the hot sun. Here in Alsace, France, it was January and cold, the barn was smaller than a house, and it was "thrashing time"! Those old Alsacian men and women were gathered in a circle flailing wheat on the bare ground in the center of an old barn. It was a scene out of the Bible!

Saturday afternoon my company pulled in, a rough-looking unit of troopers. The men looked dazed as they got off the trucks and tried to fall into some kind of platoon formation. There was very little talking, and none of the joking or cocky kind!

For the next six days we rested up and regrouped, but it took us the whole 38 days we spent in Alsace to work off the effects of the Battle of the Bulge.

Rennie Howard, "Big" Holly and Marvin Milligan were sure they knew why we were in Alsace—to stop Hitler's try at another breakthrough. On the first morning, Sunday, Holly said, "Hey, look around you! Who don't you see any more? Where is Kelly? Haddick? I don't see W. O. Bird, F. J. Folley or Floyd Marquart. There is no one to take their place!"

We weren't afraid that the new men wouldn't be as good as the old-timers they replaced, but that they wouldn't have time to get the training they needed. They would be canon fodder.

When our division dropped into Holland we had just over 15,000 enlisted men and officers. Here in Alsace, on the first of February, we were down to 9,600 men. We were missing the equivalent of one battalion in each regiment.

We learned that Jerry had struck south of Haguenau, had crossed the Moder River in two places and had cut up one company in the 222nd Regiment from the 42nd Division. Today we were moving up.

"Here we go again, Sergeant Black," said "Big" Holly as we struggled aboard the GI trucks loaded down with battle gear. It was not the front lines just yet. The 502nd would start out as the division reserve. We bivouacked at Alteckendorf within artillery range of the enemy. The 501st and the 327th Regiments drew the first front-line duty for the Division in Alsace. Our Division replaced the 42nd Infantry Division along the Moder River just west of Haguenau.

Back to France

Although we didn't see front-line duty until February 4, we spent anxious days in a small village that has no name any more. The village was one street wide, and that street ran uphill all the way from one end of town to the other. My squad was in one room of a house in the center of the village. Sergeant Hollingsworth and his squad were in the first house at the bottom of the hill.

Our trouble began the moment we moved in and took over the village. The people did not like us. We could tell from the start that they were pro-German. They "spoke the Deutsch" and even flew the German flag until we made them take it down.

I don't know why the people in this tiny village got their back up against us. Maybe we took the wrong people's houses to start with. Or maybe the German breakthrough two days earlier gave them hope that we wouldn't be in their area very long.

For the next several days the "north enders" (villagers at the top of the hill) kept running up the German flag after every heavy artillery attack by Jerry. As soon as we paratroopers showed up in the street, they would take the flag down again.

On our third day Holly's house was hit with artillery fire, and he had to move to another house. The next day my squad's house was hit, and I had to move out.

I wasn't keen on staying inside houses in combat, but it was still winter. For two days at the end of January it was colder than the coldest in the Bulge. Our orders were to "cut down on frost bite and stop trenchfoot." And put a stop to the pro-German carrying on.

Finally, on Sunday, Platoon Sergeant DeWitt passed the word that we were moving up in the morning.

Our Company assembled in the early morning of February 4 decked out in full-field battle dress to march on line. It had started to warm up, but there was still lots of snow on the ground. Snow drifts had been plowed back from the roads so many times that snow on each side of the road was ten feet deep in many places. It was like walking through a tunnel without a roof.

Snow was melting with the warmer weather, and small streams were overflowing their banks. On our first day out, we held a six-mile stretch on the front—every inch along the Moder River. In dry times the river was about twenty-five or thirty feet wide. Now it was more than two hundred feet wide and instead of slow and shallow it was swift and deep.

My good friend W. O. Bird joined us after being gone a month. He took over Sergeant Folley's Third Squad. Private First Class Kent Lee Master, who had been with the Fourth Squad when he was wounded in Holland on September 19, joined us in the Second Squad. Even with the replacements there were gaps in every unit, and all the old-timer troopers were being stretched thinner and thinner in the ranks. About six hundred paratroopers came to the division from Camp Mourmelon and were divided among our three regiments. These men were qualified jumpers but untrained in airborne tactics.

A platoon runner came over to my billet with the message that I was wanted at Platoon command post right away. Sergeant DeWitt began talking the moment I walked in the door. "This is Sergeant Black, Squad Sergeant of the Second Squad," he said. "For the next two days he will be in charge of you new men. He is going to give you some front-line training. You will do what he says; it might save your life!"

Then he turned to me. "Sergeant Black," he said, "Captain Cody wants all the new replacements to have at least a week of front-line training before they man the foxholes. You will have them Monday and Tuesday. Sergeant Hollingsworth will have them Wednesday and Thursday. Any questions?"

"Yes! What the hell do I do for front-line training?"

"Take them for a walk along the front lines, Sergeant!"

That's exactly what I did for the next two days. It turned out to be fun for both Holly and me. We didn't walk right along the front line, but maybe a hundred yards behind it, sometimes on high ground where Jerry could see us.

There was still snow on the ground in most places and quite heavy in wooded areas. Along the Moder River we faced the great Haguenau Forest that covered an area fifteen miles wide and five miles deep. Jerry was dug in deep in the forest. We had the high ground, but the enemy had the cover. In many places the dense evergreen forest came to the edge of the Moder River.

Some sharp trooper figured out that by using searchlights a few miles in our rear on dark nights, the beams shining in the sky would reflect on particles in the cold air and make "artificial moonlight." The lights could be controlled to illuminate any given sector of our front lines. The search lights added to the spectacular show.

Down by the Moder River we dug individual foxholes a few hundred yards back from the river. Even on high ground the February thaw brought flooding to our foxholes. In Bastogne the ground stayed frozen, and with hay and straw a trooper could stay dry. Here in Alsace there was water everywhere, and it was still deep in winter.

We carried sandbags in after dark, but they were of little help. In daylight hours we had to stay down in our foxholes because of intense enemy shelling and were soaked to the bone. At night we got out of our water-filled holes and sat on sand bags. My squad went through two days and nights of this hell.

Shortly after dark the second day the "B" Company marched past my foxhole carrying boats down to the swollen river. They were planning to cross the river to try to capture German prisoners and would cover some three thousand yards on their combat patrol. For once I felt someone had it worse than me. They would be working deep in the Haguenau Forest, and the worst patrol of all is one where you go stumbling around in a forest.

As it worked out, they could not get across the flood-stage Moder River in any kind of force because they simply couldn't control their boats. Some troopers tried to swim, but that was worse. The mission was called off, and the men marched past me again.

Our Division laundry was in full effect, and I was given time to clean up and put on a dry uniform before taking a new front-line position.

From my new dugout I had a great view of Jerry's front line. By daylight we could see each other's steel helmets sticking out of the foxholes. That seemed to be OK for both sides. "But," I said to my men, "don't get up and walk around or you'll draw '88' fire for damned sure."

By now my Second Squad was down to five men. I put two men on the machine gun in a dugout by themselves. With me in the big dugout was my assistant squad leader, Jumpknife Milligan, and a rifleman who had joined us in Alsace. We spent the next five days together.

Corporal Milligan and I laughed and joked about the "old days" before the war. With our new trooper, who was very young, we had an eager audience, and we poured it on. Corporal Milligan liked to tell the new men when he thought they were getting careless. "Hey," he would say. "Keep your eyes on Sergeant Black and do what he says. He hasn't had a scratch." But on Thursday, February 15, Milligan didn't get a chance to tell the new men to listen to their squad leader.

Around 0800 hours (8 a.m.), our 2nd Platoon runner brought two replacement soldiers to my dugout. "DeWitt said these two men are to join your squad, Sergeant Black," the runner said. "They have your squad's food and water ration for today." The runner left on the double, knowing the problems of being on the front line during daylight hours.

One of the new soldiers was small and very young; the older man was average size and had an Air Force patch on his GI overcoat. I took notice of all of this in the short time they stood exposed to the enemy, looking down into my dugout.

"The very first thing you have to learn out here, men, is to keep your head down," I said. "Protect yourself and your rations. Hand that water and food down here, and then get in here with me until I figure out what to do with you."

The little guy wasted no time, but the other one laid his rifle in the dirt, took off his steel helmet and sat down on the roof of my dugout. "I'm not afraid of the damned Germans!" he said.

I started to say, "Our here, one man's mistake can be everybody's problem—"

"Shhh-wham!"

There was only time to duck my head and dive into the dugout. Hell, the 88 shell landed just ten feet away, halfway between my dugout and my machine gun crew's foxhole. The shell slammed into the ground and sprayed deadly shrapnel between the two holes.

I waited for a follow-up. It was deathly quiet, and the sickening smell of gun powder hung in the air. The new soldier, the little guy, was lying close to me shaking like a leaf. In a whisper he said, "Who—what was that?"

Milligan answered him. "That's what Sergeant Black was talking about, my boy! That was the bastard's 88s!"

Suddenly I remembered the Air Force patch—that cocky guy on my dugout roof who was showing us how brave he was. I scrambled on my knees to the opening of the dugout to look for him. He hadn't even bothered to duck his head and had taken the full blast of the 88 millimeter shell. He was bleeding everywhere—nose, mouth, ears, eyes. A big piece of shrapnel had caught him in the mid section, and that alone would have killed him, but slowly. He was already dead from the concussion he took full blast.

Only as a gesture, I called for the "meat wagon" and our medic.

Damn! It was senseless. The soldier didn't have to prove anything to me. I turned to the young boy and said, "Where are you two from? And what was his name, by the way?"

Still shaken, the soldier said, "I just got here from the States. A-A-A Sergeant, Sir! I don't know who he is or where he came from, Sir." He sensed something was wrong. "Is he all right, Sir?"

"No, he is not, soldier," I said. "He is dead! See for yourself!"

Milligan took over the instruction. "That, young man is lesson number one: Do as you are told. Lesson number two is, we are all enlisted men out here. There are no commissioned officers in the front-line foxholes. No one out here rates a 'Sir'!"

By then Milligan had made up his mind what to do with the new soldier. "Sergeant," he said, "my machine gun crew can use an ammo bearer. Why don't you send him over to them. They have plenty of room for three men."

"Good idea," I said. "Take him over. What's your name, soldier?"

"Tom Yates."

(Yates survived to go on to jump school and get his wings and jump boots. He came back to the squad and served out the war.)

The rest of my front line days dragged by and on Sunday, February 18, the 3rd Battalion along with my "C" Company were pulled off the line and replaced by the rest of our First Battalion plus one company of the Second Battalion. My company went into Regimental reserve.

We noticed on the front lines that Jerry was a copy cat. Every time we sent out a patrol, they did. If ours was big, theirs was, too. When we went for small squad-sized patrols, they did, too.

The ordinary German was a good soldier but a dummy about some of his copy cat ideas.

Whenever there was a stalemate and we just had to know what Jerry was up to, we would set out to get prisoners. Any prisoners—the more, the merrier. It was inevitable that Sergeant Black, Squad leader of the Second Squad, 2nd Platoon of "C" Company, would lead a patrol in the great war.

I didn't like the idea of us front-line foxhole soldiers doing patrol work for the rear echelon people. They had S-2 sections at the regimental level with their own "pathfinders" who had volunteered back in England for that kind of work, and they were good at it.

About 1100 hours (11 a.m.) on Tuesday, February 20, Sergeant DeWitt said to me, "Report to First Sergeant Grotjan for a key job the company has planned for tonight."

I got back with Corporal Milligan, Private First Class Flanagan and Lee Master and one other man (I think it was Corporal O'Neill.)

That afternoon the First Sergeant took the five of us to an empty room where he said we would stay until time for our patrol to department. he said someone from the regiment would stop by later in the afternoon to brief us. Meanwhile we were to relax and take life easy for the rest of the day. Patrol wouldn't begin until 2300 hours (11 p.m.).

It wasn't easy to relax around company headquarters. There was too much action, and someone was always coming into our room. At least six times noncommissioned officers stopped in. Hell! If they were so worried I couldn't do the job, why didn't they go themselves?

Back to France

Far too soon it was time for me to lead our patrol. Two jeeps picked us up, and away we went without any fanfare. They drove us straight to our jumping off place, where I marched my patrol a hundred yards to the last outpost. The men at the outpost knew we were coming through on our way to no-man's land. I paused there long enough to set a time for the outpost Sergeant to call in the artillery flares once my patrol reached the river.

I said to the outpost Sergeant, "Remember who I am—Sergeant Black, from "C" Company—because we will be coming back through here before daylight. Ask some questions before your men start shooting. We just might have some Germans with us."

"Keep your eyes glued on me," I said to my men, "and no talking from now on. Milligan, you bring up the rear. Let's move out!"

A wire fence with wood posts ran from the outpost all the way downhill to the river. It would give us a perfect guide out and back and some form of concealment. We had more than six hundred yards to go before reaching the water, which was still over its river banks.

As we were moving along at a normal gait, the memory of that night in Holland when it seemed the fence posts were moving on me came clearly to my mind. I had held my fire, trying to catch those "posts" in the act. Maybe that would work here in reverse. It couldn't do any harm to try. I threw up my hand and stopped my patrol. After motioning everybody down, I told each trooper my plan.

We would move rapidly in short bursts of thirty yards or more. Then I would throw up my hand, and we would all stop and duck down for a minute or so before resuming the next thirty-yard rush. My plan worked well; not a shot was fired, and soon we were at the water's edge.

We held up for several minutes waiting on our artillery flares. At this point I heard movement noise by the Germans. It sounded like several people walking in water, and the noise came from upstream about thirty or forty yards on the other side of the fence. It was too dark to see them against the heavy wooded forest.

I looked at my GI watch. It was the exact time for our artillery flares to be shot off.

I began to count: "One, two, three..."

"Pop! Pop!" Suddenly it was light as day. Through the fence I saw the enemy patrol make a dash for dry land. I counted six of them before they went down. The last German did not make it to dry land and went down in less than a foot of water. I saw his helmet shining from the flares overhead floating slowly down the river.

I did not speak until the flares had burned themselves out. "Did you see Jerry?" I asked.

Corporal Milligan spoke up. "Hell, yes! It's a damned machine gun nest straight ahead. They are just across the river. I counted two of them. They didn't see us. We can capture the bastards, Sergeant!"

"I was talking about a Jerry patrol. Didn't you see them off on our left flank through the fence here?" I said to Milligan. Then I said to Flanagan, "Didn't you see them? There were six of them!"

"No, but I saw that Jerry machine gun nest up ahead clear enough," Flanagan whispered. Then he pleaded, "You aren't going to try to take that machine gun nest with a frontal assault, are you, Sergeant?"

I realized I'd made a big mistake by not looking toward the German lines when the flares went off. I would not get a second chance. Now I must rely on what Corporal Milligan's eyes had seen.

Marvin Milligan was as sure as James Flanagan was that there was a Jerry machine gun nest straight ahead. The only difference of opinion was how we should capture it.

"Wade the river and rush them straight on! They don't call me 'Jumpknife' for the hell of it," said the Corporal.

"Try that, and we'll be the only ones captured or killed," Flanagan said.

I whispered back, "For the time being that machine gun nest does not worry me, men. We've got to lay low right here until that German patrol gets out of here. I sure don't want them to know where we are. If they cut in behind us, we are in big trouble."

We five Americans sat down along the fence row and waited for time to pass, watching in all four directions. After about half an hour, two rifle shots rang out from the outpost we had passed earlier.

"It's the Jerry patrol! They've hit our lines! Stay on the ball! They may come right down this fence row! Be ready!" I whispered out to my patrol.

For another half hour all I heard was the heavy breathing of five paratroopers from "C" Company. I saw nothing of the German patrol. My GI watch showed 0130 hours (1:30 a.m.), and I knew I had to get on with my task. I decided to move on the machine gun nest. I told the men I was moving straight across the river at the gun and to follow close behind. "If they open up on us, beat it back across the river and give each of us cover fire from there."

I turned around and started wading into the swollen Moder River. At first it was ankle deep, but after several carefully placed steps I was in over the tops of my jump boots. I went on slowly, trying hard not to splash water for fear that the German machine gun crew would surely detect us. Suddenly I plunged into water above my belt line. I had reached the floor of the main river's channel bed, a solid footing. My movements now were fluid, almost like swimming. Once I went, closer and closer to the enemy, praying that they would not hear us. I held my submachine gun at eye level, just out of the water.

Maybe it was curiosity, maybe habit, but something caused me to turn and look back to see if my men were coming behind me. I stumbled and slapped the water hard with my left hand in an attempt to keep from falling and to hold my gun high and dry. The action kept me from falling, but it was a sharp noise, too sharp to escape an enemy long on the alert.

"Burrrppp! Burrrppp! Burrrrppp!" Water splashed off to my right as if a handful of gravel had hit the river with each burst. The fire flash from the muzzle wasn't more than fifty yards in front of me. The cry of the enemy was paralyzing: "Halt Kamerad! Halt! Kommen Sie Hier! Kamerad! Halt!"

"Beat it!" I yelled and waved my gun at my men. "To the rear!"

Neck deep in water, I was tempted to swim for it, but I needed my submachine gun. I struggled back upright, on foot.

Corporal Milligan reached dry land first and opened up on the enemy gun. He was firing at their fire flash and cutting it close to us men still struggling back in the water. He gave me a close shave. I was caught in the cross fire because by now there was a steady stream of fire coming from Jerry, who was zeroing in on the sound of splashing water.

As each of my men reached dry land, he hit the dirt and opened up on the machine gun nest. I was the last to make it to dry land. I went down spread eagle and began to fire at the enemy nest across the water.

Suddenly a horrifying scream of pain rang out from the enemy's outpost station, and the German machine gun nest stopped firing. "Hold your fire!" I called out. No one moved a muscle for several seconds. All I could hear was the heavy breathing of myself and my own men.

After about a minute I said in a low whisper, "We must have hit the gunner. Now's our chance to get out of here. Milligan, fall back along the fence for one hundred yards. Watch our rear for the enemy patrol. Go one man at a time—slow—and stay close to the fence. I'll cover from here. Check your ammo first. Did anybody get hit? Good! Good! How in hell did they miss us? OK, now. One at a time—go slow! Remember they know where we are. Be ready! Let's go, Jumpknife!"

One at a time my patrol fell back along the fence row. When they reached Corporal Milligan they waited for me. At last I made it, and we were all safe. There were still some rifle shots and a hand grenade popping here and there across the river, a sure sign we'd made Jerry nervous.

Private First Class James Flanagan was the first to speak to me as we huddled close together. "Sergeant Black," he said, "I'm freezing to death!"

Our teeth were chattering, and we were soaked to the bone. My GI watch said it was 0200 hours (2 a.m.) My jumpsuit was frozen stiff.

Back to France

Our adrenaline had been pumped up so high that our blood had been warm on the way out, but now we were feeling the effects of the cold winter night.

"This patrol has ended," I said to my men. "We have got to get back and get out of these wet clothes, and I mean now! Follow me!"

I wasted no time moving back along that fence row and did not need to look back to see if my men were keeping up. Milligan was pushing them so hard that Flanagan was literally on my heels half the time.

Soon we reached our friendly outpost. Along with the password, I said, "This is Sergeant Black and his patrol from 'C' Company coming back from a lousy Kraut hunt!"

The outpost Sergeant said to me, "The regimental people told me to tell you, Sergeant, that you and your patrol did a fine job forcing that German patrol into our lines. We captured four of them without a fight. Also, they have a jeep waiting for you on the roadway. By the way, Sergeant, what was all that firing about down by the river?"

I told my men to go on to the jeep and then filled the sergeant in on what had taken place. I told him we were freezing from being wet and would have to keep moving.

At the jeep we were happy to find GI blankets someone had thought to bring for us. They helped, but we were thoroughly cold now. I told the driver to step on the gas. We had to get back where it was warm. The next thing I remember is sitting back in the warm room at Company Headquarters, stripped of all clothing and wrapped only in a blanket. Our platoon medic kept hot coffee running through each of us.

None of us suffered any ill effects from our adventure.

28

Filling in the Ranks

The 502nd Parachute Regiment was the first in the Division to be relieved. We moved to a place called Buhl and from there boarded trucks for Sarrebourg. On February 27 we boarded a train at Reding Station and headed back to Reims, France, and Camp Mourmelon.

The day was clear and warm, and we knew spring was not far off. We passed through a vast farm area with a group of houses every now and then. I could see huge tractors plowing the fields, probably preparing for spring wheat.

At one point we took a convoy break right next to one of those groups of farm houses. When we got off the trucks to stretch our legs, kids of all ages poured out of the houses. We GIs started giving away candy, cigarettes, chewing gum and K-rations—a sure way to put smiles on their faces.

We reached Sarrebourg after dark and stopped along a railroad track at Reding station where we took our first train ride on the continent. Not exactly in style. The train was made up of box cars. When we pulled the doors back we saw they were full of straw for us to lie on. Some smart dude said, "They hold forty soldiers or eight horses."

"Damn it, Black!" said "Big" Holly, putting it in perspective. "Can't you see what's happening to the Elite 502nd now that the old-timers are almost all gone?"

We stretched out on the soft straw with the doors closed to the chilly night air.

Holly continued his explanation. "Remember, we started out from the States on a Luxury Liner. Then we rode beautiful trains in England. They flew us first class to Normandy and Holland. Then what happened? They put us on cattle trucks and sent us to Bastogne. Now they bring us back like a bunch of pack horses. When is this damned war going to end, Sergeant Black?"

I did not answer. The boxcar was a lot more comfortable than riding in the back of an open truck, and warmer, too. Given a choice, I want to see where I'm going, but I'd already seen this country. In a couple of minutes I was asleep.

As our train rolled to a stop we were greeted by music from our 502nd band playing our 502nd marching song. A feeling of heroic pride swelled up in our hearts.

From the train station at Mourmelon we rode in trucks to our new campsite. No longer were we to use the wood barracks of last December that we had worked so hard to make livable. They were now an army hospital. Instead, the "heroes" of the Bulge would live in pyramidal tents with all the trimmings that go with living in a tent city.

To all of us in "C" Company, the sight of those cold tents was a devastating blow. Hell! For the most part, our quarters in combat were better.

We were to stay there only 32 days, and the tent city met the overall objectives of the division, but we all felt we deserved better.

There were eight troopers to a tent, and my Second Squad with Sergeant Hollingsworth's First squad took over three tents. Each tent had a noncommissioned officer in charge, mostly old-timers.

Filling in the Ranks

After the shock wore off, it didn't take long to iron out most of the wrinkles. The beds were double-deck wood beds with heavy fence wire for "springs." Each tent had a small low-boy coal stove.

From the first day, training in infantry tactics was the name of the game. Most of the new men were lacking in this type of combat training. For us old-timers playing at making war wasn't any good for us. We had been taught well, we could still fight, and we could still lead. Most of the training was done by new officers just out of jump school. It was much too realistic. In 38 days at Alsace we of the 502nd had twenty-two casualties, including four who were killed. In training at Camp Mourmelon, twenty enlisted men and officers were wounded, and two officers were killed. All of the casualties were from accidents with short rounds and hand grenades.

We began six weeks of training on March 5. The Rhine River jump was no longer in our division's plans. The 17th Airborne Division would make that jump instead, on March 24. For now our Division was being pushed to the limit with training for the 15th of March when we would "pass in review" for General Eisenhower.

We had received word that we were to be awarded the "Distinguished Unit Citation" from the President for gallantry in action. We were marching to music, at all levels of all units at every spare moment. Besides marching, the clean up for a great parade was under way. Spit and polish, no less.

The Division had a mission of pride at stake and fifteen days to get ready. Our rifles were in a terrible condition. Linseed oiling and rubbing began in dead earnest. Our leather slings were dry and cracked; rust and dirt had been left on too long. Our pistol belts needed hand scrubbing in boiling water with a harsh soap. Our uniforms had to be washed and pressed, and all the new stripes and insignias had to be sewn on everything. Our battle ribbons were a must. Our jump boots had seen a hard winter, and it was a real chore shining them, but by March 15 every pair had a mirror-glass look.

On the day before the parade we were told that the "outstanding" company of the parade, as selected by the Regimental Commanding Officer, would be honored by having Marlene Dietrich join them for noon chow on Monday, March 19.

At Monday morning revelry, First Sergeant Grotjan read an order signed by Colonel Chappuis stating that the "C" Company had been selected as the outstanding company in the Regiment and would be honored at the March 15 parade. After the company roared its approval, Sergeant Grotjan looked straight at Sergeant DeWitt and said, "Captain Williams has declared your 2nd Platoon, Sergeant DeWitt, to be the company winner. Then he looked at me, standing at the head of the Second Squad, and said, "Sergeant Black, Captain Williams has picked your squad as the best in the company!"

Somewhere in the mass of 12,000 "Screaming Eagles" I participated in that grand review. It was the most thrilling event of my life.

The band at the far right hears the call, "Strike up the band!—Forward—March! Left turn—March!"

The band moves past the reviewing stand and then back to their stationary playing position in front of the stand. Then begins the parade of each unit in its long march past the stand and back around the huge parade grounds to the beginning place.

"Forward—March! Left turn—March! Eyes—Right!"

The 502nd Parachute Infantry Regiment is on the far left, and my First Battalion is the last to pass in review.

The band plays our 502nd marching song, and goose pimples are everywhere. My eyes catch the parachute-decorated reviewing stand and from right to left I could clearly see Presidential Secretary Stephen T. Early, Generals Ridgway, Brereton, and Taylor; and the head man himself, General Dwight D. Eisenhower.

"It is a great personal honor for me to be here today," Eisenhower began. "Never before has a full division been cited by the War Department in the name of the President for gallantry in action."

The General continued, "As far as I know there may be many among you that would not rate Bastogne as your bitterest battle. Yet it is entirely fitting and appropriate that you should be cited for that particular battle. It happened to be one of those occasions when the position itself was of the utmost importance to the Allied forces. You, in reserve, were hurried forward and told to hold that position. All the elements of drama, of battle drama, were there. You were cut off, you were surrounded. Only valor, complete confidence in yourself and in your leaders, a knowledge that you were well trained, only the determination to win, could sustain soldiers under those conditions. You were given a marvelous opportunity, and you met every test."

At 1130 hours sharp (11:30 a.m.) on Monday, March 19, the "C" Company stood in formation waiting for the movie queen from Hollywood to arrive for our important dinner date. With our new honor, the 2nd Platoon was placed at the head of the company instead of in the middle, and our entire company wore the "overseas cap" instead of the steel helmet, a battalion trademark.

As we stood in formation, waiting, Sergeant Grotjan decided to give us some good news he had been holding for later in the day. He was handing out four seven-day furloughs in my "C" Company: one to the Mediterranean Riviera, one to Paris, one to Brussels, and one to London. I don't remember who went to the Riviera or to Brussels, but Holly was headed for Paris, and I was bound for London.

We stood in line for a half hour before a load of show people drove up and came to a stop. All of them were wearing some combination of army clothes. God, if there was a woman in that bunch, it didn't show!

We had visions of movie queens in slinky see-through evening gowns or bathing suits, but never in men's GI garb! Out of the jeep stepped two ordinary women from the Marlene Dietrich show. Both were wearing men's combat boots, GI wool off-duty pants with matching wool (itchy) shirt and tie, and a ridiculous off-duty cap at a cocky angle. One of the women wore a men's GI combat jacket and had jet black hair. The other woman I did recognize in spite of her dress. She was wearing an army tanker's jacket and had blonde hair. She was Marlene Dietrich.

Sergeant Grotjan introduced himself, Sergeant DeWitt and us four squad leaders. Somewhere in all of those introductions they forgot to tell Miss Dietrich that she was to eat lunch with the Second Squad.

Off to chow we marched with the whole camp looking on. Damned if we weren't a bunch of proud troopers on that day. However, at the mess tent, disappointment set in on me and my

Second Squad. We got caught up in the old army game. Someone pulled rank on us. The handsome devil sitting next to Miss Dietrich in the official photos was Sergeant Grotjan and one soldier away was Sergeant DeWitt. Not one Second Squad man sat at that table for eight. We were seated at the next table.

With so many losses of key officers, reorganization at top levels was under way. Even Majors and Colonels had been lost. Captain Cody left "C" Company for the Regiment. Captain Williams from our First Battalion Headquarters Company came down to head up "C" Company.

29

Slam the Door

Over the next seventeen days I covered five countries traveling by truck, French trains, U.S. Navy ships, English trains, cars and subways. W. O. Bird saw Holly and me off by the main gate at noon chow time. Holly would spend only a few hours in Paris with me, and then I would head for London for my seven-day leave. We were in no hurry to get back to "tent city," and it was a good thing. Transportation systems throughout Europe were devastated by bombs and artillery. Bridges, train stations and even roadbeds were shut down. This plus the fact that furloughs for staff sergeants were not the highest priority for the military slowed us down on our "vacation" travels.

Our GI truck rolled up in front of a big French hotel in the center of Paris. The hotel had been leased by the U.S. Government for American troops on pass in Paris. This is where Holly would make his headquarters for his seven-day stay in this great city. I said good-bye to Holly over Red Cross coffee and doughnuts in the coffee shop.

A group of us heading for England met at a Paris railroad station and then headed for Le Havre, France, a seaport on the coast of France in the Normandy Province. It wasn't a fast trip, but a comfortable one. We were traveling on a first-class train. Our car was compartmentalized, and only American soldiers occupied it. Many French civilians were riding elsewhere on the train.

After dark our train traveled even more slowly. Much of the time we spent parked on side tracks waiting on other trains. Most of those trains were supply trains headed for the front. On March 21 General Patton's Third Army had crossed the Rhine River, and three days later another huge river crossing was completed.

In Le Havre we were taken by GI trucks to a beautiful resort hotel the army had taken over. I had two days to prepare for my seven-day visit in London. Instead of drawing fighting equipment, I drew "furlough" equipment getting ready for my trip to London. This meant a new uniform, a haircut and shower—and a paymaster on hand to make sure I had enough money. I took all the pay they would give me. PX rations were available, too, and I took on more just for the hell of us.

We set sail for England in daylight Friday and were at sea throughout the night. In the early morning hours of Saturday, March 24, we landed at Southampton, England, and I boarded a train. Before noon my furlough officially began, for I had reached London!

I picked a hotel in Leicester Square with a large entrance, a big lobby, and a sitting room and dining room off the main lobby.

The joy of being on furlough was the right to sleep in as well as the right to stay up late. I did this to excess every day and night I was in London.

I filled my furlough with walks in the park in the daytime, rides on the double-deck bus, dancing with girls, and "pub hopping" after the dance halls closed.

A holiday, Easter Sunday, happened to follow our seven-day furlough, so we all took one more day. We set sail for Le Havre by noon on Monday and were back in France on the morning of Tuesday, April 3. This time we didn't stay at Le Havre but boarded a train for Paris, where we spent one "free" night.

Slam the Door

At Reims the G. I. trucks were waiting for us, and I took the truck to Camp Mourmelon. At Division Headquarters I learned that the 101st Airborne Division had pulled out of Camp Mourmelon and had moved to the "Ruhr Pocket" along the Rhine River in Germany. All that was left of my division were the 501st Parachute Infantry Regiment and a small rear echelon headquarters staff. I had missed them by just one day.

From Reims, France, I rode on the back of a GI truck through Luxembourg and Belgium to Aachem, Germany. By Thursday I had caught up with my "C" Company in division reserve on the west side of the Rhine River a few miles north of Cologne. The front lines ran along the river for some twenty miles, from Dusseldorf to Worringen, where we met up with the 82nd Airborne Division.

For the first time we were inside Germany, the "Father Land," as Hitler called it. The sector occupied by the Division now extended twenty miles deep and fifteen miles long. Inside the area were many villages, towns, and the big city area of Munchen-Gladbach, Rheydt and Odenkirchen. The city area alone was occupied by 200,000 people.

Nobody was sure what to expect from the German people. Even though the war had moved through here up to the banks of the Rhine River, the only signs of fighting that we could see were spring-dug deep trenches along one of the main roads. It gave the impression that the home guard of the German people might be planning to make a last-ditch stand as their army fell back.

The company posted a walking guard day and night, in the center of the street, one every one hundred yards. Nobody went outside after dark—Yanks or Germans!

My billet was a two-story wood frame house with a lawn on four sides. It has six rooms, four at ground level and two upstairs. I used three of the downstairs rooms for my Second Squad and took a bedroom upstairs for myself. My plan was always to clean out everything we did not need or might harm in some way. Rugs, tables, stands, chairs, pictures and so on I stored in a spare room. We were using our sleeping bags and slept on the floor. My house had centralized steam heating.

A new trend was starting among us top-ranking noncommissioned officers. We began separating ourselves from the men under us in our living conditions. This reached the point that we ate separately, even if only at a special table set aside in the mess hall.

I wanted to know how Holly had made out in Paris. I started the big hillbilly off by telling W. O. Bird that I had "broken down" over a few glasses of wine in Paris with Holly before I left for England. "The last time I saw this big guy," I said, "was as he rode off in the back of a horse carriage on his way to 42 Blondell."

That's all it took to get Holly started. "Boy! What a place that 42 Blondell is! Wow!"

"Did that big blonde gal throw you out, too? What an Amazon she was, wasn't she, Bird?"

"Sure was," chipped in W. O. Bird. "She threw us both out."

"I sure wouldn't want you to make her mad at me. Damn, my arm still hurts where she squeezed it the first time she pushed us out in the street."

"Watch it, Sergeant Black," Holly said. "You are talking about the girl I love."

"What?"

"That's right. My French girlfriend, Joan Blondell."

Sergeant Bird and I looked at each other in total disbelief. Bird spoke first. "You mean she didn't throw you out?"

"No! As a matter of fact, she was real nice to me. She had me go over in a corner and sit at a table after she made a French couple get up and leave."

Now it was my turn. "Let me start over. Holly, you mean to tell me they let GIs in 42 Blondell now?"

"No!" he said.

"OK, OK. We'll shut up," I said. "Tell us all about it. Tell us how a hillbilly from North Carolina got into a place in Paris where two boys from up north could not."

Sergeant William T. Hollingsworth proceeded to lay it on us, vintage "Big" Holly. He told us that the cab driver had wised him up on how to get inside 42 Blondell. The cab driver took him to the back door of the cafe and told him to say, "Tell Joan, Louis sent me."

Slam the Door

"Everything went like clockwork," Holly said. "Until someone came back and said, 'Joan wants to know who you are.' Well, I thought, why lie? So I said, Big Holly from the Bear Country!' Believe it or not, men, but that brought the big blonde herself. She took one look at me, and it was love at first sight.

The big blonde took him inside and set him up at the table in back and kept him all to herself. "Hell, men," Holly said, "I never paid a dime of my own money the whole seven days I stayed with her. Of course, I gave her all the PX goodies I had in my musette bag."

You could not make up a story that good.

Live ammo was always used on guard duty, and the importance of safety was continually stressed. But once in a combat zone, it wasn't a good idea to keep riding the men, even more so if they were "old-timers." After four campaigns in the war, many of the troopers were carrying an extra weapon, usually a foreign pistol.

James Flanagan had picked up a Belgium-Browning revolver in Normandy and managed to hang on to it most of the time. Here in Germany he had made a trade with a friend from another company and had to wait for his friend to run out of money in order to get his weapon back. We had just come off guard duty and were back in my squad's house. Flanagan had unloaded his "Browning" and was playing with it as he had done many times in the past.

Just as I had done before, I again cautioned Flanagan to watch out for the men around him when he played with that revolver.

"But it is unloaded, Sergeant Black!" he said.

My upstairs room was just above the room my men used as a living room. I had lain down on the bed in my sleeping bag and was almost asleep when "BANG!"

It sounded like the room below me was blowing up. I sat straight up in bed and waited. It was one of those times in my combat experience when I was certain I knew without seeing exactly what had happened.

It was deathly quiet. Then, faintly, faintly, came the call, "Sergeant Black! Sergeant Black! I shot myself. Where are you, Sergeant Black?" It was James Flanagan calling me.

I got up off the bed and moved slowly to the stairway and started carefully down the stairs. I think I wanted time to calm myself down so I wouldn't be too harsh with him.

When I was far enough down the stairs that I could see into the living room there was Flanagan standing in the center of the room holding his left hand at the wrist. He had shot himself in the fleshy part of his left hand. "Didn't I tell you what was going to happen?" I said. "Goddammit, Flanagan! Why didn't you listen? Now the war *is* over for you."

Then I took over and started to act. I shouted, "You, get going to Company for a doctor. Bring back a medic. Hurry! Sergeant Milligan, get a towel. Take off Flanagan's belt, one of you men. Hurry it up! This man will bleed to death if we don't move fast. Get a chair over here, somebody. Sit down, Flanagan, before you faint. Hey, you! Come here! Help us!"

It was a rude awakening for those of my men who were new since Bastogne. Some had not even seen a gunshot wound. A few were in shock from the sound and all the blood spattered around. Bad as it was, it was a hell of a lot better than our house's being hit by an artillery shell.

Flanagan kept trying to explain what he had done. "It was a dumb trick," he said. As we worked to stop the flow of blood, the medic ran in and not far behind him the "meat wagon" and a doctor. Before we could think about what was happening, Private First Class James Flanagan was gone, and in full battle gear.

As the ambulance driver was closing the back door and I was moving out of the way, Flanagan said, "Slam the damn door! I don't want to fall out and kill myself!"

I stood there thinking, "That big paratrooper Flanagan was leaving the same way he arrived, with the slam of a door!"

30

Bales of Silk

With chow call came the order to pack up and be ready to move in the morning. A new phase of the war was to begin for the 502nd Parachute Regiment. We were now the "military government," the Army of Occupation in charge of "displaced people."

These displaced people (soon called DPs) were Europeans who had come to Germany against their will to work for the German war effort. They were Poles, Russians, Yugoslavs, French, Italians, Dutch, Belgians and Czechs, both men and women and of all ages.

We rode through the city of Munchen-Gladbach on a beautiful spring morning on the back of open trucks. It was a manufacturing city, and the railroad and factory areas had been heavily damaged by air strikes, but the housing areas were mostly untouched. We stopped in an area of modern two-story houses with yards around them. We could have been anywhere in America.

First Sergeant Robert Grotjan had the men fall in along side the trucks on one of Munchen-Gladbach's main roads.

Captain Williams proceeded to tell us what we were in this big city to do. It was the first time I had heard the term "DP."

"We are here in Munchen-Gladbach acting as the Army of Occupation," he said. "Hard as it may sound to you men, our job is to protect the German people from their own terrible deeds. That is, to keep the DP's from harming them. Lord knows, they want to get even, and I don't blame them!"

Sergeant Grotjan took over. "We are soldiers, men. We take orders. We carry them out. We do not question why! Our job here is to stop the killing, not to do the killing! We are to maintain order in this big city. The whole First Battalion is here. We will be pulling guard duty, but those details will be passed on to you from your own NCOs in due course. For the time being, 'C' Company will take over this area of the city. There is one bit of good news, men. The Captain has assured me that we have the pick of the fine billets. There will be no ass-kissing of Germans by the 101st! Take any one of these houses you squad leaders choose." Then the First Sergeant called all the platoon sergeants over to assign them streets.

By the time Sergeant DeWitt came back I had my house picked out, and so had Sergeant Hollingsworth and W. O. Bird. Sergeant DeWitt would do his own picking.

Once my squad was in front of the two billets, I assigned the men to Sergeant Milligan and told them to stow their gear before they went "house hopping."

The scene was like an old movie re-run. As if by pre-arranged signal, forty troopers came running out of eight 2nd Platoon houses in every direction down the street and into the houses, as if each trooper wanted a house all to himself—and got it! If someone beat you to that house, you went on to the next one. I stood on my front porch watching the men run. When I saw W. O. Bird and "Big" Holly standing on their porches, too, I said out loud, "What are we waiting for? Come on!"

All three of us joined in the search. I was halfway down the block and across the street when I found the house of my choice. It must have been the home of a professional German; a

Bales of Silk

plaque near the doorway was in plain view for anyone to see. I could not read German, so it meant nothing to me. In I went.

We all carried our rifles or a firearm of some kind and struck fear in most of the German civilians we came across. I opened the front door into a hallway. Noticing a sign on the door to my right, I decided to explore that room first. It was the office of this German professional. "This is some kind of doctor's home," I thought out loud. "This German will have means! I've hit the jackpot!" I set my M-1 rifle against the wall near a huge old-fashioned desk and started pulling out drawers. I came across a drawer full of fountain pens. I took one out and put it between my teeth. I went on pulling out drawers and was bent over clear to the floor when the door banged open behind me. I heard a very stern voice saying, *"Vas ist los?"*

I didn't understand a word of German, but when you get caught doing something wrong, any language of the one offended is easy to understand.

I straightened up and turned around to meet a very distinguished looking old man. He was upset. For a moment I froze! I'd been caught with a mouth full of his fountain pens! If the old man had been a German soldier, I was dead. But he was not!

I leapt for my rifle. As I did so, I rammed a shell into the chamber all in one motion, an automatic move on my part. My action unnerved the old German, and he hastily beat a retreat into the hall. I went after him. It was my turn to get mad. I yelled at him as I pushed him out of his own front door, "Get the hell out of here before I shoot you down like a dirty, sneaking dog!" He was now leaving, and that was a good thing for both of us. I had come close to killing that old man, or at least bashing his head with the butt of my rifle.

I stood on the front steps and watched the owner of this house run for his life. "Hell, what is the matter with me?" I thought. "The war is over for these people! Hell, how can we get even with them without becoming like them?" I took the pen out of my mouth, threw it into the house and walked slowly back to my billet.

Once inside "my" house, I found myself all alone. I sat down in a chair with my M-1 rifle across my knees, shaken by what had happened. I felt guilty for what I was doing and because I had almost killed an old man. "God damn this war!" I said. Without moving the rifle from my knees I yanked the automatic ejection mechanism back and forth until all eight shells lay at my feet.

I looked out the window. No one was in sight. Everyone was inside these well-off German people's houses, looting. "These God-damned wars are all backwards," I said. "These civilians of all the warring countries, the ones who never do the fighting, are the ones who have everything to gain or lose. They should have to do the fighting. Then there would be no wars. How have they been able all these years to turn the youth into tin soldiers so we can do their dirty work? It sure as hell isn't for money. That old German had a drawer full of fountain pens, and I don't have any!"

During the next two days First Sergeant Grotjan informed us noncommissioned officers of the rules and regulations laid down for the Army of Occupation. One rule was so ridiculous that only high-ranking political and military powers could have dreamed it up. That was the "no fraternization" rule. To us in "C" Company, it meant "Don't get talking to any German people, young or old." The penalty would be six months and two-thirds of your pay—and that's for the first offense! They meant it, too, and a few paid the price.

"Big" Holly had not yet found looting to be against his principles. Still, he was never one to take things just for the sake of taking. He was always looking for something that had to do with hunting—guns or knives. No one ever found anything of value. These European people had been through many wars and weren't dumb.

Nevertheless, Holly went over to snoop around in the factory area over a mile away. When Holly got me off to himself at noon time chow, I could see the child-like look of excitement all over him. Sure it was true, he had found something of value.

"I tell you, Black," he said, "it has great value! I'll give you half of it if you go with me after chow call is over."

"What is it?" I said.

I could have saved my breath. He was not about to tell me yet.

As soon as chow ended and we were both free, off we went for the railroad yards and the Munchen-Gladbach factories. For the life of me I could not see how anything of value could be left in those buildings. To call it a "devastated site" would be a proper statement to put in a military report.

"Big" Holly led the way at a fast clip using a shortcut. We came back out of a back street above the railroad factory sites. "There it is right down there!" Holly said.

"What the hell is it?"

I'll swear there were nothing but bomb craters, twisted rails and burned-out buildings with smashed windows. There wasn't a sign of life anywhere. This place was dead and had been for some time. "Isn't it beautiful?" Holly said.

"What? Tell me what it is. I might step on it."

"I can see it from here."

"See what?"

"There! In that big building. The one with part of the roof left on it."

I could see nothing. Since I'd come this far, there was only one thing to do—go down with the big Sergeant. The place was a wasteland. Cleaning it up would be a long, hard task. For the first time I thought about all the work ahead for Europe after the war ended. "Will there be any people left?" I said outside.

"You'd better ask Hitler," Holly said. "God didn't have anything to do with this!"

Inside the building we went up a long steel stairway to a second-floor warehouse. There, stacked to the ceiling under the only good roof left in the entire area, were rows and rows of large bales. They looked like cotton bales to me.

"That's it!" Holly said.

I walked up to a bale and saw it wasn't cotton, but I'll be damned if I was going to say, "What is it?" one more time. So I acted as if I was inspecting every bale.

That must have pleased William T. Hollingsworth because he got excited. I was still waiting for him to tell me what it really was when finally he said, "Did you ever see so much raw silk in your life, Sergeant Black?"

"No, I don't believe I have."

I was stunned by Holly's next question. "How are we going to get all of these bales back to Horseshoe, North Carolina, Sergeant?"

That was a question I wasn't ready for, so I went on with my inspection. He followed me around and finally said, "Do you have any idea of what the price of just one of these bales is, Black?"

I almost lost my temper. "Hell, no! Goddammit, Holly, I don't know the going price of a bushel of wheat, not to mention a bale of cotton. How in the world would I know what the price of raw silk is?"

"Well, Sergeant Black, I do. Each one of these bales of raw silk figures to be worth a million dollars. Of course, that is as 'finish material,' you understand." William T. Hollingsworth was speaking as if he had been in the textile business all his life.

I was thinking fast. How could I walk away from all of these millions of dollars without hurting "Big" Holly's feelings or making him mad?

We both knew we couldn't pick up a bale, much less put one in our pocket and walk away. That was my first and last thought about raw silk.

Back in our company area W. O. Bird told us that the Platoon Sergeant was mad as hell with us two Squad Sergeants. "Something about leaving the company area without telling anyone where you were going." Once again Holly and I were on DeWitt's shit list. Although he did not pull us in and dress us down, we knew by the harsh looks he gave us and the number of night-time guard duty details he gave us that he was most unhappy with us.

At our next Company formation First Sergeant Grotjan handed down the order that no one would leave "C" Company area unless told to do so. As he put it, "There is too much wandering around. Two troopers were seen down by the railroad this afternoon. That's not even our area of responsibility. Speaking of responsibility, 'C' Company will take over the security of the

Bales of Silk

DP's depot in the main part of the city. You will be prepared to move out on foot at 0600 hours tomorrow morning (6 a.m.). Just in case any of you are still superstitious after all we have been through, tomorrow is Friday the Thirteenth!"

So we marched clear across town to take over a new job for seven days.

The "depot" was set up in the central part of the city in a three-story row-type apartment building. All of our "C" Company troopers were billeted in single-row houses across the street from the depot. We would pull guard duty, which was simply to let no one in or out. All the needs of these people were in the hands of the Regiment—food, health, laundry, as well as sorting out where they were from and starting in motion the day for their return to their home countries.

Most of this work was easy and a welcome change of pace. It meant that the war was over for these people. They could now smile. It was a good thing to see.

31

Schnapps by the Barrel

Of course the 101st weren't going to Berlin. We were moving by train to southern Germany to join the Seventh Army in the fight for the "National Redoubt" where General Eisenhower believed Hitler would make a last, hard stand.

The "National Redoubt" is twenty-four miles long and eighty miles deep and is made up of extremely mountainous terrains in the western half of Austria. A small piece of Italy and German also lay within the area. The real prize was a place called "The Eagle's Nest" at Berchtisgaden. This was Hitler's hideaway in the extreme southern point of Germany.

On April 14 General Taylor was advised that the "Ruhr Pocket" was about to collapse and to be prepared to move into southern Germany. Four days later it fell into Allied hands. A total of 325,000 German soldiers plus huge stores of their supplies and equipment were captured. Our casualties totaled 50 officers and enlisted men, including ten who were killed.

Division trucks pulled out early Friday morning on a 150-mile trip to Merchingen, Germany, about sixty miles due west of

Nuerenburg. Most of the 101st took the slow, long route using railroad trains equipped with the "40 and 8" boxcars we had become familiar with.

We left the Rhine River Valley and headed into Germany's uplands. We arrived late in the evening at the tiny country village where we were to set up. I pulled the first night's guard duty before I had time to reconnoiter the area, but the hours of the night went smoothly. Slowly I was becoming convinced that we had nothing to fear from the German civilians.

The second night Sergeant DeWitt put Holly on guard duty with two strict orders: A curfew for all German people ("No one is to be outside after dark—no one!"); and "All Sergeants of the Guard will maintain a strict liaison between each platoon and Company Headquarters."

Guard duty would be on a platoon-by-platoon basis. More to the point, it would be on a combat basis: shoot first and ask questions later! "Jumpknife" Milligan was named the "Corporal of the Guard" for the platoon. That meant two hillbillies—Milligan and Holly—were in charge of keeping the peace.

To those two hillbillies the taste of "White Lightning" (Schnapps) made them homesick. The brew was made of potatoes and was clear like corn liquor. I thought it tasted awful.

It all began as a nice gesture by the old farmer who owned the house where Sergeant Hollingsworth's squad was billeted. The farmer and his family had moved out of their house into the barn, which was actually part of the house. The main house was at ground level facing the street with a two-story barn linked to the back of the house. The farmer hid his Schnapps barrel in the haymow. He offered Holly a drink of his best and asked for Holly's canteen cup so that he could bring a drink to him. He should have left by the front doorway, but he used the door into the haymow. Holly watched through the keyhole. What he saw was a huge barrel covered with hay—a hundred gallons in it if it had a drop.

When Holly came over to my squad's house next door at dusk he was already drunk. He came over to offer me a drink, or several drinks. "Come on, Black!" he said. "Bring your canteen with you. I've got a barrel of Schnapps at my place!" Holly

Schnappes by the Barrel

whirled around to leave and bumped straight into "Jumpknife" walking through the doorway. They both landed on their asses.

The Sergeant and the Corporal of the Guard were both drunk, and it was getting dark. "Goddammit, Holly," I said. "You are on guard duty! You are the sergeant of the Guard. Man, they will shoot you at sunrise!"

"Big" Holly was standing up now, but "Jumpknife" was not.

"Hell's fire, Milligan," I said. "You are the Corporal of the Guard!"

Sergeant Hollingsworth helped Sergeant Milligan off the floor. Then he said, "Come on, 'Roundhead.' We're on guard duty. Let's go out and shoot some Germans!"

Sergeant Milligan said, "Wait 'till I go back and get another canteen of Schnapps. I spilled mine. We'd better shoot that old farmer first, Holly." With that they both left.

I wish I could have walked away, but my instincts wouldn't let me. Hell, they were my good friends. I couldn't let them screw up now!

I went next door to Holly's house to try again. I decided I could go along with them, take a drink of Schnapps as "Big" Holly had asked and spend the whole night trying to keep them out of sight and hoping that no trouble was in store.

By the time I walked in, the trouble for the night was already under way. The doorway out of the house into the haymow was open, and from it came shouting, both in German and English. I walked over and peered in. There was the scene I had feared.

"Big" Holly had uncovered the Schnapps barrel. He had a canteen cup in each hand and was filling them to the brim. "Jumpknife" Milligan had the old German farmer down on all fours in the hay, begging for his life. Holly had the barrel of his Thompson submachine gun resting on the shoulders of the farmer and pointed at the back of his head. They were going to kill that old man if I didn't stop them.

I was furious with both sergeants. "Jesus Christ, Milligan!" I yelled. "What the hell is the matter with you? Put that gun away! Take your damned drinks and leave that old man alone! You men are on guard duty, goddammit. Wake up before you kill somebody!"

Both men seemed startled. They gave up what they were doing and came back into the house. Holly offered me a drink, but I refused. "I came over here to have a drink with you two and try to talk some sense into you," I said. "But you guys are crazy drunk, so I'm getting out of here. I hope Sergeant DeWitt doesn't need the sergeant of the Guard tonight."

Back in the street headed for my billet, I noticed that it was pitch dark now. I also heard noise coming from the back of Hollingsworth's house in the barn area. Holly caught up with me. I said, "What's all that noise coming from behind your house?"

"It's good riddance!" he said. "That old German farmer is moving his family out."

"What?" I yelled as I headed for the barn area.

When I turned the corner I saw a scene out of a fairy tale. The good guys had turned into the bad guys, and the bad guys were the ones I felt sorry for now.

The big wide barn door was standing open, and light from inside the barn lit up the outside area like the day. The old man's woman had a child in each arm. Both were crying, and so was the old woman. She was gathering the other children around her, apparently preparing to leave and take them all with her. The problem was that they were so scared she couldn't make them listen to her. There must have been eight or ten kids running in all directions in and out of that barn, not sure if they should go with the woman or stay with the old man.

"Goddammit, Holly," I said. "You know the orders for the day. No Germans outside after dark. You'd better get them all back inside that barn somehow!"

I don't know if the scene got to him or whether it was my words to him, but "Big" Holly came to his good senses and started herding all of the kids back into the barn. "Jumpknife" was still up in the haymow, brandishing his gun and spouting epitaphs. It was useless for me to hang around any longer. As I left I could hear Milligan saying, "Tell it to the Fuhrer, that godamned Adolf Hitler. He likes kids! Poop, right in the Fuhrer's face!"

I went back inside my billet and went to bed for the night.

The next day when the First Sergeant questioned Platoon Sergeant DeWitt about the fact that some German civilians were said to be outside after dark, DeWitt answered, "I doubt that. My Sergeant of the Guard made no such report to me."

Sergeant Hollingsworth decided to make chow call and cut through the back farm yards straight down the hill among the farm buildings. As he stumbled along, half hung over, a rifle bullet cracked past his ear and ripped into the side of the barn nearby. From somewhere up the hill came the rifle's report.

Sergeant Bird took one look at Holly and said to me, "Something is wrong with Holly this morning. He is only having coffee. Here he comes over to our table. A beautiful morning here in the ETO, Sergeant!"

Holly looked at W. O. Bird as if he was nuts. "What are you talking about? It's a terrible morning. I guess nobody has taken a shot at you, yet. Watch your step going back from breakfast. These damned krauts aren't ready to quit yet. One of them took a shot at me on my way down here."

Sergeant Bird changed his tune. "Dammit, Holly," he said. "Watch your step. Better stay in Company formations when you can. Try not to go out alone. You don't want to get killed by a stray bullet. This war's about over."

This was good advice, but I could not leave it at that. "Stray bullet—hell! Holly knows that they're shooting at him."

Bird didn't even look at me. He kept his eyes all the time on Holly and said, "A little too early to start celebrating, isn't it, Sergeant?"

"That rifle shot scared the hell out of me, Black!" he told me a few minutes later. "Somebody in this town is trying to kill me. What in hell am I going to do? By the way, what did I do last night, Sergeant Black?"

Late in the morning the old Catholic priest, the father of the flock of local believers, came to pay a visit on Sergeants Hollingsworth and Milligan. Someone had given the old priest their names, and the priest had gotten permission from the First Sergeant to speak to them in private. He told Holly and Milligan that the consensus among the townspeople was that they did not like their little children being scared by drunken soldiers. He said he had spent some time in the U.S. back in the 1920s and knew that the "humanity" of the American people was not in favor of scaring children. He said his people would drop the matter with a personal apology by the two sergeants.

At 1200 hours (12 noon) sharp the church bell rang, and all the townspeople gathered to hear the two American sergeants say they were very sorry for the previous night's trouble. "Jumpknife" Milligan didn't go without fortifying himself with a few drinks of Schnapps, but "Big" Holly did not take a drink and made only a very short statement of apology.

As always, Milligan's fortification made him bold with his tongue. He gave the German people a little speech that probably only the old priest understood. It went like this, "No Yankee soldier, and that includes me, ever wants to scare the German kids or their mothers. But that doesn't hold true for their dads! Didn't the Fuhrer tell you people there's a war going on? Hell, he's had me scared for five years! I make no apologies to any of you men!"

The "man" in the old priest took a liking to those two Americans, and he visited them each night and morning for the three days we stayed in his town. On our last day we had a baseball game at the edge of town in a flat pasture, and he came to watch us play.

32

When Your Home Isn't Your Castle

We boarded open-air Navy jeeps ("Dukws") for a place called Memmingen, Germany, some two hundred miles straight south and deep in Bavaria. The city had been taken by the 44th Division on April 26, the day before we arrived. We rolled down the Autobahn at 40 miles while hundreds of German soldiers marched four abreast down the grassy center of this beautiful highway. They wore no helmets, carried no rifles and were marching away from the front lines. Now and then a German fighter plane appeared overhead, and I was amused to watch while two of these planes used the northbound lanes as a runway for landing. The German soldiers with the planes taxied them off to the side and then joined the ranks of their countrymen in surrender.

Our "C" Company drove through Memmingen to a small village near the front lines where the 44th Infantry Division was in force. A problem emerged: soldiers from two American divisions were in the same area.

A Major for the 44th was upset because he hadn't been told that we were going to share "his" town for the night. While we were lined up standing in the rain and waiting for orders we heard the Major from the 44th arguing with Captain Williams, who had received his orders from Major John Hanlon, the First Battalion Commanding Officer for the 502nd Parachute Regiment.

"Sergeant," Captain Williams began. "Call the company to order! Now hear this! This Company will spend this night inside these German houses right here. You Squad Sergeants take over every house that isn't in the hands of someone from the 44th Division. Any questions, Sergeant?"

"Yes!" said the First Sergeant. "What do we do with the German people we find?"

"Put them out in the streets. This town belongs to the 44th Division. Let *them* take care of them, Sergeant!"

"Yes, Sir!" The First Sergeant saluted smartly, then turned to the Platoon Sergeants. "You heard the captain," he said. "Carry out the orders." The three Platoon Sergeants put their heads together about which houses each would take, and soon we Squad Sergeants were moving the Germans out into the streets.

The Major for the 44th Division watched all this with his mouth open. For some reason he had not yet moved his men into the houses. This was a real triumph for "Jumpknife" Milligan, and I gave him the reins. With that the captain endeared himself in Milligan's eyes for the rest of the war. Milligan set about clearing houses for the First, Second and Third Squads, a task most of us would rather not do.

As the U.S. forces swept toward Austria, many German civilians were uprooted. Somehow Milligan and his men overlooked the old woman in the house assigned to me and my squad. The house was old and had been added onto within the past few years. The old woman who owned this house had not intention of running anywhere. She owned this house, and she was going to stay in it!

My squad had settled into the house, and even "Jumpknife" Milligan was relaxing, waiting for the chow call. Private Yates went back into the newest part of the house to snoop around.

"There's an old lady in there!" he said as he ran back to me.

"What is she doing back there?" I asked.

"She is sitting in the center of a large bed with her arms folded, and she doesn't look like she is going to leave," Yates said.

"What?" roared Milligan, jumping out of his chair.

"Now wait a minute, Milligan," I said. "Let's find out what is the matter with her before we have her shot."

"Shot! By God, I can do that, too, if I have to. You know what Captain Williams said: 'Every damned German out in the streets!'"

"Well," I said, "let's go back and take a look at her first."

Milligan and I went back to the room where the woman was seated in the middle of a large four-poster bed. She was a beautiful lady at least seventy-five years old, and she looked like "everyone's grandmother." She called for her English interpreter, a young German girl, who was near by. Through her interpreter she told us that her husband had just been killed by bombs, two sons had died in the war, and two grandsons had just been killed in action with the Americans. It was enough. All she had left was the house. She was not going to give it up, Hitler be damned!

"Tell her she can stay in this room only," I said to the German girl. "She must not go outside in the hours of darkness." Then to Sergeant Milligan I said, "Post a guard on her door for the night. See that no harm comes to her. That's an order!"

We in "C" Company moved out onto the line by 0800 hours (8 a.m.) under a steady, cold rain falling and the possibility of snow just ahead. I was grateful for warm clothing our Supply Sergeant had re-issued us the day before. Our strategy in the farmlands was to "advance as skirmishers." The audacity of such an attack almost always forced the enemy to fire erratically, which helped build the confidence our troopers needed to press the route of the German army.

Jerry was falling back in total chaos. Any resistance they offered was only a token of what they had been giving us before. It was the weather that made this a miserable day, although at sunset the skies cleared off for a beautiful evening.

About 1800 hours (6 p.m.) the cry rang out, "Halt! Dig in and hold!" We were crossing a large dairy farm with a beautiful new dairy barn in the center of it. After digging my foxhole, I gave in to my farming instincts and walked over to the big barn on the pretense that I was inspecting my squad's foxholes. The doors into the barn were open, so I peered inside. The dairy workers saw me and invited me inside.

At least a hundred cows were standing in that barn, row upon row across the width of that barn. They were all Brown Swiss cows, all big and in great shape. The workers came up to me and patted me on the back or stuck out their hand to shake mine. Then they stood around me smiling.

The world over, farmers milk cows night and morning. I, a Yank paratrooper sergeant, had disrupted the big dairy's night milking. A woman walked over to where I was and spoke in a harsh tone to the workers. Some took off in a hurry, but a small boy pointed to my stripes, touched my rifle and said something to her. Nobody moved. She walked away without saying anything more.

The next morning I learned that it was a state-run dairy farm that used slave labor. All the workers were Displaced Persons from several countries—men and women, and even children.

At this point the German armies were caving in so fast that our military governments couldn't keep up. Some of the gaps that resulted during the transition were harmful to the people of the country. The flow of milk was one.

I spent the night in my foxhole near the big barn thinking that the cows had it better than I did. They were inside, out of the weather. I didn't know it then, but this was the last foxhole of the war for me.

After hot chow the next morning, our "C" Company pulled away from that beautiful dairy farm. We were moving on our own this time into a small town we would enjoy all to ourselves. It was a tiny village, clean as a pin and deep in a picturesque valley with a lone church steeple standing boldly against the sky. We were still in Germany, but Austria was only a few miles away.

33

Unconditional Surrender

War had not made a mark on this village because it was far from the "madding crowd" of war mongers. Every house looked prosperous. Besides farming and related business, the village must have been a tourist haven for German middle-class people seeking a change of pace from the big city.

Captain Williams headed up more than one deer-hunting party during our five-day stay, and we enjoyed venison every day.

Tuesday, May 1, dawned with a snowstorm. Besides the hunting party, another party happened because of a big discovery by Sergeant William T. Hollingsworth. "Big" Holly had been down in his basement, no doubt looking for exactly what he found: a "secret" wine cellar. Holly had hit the jackpot! Somehow he kept it quiet until Tuesday morning.

At the first sight of snow on this day one of my men woke me up by calling upstairs to my bedroom and telling me to look out the window. "Someone is on the way up to our place!" he shouted.

"Who is it?" I asked.

"Don't know, but he sure is a hell of a big guy!"

I rolled over and looked out the window. That big head gave him away. It was Holly coming to come and tell Bird and me about his find. One look at him and I knew what he had found. He was drunk and had a bottle of vintage champagne in each pocket: two bottles in each thigh pocket, one in each hip pocket, one in each jump jacket pocket, and over all of this he had on his big Army overcoat with a bottle in each of its pockets! That made ten pockets in all. I hadn't seen that much champagne in all of France. If Holly wanted to keep that wine cellar a secret he was going about it in the wrong way. Everybody in town could hear those bottles tingle.

Holly plays his game out on me, as usual. Here he comes, all the way upstairs to my bedroom. That was something to see! Before I get out of bed I have to take a drink of champagne. He tells me he's never seen so much to drink. I try to remind him of all those barrels of wine back in Normandy. He just laughs and said, "I mean, all of it in bottles, Sergeant!"

The two of us drank a whole bottle before I got out of bed. Then he thought Sergeant Milligan ought to have a taste, so we called him into my room for a morning eye opener. That's when all the celebration started.

Between then and Saturday morning, May 5, 1945, I lost all track of time. Our men started following the radio accounts of the fall of Germany. The first news I remember was, "The Russians captured the Reichstag last night in the Battle of Berlin!" A great reason to celebrate!

"Hamburg radio has announced that Hitler has died in Berlin!"

Our men kept bringing in news reports:

"Admiral Doenitz is Hitler's successor!"

"Munich has fallen!"

"The First French Army crosses the Austrian frontier!"

"The American Fifth Army in Italy is near the Brenner Pass."

"General Zhukof demands unconditional surrender of Berlin!" (He gets it.)

"General Krebs commits suicide."

"Goebbels has his wife, his six children and himself all shot to death!"

"The unconditional surrender of all German forces in Italy goes into effect!"

"The British, under Field Marshall Montgomery capture Hamburg!"

"The XVIII Airborne Corps with the 82nd Airborne Division reach the Baltic Sea!"

"Holland and Denmark are free at last!" (A loud Hurrah!)

"Salzburg surrenders!"

"Innsbruck surrenders to our VI Corps!"

"The 101st goes after Berchtesgaden!"

All of these radio reports fed the fires of our celebration. I am sure that no one enjoyed the end of World War II in Europe more than the 2nd Platoon of the "C" Company.

On May 1 Holly would not let me go back to sleep, and I didn't want to after one of my men ran upstairs to tell me the report of the death of Hitler and Eva Braun, his fraulein. Then it was off to tell Bird. That was worth a bottle apiece, at least.

Eventually Holly's pockets ran dry, and we headed for the wine cellar, the first one I'd ever seen. It was hard to believe that one household needed that much wine. But that was not our concern. We owned the wine cellar now, when the celebration counted!

The news of the wine cellar spread all over the whole company and even drew the big people. Holly was no wine expert, but he knew a good thing when he tasted it. After sampling several kinds of wine in the wine cellar, he assembled his own supply and set up his own wine cellar over at W. O. Bird's house, in case the higher ups decided they wanted it all.

Hollingsworth's billet was no place for a celebration. There were too many interruptions. My billet was out of the center of activity. Sometime after dark on May 1, I made it back to my house, where I stayed until we moved out again on Saturday morning five days later.

I didn't leave my house even to go to chow on Wednesday, Thursday or Friday. Not that I didn't eat. We ate practically all the time. The reason I stayed in the house was due to some squad planning on my part. First I made some key appointments.

First appointment: Head of Wine Supply—"Jumpknife Roundhead" Milligan. We never ran out of champagne and always took a new bottle as a gift to the Mess Sergeant and his cooks.

Second appointment: Head of Chow Procurement—"Jumpknife Roundhead" Milligan. We always had plenty of food: deer, a stray cow or pig that got lost. Milligan claimed to have been part of the Mess Sergeant's "cow shoots."

Third appointment: Head of Entertainment—"Jumpknife Roundhead" Milligan. He was absolutely irreplaceable.

These were the greatest days of the whole war. I knew the war was over. Maybe the men at or near the top were itching to get on the Japanese kill, but the enlisted men and line-company officers in the "C" company were simply overjoyed. We celebrated every news report. We toasted every officer, from General to Private. This joy and celebration went on for four days and nights. The whole 2nd Platoon was caught up in it. We were left alone by the rest of the Regiment.

By Friday afternoon we were a sorry-looking lot. My squad was spending most of its time in our living room glued to our one radio. The room was small, and the men sat or lay in every available spot. Movement meant disrupting or stepping over someone. Drinking slowed down to the point of forgetting to fill your glass. (Yes, we found glasses to use long ago.)

Milligan had left for Holly's to get our nightly supply of wine, and I was sure it was he when I heard noise out in our driveway. To Private Yates I said, "Go help Sergeant Milligan in with the wine." All those front steps with the snow on Tuesday and Wednesday had made a real obstacle course.

On the double Yates came back to report that it was the captain. "Everybody keep your mouth shut. Let me do the talking," I said. I was the soberest one of the lot.

I moved out of the living room into the hall vestibule. There was a knock on the door. Hmm. That was a strange thing for a Captain to do.

I opened the front door, and there stood the new Regimental Chaplain. His captain's bars and the church cross on his shirt collar gave him away. He stuck out his hand and said, "I am the Protestant Chaplain for your 502nd Paratrooper Regiment. May I come in and visit you and your men?"

"Half my men are Catholic, Sir," I said, hoping that would discourage him from going inside.

"I find that in the Airborne everywhere I go, Sergeant," he said. "What are you?"

"I'm a Lutheran, Sir," I said.

"Good doctrine to put your faith in, Sergeant. I'll just pop my head in and let your men know I'm in their midst."

I went ahead of the chaplain to tell my men. After calling them to attention, I said, "This is the Protestant Chaplain for our Regiment. He wishes to speak to you."

He told the men to relax and said he was sorry that we had lost our fine Chaplain Hall, that he was sure that God was looking after him and that someday soon we would all be back with our loved ones. Then he asked us when we had last been to church.

It was unbelievable to learn that most of my men could not remember when. Out loud I said, "We were near the Reims, the great Cathedral, at Christmas and Easter and missed both times."

The loss of Chaplain Hall was in Holland. My God! Had that been the last "church call" for us Protestants? As I stood near the door into the hallway, the Preacher said, "Well, gentlemen, we shall put a stop to this non-church-going Regiment. You will hear from me again!"

As the chaplain started to leave the room I paid my respects to his rank (captain) by calling out "Tench-Hut!" The Chaplain froze at attention in his tracks in the doorway. Looking past me toward the front door he could see what I could not. Somebody was opening the door from the hallway into the room, pressing against the chaplain. (The door opened into the room.) I stood frozen, blocking the door, waiting for the captain's return salute.

I heard bottles jingling and saw one drop to the floor. It was "Jumpknife" back with the wine. He was backing into the door trying to open it and had not yet seen the chaplain. In the dead silence he said, "Jesus Christ! It's crowded in here." He reached down and picked up the bottle of wine, one of eight he had carried back from Holly's. As he did so, his rifle barrel caught the porcelain crucifix that hung on the wall near the door. It fell to the floor and broke into several pieces. Looking down at it, Sergeant Milligan said in a flat voice, "The Holy Ghost has fallen!"

By now I had moved around the door so that I could see. Milligan straightened up and looked right at the captain, still holding his hand salute at attention.

Milligan snapped to attention, bringing his right hand to a sharp airborne salute—right in the chaplain's face. As he did so his M-1 rifle slid down his arm and hung there by its leather sling. Every bottle in his pockets tingled.

I could see this was never going to end if I didn't do something. "Sergeant!" I barked. "Get out of the chaplain's way! He wants to leave."

Sergeant Milligan backed up out the door. The Chaplain ducked out the doorway, into the hall and out into the driveway. I followed him to his jeep where the driver was waiting. Before getting into the jeep he turned to me and said, "Sergeant, why did you yell 'Attention!' back there in the room?"

"To pay our respect to your rank, because you were leaving, Sir!" I said.

"Oh!" he said. "I thought it was for that man coming in. Maybe he was the colonel or higher up!" He shook his head. "I guess I never will understand this army life. Sometimes it makes me mad enough to swear. By the way, Sergeant. That fellow was shook up pretty bad. Who was he? Tell him I'm sorry if it was because of me!"

The jeep jerked out of the driveway and was gone. If the chaplain had "church call," we never heard about it!

34

Alles Kaput!

The next morning after a meeting with the First Sergeant at the company the company Headquarters, I had a few facts to share with my men. First, that the celebrations were over. Our Division had been moved into the XXI Corps, which had been on the attack to capture Berchtesgaden (Hitler's Nest) since May 2. I announced to my men, "Word has it this morning that the Third Division beat us in. Their Seventh Infantry Regiment entered last night, and our 506th troopers entered this morning. The word, men, is 'Alles Kaput!' There is nothing left to fight for!"

As we stood by ready for the trip across our first mountain range, up drove several open-air German trucks. All the drivers were German soldiers, and they all had their damn uniforms on except for their steel helmets. Maybe they were there somewhere in the cab of the truck, for all we knew.

Our first trip into the Alps was one anxious moment after another as we rounded hairpin curve after curve. Not one curve had guard rails to protect vehicles from running off the road and landing hundreds of feet below, and all along the route were signs of many German trucks that already had.

It was bad enough to have Jerry drive us over the mountains into Austria; it was worse than that to have to ride in his rotten equipment. "Big" Holly was downright upset and kept saying so the whole trip. Once he said to our German driver, "You wreck this truck going over these mountains and I'll shoot you dead, for damn sure!"

"Jumpknife" Milligan was worse. He was downright furious and never took his eye off the driver behind his truck. He kept a round in the chamber of his rifle and pointed the barrel at him the whole trip.

W. O. Bird and I talked Sergeant DeWitt into having a "truck guard" on duty at all times. We weren't about to take a chance on any of the Germans being fanatics. We were too close to making it through this war to let something stupid happen now.

I kept telling Bird this was against the Geneva Convention that set the rules of war for the western world. "Damn it, Bird," I said. "We are always preaching about setting good examples and living by the rules, then we break them just like our enemies. Once a soldier is out of the war and captured, he is not to be used to help his enemy defeat him. He is a prisoner of war! He has a duty to his own country to try to escape, and if he is a good German soldier he will try to take a truckload of Yanks with him!"

"Not this truckload, Sergeant," W. O. Bird answered me. "You guys be ready to jump off when I yell."

We had over a hundred miles to go, most of it in high country. We skirted around three mountain ranges before reaching the range we had to cross to get into Mittenwald. It took most of the day. Some of those damn German trucks broke down. When that happened we had our troopers get on other trucks and left the driver with his truck waiting for help later on.

Dropping down off the mountains into the valley, we were treated to a spring-like scene that was truly beautiful. The snow was gone. Grass and wild flowers colored the hillsides down to the floor of the valley where the small village lay. It was a picture only God could paint.

On Sunday, May 6, we learned, the German Army surrendered in front of our XXI Corps. General Taylor took the surrender of XII SS Corps the next afternoon, and a German General surren-

Alles Kaput! 357

dered his LXXXII Corps to the 506th Parachute Infantry Regiment the same day.

German radio announced that an Armistice had been signed at 0241 hours (2:41 a.m.) on May 7, 1945, ending the war. There was joy in the camp, and a few rifle shots rang out in our town. But there was no word from ETO headquarters all day long.

Sometime in the afternoon an order came down without explanation from First Sergeant Grotjan. "All personnel—repeat—all personnel of the 'C' Company will put on their O.D. (off-duty) uniforms less jackets. Ties and overseas caps will be worn—jump boots with pants bloused, as per airborne authorization. Be ready to fall out for company inspection in fifteen minutes!"

With the cold weather we had run into by moving through the mountains the men had been wearing their off-duty uniforms under their jumpsuits. The problem was ties and overseas caps. There weren't enough for everyone. After standing in full company formation with all officers in place, we speculated that we were going to hear a war-ending announcement.

Up drove a military police jeep from the Division with four people in it: the driver, a Sergeant from the Military Police; a First Lieutenant and a Major from the Division; and a young German girl, maybe sixteen years old.

Captain Williams saluted the Major, who asked the captain to call his Company to attention. The Captain did. The Major then said, "Spread your ranks one pace apart, Captain."

Captain Williams moved to the head of the 1st Platoon2nd Platoon. "The entire first rank—two paces. Forward—March! The entire second rank—one pace. Forward—March! The entire fourth rank, a-bout—Face! One pace, Forward—March! A-bout—Face! The entire third rank—Stand—Fast!"

The Captain then fell in behind the party of four, who walked slowly behind each rank. We stood at attention; not one word was said. After passing through all four ranks, they went back again, this time looking into our faces.

When they finished looking over the company, the Major turned to the Lieutenant and said, "Ask the girl if the soldier is in these ranks."

The First Lieutenant spoke in German to the girl, who nodded her head, "Yes!"

The Major said, "Go with her and have her point him out!" They did. He was in the second row!

"Sergeant, arrest that soldier for rape!" the Major said.

At Company formation on May 8 the captain read the main content of the telegram from the Supreme Allied Headquarters in Reims, France, and signed by General Dwight D. Eisenhower:

"A Representative of the German High Command signed the unconditional surrender of all German land, sea and air forces in Europe to the Allied Expeditionary Army Forces and simultaneously to the Soviet High Command at 0141 hours, central European time, 7 May, under which all forces will cease active operations at 0100 hours, 9 May."

Captain Williams continued, "The President of the U.S., Harry S. Truman, has declared 9 May to be V-E Day, the day of victory in Europe." Then as if it was just another day in the life of "C" Company, he said, "Gentlemen, you have the next hour off to eat your breakfast, after which there will be one hour of calisthenics.

"There will be no formation for chow this morning. Each trooper may go at his pleasure," First Sergeant Grotjan said. "Chow is being served now in the driveway behind the company command post. The uniform for calisthenics will be the combat jumpsuit, less the steel helmet. Dismissed!"

There was no shouting, no jumping for joy, not even many smiles. The formal announcement had come a little too late.

While enjoying chow Holly asked Sergeant Curtis DeWitt, "What happens now, Sergeant?"

"I've thought about this day for a long time," Sergeant DeWitt said. "I knew we would win. Hell, there was no question of that! Our country is on the side of peace. The question is, once we win it can we preserve it?" He paused to take a drink of coffee from his canteen cup. He made an awful face and went on. "The 101st Airborne, and I mean us, the 'C' Company, will be part of the army of occupation for the next few weeks. Some of these godamned Germans are hard-nosed SSs—Super sons of bitches. You boys know them. Hell! I don't mean to call you 'boys.' You are all men now.

There isn't a boy left in this company." The Sergeant stared into his cup for a long time. We knew he had more to say and waited.

"If I don't miss my guess, men," he said, "these next few weeks are not going to be easy. The Captain is on his way right now up to Regiment to be briefed on the job they want us line companies to carry out. You know damned well these mountains make good hideouts, Holly. You do, too, Milligan. There has to be some 'big shits' in hiding around here. We'll have to go in and get them. We'll use as small a unit as possible. I see us using a lot of squad- and platoon-sized patrols, backed up by the company if a fire fight breaks out. But it is over. The terrible fighting of the war in Europe ended yesterday.

Bob Marohn broke the long silence that followed. "What about the other war?" he asked.

"What other war? This is the only war that matters. The great task was here in Europe. Winning the war was the first half. Now we must win the peace. That is sure to mean a large standing army of occupation. No way will we let Jerry up off the floor this time! You remember a guy named Winston Churchill, don't you? You haven't forgotten what he said about the Russians, have you? Make no mistake, men. The Red Army has proved itself, and it is going to be interesting to watch the 'big lion' and the 'big bear' going at it. Remember, men, there is no Roosevelt to referee anymore."

Before noon our whole company boarded trucks headed out of Mittenwald on our way south.

35

Crashing an SS Party

Captain Williams' words were still ringing in my ears a mile on our four-abreast march down the gravel road. He had said to Lieutenant Wall, as he left him off in front of us, "Goddammit, Lieutenant, kick the son-of-a-bitch out if you have to shoot three or four of them! That's an order, Lieutenant!"

Looking over at the other Sergeants, including DeWitt, I didn't pick up any comments. Each sergeant just shook his head in a negative way. The Captain's order indicated that trouble lay ahead. If so, marching close order four abreast was not very smart.

The road made a long sweeping curve and left the wide valley behind. After about four miles the valley narrowed to a few yards on either side of the road and the stream running alongside it. At the five-mile point the mountains were reaching down to the road and stream from both sides. I had a sudden feeling of being closed in. It looked to me like the road was coming to a dead end up ahead, and I had the feeling of being led into a trap.

At the sixth mile we learned what we were in for by looking up on the hillside. A mountain resort hotel sat just off the road, a picturesque structure built into the mountainside. It was a three-story Bavarian style building with balconies running around each floor. Standing on each of the balconies were several SS troopers in black uniforms and a lot of pretty, young girls.

A ripple of tension ran back through the platoon when we turned into the hotel driveway and Sergeant DeWitt called for the platoon to halt. Then he turned to Lieutenant Wall and said, "What are the orders, Sir?"

"The Captain wants these black-shirted Germans kicked out of this building and off these grounds—now! And I mean kicked out! They were told to be out of here hours ago."

Sergeant DeWitt moved sharply to the head of the platoon, still in close order. Then he shouted, "Platoon—Tench—Hut! Fix—Bayonets!"

There must have been forty SS soldiers in plain view, thick on the west balconies. Several stood at the top of the driveway along the barn. Three stacks of German rifles lay by the barn within their reach. Most intimidating to us was the German machine gun sitting on its bipeds ready for action. I saw that it was loaded and pointed straight down the driveway where we now stood. Of course, standing at the head of our column were Holly, me, Bird and Marohn. All four of us were looking down the barrel of that deadly gun, and two SS soldiers were standing less than three feet from it.

With Sergeant DeWitt's command to "Fix Bayonets" there was a rustle of action as the troopers bumped into each other to unsling rifles and quickly draw the bayonets, placing them on the rifles and then snapping back to attention.

While the platoon was fixing its bayonets, the sergeant was surveying the landscape. He moved off to the side of the formation to get a better look at the SS troops.

"Platoon—Port arms! First Squad—move up the hill to the left! Fourth Squad—up the hill to the right! Second Squad—spread out here in the driveway! Third Squad—start moving these bastards down through our ranks, out onto the road. Use your bayonets until they get the point of what we want.

Sergeant W. O. Bird marched straight up the hill to the German machine gun. With his M-1 rifle at fixed bayonet he pointed first at one and the other belly of the two S. S. troopers. They did not move a muscle. Bird stuck the toe of his right jump boot under the machine gun's barrel and sent the gun flying backwards end over end.

Bird then reached out with his huge left hand, took hold of one of those troopers by his uniform and sent him flying bodily through the air down the hill between our ranks. The other German soldier was frozen with fright. With his rifle held out straight in his right hand, Bird pressed the bayonet into that trooper's side. He was not gentle and jabbed him several times, pushing him the way he wanted him to go. As the German passed me I could see blood staining his uniform.

If Sergeant DeWitt had gotten their attention, Sergeant Bird had given the Germans the message. The 2nd Platoon's quick response to DeWitt's orders caught those SS troops so that they couldn't act if they had been planning to.

Sergeant Bird now began giving out orders to his Third Squad. "Move those Germans over by the barn down through the Platoon! Hurry it up—Don't let them react. Hey, you trooper! Grab those German rifles and get them away from here! Let's go! Move 'em out, men! Move 'em out!"

Bird went over to help the trooper with rifle detail. Holding his own M-1 in his right hand as if it were a match stick, he took hold of a stack of German rifles with his left hand, carried them at arm's length for several yards and dropped them in a pile behind our line. I was amazed at Bird's strength. In that one hand there were ten guns! I know because I turned around and counted them in the pile next to me where he dropped them.

Sergeant Marohn ran up the steps to the third balcony taking three at a time. At the head of the stairs a tall SS Sergeant was blocking the path of the other SS soldiers behind him. So far none of the Germans had made a move to leave the balconies, nor had any of the girls, but they were stirring around and nervous by now.

Sergeant Marohn was a big man, too. He said to the S. S. Sergeant, "The war's over, Kamerad! Vamooose! Get the hell down the stairs, I said!"—Whaaam! Bob Marohn decided that the SS Sergeant was going to be a problem, so he dealt with it SS style!

The butt of Marohn's rifle caught the black-shirted soldier square on his jaw. The force was so great he toppled over the railing onto the ground below the second balcony. Blood spattered over the girl standing next to him. She went hysterical and jumped over the railing after him.

Now those hard-nosed German soldiers understood what we were there for. Bounding up the stairs, onto the balconies and into the hotel went several paratroopers. Both SS German soldiers and their girlfriends ran for their lives now. The girls ran in all directions. Many fell down the steps, tripping over their high-heeled shoes. A few went back to their rooms for something they'd forgotten.

Every German soldier and his girlfriend had to pass out the back of the hotel through our gauntlet. By now Holly and I had arranged our squads to make a gauntlet clear out to the road. No SS trooper made it to the road without a bayonet prick or two. Some of those pretty young girls felt a sharp point also.

Suddenly Sergeant Milligan appeared on the second floor of the balcony. With him was a tall good-looking SS officer, a young Lieutenant in shirt sleeves. Milligan was carrying his jacket. A beautiful blonde woman, older than the other women and a German, I was sure, stood next to the officer.

All the other German soldiers were on the road by now, having run the 2nd Platoon gauntlet. Milligan told us later that he found the officer and his beautiful fraulein in a room together on the far side of the hotel.

The SS officer stood there, surveying the humiliating defeat of his unit at the head of the steps. He scowled at several of us noncommissioned officers, and to myself I thought, "If looks could kill, that bastard has just eliminated us!"

Sergeant DeWitt broke the spell. "Sergeant!" he said. "Get that son-of-a-bitch out of there!"

Crashing an SS Party

Sergeant Milligan put his right foot in the small of the lieutenant's back and gave a great push. The SS officer landed clear out in the driveway, right next to where Holly and I were standing. He was face down in the gravel. With the quickness of a cat, "Big" Holly put his bayonet on the lieutenant's neck. He didn't even try to get up. Holly's action was not a mere gesture; it, too, drew blood.

Back at the head of the stairs the blonde fraulein watched her lover get rough treatment. She was wearing a mink coat that reached to her knees. Unlike the other girls, this woman was not scared. The SS officer was her man. She was a true lover and no one—not even a Yankee soldier—could mistreat him! You just knew from looking at her that she'd been through a lot of the war with him. She stared off into space over our heads.

Suddenly she turned on Milligan, striking at him with her right arm. He was to quick for her and parried her arm with his rifle. That hurt! Then she tried to kick him in the balls. That was a mistake. "Jumpknife" grabbed her foot, pulled her off balance and sent her on a backward fall clear down the stairs where she landed on top of her lover boy. At least it was a soft landing, but it wasn't very lady-like. She did have her pink "step-ins" on, as the whole 2nd Platoon could see, and that saved some of her vanity.

"Big" Holly took his bayonet away from the lieutenant's neck and motioned for him to get up. The blonde fraulein scrambled to her feet, now missing the high-heel shoe Milligan had pulled off when he grabbed her leg. She kicked the other shoe off and reached down to help her boyfriend up. Once the SS officer was on his feet, he and the fraulein took time to try to make him look presentable. With her uninjured hand she brushed off his uniform.

Before these two Germans began their walk through the 2nd Platoon, they glared up at Sergeant Milligan. It was Milligan's greatest triumph. He tossed the lieutenant his jacket.

On Wednesday morning, May 9, we learned what our main mission in this valley was. A small arms dump was located down the valley about a half a mile past this hotel. It would grow to become a huge pile of military and civilian firearms surrendered to the Allied Powers—rifles, shotguns and pistols of every description. The 2nd Platoon would pull guard duty of this dump.

While the small arms were being brought in and piled high on our dump, some of our American officers agreed to let the SS unit in our area stand guard at the dump with us. We used a squad four hours at a time, and Sergeant DeWitt had us draw straws to see who went first. Of course, it was me and my Second Squad. "I might as well go and find out right now if this war is really over," I said to "Big" Holly.

"Better keep a close eye on 'Jumpknife,' Sergeant," Holly said. "Those SS troopers won't forget what he did to their Lieutenant. Be damned careful now, and don't stir up a hornet's nest anymore than we have. My squad is on duty next, you know!"

I did not know all the local surrender terms. When I saw the German guard detail coming down the road, marching in step carrying rifles, I was shocked and even more so when they turned into the dump driveway right beside my squad. There were eight SS soldiers, and they all stood in a row at parade rest just looking at us Yanks. We stood within ten yards of each other. No one said a word the whole four hours.

They were dressed in their black dress uniforms with steel helmets. We wore our green combat jumpsuits and in some cases they were not even clean. To tell the truth, those German soldiers put us to shame, and I began to wonder who really won this war. I realized as never before that the U.S. is not a military nation, and I hope we never become one, but for the next few days I saw how good a military nation looks even in defeat!

Mutual respect soon took over, and by the second day we looked sharp on guard duty. The game to see who could outshine the other side had started. Each day it got worse for us enlisted men until it was "spit and polish" and marching everywhere at attention. It got to the point that we were drawing the attention of the high-up officers. I soon found out why. Our dump had the choice pick of small arms for miles around. The officers drove in from miles around in their staff cars and jeeps to do their own picking from the pile.

Crashing an SS Party

A new order from the highest echelons reversed that order on "war souvenirs." Now you could send them home. They had to get rid of all those German "spoils." What better way than to have several million GIs build wooden boxes and fill them with the losers' tools of war? I wonder if the same genius in the War Department figured out the "wooden box" as well as the size of that box.

I went to work like everyone else building a wooden box in my spare time. I think the outside dimensions of the box were 8 inches by 10 inches by 42 inches. We weren't to send ammo of any kind home (although some did). Otherwise you could put almost anything in that box that was a souvenir of the war. And you could send as many boxes home as you could build. The point was that the items had to be small to fit in those boxes. I sent home a rifle, a bayonet, a helmet, a belt, a telescopic sight, a pistol, a T-shirt with a swastika on it, German war medals and other things. My box was still not full, so I added pieces of parachutes. There was still room to spare, so I went into my bedroom and took a bedspread to complete the job and keep things from rattling around.

By Saturday I knew for sure that the war in Europe was over. It was the end of SS soldiers standing guard, and the day that the Battalion asked troopers to go on "special duty" as carpenters. Some did—building boxes for officers!

36

In Hitler's Back Yard

As rear-echelon people moved up to assist in changing from a wartime footing to a reign of peace for the people of Germany and Austria, our early jobs of guarding "dumps" came to an end. We "lone combat" units moved on to rid the mountains of stray enemies.

For a week we worked on both sides of the German/Austrian border hunting "war criminals." Some of our prizes the 101st succeeded in bagging included two who were among the twenty-four war criminals who went on trial at Nuerenburg. They were Robert Ley, the Nazi Minister of Labor, and Julius Streicher, a high-ranking Nazi "Jew baiter." Both of them were hanged at Nuerenburg.

Also, we picked up Karl Albrecht Oberg, the "Butcher of Paris," a lieutenant general of the SS, and the chief of the German SS in occupied France. The biggest military individual we captured was Field Marshal Albert Kesselring, Commander-in-Chief of the German armies.

We were also-rans in the competition to bring in the biggest of all German Nazis—Adolf Hitler and Herman Goering. The

506th regiment in our division lost out to the 36th Infantry Division to seize Herman Goering.

But for one day, Adolf Hitler belonged to the 2nd Platoon of the "C" Company in 502.

My 2nd Platoon less my Second Squad, went on out of town up the valley about a mile and climbed the mountain to a small settlement above Hutte. I was out of town in a big farmhouse with my squad, a farm that claimed the land to the whole valley. The farm lay as flat as your hat for five hundred acres. The First Sergeant asked me to find some form of recreation for the company. The farm area was ideal for playing softball, so we arranged softball games every afternoon. I loved playing ball and was happy to stay with the company and the Battalion in Rhiet in Winkle.

On a Wednesday morning, I think it was May 16, there was a lot of excitement at the company command post. Jeeps and trucks were running back and forth all day long. All I could find out was that there was some action up the valley with the 2nd Platoon. Later in the afternoon I'll be damned if "Big" Holly didn't go by my house riding in a jeep. Smiling from ear to ear, he yelled to me, "See you back in the States, Black!"

I immediately sent Milligan up to the CP to find out what Holly was up to. "Jumpknife" came running back with an incredible story. "Sergeant William T. Hollingsworth is being interviewed by Stars and Stripes (military newspaper)," he said. "Something about Holly's finding Hitler up there in the hills where the 2nd Platoon is!"

Before Holly's "discovery" had a chance to soak in, I saw our Battalion surgeon go by in his jeep. He didn't look like a "bundle of joy," but he never did. Soon after that "Big" Holly came walking by and stopped at my house. He was subdued by now.

"I'll tell you," Holly said to me. "For a while there today I thought old 'C' Company was going to be famous. We captured Hitler back up there in them hills where Bird and I are camped out. You remember Tennessee hills, don't you? Those hills are about the same, where we are. We thought we had him for sure. But it turned out to be one of his look-alikes. Damn if it wasn't exciting there for a while—all those jeeps ramming up that mountain and big shots coming and going. But like you always say, Black, that's life in the ETO. One minute you can be a hero and they'll haul you around in jeeps; the next minute you're nothing but a dumb GI and they make you get out and walk back!" Sergeant Hollingsworth started walking back to his camp. Down the road he turned and said to Milligan, "Hey, you flatland farmers! Come up and see us hillbillies sometime!"

The war was over, but peace was not under control. Shooting accidents began occurring. In my own Company 'C' four troopers accidently shot themselves in one week. None were killed, thank God. Also, there were wrecks by GIs driving unauthorized vehicles, and one 506 officer was killed when he crashed trying to fly a Luftwaffe plane.

In the last two weeks of May there were seventy wrecks among the 101st Airborne in these mountains. For a six-week period after the war ended, our division had a total of eleven enlisted men and two officers killed.

Those of us in the 502 never had it too good in the 101st. The "frying pan" in Alabama's Fort Benning was a hell hole. The Fort Bragg area wasn't much better. Maneuvers in Tennessee put us in pup tents in Indiana's bare fields near the steaming Ohio River during the hot summer of '43. We did not sail smoothly—or quickly—to England. Nor were our homes in England like castles. And France after Alsace was "tent city."

Now here in the great tourist country of German and Austria, the 502 did not stay in the luxury resort towns such as Badgastein, Bad Reichenhall, Berchtesgaden and Zell am See. No, our assigned quarters were fifty or sixty miles away from those lovely sites.

We spent all of June in a town between Kitzbuhel and Kossen, with a railroad running along the main road to Zell am See. Early in July we moved south, deep into Austria, along the Salzach River to a small village called Uttendorf where we spent the rest of the month.

The highlight of the month of June was seeing the first "high-point" men leave the company for the States and home. A point system had been developed to start mustering out of the army, with the older men leaving first. The system gave men a point for every month in service, points for months overseas, points for medals and combat missions. Anyone with 85 to 120 points was a high-point man. These men started leaving for home in mid-June, and the pace picked up faster in June.

Sergeant W. O. Bird was an example of a high-point man with three purple hearts and the bronze star, which gave him twenty points more than "Big" Holly or me. Bird left for home in late June. Officers left the service in large numbers during these first months, not career officers and not the highest-ranking officers, but the First Lieutenants, Captains and Majors who had spent more time in the service and had more medals to their credit.

Rank had privilege, but they had earned it.

One of the first to go with high points was Curtis DeWitt. What a party we had for him! It lasted all night, and when the truck pulled up for him, he wasn't going to go! We had a hell of a time getting him on that truck. In the end, the captain had to order him to get on that truck. W. O. Bird was now the acting Platoon Sergeant and probably saved Sergeant DeWitt from a court martial by picking him up bodily and literally throwing him onto the truck. (DeWitt went home for a while, but re-enlisted later!)

At the end of June, Bird left the company. DeWitt had recommended Bird as his successor, but he left before the paperwork could be started on his new rating. As W. O. Bird left for home he turned my name in for 2nd Platoon Sergeant, and I took over the Platoon.

A few days before Sergeant Bird headed for home, the 2nd Platoon took a 48-hour rest leave at a beautiful lake high in the Alps with a new hydroelectric plant on it. There was a large inn at the water's edge with boating, swimming and horseback riding. Holly and I rode horseback up to the snow-capped peak of a mountain.

Only a few days earlier the German Wehrmacht had used this mountain retreat for the rest area, and that "German smell" lingered in the house.

It was the last time Bird, Holly and I were together, just the three of us. We had been through a lot together over the past two and a half years. It was the greatest friendship I would ever know, and I knew it back then. We had survived a great war without getting a scratch. Holly was a hillbilly, and I was a farm boy. Neither of us was military in a professional sense. We both went home and stayed within eyesight of where we were born.

Holly left the 2nd Platoon on his way home just as Bird did—with a firm handshake and "Be seeing, you, Black!"

What a surprise it was for me when my first cousin, Bob Black, drove up to the mountain retreat in a weapons carrier. He was Sergeant Robert Black. We'd grown up together, although Bob was three years older than me. He had been one of the first in the county to be called up and had ended up in the Signal Corps with General George S. Patton in California. He crossed Africa with General Patton and went on with him for "Operation Torch," the invasion at Casablanca on November 8, 1942; "Operation Husky," the invasion of Sicily on July 10, 1943; and "Operation Dragoon," the invasion of southern France on August 15, 1944. Bob spent two nights with me. Bird, Holly and I took him on a little "fraternizing" tour up the valley on his second night.

W. O. Bird left "C" Company the same day my cousin Bob headed back to his outfit and, with 111 points, on his way home.

I took over the job of Platoon Sergeant, but we had little to do as far as training and conditioning were concerned.

"Jumpknife" Milligan became interested in trains. He was always down at the railroad yard at our village trying to get one of those engines to run.

Finally Milligan was able to fix up one of the many engines that had been deserted by the Germans. We used Milligan and his engine to travel to and from our intra-company softball games along the railroad line. Once we went as far as Zell am See to play a team from the 506. By now "Jumpknife" was calling himself the "'C' Company Engineer—head of transportation.

With this rail line still out of use, no one seemed to object. Milligan started out pulling just one flat car, but the captain got the idea that we could move the whole company at one time. Now "Jumpknife" thought he'd moved into the big leagues. He could show the big boys at Battalion his abilities as an engineer.

Sergeant Charles Tinsely told me to pass the word to Sergeant Milligan that he was to have a full head of steam up by 1000 hours (10 a.m.) the next day so that he could pull eight flat cars, since "B" Company was going to ride along with us. That night Milligan was a nervous wreck. Sergeant Bob Marohn and I tried to calm him down with an extra drink or two, but he was still worried.

It was a beautiful day, and our "C" Company got off and rolling on the track at precisely 1000 hours, with the captain's cry, "Roll 'em, 'Jumpknife!'"

"Jumpknife" gave a toot on the whistle, and the whole train jerked forward. Everybody gave a cheer, and "Jumpknife" Milligan looked back at me with a big smile. This was his day!

We rolled easily down the line to "B" Company, where Milligan eased to a full stop without a single jerk. "God, that was smooth," I said to Sergeant Marohn.

Marohn yelled, "Three cheers for 'Jumpknife' Milligan!"

Everybody cheered.

Sergeant Milligan was embarrassed, and as the troopers from "B" Company were boarding, he climbed out of the cockpit. Pretending to be inspecting the wheels, he came back to the third car, ours. He said to me and marohn in a whisper, "Hey, hold it down. This part of the trip was easy. The next ten miles are hell! All up grade. I don't think I have enough steam!"

"Aw, hell! You'll make it, 'Jumpknife.' Pour on the coal. You're doing great," said Sergeant Marohn.

Everybody was happy and had been enjoying the ride, but I knew Marvin Milligan better than anybody else, and I knew something was wrong. I wasn't about to pour on cold water, so I took up the chant of the "Wabash Canonball."

Once more, the cry of "Roll 'em!" by Captain Williams. Then the toot of the whistle and a double jerk started us rolling toward Zel am See. You could still hear us chanting, "Listen to the rumble, listen to the roar, as she glides along the woodland, over the hills and by the shore." Even the "B" Company troopers joined in on the singing.

The last ten miles flew by, and up ahead we could see the rest of our Battalion standing in formation out in an open field. There was one sharp rise and a few hundred yards before we got to the formation. "Jumpknife" was afraid he couldn't keep enough steam up and wouldn't make it over the hump, so he had his firemen pouring on the coal for the last ten miles.

Milligan took us across that hump with flying colors. It was more like a ski jump. The men from "B" Company, in the eighth flat car, all left their seats. In fact, some of the men from "A" Company, who were watching from the field, said that the wheels of that last car all left the tracks. We were doing at least forty miles an hour when we blazed past the reviewing stand.

Once off the hump it was only a couple of hundred yards to our stopping place. When Milligan saw Major Hanlon wave his arms for him to stop, that is exactly what he did. He put on the brakes!

The only brakes that worked on the train were on the engine. Sparks flew! The screen of steel on steel was deafening. As we flew by the Battalion in formation, many of the troopers watching us put their fingers in their ears to shut out the horrible noise.

By the time Sergeant Milligan got us stopped we were out of sight of the Battalion formation. Worse than that, Milligan could not get the brakes to unlock so he could back the train up. So all of us had to march back and were a little late.

While Milligan and his fireman stayed with the train trying to free the brakes, the rest of us heard General Taylor's little speech. The part of the speech that stuck in my craw was based on the misconception that the nonprofessional GI (commissioned officer or not) had a burning desire to be on the "Japanese kill" once the war in Europe ended.

At the end of his speech General Taylor said he would not rest until he had won the right for the 101st Airborne Division to lead the invasion of Japan. To a man, every trooper in the Battalion booed.

That made the General mad! He proceeded to lecture us about the "military mind." "War," he said, "is what a General studies for. War is how a General will advance. There is a war going on in Japan. I'm a General, and I want to be in it."

He went on to say that he had spent his earlier years in the military in the Orient, that he understood their ways and felt he could help win the victory over the Japanese.

The General was the first to notice Milligan's train as it moved slowly toward the reviewing stand. There was an awkward pause as the General decided he was through talking. He climbed down off the stand, walked to his jeep, got in, and he and his driver drove off. I don't remember another speech by General Maxwell D. Taylor, and I don't think I ever saw him again.

Sergeant Milligan ran all the way from the train to the "C" Company, which was still in formation. He saluted the captain and said, "You wanted to see me, Sir?"

The captain said, "Is your train going to be safe to go back on, Sergeant?"

"Yes, Sir!" the sergeant replied. "I'm ready to load when you are, Captain. Sir!" He started to back away with a hand salute and backed right into Major Hanlon.

"Watch where you're going, Soldier!" roared the Major. Then he said, "Sergeant! You're out of uniform! Where is your helmet? What kind of headgear is that?"

Captain Williams stepped between the two men and tried to keep things from going sour, but the damage had been done. It was "C" Company's last train ride in Austria. The next day an order was read ending all unauthorized vehicle use.

After that Marvin Milligan didn't give a damn about anything military. He no longer cared for his squad, and as far as he was concerned, the 502, the great Regiment he knew and loved, no longer existed. He merely waited for his turn to go home. I said good-bye and never saw him or heard from him again.

On July 3 we moved deeper into Austria to the village of Uttendorf on the Salzach River on its way to Salzburg and the Danube River.

The whole 4th Squad moved in with me, and Bob Marohn and I were together for a short time until it was time for him to head for home. I threw a big party for him. Like all the old-timers, at the last minute he didn't want to go and cried like a baby. Of course, he was as drunk as hoot owl by then.

When we got up the morning of July 4, 1945, it was snowing like the devil. We stood in formation in a blizzard before going off to chow. By the time we were through with breakfast it had stacked to four or five inches on the ground.

In the middle of the day the sun came out. Everybody in Uttendorf was on skis until the snow melted, and that included every trooper in "C" Company who could find a pair of skis.

In Hitler's Back Yard

Every house in Austria had several pairs on hand. Skis in Austria were like bicycles in England.

The sun was hot when it came out, and by noon all the snow was gone.

I'll never forget seeing Charles Tinsley, now a First Sergeant, at the top of the hill in the main street of the village of Uttendorf. I was resting up on the second floor balcony of my house from my first and last experience on skis.

Tinsley had his shirt off but was wearing his steel helmet. His skis were pointed down hill, and he was posed for his downhill run like he was in the winter Olympics. He gave a yell that was meant to be a Swiss Yodel and pushed off. He was all over the street, from the picket fence on one side to the one on the other side.

At the bottom of the street where our house set, the street made a forty-five degree to the left, ran level another hundred yards and dropped off sharply downhill for another two hundred yards where it dead-ended on the highway running along the river. The total distance was over half a mile.

My guess is that Charles Tinsley, who was from Baltimore, had never been on a pair of skis before.

He was still on top of those skis coming into the turn in front of my house. I was sure he was going to crash into our house and kill himself, but just at the right moment he leaned to the left and made a perfect forty-five degree turn. He continued on down the street, gaining speed.

I watched the First Sergeant sail all the way down to the highway and over the fence where he landed on the seat of his pants in the river on the other side of the highway.

37

The Last First Sergeant

By the middle of July only Charles Tinsley and I were left of the old "C" Company. Even Milligan and Marhon were gone by then. Captain Williams left, and then Major Hanlon. Captain Gregg arrived from 501 near the end of July to take over "C" company.

Handing out rank by the mere process of elimination ended late in August, but I got in under the wire. For some reason Charles Tinsley's number came up sooner than we expected, and he headed for home before the end of July. Before he left he turned my name in to Captain Gregg for First Sergeant. Since Captain Gregg didn't know me any better than the rest, he took Tinsley's advice.

Before I replaced Tinsley as the acting First Sergeant, an order came in for a detail of troopers from my 2nd Platoon to "ride shotgun" (guard) on a trainload of Hungarians, Czechs and Poles—all displaced persons going back to Budapest and Warsaw. Some of those "displaced persons" had already gotten the point about the "Russian influence" in the countries where the train was headed and refused to go home.

My men would be crossing into the Russian sector and would see a lot of country for the week of the detail.

I wanted to volunteer myself, but I already knew of Tinsley's plan to put me in for First Sergeant, so I decided not to sign up. At the start of my new rank there was a little detail about two squads of men listed on "train guard duty." After two weeks Captain Gregg began raising hell with me to find out where they were. I ran into a stone wall at Battalion, but Regiment finally picked up the ball and started checking through diplomatic channels all the way back to Washington.

After three weeks rumors were going the rounds that the men had been killed going through the Russian sector, but they showed up in Uttendorf just in time to pack up for the Division's move.

The stories those boys told us about the Russians were eye-openers for the years to follow. The Russians weren't trusting anybody now, including the Yanks, and backed that up with action. When the train reached Budapest the Russians took over and placed our American troopers in a big hotel and kept them under guard as if they were under a house arrest. They had plenty of food and were treated as heroes, but they could not leave the hotel.

On July 30 we started the move back to France, and by August 2 we were settled in an old French army post in the village of Auxerre about 110 miles southeast of Paris. This was a beautiful old city of about 25,000 people that dated back to the days of the Roman Empire. The narrow streets were cobblestone, and there were cathedrals everywhere.

I was the acting First Sergeant for "C" Company for three weeks before the full rank came through. I sewed the new stripes on my uniform on August 16 and was the First Sergeant for four months, until November. I was the last one in "C" Company to hold that rank.

My tasks were to deal with the changes in personnel and airborne training for the war in Japan. My main problem was dealing with all the gripes from GI trainees, including all of the company's noncommissioned officers. The day we booed General Taylor came back to me. He was wrong that day. Japan did not belong to the 101st Airborne; that was the show for the 11th Airborne Division and the U.S. Marines.

The Last First Sergeant

The power that came with my new rank was awesome. I no longer lived with the men or even ate with them. I didn't go to the fields with them and had real contact with only a very few men. Instead of looking up, I was looking down. It was certainly more comfortable, but not nearly as much fun.

With the end of the war in Europe many "dear John" letters came to the First Sergeant's incoming mailbox. Some were sad indeed; the girls had waited until the very last to tell some trooper they had lost their love. Most had found a new lover, and many times it was a wife writing. Some wrote to the First Sergeant to try to keep that trooper overseas because she didn't want to face him! Not all of the letters came from the U.S. Some were from English girls with babies who were a year old by now. "That Yank promised to marry me..." The hell of it was, he was already married!

There were some sweet romances that came out of the war. Private Frank L. R. Hare joined my squad at Mourmelon, France, in time to make Bastogne but froze his feet badly. He ended up as my "C" Company cook now in Austria. "Rabbit" had met Jolanda Konigsberger in London and had fallen in love with her. "Rabbit" came to me asking for furlough time so he could go to England to see her. He said he was thinking about getting married. I tried to talk him out of it and told him he couldn't marry anyone out of the States without the captain's OK. Still, we gave him a furlough to go see Jolanda.

Frank Hare knew a good thing when he found it. When he came back from his furlough he had made up his mind that he wanted to marry Jolanda. He came into the orderly room in Auxerre and asked to see Captain Gregg. To my surprise, the captain said it was OK and gave him another pass back to England to get married right away.

The 101st Airborne should have gone home intact. We should have marched down the main streets of America. The people back home deserved it. Instead, we were torn apart, piece by piece, until we were completely broken up in a French town that hated us.

In early September an order came down from Division: "Jump or lose your jump pay!" (fifty dollars.)

When the time came to answer yes or now, I didn't hesitate. "Yes!" I told Captain Gregg. "I'm the First Sergeant and must lead by example."

On September 17, just one year from our Holland Jump, I made my last parachute jump.

As a member of the "command group" I was treated special. We weren't supposed to stand around and waste time. I jumped from a C-47 plane with only six other First Sergeants in it. It had been raining all day, and I landed in a plowed field, clear up to my knees in mud.

My landing was soft, but then I had to march half a mile out of that field. On the edge of the field at the roadway, two 101st Red Cross girls were waiting with smiles, coffee and doughnuts.

I was sent to a lake-side resort in the French Chateau country to attend an NCO school. When I got back from school, an order was waiting for me on my desk from Major Fitzgerald, the Battalion Commanding Officer. The order notified me that I was to be awarded the "Bronze Star" medal and that there would be an awards parade Saturday morning in honor of me and a few other men from the First Battalion.

From the middle of September on, my men were scattered all over Europe in every kind of class the Army could invent. Even if they didn't have tools, textbooks, teacher or classrooms, they were going to school. Tents in open fields became school rooms for our men. There was even a class in ballroom dancing out in the hayfields—with no girls to dance with!

With October thoughts of "back to college" came to many, and a few were lucky enough to get into European colleges for some of their studies.

About the time I was feeling that everybody had it better than me, Captain Gregg said to me, "Can you be ready to go to Paris in half an hour, Sergeant?"

"Yes, Sir!" I said.

"Take this over to Regimental Headquarters," he said, handing me a piece of paper. "They have a seven-day command group furlough to London waiting for you to pick up. This paper will allow you to draw the English money you need. Have fun. See you in a week. Now get out of here!"

The Last First Sergeant

Half an hour later I was speeding out of Auxerre in a jeep with my own private driver. We were racing for Paris faster than I liked for the 110 miles of the trip so I could catch a special plane for London. My driver kept saying, "We must catch a plane, Sergeant. The war is over. Now they fly on schedule."

Up in that airplane, seated facing the same way the plane was flying, I realized the war had truly ended. During those seven days in London I began to think about home. I chose a small hotel in the center of the old city and spent a lot of time reading and writing letters. I did not run around at night as I had in the past, just took in a movie a few times.

I kept thinking about old girl friends, all of those girls who had taken time to write to me during the past two and one-half years. I'd never given a thought to marriage because of the "danger game" I was in, but I asked them all to wait for me.

One of those girls was head and shoulders above all the rest. She was three years younger than me and was still in high school when I left the States. She was beautiful, had a stunning figure, a lovely dancer and a marvelous smoocher. She'd written me more letters than anyone else, even my mom. Her letters were never mushy, always full of hope and news of life back in the States. Now she was a college sophomore at Ohio State. Every day in London I wrote long letters to the girl at Ohio State. By now I was sure I was in love with her.

On my trip back to Paris my thoughts were only of going home. When I arrived back at Company Headquarters in Auxerre and heard the news from the clerk, Corporal Freeman, that the point system had finally reached my number, 82, I was ready.

I left Europe on November 4, 1945, traveling by ship from Antwerp, Belgium, to Boston, arriving on November 15, 1945, in time to be home for Thanksgiving Day.

I'm sorry the great 101st Airborne Division did not come home intact from the European theatre. For me, as the last First Sergeant of "C" Company in World War II, the honor of leading her home would have been great.

The truth is, my "C" Company died in Auxerre, France, in November 1945, and I was her last First Sergeant.

Above: 1st Sergeant Layton Black receiving the Bronze Star at Auxerre, France, from Major C. R. Fitzgerald, Commander, 1st Battalion, 502nd Parachute Infantry, 101st Airborne Division.

Top: Jeanne, Layton Black's "girl" during the war, and his wife until his death many years later.
Above: "Big" Holly, Sergeant William T. Hollingsworth.

Top: Layton Black and W. O. Bird.
Above: James Flanagan and his brother, E.M. Flanagan.

Epilogue

Much that I have heard and read has impressed me, but there are a few words that had great meaning in my life because they tell something about who I am.

"Under the Spreading Chestnut Tree" was a pleasing memory to a country boy. The Gettysburg Address portrayed the power and the glory of being an American. I cannot forget, "That we here highly resolve that these dead shall not have died in vain—and that government of the people, by the people, for the people, shall not perish from the earth. . ."

After fighting so close to Englishmen and seeing them die, I could not help but love the words of Rupert Brooke: "If I should die think only this of me. That there's some corner of a foreign field that is forever England." The powerful words of "The Battle Hymn of the Republic" continue to drive real soldiers on. "Mine eyes have seen the glory of the coming of the Lord; He is trampling out the vintage of where the grapes of wrath are stored; He hath loosed the fateful lightning of his terrible swift sword. His truth is marching on."

Then there was a tune that had great private meaning, helping to sustain me, a lonely soldier, when times were grim. "When they begin the Beguine, let them play till the stars return above you." She was the love of my life. Oh, to dance so close. To hear those lines over and over in my mind was to remember why I must come back.

In the final triumph nothing equals the flag, hand salute, "Oh say, can you see," the loud cry, "Pass in review!" and the thrill of the "Stars and Stripes Forever." God, I've always loved a parade!

What have I done since the war? Married that girl, raised two boys, enjoyed two grandkids, farmed for fifty years, worked in the lumber (retail) business twenty years and somewhere in there broadcast high school football and basketball over the radio. Hell, all of that was easy after what I had been through. And it was fun.

Please, God, tell all those wonderful men who missed out on the last fifty years that I have never forgotten them.

Airborne all the way. Layton Black, Jr.

Appendix I

A Guide to WWII Rhetoric

Each great war in history has its own style of rhetoric. I'm not talking about the vernacular of the period. I mean the manner of expression between leaders and soldiers. No organization I know used more abbreviations than the military, and no one was more familiar with all of these terms than a First Sergeant. Here are some of the most common abbreviations and their meanings.

GI Government Issue Everything given to a soldier by the USA in World War II. The term meant that a soldier was "very" military—by the book. Also, the name of the American soldier of World War II.

ETO European Theater of Operations

SHAEF Supreme Headquarters Allied Expeditionary Forces

OKW German Supreme Headquarters (Hitler's Military Board)

CP Command Post

CO Command Officer

Co. Company

Bn. Battalion

Reg. Regiment

Div. Division

Plt. Platoon

DZ Drop Zone

LZ Landing Zone

LD Line of Departure

MLR Main Line of Resistance

TO Table of Organization

DP Displaced people

POW Prisoner of War

KP Kitchen Police

MP Military Police

OP Outpost

FO Forward Observer

SS German Storm Trooper

M-1 American Rifle

88-MM German Artillery gun—an "88"

MM Millimeter

AWOL Absent Without Leave

KIA Killed in Action

MIA Missing in Action

WIA Wounded in Action

S-1 Personnel Office (adjutant)

S-2 Intelligence Officer

S-3 Operations Officer

S-4 Supply Officer

DSC Distinguished Service Cross (medal)

H-Hour Hour of attack

D-Day Day of attack

D-Plus Counting of days after attack

R.W.D. History of the 101st Airborne Division

"Booby Trap" An explosive wired to something misleading to the enemy

GIR Glider Infantry Regiment

PIR Parachute Infantry Regiment

TD Tank Destroyer

LST Landing Ship, Tank

MG Machine Gun

SP Self-propelled gun

Appendix II

Military Organizational Structure

Division. Self-contained organization within a military branch. Equipped for long-term combat. Divided into regiments.

Regiment. Next organizational unit below a division. Consists of two or more battalions. Head is a Colonel.

Battalion. Consists of two or more Companies and a Headquarters.

Company. The smallest administrative unit. Includes two or more battalions. Head is a Captain.

Platoon. Subdivision of a Company. Head is a Lieutenant.

Squad. Smallest tactical unit (often 12 to 15 men).

The Last First Sergeant